I0123811

Diversity in Leadership

Australian women, past and present

Diversity in Leadership

Australian women, past and present

Edited by Joy Damousi, Kim Rubenstein and Mary Tomsic

Australian
National
University

PRESS

ANU PRESS

Published by ANU Press
The Australian National University
Canberra ACT 0200, Australia
Email: anupress@anu.edu.au
This title is also available online at http://press.anu.edu.au

National Library of Australia Cataloguing-in-Publication entry

Title: Diversity in leadership : Australian women, past and
               present / Joy Damousi, Kim Rubenstein, Mary Tomsic, editors.

ISBN: 9781925021707 (paperback) 9781925021714 (ebook)

Subjects: Leadership in women--Australia.
               Women--Political activity--Australia.
               Businesswomen--Australia.
               Women--Social conditions--Australia

Other Authors/Contributors:
               Damousi, Joy, 1961- editor.
               Rubenstein, Kim, editor.
               Tomsic, Mary, editor.

Dewey Number: 305.420994

All rights reserved. No part of this publication may be reproduced, stored in a retrieval system or transmitted in any form or by any means, electronic, mechanical, photocopying or otherwise, without the prior permission of the publisher.

Cover design and layout by ANU Press

This edition © 2014 ANU Press

Contents

Part V. Women and culture

Part VI. Movements for social change

Introduction

Joy Damousi[1] and Mary Tomsic[2]

Prime Minister Julia Gillard spoke passionately in Parliament on 9 October 2012. Many people around the world took notice of what has come to be called her 'Misogyny Speech'. By the following day, footage of the speech had been viewed more than 300,000 times online, 'Gillard' was one of the top trending words on Twitter and newspaper headlines around the globe reported the speech.[3] Just more than one year later, the video clip on YouTube had been viewed more than 2.5 million times. This speech was clearly 'heard around the world'.[4] The Liberian peace activist and Nobel Peace Prize laureate Leymah Gbowee spoke of her excitement in watching the speech and the high value she placed on it as an example of a woman leader breaking the bounds of public priority to make a personally political statement about the still radical idea of misogyny.[5]

In this speech, the leader of the nation plainly named what she saw as the sexist and misogynistic actions and comments of the Leader of the Opposition, Tony Abbott. She declared Abbott to be the embodiment of 'what misogyny looks like in modern Australia'. In the speech, Prime Minister Gillard said she was personally offended by sexist acts, and later: 'I could not take the hypocrisy of the Leader of the Opposition trying to talk about sexism ... I was not going to sit silent.'[6] This speech is significant for many reasons, but in the context of this book's focus it is a clear example of activism. Here we see a woman holding a recognised and formal position of leadership, publicly calling someone to account for sexism generally, and specifically against her. In September 2013, Julia Gillard spoke publicly as to how, when she first became prime minister, she had not wanted to place any particular public attention on her sex because 'it was just so obvious, it was going to be commented on and it was going to be so much of what came to define my Prime Ministership without me constantly pointing to it'. But despite her lack of attention to her sex she felt the burden of a 'misogynist underside' emerge. She described the particular parliamentary

---

1   The University of Melbourne.

2   The University of Melbourne.

3   'Gillard's Misogyny Speech Goes Global', *ABC News Online*, 10 October 2012, http://www.abc.net.au/news/2012-10-10/international-reaction-to-gillard-speech/4305294. For the YouTube video of the speech, see: http://www.youtube.com/watch?v=ihd7ofrwQX0.

4   'The 2013 Time100 Poll', 28 March 2013, http://time100.time.com/2013/03/28/time-100-poll/slide/julia-gillard/.

5   'Nobel Laureate Leymah Gbowee Praises Gillard's Misogyny Speech', *ABC News Online*, 9 April 2013, http://www.abc.net.au/news/2013-04-09/nobel-peace-prize-winner-leymah-gbowee-on-the-drum/4619274.

6   Jacqueline Maley, 'I Give as Good as I Get: Gillard', *Age, Daily Life*, 11 December 2012, http://www.dailylife.com.au/news-and-views/dl-opinion/i-give-as-good-as-i-get-gillard-20121210-2b4p5.html.

debate as a 'crackpoint' in her thinking: 'after everything I've had to see on the internet, after all the gendered abuse that I've seen in newspapers, that has been called at me across the dispatch box, now of all things I've got to listen to Tony Abbott lecture me about sexism.'[7] Here in this speech, and the context of it, is one prominent example of the entanglement between 'the personal' and 'the political' that women acting in the public sphere readily encounter. The cause of these sexist acts and statements towards Prime Minister Gillard can be explained as misogyny (at worst) and unease (at best) against a woman holding such a conventionally recognised position of authority. Judith Brett has described Prime Minister Gillard's speech as 'fighting back' against 'the misogynist fantasies of so many men … projected onto [her] on a daily basis'.[8]

The immense interest in Gillard's Misogyny Speech demonstrates how timely it is to broadly consider ideas about and experiences of women and leadership. And in doing this, we are not only interested in women's leadership in public and readily recognised positions, such as that of prime minister. Instead we are interested in exploring the diversity of leadership roles that women have undertaken in the past and today, to more fully appreciate how involved women have been in leading society, while simultaneously also examining the obstacles that stand in their way.

This collection developed out of an Australian Research Council Linkage Grant, 'Australian Women and Leadership in a Century of Australian Democracy'. The researchers involved in this project were interested in uncovering and examining women's leadership within movements for social and political change in Australia since white women were granted political citizenship in 1902 of the newly federated Commonwealth of Australia. This research has revealed 'the diverse ways that women have performed leadership'.[9] In addition to adding women's experiences to the historical record, the analysis of specific examples of women's leadership reveals many inconsistencies and complexities that demand sustained examination.[10] As part of this same project, *Diversity in Leadership: Australian Women, Past and Present* further develops new understandings of historical and contemporary aspects of women's leadership since Federation in

---

7 'Julia Gillard in Conversation with Anne Summers', 30 September 2013, http://australianpolitics. com/2013/09/30/gillard-summers-conversation-sydney.html, quote from 'Watch Gillard Comment on Her Misogyny Speech'.

8 Judith Brett, 'They Had it Coming, Gillard and the Misogynists', *The Monthly* 84 (November 2012), http://www.themonthly.com.au/gillard-and-misogynists-they-had-it-coming-judith-brett-6770.

9 Rosemary Francis, Patricia Grimshaw and Ann Standish, 'Identifying Women Leaders in Twentieth-Century Australia: An Introduction', in *Seizing the Initiative: Women Leaders in Politics, Workplaces and Communities*, eds Rosemary Francis, Patricia Grimshaw and Ann Standish (Melbourne: eScholarship Research Centre, University of Melbourne, 2012), http://www.womenaustralia.info/leaders/sti/index.html, 13.

10 Fiona Davis, Nell Musgrove and Judith Smart, 'Introduction', in *Founders, Firsts and Feminists: Women Leaders in Twentieth-Century Australia*, eds Fiona Davis, Nell Musgrove and Judith Smart (Melbourne: eScholarship Research Centre, University of Melbourne, 2011), http://www.womenaustralia.info/leaders/fff/index.html, 12.

a range of local, national and international contexts. The aim of the chapters in this collection is to document the extent and diverse nature of women's social and political leadership across various pursuits and endeavours. We suggest the actions documented and analysed in the collection should be understood as cases of political activism, which are examples of women enacting their civic citizenship, even when those rights were not legally bestowed, as was the case for Indigenous women.

The previous Governor-General of the Commonwealth of Australia, Her Excellency the Honourable Quentin Bryce AC CVO, recently delivered the 2013 Boyer Lecture series. In these, Bryce spoke of the importance of listening to people's stories and then, in her role, echoing these stories around the nation. She described the power of 'real life stories, once heard, we can never walk away from'.[11] One of the arguments made in this lecture series was of the key role people's stories play in building neighbourhoods, in practising good leadership, good citizenship and participating in a democracy.[12] These stories, she suggests, should be understood as examples of people's actions and agency. This same argument can be seen in the contributions to this collection. The chapters are similarly a collection of stories—women's stories. Some are presented as single or multiple life stories while others are stories of movements and organisations, but all are examples of women's actions, agency and ultimately leadership.

While leadership is an overused term today, how it is defined for women, the context within which it emerges and how it changes over time remain elusive. Moreover, women are exhorted to exercise leadership, but occupying leadership positions for women comes with challenging issues of acceptable behaviour for women in these positions and what skills women are perceived to need to be successful leaders. These complex and conflicting ways in which leadership is enacted are examined in this collection. The volume is divided into six parts to capture the diversity of women's leadership, but also to identify the complexity and nuance of women's leadership in various historical and contemporary contexts. These are: feminist perspectives and leadership; Indigenous women's leadership; local and global politics; leadership and the professions; women and culture; and movements for social change.

The purpose of the book is threefold. First, the aim is to identify outstanding women leaders to demonstrate the significance of the intervention and activities in their field of interest. In doing this some of these women have inspired the actions of others within a range of activities. In uncovering the experience of women the intention is to record the outcomes of women's achievements. Second,

---

11 'Joining the Neighbourhood', *Boyer Lectures 2013: Back to Grassroots*, 3 November 2013, http://www. abc.net.au/radionational/programs/boyerlectures/.

12 These ideas are developed further in Kim Rubenstein's Epilogue to this collection.

we draw together a group of leading scholars with interdisciplinary expertise in various fields including history, Indigenous studies, political science, law and heritage, and in so doing provide a wide perspective on understandings of women and leadership. Finally, this volume raises the question regarding the perceived fragility of women's capacity to take up leadership roles since white women gained full citizenship. The experiences of the women examined here clearly show how many attempted to define a different kind of leadership culture that challenged a masculine model on which leadership is conventionally based.

The collection begins by examining feminist interventions into understandings of leadership. The chapter by Amanda Sinclair grounds *Diversity in Leadership* by articulating a rigorous theoretical framework for the specific case studies of women's leadership that follow in the collection. Sinclair identifies key questions regarding how leadership is defined and the need to interrogate the very construction of leadership itself. What is leadership, she asks, and why is it that so many of women's contributions to public life have not been recognised as such? Aboriginal leader Lillian Holt has argued that leadership is a white male idea. Many women feel deeply ambivalent about leadership—about what it signals, symbolises and seems to require. Sinclair argues that while this ambivalence is well founded, it is equally important to mount a feminist argument for and conceptualisation of leadership. To this end, this chapter looks at the construct of leadership itself. Leadership as an idea has enjoyed enormous popularity over the past three decades or so: across many societies and sectors we hear a call for more 'leadership'. What does this mean? How societies and groups define leadership depends on their history, cultural myths and ideologies. This creates and has created profound problems for women as leaders. Highly visible and effective women in public life have often not had the term leader bestowed on them. To further complicate matters, many women are sceptical about the term leadership—they do not want to be labelled a leader because of what it connotes: the out-front, tough and stoic male hero. Sinclair proposes a feminist reconceptualisation of leadership that goes beyond women performing against pre-existing criteria of leadership, or the 'add women and stir' remedy. She suggests that alongside our efforts to have women recognised as leaders, we need to use our findings to interrogate and contest received wisdom about leadership. We need to build into understandings of leadership and leaders more explicit notions of power, sex and gender. Our interest in women's leadership should be more than just adding women in, but be more reforming, and shift public images and imagination about what good leadership is and how it can be executed.

In pursuing this line of inquiry and interrogating the very definition of leadership and exploring its different forms, expressions and manifestations, Part II of the collection identifies distinctive leadership practices of Indigenous women. Gwenda Baker, Joanne Garŋgulkpuy and Kathy Guthadjaka explore this theme in their chapter on 'Guthadjaka and Garŋgulkpuy: Indigenous women leaders in Yolngu, Australia-wide and international contexts'. This chapter examines the extraordinary growth in political leadership over the past 30 years amongst Indigenous women from remote communities in Australia. Kathy Guthadjaka and Joanne Garŋgulkpuy are Indigenous women who have taken up key leadership positions in their communities on Elcho Island, a remote island off the Northern Territory. The chapter demonstrates that these women are representative of an Indigenous Australian phenomenon: the intense participation in democratic affairs by Indigenous women. In providing leadership, a continuing conversation on governance and an interaction with Western systems of thought and administration, Guthadjaka and Garŋgulkpuy, it is argued, have been pivotal in promoting a wider level of political inquiry and activity within their communities. This chapter demonstrates how locally developed strategies are more likely to be accepted and are more likely to achieve positive outcomes. It also considers how their locally developed strategies can be used by other local and international groups who seek to explore and implement their own ideas.

Aunty Pearl Gibbs provides an exemplary case study of political leadership of an Aboriginal rights activist. Rachel Stanfield, John Nolan and Uncle Ray Peckham focus on the work of Pearl Gibbs, a prominent Aboriginal leader of the twentieth century. Pearl Gibbs began her activism focusing on women's issues. Her early work assisted young Aboriginal women, members of the Stolen Generations, working in situations of exploitation as domestic servants in Sydney homes. Pearl Gibbs' career then expanded into national campaigns for Aboriginal rights, where she worked with prominent Indigenous activist William Ferguson in the central west of New South Wales. As her leadership role developed, she began to break down gender and racial barriers, becoming the first woman to serve on the NSW Aborigines Welfare Board and the first Aboriginal woman to hold a ticket in an all-male trade union. The chapter outlines the contribution Aunty Pearl Gibbs made in encouraging Aboriginal activism on the international stage, detailing her formative influence on the life and work of Uncle Ray Peckham as a young man, including Pearl Gibbs' role in his attendance at the World Youth Festival in Italy in 1951.

In both global and local politics, women have in various ways assumed myriad models of leadership, taking up different causes and campaigns, and this is the focus of Part III of the collection. As Marilyn Lake demonstrates in her chapter, international mobilisation exerted a powerful attraction for women leaders as Australian women joined their sisters around the world from the beginning of the century to campaign for full equality on an international basis in economic, political and social domains. Australian women such as Vida Goldstein, Muriel

Heagney and Mary Bennett could take on leadership positions as a result of their internationalism, which also worked to strengthen their political position at home. Women such as Jessie Street were able to forge networks and access resources that led to them taking pioneering roles, for example, in domestic campaigns for racial and sexual equality. Jessie Street became vice-president of the Status of Women Commission at the United Nations and both she and Bennett played major roles in campaigns for recognition of the human rights of Aboriginal people and the passage of the 1967 referendum on Aboriginal affairs. Australian women also used international organisations, ranging from the League of Nations and the International Labour Organisation to the United Nations to strengthen their campaigns at home for economic and political equality, for equal pay, equal opportunity and affirmative action. In doing so, they defined a form of political leadership that was formed through an internationalist engagement.

Susan Harris Rimmer similarly points to the contributions of Australian women who have been successful in promoting social change using international forums, particularly the United Nations. Based on previous research and new interviews—with Elizabeth Evatt, Hilary Charlesworth, Carolyn Hannan, Caroline Lambert and Erika Feller—she describes the different ways in which these women have displayed leadership for women's rights on the world stage. Rimmer questions whether Australian domestic reforms can and should be pursued through international processes, and/or whether international progress can be a goal in its own right. What is the measure of successful leadership in the international sphere? Rimmer argues that domestic reform and engagement with the UN system can be a mutually enriching experience. The women whose careers she discusses have been innovative in their use of the international system or have created new ideas about international law and practice. Their experience has some common themes: the need for both patience and determination; the key role of good gender analysis as opposed to general gender awareness; and the importance of strategic thinking. The last can range from improving decision-making machinery in the interests of women to changing the way the reform agenda is formulated. Rimmer concludes that these stories of leadership at the international level need to be told, especially as the feminist movement in Australia undergoes generational change. Australian advocates for women's rights should consider using international processes as one of their tools but with full knowledge of the limits to achieving transformative change in this way.

Other campaigners developed their leadership qualities and attributes around local politics and as individual campaigners. Bertha McNamara (1853–1931) stood unsuccessfully for Labor preselection for her party's senate ticket in 1928. Had she been elected, she would have been the first woman in the Australian

Parliament. Often remembered more for her relationships by marriage with the writer Henry Lawson and the populist politician Jack Lang than for her own achievements, she was a strong voice for parliamentary engagement in the Labor movement in New South Wales in the early part of the twentieth century. She was also a writer, whose short stories and pamphlets drew on the socialism of Edward Bellamy, and a bookseller whose store provided an important focus for many in radical circles in New South Wales. Michael Richards considers the ephemeral evidence of her life and work, and contributes to a discussion of how such stories can be told in a museum. Richards argues that although recognition of the first cohort of women elected to parliament must be paramount in history museums, such institutions should also pay close attention to the often-overlooked women who first nominated unsuccessfully for election—the pioneers in testing the openness of the first democracy in the world to allow women to stand for parliament.

Judith Smart and Marian Quartly explore the development of women's collective activism and civic awareness in Australia through the formation of National Councils of Women in all States between 1896 and 1910, culminating in the National Council of Women of Australia (NCWA) in 1931. Linked to the International Council of Women (ICW), and through it to the League of Nations and later the United Nations, the council movement provided an umbrella structure under which existing women's groups could discuss matters of common interest, gather and exchange information in order to promote peace and general wellbeing. Though the NCWA included radicals among its affiliates, the feminist face it presented was self-consciously moderate, emphasising information, education and cooperation rather than activism, agitation and opposition. The founding objectives dedicated the organisations to 'unity of thought, sympathy and purpose' among women 'of all classes, parties and creeds' and to 'the application of the Golden Rule to society, custom and law'. But membership of the ICW also committed the NCWA to a broad equal rights feminist agenda. Until the mid 1970s, it was the major voice of mainstream women's views in government and community forums, and the number of affiliated organisations enabled NCWA leaders to claim they represented the views of more than a million Australian women. Through its ICW affiliation and its participation in regional conferences, the NCWA was the strongest non-governmental organisational channel through which Australian women could speak and be heard internationally. In their chapter, Smart and Quartly examine the constraints this broad leadership role placed on national presidents from the 1930s to the 1970s and the means they employed to minimise conflict and to inform and lead their diverse membership on issues of equity and justice to which ICW affiliation committed them.

Finally in this section, Nikki Henningham demonstrates how women with disabilities have developed particular distinctive leadership styles and approaches to agitate effectively for their rights. The International Year of Disabled Persons in 1981 was a crucial year for the disability rights movement in Australia, not only because it helped to 'mainstream' important issues but also because it reaffirmed the importance of people with disabilities taking control of their own organisations and leading their own projects. Within this context, Australian women with disabilities took inspiration from activists from overseas and were at the forefront of a push to inject a feminist perspective into the thinking of disability advocacy organisations such as Disabled People's International (DPI). Women like Margaret Cooper, Lesley Hall and Sue Salthouse have played a significant role in shaping policy to improve the lives of women with disabilities on the national and international stages. The advocacy organisation in which they have all occupied leadership roles at one stage or another, Women With Disabilities Australia, has been recognised by the United Nations for its work on behalf of the rights of women with disabilities. This chapter traces key themes in the gendered development of the disability rights movement in Australia and abroad, focusing on the role played by individual women with a global presence. It discusses key individuals and their leadership styles, in a context where they quickly came to realise that existing frameworks within the disability rights and feminist movements did not accommodate the needs of women with disabilities.

The theme of women and the professions past and present offers an opportunity to explore how professional work has often demanded that women's leadership is understood in different ways to that of their male counterparts. This is the focus of Part IV of the collection. Joy Damousi examines the careers of the first three Australian female factory inspectors—Agnes Milne, Margaret Cuthbertson and Annie Duncan—as a way of exploring an aspect of Australian women's leadership within the professions during the early twentieth century. By adopting the perspective of administrative leadership embedded within an organisational structure, Damousi examines how female factory inspectors administered the *Factory Acts* as a form of leadership. In the context of the rapidly shifting industrial and urban landscapes of the late nineteenth and early twentieth centuries, the role of the female factory inspector invites an analysis of the concept of 'leadership' within the framework of administrative leadership. Damousi argues that there is a need to develop a historically grounded understanding of leadership, which encompasses the opportunities available to women at that time and the diversity of their activities towards bringing about social change for working women. In this chapter, leadership is explored through different models of social change at a time when the position of female factory inspector came with considerable responsibility and direct influence, as administering the *Factory Acts* could have a distinct impact on improving the conditions of working women.

Shurlee Swain explores how in the nineteenth century, religion and philanthropy provided another avenue through which women were able to move beyond the confines of the home and exercise leadership in their local communities. This chapter examines the intersections and fissures that developed in these interlinked areas as a result of professionalisation and secularisation during the twentieth century. Australia provides an interesting case study in this area. At the beginning of the century its early enfranchisement of women provided alternatives to philanthropy as a way of bringing about change, but this was countered by the relatively slow progress of professionalisation, particularly in the area of social work. The focus of the chapter is on the shifting relationship between professionals and volunteers in articulating claims to leadership in the arena of welfare and social policy. It asks what factors particular to Australia created the space for the emergence of a significant number of younger female social entrepreneurs when the welfare state began to contract as the century came to its end.

In another context, Patricia Grimshaw and Rosemary Francis consider the leadership of women who have held positions and exerted influence in Australian universities since the early decades of the twentieth century to current times and offer brief biographical profiles of several women. There were few women who held lectureships or senior administrative positions in Australian universities before the onset of World War II, but those who found such employment were often remarkable scholars and teachers whose participation was significant in influencing others to follow in their paths. The areas where women gained positions widened from the humanities and science emphases of earlier decades into major professional areas such as education, medicine and law. In comparison with other Western countries such as the United Kingdom and the United States, in Australia, the entry of women to academia remained slow. Australia remained a provincial country, which, despite bursts of progressive legislation, was relatively socially conservative and continued to emphasise the value of marriage and domesticity for its predominantly Anglo-Australian women. Under the pressure of the vigorous women's movement of the late 1960s and 1970s, and the affirmative action legislation of the 1980s, social attitudes underwent a marked change that allowed for a fracturing of the domestic ideal for married women—especially notable for those with children. Women since the 1990s have held a wealth of leadership positions, so that outstanding women leaders emerged not only within a breadth of disciplines but also in the previously male province of academic administration, including the first female vice-chancellors. The year 2009 saw the first Australian woman academic, scientist Professor Elizabeth Blackburn, receive a Nobel Prize.

Within cultural forums, women's leadership has been in evidence in a range of ways, and this is the focus of Part V of the collection. Beginning this discussion is Libby Stewart's chapter, which notes how female political leaders in Australia, and in other parts of the world, are often portrayed in superficial ways. Their appearances in brief television grabs or newspaper articles to explain policy or programs are often subjected to comments about clothing or hairstyles, which trivialise their efforts and demean their leadership credentials. Studying the material culture of female political leaders can reveal much more about these women than is often conveyed in the public arena. The women's suffrage movement has left a wealth of items, such as jewellery, medals and board games, which convey the depth and seriousness of the women who drove its activism during the nineteenth and twentieth centuries. Less obviously important but equally revealing are items like election T-shirts, presentation plaques, cartoons and photos, which make up part of the valuable heritage of the lives of female political leaders. The Museum of Australian Democracy holds many of the items mentioned here and this chapter analyses, through a study of some of the museum's collection of objects relating to female political leaders, the complexities of women's struggle for political representation and leadership both in Australia and elsewhere.

Other cultural forums provide evidence of women's advocacy and activism as a mode of leadership. As Mary Tomsic demonstrates, concerned women have publicly and actively taken an interest in the types of screen entertainment available for children in Australia since the 1920s. A number of women presented evidence at the 1927 Royal Commission on the Motion Picture Industry about the effects of films on children. In doing so the types of entertainment that these women believed to be appropriate for the nation's children were articulated. This interest continued to grow, and in particular the introduction of television into Australian homes from 1956 provided an impetus for more activity. While work in the area of children's film and television has not been the sole domain of women, it is women's social activism that has proven to be a significant force. Women's leadership has taken a number of forms, and has pursued differing political and social agendas. Despite this, what remains consistent is the understanding of children as important viewers, whose entertainment should be taken seriously. Whether as social/community workers, interested mothers, academics or film workers—all the women have in their own ways advocated for 'good' entertainment for children. What is suitable and good entertainment is contentious and historically specific, but significantly, adults campaigning for children's entertainment is social action carried out on behalf of others. It is argued that this helping work by women can be understood as a means of enacting children's social citizenship. In this chapter Tomsic examines some specific instances of women's involvement with censorship and the royal commission, and in doing so she highlights the varying approaches taken and the vast amount of (mostly unpaid) labour that has been carried out by women exerting their influence in the public sphere with the aim of improving screen entertainment available to Australian children.

In her chapter on women and literary leadership, Susan Sheridan poses the question: in what ways have twentieth-century Australian women exercised leadership through their literary work? Poets and novelists like Judith Wright, Henry Handel Richardson and Christina Stead are well known for the memorable stories and images conveyed by their writing, and it could be said they offer models of individual achievement. Others have led public opinion in more conventional ways, furthering the cause of Australian literature by advocacy (Miles Franklin) or by exercising their influence as editors (Beatrice Davis at Angus & Robertson publishing company). Sheridan explores how women have been active in establishing and running three writers' associations, the Fellowship of Australian Writers (established in 1928 and dominated in the 1930s by Flora Eldershaw and Marjorie Barnard), Sydney PEN (founded in 1931 by Ethel Turner, Mary Gilmore and Dorothea Mackellar) and the Australian Society of Authors (founded in 1963, with Barbara Jefferis as its first woman president in 1973). In these cases of women's leadership, they were not organising on their own behalf as women, but as writers, for writers of both sexes. And in doing this, they established social and political networks to work towards improving the opportunities and income prospects for all Australian writers.

In the final part of this collection, movements for social change are explored. Aspects of women's leadership are examined through concepts of consensus, career trajectory of women leaders and patterns of women's leadership. Marian Sawer and Merrindahl Andrew argue that participatory democracy was a catchcry of the student movements of the 1960s but too often concealed the continuance of gender hierarchies. The women's liberation movement reacted to this contradiction, seeking an alternative to male models of leadership and organisation. The 1970s saw a sustained attempt to institutionalise these new organisational norms in the women's services established in many Western democracies.

Traditional forms of leadership were associated with hierarchy and the subordination of women. Instead of leadership being seen in terms of the attributes of an individual, the new direction was to look at the functions of leadership and how they could be democratically shared within a group. Functions included not only setting and achieving goals but also maintaining group morale and nurturing members. The concept of shared leadership was embodied in the flatter structures adopted by women's movement organisations (matrices rather than hierarchies) and the emphasis on democratic process and consensus decision-making. This philosophy was seen both as reflecting preferred female ways of organising and as supporting the empowerment of women.

The idea of shared leadership became important in the movements for social change in which women were playing a central role, including the environment and consumer movements examined here. In these movements it was rare for women to be willing to be described as 'leaders' in the traditional sense. In transnational organisations such as the United Nations, the kind of expertise required for effectiveness might seem distant from the practice of shared leadership; however, as shown in Rimmer's chapter on feminist engagement with the United Nations, there are common elements aimed at the empowerment of women, whether through information sharing or the emphasis on more inclusive processes.

Jane Elix and Judy Lambert examine women's activism in the environment movement since the 1970s. Charismatic leadership, they note, is highly valued in the environment movement, but leaders are also usually expected to respect and work within low-hierarchy structures, undertake extensive internal consultation and demonstrate inclusive decision-making. Leaders also often take on significant managerial and fundraising roles at the same time as being involved in high-stakes public campaigns. This chapter examines patterns of female leadership within the environment movement, primarily through analysis of interviews with 34 women leaders who were involved in the movement from the 1970s to the present. During this time women have been active participants and leaders in community environment groups at local and regional levels, and in State-based environment organisations, but their presence in national leadership roles has been much less obvious. Elix and Lambert consider how women leaders in the environment movement combine leadership with family responsibilities; whether the expectations placed on such leaders—including high levels of commitment over long periods—are compatible with women's lives; the differences between women's and men's leadership in the environment movement; patterns in the career trajectories of women leaders in the environment movement; and the impact of feminist values on women leaders' self-perception.

In the final chapter, Jane Elix and Kate Moore argue that with the creation of the National Consumers' League by Florence Kelly in the United States, political action by consumers has been largely identified with women. This coincides with the gender stereotyping of consumption as a female activity, in contrast with the masculine (and more heroic) domain of production. The consumer movement is composed of many different types of organisation, all of them feminised to some degree. In Australia the largest is probably Choice, whose flagship magazine receives extensive media coverage. Women founded Choice and have shaped its direction. Similarly, women dominated the board of management and staff of the former peak body for consumer groups, the Australian Federation of Consumer Organisations (1974–94), briefly renamed the Consumers' Federation of Australia (1994–96). Turning to government, we find that consumer affairs is also a portfolio characteristically held by women. The consumer movement has been largely absent from the social movement literature, perhaps because of its gender but also because its repertoires have rarely included the kind of disruptive protest events that have attracted male scholars. This chapter redresses this invisibility and explores the patterns in women's leadership across different consumer sectors through interviews with women leaders.

* * * *

Collectively, the chapters of this book point to the ways in which the definition of leadership, and who is defined as a leader, is a historical, social and cultural process. Without taking these factors and processes into account, our knowledge of women's engagement with leadership is diminished. It is through adopting a historical and social perspective on women's leadership that we can more fully explain how women's leadership has often gone unnoticed; it has frequently been labelled as community organising or something else. In addition to this, women themselves have often eschewed the term, choosing instead to describe their achievements in collective terms. The studies here provide examples of the diversity and range of women's leadership and demonstrate their significance in inspiring the actions of others within local, national and international contexts. It is by seriously and broadly interrogating the actions and work of women that we can begin to unravel the powerful discourse of leadership and consider the diversity of modes in which leadership is carried out and the range of women who have worked towards guiding social change.

References

Brett, Judith. 'They Had it Coming, Gillard and the Misogynists.' *The Monthly* 84 (November 2012). http://www.themonthly.com.au/gillard-and-misogynists-they-had-it-coming-judith-brett-6770.

Davis, Fiona, Nell Musgrove and Judith Smart. 'Introduction.' In *Founders, Firsts and Feminists: Women Leaders in Twentieth-Century Australia*, edited by Fiona Davis, Nell Musgrove and Judith Smart, 1–12. Melbourne: eScholarship Research Centre, University of Melbourne, 2011. http://www.womenaustralia.info/leaders/fff/index.html.

Francis, Rosemary, Patricia Grimshaw and Ann Standish. 'Identifying Women Leaders in Twentieth-Century Australia: An Introduction.' In *Seizing the Initiative: Women Leaders in Politics, Workplaces and Communities*, edited by Rosemary Francis, Patricia Grimshaw and Ann Standish, 3–14. Melbourne: eScholarship Research Centre, University of Melbourne, 2012. http://www.womenaustralia.info/leaders/sti/index.html.

'Joining the Neighbourhood.' *Boyer Lectures 2013: Back to Grassroots*. 3 November 2013. http://www.abc.net.au/radionational/programs/boyerlectures/.

'Julia Gillard in Conversation with Anne Summers.' 30 September 2013. http://australianpolitics.com/2013/09/30/gillard-summers-conversation-sydney.html.

'Gillard's Misogyny Speech Goes Global.' *ABC News Online*, 10 October 2012. http://www.abc.net.au/news/2012-10-10/international-reaction-to-gillard-speech/4305294.

Maley, Jacqueline. 'I Give as Good as I Get: Gillard.' *Age, Daily Life*, 11 December 2012. http://www.dailylife.com.au/news-and-views/dl-opinion/i-give-as-good-as-i-get-gillard-20121210-2b4p5.html.

'Nobel Laureate Leymah Gbowee Praises Gillard's Misogyny Speech.' *ABC News Online*, 9 April 2013. http://www.abc.net.au/news/2013-04-09/nobel-peace-prize-winner-leymah-gbowee-on-the-drum/4619274.

'The 2013 Time100 Poll.' 28 March 2013. http://time100.time.com/2013/03/28/time-100-poll/slide/julia-gillard/.

Part I
Feminist perspectives and leadership

1. A feminist case for leadership

Amanda Sinclair[1]

On 10 October 2012, Australia's then Prime Minister, Julia Gillard, addressed the Australian Parliament in response to a motion put by Opposition Leader Tony Abbott. While the motion concerned the future of disgraced Speaker, Peter Slipper, Gillard's speech was a call to, and invocation of, feminist leadership. Gillard used the occasion to draw attention to a concerted campaign of misogynistic, sexist attacks from the Opposition and some of their associates, not just towards herself but also towards Australian women in general.

Julia Gillard's speech followed earlier concerns expressed by prominent feminists—for example, Moira Rayner and Anne Summers—about the escalating sexism in public commentary about the prime minister.[2] For example, Summers argues that a new and contagious level of misogyny has been given voice via social media sites, evidencing a level of discrimination and bullying that would be treated as illegal were it to occur in a company.

Why can the prime minister's speech be seen as a call to and example of feminist leadership? I argue in this chapter that feminism brings with it an insistence on facing squarely several things. First, it demands we look at the sustained, yet routinised and systemic way in which women are demeaned, discriminated against and subordinated because of their sex. Second, feminism helps us understand why the special category of women with power (leaders) will attract particularly vicious and brutal efforts to drive women into silence or submission. Third, feminism brings us theories and ways of comprehending the 'underbelly' of leadership: the hubris that often takes sexually exploitative forms that we have seen played out in the demise of America's Central Intelligence Agency chief David Petraeus. Gillard's speech invited listeners to notice the pernicious and insidious ways sexism continues to work against women, and to see how public platforms of leadership are often used, consciously and unconsciously, to advance this agenda. Women's efforts towards leadership take place against the backdrop of women's subordination. For example, women's bodies are scrutinised and routinely measured against sex stereotypes, portraying them as less leader-like.[3] Though some may argue that instances of outright discrimination have

---

1   The University of Melbourne.

2   Moira Rayner, 'Gillard, Bligh and Leadership in a Crisis', *Eureka Street*, 7 January 2011; Anne Summers, 'The Political Persecution of Australia's First Female Prime Minister', Human Rights and Social Justice Lecture, University of Newcastle, 31 August 2012. See also Amanda Lohrey, 'A Matter of Context: Gillard and the Press Gallery', *The Monthly* 84 (November 2012); and Judith Brett, 'They Had it Coming: Gillard and the Misogynists', *The Monthly* 84 (November 2012).

3   Amanda Sinclair, 'Body Possibilities in Leadership', *Leadership* 1(4) (2005): 387–406; and Amanda Sinclair, 'Leading with Body', in *Handbook of Gender, Work and Organization*, eds E. Jeanes, D. Knights and P. Martin

been reduced, there is plenty of evidence of emerging forms of media in which women are routinely derogated and treated as sex objects. This backdrop shapes how women are seen, and their experiences in public life, in turn affecting their appetite for leadership.

While leadership has become a popular ideal, there have been few explorations of both the problems with and the possibilities of leadership from a feminist point of view.[4] If gender is recognised as an issue, it is through noting women's 'lack of fit' for leadership, or the need to make 'the business case' for appointing women more persuasive. It is understandable that women and especially feminist leaders and scholars have been wary of leadership. Leadership as the lionisation of the achievement of individuals in powerful, privileged positions is the antithesis of what many women have fought for. Indigenous leader Lillian Holt echoes the views of many when she suggests 'leadership is a white male idea'.[5]

Yet the argument of this chapter (and indeed to some extent this collection) is that while we might oppose traditional constructs of leadership, women have a strong interest in the broader phenomena of leadership. How have women influenced and changed the public agenda and improved the life experiences of the people around and following after them? Precisely because leadership has become such a powerful discourse, with people at all levels of society being urged to undertake more leadership, it is vital to deconstruct, interrogate and reapproach leadership from a feminist point of view.

In the first part of this chapter, I define and provide a short history of leadership, including the rise of interest in women and leadership. In the second part of this chapter, I explore leadership from a feminist perspective. Scholars and those with a feminist perspective have been conceptualising and critiquing organisation, management and leadership throughout the period of leadership's ascendancy. Women activists and leaders have, and are, reorienting our understandings,

---

(New York: John Wiley & Sons, 2011), 117–30.

4   Exceptions include studies of feminist organisation that discuss leadership tangentially. See, for example: Myra Marx Ferree and Patricia Yancey Martin, *Feminist Organizations: Harvest of the New Women's Movement* (Philadelphia: Temple University Press, 1995); Marta Calas and Linda Smircich, 'From "the Woman's" Point of View: Feminist Approaches to Organization Studies', in *Handbook of Organization Studies*, eds Stuart Clegg, C. Hardy and W. Nord (Thousand Oaks, Calif.: Sage, 1996), 218–57; and Karen Lee Ashcraft, 'Organized Dissonance: Feminist Bureaucracy as Hybrid Form', *Academy of Management Journal* 44(6) (2001): 1301–22. On feminist perspectives on leadership, see, for example: Susan Carroll, 'Feminist Scholarship on Political Leadership', in *Leadership: Multidisciplinary Perspectives*, ed. Barbara Kellerman (Englewood Cliffs, NJ: Prentice Hall, 1984); Jill Blackmore, 'Disrupting Notions of Leadership from Feminist Postcolonial Positions', *International Journal of Leadership in Education: Theory and Practice* 13(1) (2010): 1–6.

5   Quoted in Amanda Sinclair, *Leadership for the Disillusioned: Moving beyond Myths and Heroes to Leading that Liberates* (Sydney: Allen & Unwin, 2007).

public images and imagination about what good leadership is. Drawing on this work, I make a 'feminist case' for how leadership should be recognised and researched.[6]

Leadership: Definitions and a brief history

Leadership is not a position or a person but a process of influence, often aimed at mobilising people towards change—for example, in values, attitudes, approaches, behaviours and ideologies.[7] Recent research on 'adaptive leadership' explores how to exercise leadership with less authority (the formal power that comes from position). Scholars with an interest in adaptive leadership focus on complex public policy and community problems, where the leadership task might involve, for example, supporting groups to face realities and accept responsibilities, creating opportunities and encouraging aspiring leaders to foster social learning or sustainable problem-solving.[8] In this version, leaders are less likely to be out front, telling followers what to do, and more likely to be in groups, working from within, between, sometimes on the edge or from below.

Leadership therefore can be exercised by individuals located in the middle or at the bottom of organisations, by people without formal authority as much as by CEOs and prime ministers. These views of leadership are consistent with feminist formulations. For example, in her feminist analysis of political leadership, Susan Carroll defines an effective leader as 'one who empowers others to act in their own interests, rather than one who induces others to behave in a manner consistent with the goals and desires of the leader'.[9] Leadership is only comprehensible in relation to its educational, empowering and nurturing effects for followers.

Yet these understandings of leadership are recent views. Scholar Joe Raelin observes there is a 'long history in institutional thought and practice of considering leadership as an individual property'.[10] Further, when you ask

---

6   The title of this chapter draws on Kathy Ferguson's critique of bureaucracy titled *The Feminist Case against Bureaucracy* (Philadelphia: Temple University Press, 1984). In contrast with Ferguson, who argued that the logic of bureaucracy was fundamentally antithetical to feminism, I suggest there is value in applying a feminist lens and intent to leadership. See also Hester Eisenstein, 'The Australian Femocratic Experiment: A Feminist Case for Bureaucracy', in *Feminist Organizations: Harvest of the New Women's Movement*, eds Myra Marx Ferree and Patricia Yancey Martin (Philadelphia: Temple University Press, 1995), 69–83.

7   Mary Uhl Bien, 'Relational Leadership Theory: Exploring the Social Processes of Leadership and Organizing', *The Leadership Quarterly* 17 (2006): 668.

8   For treatments of adaptive leadership, see: Ron Heifetz, *Leadership without Easy Answers* (Cambridge, Mass.: Belknap Press, 1994); Ron Heifetz and Marty Linsky, *Leadership on the Line: Staying Alive through the Dangers of Leading* (Boston: Harvard Business School Press, 2002); and Dean Williams, *Real Leadership: Helping People and Organizations Face their Toughest Challenges* (San Francisco: Berrett-Koehler, 2005).

9   Carroll, 'Feminist Scholarship', 142.

10   Joseph Raelin, 'From Leadership-as-Practice to Leaderful Practice', *Leadership* 7(2) (2011): 195.

people about leadership they often nominate performances of toughness or 'greatness'. And 'greatness' is an adjective that is almost always applied to men. Constructions of modern leadership remain, according to Keith Grint, 'irredeemably masculine, heroic, individualist and normative in orientation and nature'.[11] An alarming amount of common wisdom about leadership derives directly from the military. In research that colleagues and I undertook in the 1990s, one of the key themes that emerged from interviewing CEOs was the idea of leadership as combat, involving 'rallying the troops' and 'taking no prisoners'.[12] Further and particularly in the United States, which has dominated leadership research, the psychological and social sciences have been concentrating on questions about selecting and training leaders.[13] Aspects of an idealised American national character—individualism, self-reliance, competitiveness, assertiveness—have thus come to underpin much leadership theorising, development and training.[14]

The continuing appeal of notions of tough, heroic leadership is important to those of us with an interest in women's leadership because we can also notice how theories of leadership have been remarkably adaptive. As soon as a powerful critique begins to be mobilised about leadership, we see emerging a new emphasis on 'collaborative', 'empowered' or 'relational' leadership, often with sporting coaches given as exemplars. We are tempted to sigh with relief at this point and say, 'Oh, things must be changing'. But many of these manoeuvres provide a veneer of doing leadership differently, of looking more enlightened but without any systematic analysis of power, who has it and how it is reproduced in ways that render women less likely as leaders. In another example, since the late 1980s there has been a nostalgic turn to notions of transformational and charismatic leadership. While studies have shown women exhibit at least as many transformational behaviours as men, when they do so they are rarely judged as favourably as men.[15]

Interest in women's leadership

From the late 1970s and 1980s and alongside the rise of second-wave feminism and a focus on affirmative action in many Western countries, feminist scholarship

---

11   Keith Grint, 'A History of Leadership', in *The Sage Handbook of Leadership*, eds Alan Bryman, David Collinson, Keith Grint, Brad Jackson and Mary Uhl-Bien (Sage: London, 2011), 8.

12   Amanda Sinclair, *Trials at the Top: Chief Executives Talk about Men, Women and the Australian Executive Culture* (Melbourne: The Australian Centre, 1994).

13   Loren Baritz, *The Servants of Power: A History of the Use of Social Science* (Connecticut: Wesleyan University Press, 1960).

14   Barbara Kellerman, ed., *Bad Leadership: What it is, How it Happens, Why it Matters* (Boston, Mass.: Harvard Business School Press, 2004), 10.

15   For one exception, see Beverly Alimo-Metcalfe's work on transformational leadership.

began to document women's experiences of organising and influencing the public agenda, including in Australia.[16] It was also during this period that leadership as an idea was particularly taken up by business schools, management theorists and social psychologists.

It is, however, notable the two areas of thinking were rarely put together. Scholars—then and still—focus on business and politics as natural homes for leadership while neglecting women's leadership in communities and schools.[17] As Jeff Hearn and Wendy Parkin note, much of the early literature on 'women in management' was 'business oriented, American in origin and in cultural assumptions, often unduly optimistic about the immediate possibilities for change'.[18] A psychological preoccupation became common, with studies focusing on the qualities women needed in management, and whether there were enduring sex differences that meant women and men led and managed differently. The 'sex differences' approach to women in management generated considerable research from the late 1970s. Researchers concluded that there was little difference due to sex in achievement motivation, risk-taking, task persistence and other significant managerial skills. Hence, even early research demonstrated that women are not psychologically handicapped for leadership but rather face a barrage of gendered assumptions and stereotypes about their fitness for leadership, which are translated into discriminatory norms and organisational practices in areas such as recruitment and promotion.

By the late 1980s and early 1990s, a new interest specifically focused on women and leadership was emerging. Again, much of the early work came from American business-oriented researchers. Judy Rosener, writing in *Harvard Business Review* in 1990, argued that there was now a 'second wave' of women leaders who no longer had to mimic the 'command and control' male model of organisational leadership.[19] Further, they are 'succeeding because of—not in spite of—certain characteristics generally considered to be "feminine" and inappropriate in leaders'.[20] Rosener makes the case that these women are 'transformational' or distinctly 'interactive' in their leadership. 'More

---

16 In Australia, the federal *Sex Discrimination Act* was passed in 1984 and the *Affirmative Action Act* in 1986. This was a period characterised by increased opportunities for women, especially in politics and the federal bureaucracy. See Marian Sawer's research—for example: *Sisters in Suits: Women and Public Policy in Australia* (Sydney: Allen & Unwin, 1990); and also Hester Eisenstein's work—for example: *Inside Agitators: Australian Femocrats and the State* (Sydney: Allen & Unwin, 1996).

17 For an alternative view of the role of women in community leadership, see Marian Sawer and Merrindahl Andrew's Chapter 15, in this volume.

18 Jeff Hearn and Wendy Parkin, 'Women, Men and Leadership: A Critical Review of Assumptions, Practices and Change in the Industrialized Nations', in *Women in Management Worldwide*, eds N. Adler and D. Izraeli (Armonk, NY: M. E. Sharpe, 1988), 24. On the dangers of being overoptimistic about women's progress, see also Linda Blum and Vicki Smith, 'Women's Mobility in the Corporation: A Critique of the Politics of Optimism', *Signs: Journal of Women in Culture and Society* 13(3) (1988): 528–45.

19 Judy Rosener, 'Ways Women Lead', *Harvard Business Review* November–December 1990: 119–25.

20 Ibid., 120.

specifically, the women encourage participation, share power and information, enhance other people's self-worth, and get others excited about their work.'[21] This form of leadership is highly effective, she argues, and organisations should be open to expanding their definitions of effective leadership.

Rosener's argument—that women lead differently to men—elicited controversy, with researchers noting the consequences of identifying a 'feminine' or 'women's' style of leading. For example, writing that deplores the effects of stereotyping is used to create new stereotypes—for example, that women are more empathetic and people-friendly, and therefore suited to 'support' roles rather than leadership ones. Such new stereotypes are not benign. They are deployed to set higher standards for women in some areas and marginalise them in others.

Long-time scholar of women's leadership Alice Eagly observes the contradictions in much of the popular research.[22] Women leaders are identified as having a 'female advantage': showing up as consistently demonstrating qualities of transformational leadership such as 'individualised consideration', 'inspirational motivation' and 'intellectual stimulation'. They are, however, simultaneously disadvantaged by stereotypes of leadership that resemble stereotypes of men— that is, agentic, confident, aggressive and self-determined. Eagly concludes: 'men can seem usual or natural in most leadership roles … people more easily credit men with leadership ability and more readily accept them as leaders.'[23] She notes that though prejudices against women leaders dropped significantly from the 1970s and 1980s, there was evidence of plateauing or even reversal of this trend in recent years, especially in traditionally masculine fields.

Bringing a feminist perspective to leadership

Why make a 'feminist case' for leadership? In this second part of the chapter, I show how feminist work deepens, challenges and in some cases subverts understandings of leadership. Feminism as a perspective and field has undergone enormous changes through the second part of the twentieth century and into the twenty-first.[24] Initially, distinctions between radical and liberal feminism and, later, the impact of social theories such as post-structuralism, postmodernism and postcolonial scholarship have produced rich divergences in feminist thinking,

---

21   Ibid.
22   Alice Eagly, 'Female Leadership Advantage and Disadvantage: Resolving the Contradiction', *Leadership. Volume IV: 2005–2009*, eds David Collinson, Keith Grint and Brad Jackson (London: Sage, 2011), 251–72.
23   Ibid., 257.
24   See, for example: Chris Weedon, *Feminist Practice and Poststructural Theory* (Oxford: Blackwell, 1987); and Sandra Harding's discussion of whether there is a feminist methodology in 'Introduction: Is there a Feminist Method?', in *Feminism and Methodology*, ed. Sandra Harding (Bloomington: Indiana University Press, 1987), 1–14.

especially on theorisations of power and hierarchy, the agency of women and the risks of women speaking for other women. For example, feminists differ on whether women organising can, or must, dispense with hierarchy and formal leaders. Writing by women of colour, Indigenous and postcolonial scholars has critiqued the earlier assumptions by some feminists that all women share the same interests.[25] For many, a response is to recognise there are many feminisms, not one.[26]

Building on this notion of multiple and unfolding feminisms, I seek here to identify and explore some themes and emphases in feminist work that are of central importance to leadership.[27] These include the following.

1. A starting point that knowledge has often been built on male experience and is designed to serve men's interests; feminism seeks to reinscribe and reinstate the experience of women in the historical and intellectual records. Hence, feminists are aiming for change in patriarchal structures.

2. A determination to focus on power and privilege, especially manifestations of structural power in gender relations, which often escape attention.

3. A commitment to, and interest in, non-hierarchical relations in the ways groups and organisations are formed and run and in the way research is done.

4. An interest in those areas of public and private experience that traditional patriarchal accounts tend to obscure, such as theorising about bodies.

5. Enactment of reflexivity in research methods and seeking to empower others through research;[28] owning one's own context and recognising how that affects what we see and say; and a preference towards 'textual multiplicity' in writing.[29]

Women have been conceptualising and critiquing bureaucracy and organisation, management and leadership for many decades, starting with the pioneering work of Mary Parker Follet in the first half of the twentieth century. Researchers have

---

25 For example, Bell Hooks, *Feminist Theory from Margin to Centre* (Boston: South End, 1984), and *Talking Back: Thinking Feminist, Thinking Black* (Boston: South End, 1989); Chandra Talpede Mohanty, *Feminism without Borders: Decolonizing Theory, Practicing Solidarity* (Durham, NC, and London: Duke University Press 2003), 47.

26 Jean Lau Chin, 'Transforming Leadership with Diverse Feminist Voices', in *Women and Leadership: Transforming Visions and Diverse Voices*, eds Jean Lau Chin, Bernice Lott, Joy Rice and Janice Sanchez-Hucles (Malden, Mass.: Blackwell, 2007).

27 See also Judith Pringle, 'Feminism and Management: Critique and Contribution', in *New Directions in Management*, eds Alex Kouzmin, Leonie Still and P. Clarke (Sydney: McGraw Hill, 1994); and Patricia Yancey Martin, 'Feminist Practice in Organizations: Implications for Management', in *Women in Management*, ed. Ellen Fagenson (Thousand Oaks, Calif.: Sage, 1994).

28 Harding, 'Introduction'; and Michelle Young and Linda Skrla, eds, *Reconsidering Feminist Research in Educational Leadership* (Albany, NY: State University of New York Press, 2003).

29 Patti Lather, *Getting Smart: Feminist Research and Pedagogy with/in the Postmodern* (New York: Routledge, 1991).

argued that Follet challenged conventional leadership approaches and made a case for 'transformational leadership' long before James Macgregor Burns, the political scientist credited with originating the term in 1978.[30]

During the late 1970s and 1980s, as the field of contemporary leadership studies started to gain momentum, gender scholars and feminists also began to deconstruct organisational and leadership life. Instead of focusing on women as the 'other' in management who somehow needed to 'learn the ropes', researchers documented how organisations and leadership were set up to maintain a gender order in which masculinities were privileged.[31] Administrative logic and 'merit-based' principles and practices are not neutral but designed, in the words of Australian scholar Clare Burton, to 'mobilise masculine bias'.[32] Burton and others have thus argued that our focus should shift from individual women and their experiences in organisations to the structures in which they are located, including the construction and maintenance of masculinities.

Throughout the 1990s there emerged a new focus on masculinities and management. Sociologists such as R. W. Connell, as well as critical and feminist organisational theorists, began to map the cultural norms of hegemonic masculinity in how to be a manager and leader.[33] Until this time leadership had mostly been treated as a 'gender-free' zone (unless of course you were a woman, when usually one's gender was rendered problematic). In the weighty handbooks of leadership research, there were few if any entries on gender, masculinity or sexuality. In my own research in the early 1990s, I remember clearly the moment when I realised that in order to understand the obstacles to women aspiring to leadership, I needed to shift my focus from women to men.[34] I argued the need to dissect the construction of male executive cultures, including the way in which leadership was often reinforced by male heterosexuality. In contrast, women's sexuality or sense of sexual identity was seen to undermine their leadership, needing to be repressed or camouflaged. Not surprisingly, my focus on masculinities was unpopular, especially among male audiences. It has always been far more comfortable to keep the 'problem' of gender located in women and to hold women responsible for fixing their own exclusion.

---

30 Pauline Graham, *Mary Parker Follett—Prophet of Management: A Celebration of Writings from the 1920s* (Boston: Harvard Business School Press, 1995).

31 Joan Acker, 'Hierarchies, Jobs, Bodies', *Gender and Society* 4 (2) (1990): 139–58.

32 Clare Burton, 'Merit and Gender: Organizations and the Mobilization of Masculine Bias', *Australian Journal of Social Issues* 22(2) (1987): 424–435.

33 R. W. Connell, *Gender and Power: Society, the Person and Sexual Politics* (Cambridge: Polity Press, 1987), and *Masculinities* (Sydney: Allen & Unwin, 1995); Cynthia Cockburn, *In the Way of Women: Men's Resistance to Sex Equality in Organizations* (London: Macmillan, 1991); David Collinson and Jeff Hearn, *Men as Managers, Managers as Men: Critical Perspectives on Men, Masculinities and Managements* (London: Sage, 1996); and Joan Eveline, 'The Worry of Going Limp: Are You Keeping Up in Senior Management?', *Australian Feminist Studies* 11(3) (1996): 65–79.

34 Sinclair, *Trials at the Top.*

Shifting the focus from the 'problem' of women to understanding the means by which male cultures are perpetuated in leadership has therefore been a key contribution.[35] In their analysis of leadership writing, feminist organisational scholars Marta Calas and Linda Smircich argue that leadership is about seduction. The words 'seduction' and 'leadership' have common origins with the Latin root of seduction, *se ducere*, meaning 'lead' or 'to lead astray'. Calas and Smircich select and deconstruct sections of texts from four leadership 'gurus' whose work spans more than 50 years. They argue that leadership writing is complicit in reinforcing 'the homosocial libidinal economy of competitiveness and glory' as if it were the truth, and indeed, with each new discourse, a kind of deeper and more powerful truth.[36]

Many women and critical scholars have helped us see that leadership is not 'great deeds by great men' but a relational, discursive and intersubjective phenomena between people.[37] Leadership is not simply the way someone does a job or activity, but rather a series of ways of talking and understanding that is prefigured by relations of power and knowledge. Accordingly, from this perspective, leadership is already a discursively produced, privileged ideology that casts some performances as leadership and others, such as what women do, as something less than leadership. Drawing on a discourse perspective changes our understanding of leadership as a predetermined power/language position made available only to designated individuals.

Related to this, women scholars have always been centrally interested in the relationship between leadership and power. Power has been neglected in most leadership texts, which often take the view that formal power is an unproblematic accompaniment of leadership. Because of their general lack of power, women have often been more attuned to its use and effects, as well as open to theorising alternatives. How is leadership used to centralise and entrench power in an elite, or how is leadership sometimes used to unmask power and reduce oppression? Further, how is power played out in more micro, intimate relationships and how do we exercise leadership in ways that minimise dominance and oppression?[38]

One of the few areas of leadership research where women figure prominently in populations of leaders is in educational leadership in schools and universities.

---

35   Joan Eveline, 'The Politics of Advantage', *Australian Feminist Studies* 9(19) (1994): 129–54.
36   Marta Calas and Linda Smircich, 'Voicing Seduction to Silence Leadership', *Organization Studies* 12(4) (1991): 583.
37   See, for example: Jackie Ford, 'Discourses of Leadership: Gender, Identity and Contradiction in a UK Public Sector Organization', *Leadership* 2(1) (2006): 77–99, and 'Studying Leadership Critically: A Psychosocial Lens on Leadership Identities', *Leadership* 6(1) (2010): 47–65. Also Donna Ladkin, *Rethinking Leadership: A New Look at Old Leadership Questions* (Cheltenham, UK: Edward Elgar, 2010); Gail Fairhurst, *Discursive Leadership: In Conversation with Leadership Psychology* (Thousand Oaks, Calif.: Sage, 2007).
38   See, for example, Cynthia Cockburn's research of women leading the peace movement through dialogue with other women from opposing national, racial and cultural groups: *The Space between Us* (London: Zed Books, 1998), and *From Where We Stand: War Women's Activism and Feminist Analysis* (London: Zed Books, 2007).

Here women principals and senior administrators have often been at the forefront of upholding more traditional educational values against intense market and corporatisation pressures.[39] Both the women educational leaders and their researchers display a capacity to continually reflect and adjust around the balance of these tensions. Blackmore and Sachs describe their experience as one of living in contradictions—for example, between performing to new stakeholders and focusing on substantive educational and ethical issues: 'doing well' versus 'doing good'.[40]

Where women have some freedom to organise themselves differently, do feminist leadership patterns emerge? There has been extensive discussion about principles of feminist organising, particularly in international development and transnational networks, among postcolonial scholars, and feminist, Indigenous and other women's groups.[41] This research documents that women organising consistently reject hierarchy, put effort into building relationships and empowering others, and emphasise collective achievement and responsibility, rather than the leadership of individuals. At the same time, collections exploring women's leadership usually find there is considerable diversity in the way women go about the job of leading despite a common interest in transforming outcomes to better serve women's interests.[42] Partially this arises because of the contexts and constraints they must work around, within and against to do their leadership work.

Feminists and postcolonial scholars have critiqued models of leadership perpetuated by the dominance of elites and institutions such as the World Bank. A common thread is the focus on the discourses of colonialism, development and postcolonialism. Mohanty, for example, argues that genuine decolonisation that allows for the recovery of authentic indigenous values and culture is hindered by the embedded 'archive' of Western 'knowledge and systems, rules and values'.[43] She says that 'privilege nurtures blindness'. Feminist standpoint theory has advanced the idea that the perspectives of the marginalised and disempowered are a source of leadership. As Sandra Harding has also suggested,

---

39   Valerie Hall, *Dancing on the Ceiling: A Study of Women Managers in Education* (London: Paul Chapman, 1999); Jill Blackmore, *Troubling Women: Feminism, Leadership and Educational Change* (Buckingham, UK: Open University Press, 1999); Jill Blackmore and Judyth Sachs, *Performing and Reforming Leaders: Gender, Educational Restructuring, and Organizational Change* (Albany, NY: State University of New York Press, 2007); Young and Skrla, *Reconsidering Feminist Research in Educational Leadership*.

40   Blackmore and Sachs, *Performing and Reforming Leaders*.

41   For example, Ferree and Martin, *Feminist Organizations*; Kathleen Iannello, *Decisions without Hierarchy: Feminist Interventions in Organization Theory and Practice* (New York: Routledge, 1992); Helen Brown, *Women Organizing* (London: Taylor & Francis, 1992); Chin et al., *Women and Leadership*; Cockburn, *From Where We Stand*.

42   Chin et al., *Women and Leadership*; Blackmore, *Troubling Women*; Ferree and Martin, *Feminist Organizations*.

43   Mohanty, *Feminism without Borders*, 47.

standpoint research seeks to 'study up', revealing the norms and practices of dominant institutions whose impact may only be visible to those subordinated by them.[44]

Women scholars and leaders have also shown that leadership is often done in resistance and refusal from the bottom or the margins of society, rather than from formal positions at the top. Australian Indigenous scholars have increasingly documented the ways Indigenous women have enacted leadership in the face of the deliberate dehumanising sexism and racism that accompanied colonisation and which continue.[45] In her work on Indigenous women's leadership, Pat Dudgeon argues that the women she has researched, including her grandmother (Martha) and great-grandmother (Lillian), demonstrated great leadership in their resistance, in their humour and in their pride and confidence as women. Though the historical records show Aboriginal women were treated as chattels, incubators and prostitutes, these women continued to lead: to stand up and push back, to fight for their families and assert their value as women.[46]

The past decade or so has also seen critical and women scholars drawing attention to the physical, embodied and aesthetic dimensions of leadership.[47] The ideal organisation had always been portrayed as a rational, hierarchical one from which the 'disruptive' forces of sex and bodies had been eradicated. Women theorists and researchers have frequently been the ones who have dug beneath these myths to show how leadership by men often involves the performance of sexual identities, how being a successful leader is also about demonstrating hyper masculinity.[48]

This work also provides another set of explanations for the failure of leadership to be genuinely open to women. From the work of feminists and commentators like Anne Summers, we see that women, historically and now, are defined and subordinated by their female embodiment.[49] The persistence of discrimination hints at deeper causes than the rational, logical ones. Enduring and powerful

---

44   Harding, *Feminism and Methodology*.

45   See, for example: Nerida White, 'Indigenous Australian Women's Leadership: Stayin' Strong against the Postcolonial Tide', *International Journal of Leadership in Education* 13(1) (2010): 7–25.

46   Pat Dudgeon, 'Mothers of Sin: Indigenous Women's Perceptions of their Identity and Sexuality/Gender', Paper delivered at University of Melbourne, 2011.

47   See, for example: Arja Ropo and Erica Sauer, 'Corporeal Leaders', in *The Sage Handbook of New Approaches in Management and Organization*, eds D. Barry and H. Hansen (London: Sage, 2008), 469–78; Donna Ladkin, 'The Enchantment of the Charismatic Leader: Charisma Reconsidered as Aesthetic Encounter', *Leadership* 2(2) (2006): 165–79; also Sinclair, 'Body Possibilities in Leadership'.

48   For a review of some of this work, see Sinclair, 'Leading with Body'.

49   Anne Summers, *Damned Whores and God's Police: The Colonisation of Women in Australia* (Melbourne: Penguin, 1974). See also Clare Burton, *Subordination: Feminism and Social Theory* (Sydney: George Allen & Unwin, 1985).

archetypes of maternal figures are activated when women have power. These archetypes include the omnipotent, controlling mother, and the seductress intent on distracting men from noble purpose.[50]

While the contribution of the research discussed here is much wider than leadership, it shows how the concepts and assumptions underpinning leadership are skewed towards male experience and are blind towards certain dimensions of leadership such as power and bodies. The importance and value of scholarly processes in leadership of deconstruction, critique and remaking cannot be understated. They provide the foundation for problematising assumptions about leadership and the distortions popular leadership discourses produce—in the media, in scholarship and in education.

Conclusion

Attention to women's leadership is welcome on many levels. It brings into the historical and contemporary public records women's leadership contributions. It celebrates the diversity and richness of the ways that women, often blocked by sexism and patriarchal norms, have found to resist and change the public agenda and to mobilise and empower others. The potent mixes of ingenuity, daring and determination described in chapters of this book are surely forms of leadership worth documenting and learning from.

Our role as feminists, scholars and activists, I have suggested, is, however, not just to celebrate this new level of attention. Rather, a feminist case for leadership requires us to bring values and perspectives from feminist research to the case for leadership, we must do the following.

1. Draw attention to the power and privilege reproduced in leadership and leadership research. Feminist researchers need to continue to resist the tide of thinking that focuses on women and what they need to do to 'get up to speed' to improve their eligibility for leadership. They need to continue fearlessly to redirect attention to the ways dominant forms of leadership reinforce the power of a narrow white male elite and continue the oppression of the majority of women, Indigenous peoples and those from non-white backgrounds.

---

50 See, for example: Barbara Poggio, 'Who's Afraid of Mothers?', and A. Telford, 'Maiden, Mother, Mistress, Monster: Controlled and Uncontrolled Female Power and the Curse of the Body in the Early Victorian Novel— Implications of Historical Stereotyping for Women Managers', both in *Interpreting the Maternal Organization*, eds Heather Höpfl and Monica Kostera (London: Routledge, 2003); also Amanda Sinclair, *Doing Leadership Differently* (Melbourne: Melbourne University Press, 1998).

2. Notice that leadership is itself a powerful discourse, which gives attention and legitimacy to our work, but which may also skew our analyses, causing us to lose sight of important values and experiences.

3. Not collude with the biases in leadership research towards individualism and universalism. Leaders rarely act alone. Yet myth-making often lionises the 'self-made man', while neglecting the contributions of those around the leader who do the unpaid, and some argue more important, work of nurturing and caring for families. There is also a particular bias in leadership research that seeks models and rules about how to lead. Such approaches already reflect a masculinist, ethnocentric bias. Rather, leadership work is often about proceeding in ambiguity, in circumstances of 'not knowing', and being open to diverse and shifting measures of success.

4. Be reflective about who we speak for and consider the effects of our work and scholarship on others. It is important that our work on women's leadership is useful, inspiring and empowering for women with less access to power.

Alongside celebrating women's contribution as leaders, I have argued there is an equally if not more important place for the kind of challenge made by former Prime Minister Gillard referred to in my introduction. The feminist task is to draw attention to the ways social and organisational structures, and the invocation of leadership's logic and discourse within those structures, continue to devalue women and their experiences. By locating women's leadership within the wider canvas of women's experiences, we see more clearly how leadership can both support and constrain human possibility.

References

Acker, Joan. 'Hierarchies, Jobs, Bodies.' *Gender and Society* 4(2) (1990): 139–58.

Alimo-Metcalfe, Beverly. 'An Investigation of Female and Male Constructs of Leadership and Empowerment.' *Women in Management Review* 10(2) (1995): 3–8.

Ashcraft, Karen Lee. 'Organized Dissonance: Feminist Bureaucracy as Hybrid Form.' *Academy of Management Journal* 44(6) (2001): 1301–22.

Baritz, Loren. *The Servants of Power: A History of the Use of Social Science.* Connecticut: Wesleyan University Press, 1960.

Boin, Arjen, Paul 't Hart, Eric Stern and Bengt Sundelius. *The Politics of Crisis Management: Public Leadership under Pressure.* Cambridge: Cambridge University Press, 2005.

Blackmore, Jill. *Troubling Women: Feminism, Leadership and Educational Change*. Buckingham, UK: Open University Press, 1999.

Blackmore, Jill. 'Disrupting Notions of Leadership from Feminist Postcolonial Positions.' *International Journal of Leadership in Education: Theory and Practice* 13(1) (2010): 1–6.

Blackmore, Jill and Judyth Sachs. *Performing and Reforming Leaders: Gender, Educational Restructuring, and Organizational Change*. Albany, NY: State University of New York Press, 2007.

Blum, Linda and Vicki Smith. 'Women's Mobility in the Corporation: A Critique of the Politics of Optimism.' *Signs: Journal of Women in Culture and Society* 13(3) (1988): 528–45.

Brett, Judith. 'They Had it Coming: Gillard and the Misogynists.' *The Monthly* 84 (November 2012). https://www.themonthly.com.au/issue/2012/november/1351733161/judith-brett/they-had-it-coming.

Brown, Helen. *Women Organizing*. London: Taylor & Francis, 1992.

Burton, Clare. *Subordination: Feminism and Social Theory*. Sydney: George Allen & Unwin, 1985.

Burton, Clare. 'Merit and Gender: Organizations and the Mobilization of Masculine Bias.' *Australian Journal of Social Issues* 22(2) (1987): 424–35.

Burton, Clare. *The Promise and the Price: The Struggle for Equal Opportunity in Women's Employment*. Sydney: Allen & Unwin, 1991.

Calas, Marta and Linda Smircich. 'Voicing Seduction to Silence Leadership.' *Organization Studies* 12(4) (1991): 567–602.

Calas, Marta and Linda Smircich. 'From "the Woman's" Point of View: Feminist Approaches to Organization Studies.' In *Handbook of Organization Studies*, edited by Stewart Clegg, Cynthia Hardy and William Nord, 218–57. Thousand Oaks, Calif.: Sage, 1996.

Carroll, Susan. 'Feminist Scholarship on Political Leadership.' In *Leadership: Multidisciplinary Perspectives*, edited by Barbara Kellerman, 139–56. Englewood Cliffs, NJ: Prentice Hall, 1984.

Chin, Jean Lau. 'Transforming Leadership with Diverse Feminist Voices.' In *Women and Leadership: Transforming Visions and Diverse Voices*, edited by Jean Lau Chin, Bernice Lott, Joy Rice and Janice Sanchez-Hucles, 355–62. Malden, Mass.: Blackwell, 2007.

Cockburn, Cynthia. *In the Way of Women: Men's Resistance to Sex Equality in Organizations*. London: Macmillan, 1991.

Cockburn, Cynthia. *The Space between Us*. London: Zed Books, 1998. Cockburn, Cynthia. *From Where We Stand: War Women's Activism and Feminist Analysis*. London: Zed Books, 2007.

Collinson, David and Jeff Hearn. *Men as Managers, Managers as Men: Critical Perspectives on Men, Masculinities and Managements*. London: Sage, 1996.

Connell, R. W. *Gender and Power: Society, the Person and Sexual Politics*. Cambridge: Polity Press, 1987.

Connell, R. W. *Masculinities*. Sydney: Allen & Unwin, 1995.

Cregan, Christina, Timothy Bartram and Pauline Stanton. 'Union Organizing as a Mobilizing Strategy: The Impact of Social Identity and Transformational Leadership on the Collectivism of Union Members.' *British Journal of Industrial Relations* 47(4) (2009): 701–22.

Dudgeon, Pat. 'Mothers of Sin: Indigenous Women's Perceptions of their Identity and Sexuality/Gender.' Paper delivered at University of Melbourne, 2011.

Eagly, Alice. 'Female Leadership Advantage and Disadvantage: Resolving the Contradiction.' In *Leadership. Volume IV: 2005–2009*, edited by David Collinson, Keith Grint and Brad Jackson, 251–72. London: Sage, 2011.

Eisenstein, Hester. *Contemporary Feminist Thought*. Sydney: Allen & Unwin, 1984.

Eisenstein, Hester. 'The Australian Femocratic Experiment: A Feminist Case for Bureaucracy.' In *Feminist Organizations: Harvest of the New Women's Movement*, edited by Myra Marx Feree and Patricia Yancey Martin, 69–83. Philadelphia: Temple University Press, 1995.

Eisenstein, Hester. *Inside Agitators: Australian Femocrats and the State*. Sydney: Allen & Unwin, 1996.

Eveline, Joan. 'The Politics of Advantage.' *Australian Feminist Studies* 9(19) (1994): 129–54.

Eveline, Joan. 'The Worry of Going Limp: Are You Keeping Up in Senior Management.' *Australian Feminist Studies* 11(3) (1996): 65–79.

Fairhurst, Gail. *Discursive Leadership: In Conversation with Leadership Psychology*. Thousand Oaks, Calif.: Sage, 2007.

Ferguson, Kathy. *The Feminist Case against Bureaucracy*. Philadephia: Temple University Press, 1984.

Ferree, Myra Marx and Patricia Yancey Martin. 'Doing the Work of the Movement: Feminist Organizations.' In *Feminist Organizations: Harvest of the New Women's Movement*, edited by Myra Marx Ferree and Patricia Yancey Martin, 3–23. Philadelphia: Temple University Press, 1995.

Ferree, Myra Marx and Patricia Yancey Martin, eds. *Feminist Organizations: Harvest of the New Women's Movement*. Philadelphia: Temple University Press, 1995.

Fletcher, Joyce. *Disappearing Acts: Gender, Power and Relational Practice at Work*. Cambridge, Mass.: MIT Press, 1999.

Fletcher, Joyce. 'The Paradox of Post Heroic Leadership: An Essay on Gender, Power and Transformational Change.' *The Leadership Quarterly* 15 (2004): 647–61.

Ford, Jackie. 'Discourses of Leadership: Gender, Identity and Contradiction in a UK Public Sector Organization.' *Leadership* 2(1) (2006): 77–99.

Ford, Jackie. 'Studying Leadership Critically: A Psychosocial Lens on Leadership Identities.' *Leadership* 6(1) (2010): 47–65.

Graham, Pauline. *Mary Parker Follett—Prophet of Management: A Celebration of Writings from the 1920s*. Boston, Mass.: Harvard Business School Press, 1995.

Grint, Keith. 'A History of Leadership.' In *The Sage Handbook of Leadership*, edited by Alan Bryman, David Collinson, Keith Grint, Brad Jackson and Mary Uhl-Bien, 3–14. London: Sage, 2011.

Hall, Valerie. *Dancing on the Ceiling: A Study of Women Managers in Education*. London: Paul Chapman, 1999.

Harding, Sandra. 'Introduction: Is There a Feminist Method?' In *Feminism and Methodology*, edited by Sandra Harding, 1–14. Bloomington: Indiana University Press, 1987.

Harding, Sandra. *Sciences from Below: Feminisms, Postcolonialities, and Modernities*. Durham, NC: Duke University Press, 2008.

Hearn, Jeff and P. Wendy Parkin. 'Women, Men and Leadership: A Critical Review of Assumptions, Practices and Change in the Industrialized Nations.' In *Women in Management Worldwide*, edited by Nancy Adler and Dafna Izraeli, 17–40. Armonk, NY: M. E. Sharpe, 1988.

Heifetz, Ron. *Leadership without Easy Answers*. Cambridge, Mass.: Belknap Press, 1994.

Heifetz, Ron and Marty Linsky. *Leadership on the Line: Staying Alive through the Dangers of Leading*. Boston: Harvard Business School Press, 2002.

Hennig, M. and Ann Jardim. *The Managerial Woman*. London: Marion Boyars, 1978.

Hooks, Bell. *Feminist Theory from Margin to Centre*. Boston: South End, 1984.

Hooks, Bell. *Talking Back: Thinking Feminist, Thinking Black*. Boston: South End Press, 1989.

Höpfl, Heather and Monica Kostera, eds. *Interpreting the Maternal Organization*. London: Routledge, 2003.

Höpfl, Heather and Sumohom. Matilal. 'The Lady Vanishes: Some Thoughts on Women and Leadership.' *Journal of Organizational Change Management* 20(2) (2007): 198-208.

Iannello, Kathleen. *Decisions without Hierarchy: Feminist Interventions in Organization Theory and Practice*. New York: Routledge, 2002.

Kanter, Rosabeth Moss. *Men and Women of the Corporation*. New York: Basic Books, 1977.

Kellerman, Barbara, ed. *Leadership: Multidisciplinary Perspectives*. Englewood Cliffs, NJ: Prentice Hall, 1984.

Kellerman, Barbara. *Bad Leadership: What it is, How it Happens, Why it Matters*. Boston: Harvard Business School Press, 2004.

Ladkin, Donna. 'The Enchantment of the Charismatic Leader: Charisma Reconsidered as Aesthetic Encounter.' *Leadership* 2(2) (2006): 165–79.

Ladkin, Donna. *Rethinking Leadership: A New Look at Old Leadership Questions*. Cheltenham, UK: Edward Elgar, 2010.

Lather, Patti. *Getting Smart: Feminist Research and Pedagogy with/in the Postmodern*. New York: Routledge, 1991.

Lohrey, Amanda. 'A Matter of Context: Gillard and the Press Gallery.' *The Monthly* 84 (November 2012). http://www.themonthly.com.au/issue/2012/november/1354241249/amanda-lohrey/matter-context.

Martin, Patricia Yancey. 'Feminist Practice in Organizations: Implications for Management.' In *Women in Management*, edited by Ellen Fagenson, 274–296. Thousand Oaks, Calif.: Sage, 1994.

Mohanty, Chandra Talpede. *Feminism without Borders: Decolonizing Theory, Practicing Solidarity*. Durham, NC, and London: Duke University Press, 2003.

Poggio, Barbara. 'Who's Afraid of Mothers?' In *Interpreting the Maternal Organization*, edited by Heather Höpfl and Monica Kostera, 13–26. London: Routledge, 2003.

Pringle, Judith. 'Feminism and Management: Critique and Contribution.' In *New Directions in Management*, edited by Alex Kouzmin, Leonie Still and P. Clarke, 127–42. Sydney: McGraw Hill, 1994.

Raelin, Joe. 'From Leadership-as-Practice to Leaderful Practice.' *Leadership* 7(2) (2011): 195–211.

Rayner, Moira. 'Gillard, Bligh and Leadership in a Crisis.' *Eureka Street* 21(2) 7 January 2011. http://www.eurekastreet.com.au/article.aspx?aeid=24745#.U5PsJPna6m4.

Ropo, Arja and Erica Sauer. 'Corporeal Leaders.' In *The Sage Handbook of New Approaches in Management and Organization*, edited by Daved Barry and Hans Hansen, 469–78. London: Sage, 2008.

Rosener, Judy. 'Ways Women Lead.' *Harvard Business Review* (November–December 1990): 119–25.

Sawer, Marian. *Sisters in Suits: Women and Public Policy in Australia*. Sydney: Allen & Unwin, 1990.

Shaw, Jan. 'Papering the Cracks with Discourse: The Narrative Identity of the Authentic Leader.' *Leadership* 6(1) (2010): 89–108.

Sinclair, Amanda. *Trials at the Top: Chief Executives Talk about Men, Women and the Executive Culture*. Melbourne: The Australian Centre, 1994.

Sinclair, Amanda. *Doing Leadership Differently: Gender, Power and Sexuality in a Changing Business Culture*. Melbourne: Melbourne University Press, 1998.

Sinclair, Amanda. 'Bodies Possibilities in Leadership.' *Leadership* 1(4) (2005): 387–406.

Sinclair, Amanda. *Leadership for the Disillusioned: Moving beyond Myths and Heroes to Leading that Liberates*. Sydney: Allen & Unwin, 2007.

Sinclair, Amanda. 'Leading with Body.' In *Handbook of Gender, Work and Organization*, edited by Emma Jeanes, David Knights and Patricia Yancey Martin, 117–30. New York: John Wiley & Sons, 2011.

Summers, Anne. *Damned Whores and God's Police: The Colonisation of Women in Australia*. Melbourne: Penguin, 1974.

Summers, Anne. 'The Political Persecution of Australia's First Female Prime Minister.' Human Rights and Social Justice Lecture, University of Newcastle, 31 August 2012.

Telford, Andrena. 'Maiden, Mother, Mistress, Monster: Controlled and Uncontrolled Female Power and the Curse of the Body in the Early Victorian Novel—Implications of Historical Stereotyping for Women Managers.' In *Interpreting the Maternal Organization*, edited by Heather Höpfl and Monica Kostera, 104–20. London: Routledge, 2003.

Uhl-Bien, Mary. 'Relational Leadership Theory: Exploring the Social Processes of Leadership and Organizing.' *The Leadership Quarterly* 17 (2006): 654–76.

Weedon, Chris. *Feminist Practice and Poststructural Theory*. Oxford: Blackwell, 1987.

White, Nerida. 'Indigenous Australian Women's Leadership: Stayin' Strong against the Postcolonial Tide.' *International Journal of Leadership in Education* 13(1) (2010): 7–25.

Williams, Dean. *Real Leadership: Helping People and Organizations Face their Toughest Challenges*. San Francisco: Berrett-Koehler, 2005.

Young, Michelle and Linda Skrla, eds. *Reconsidering Feminist Research in Educational Leadership*. Albany, NY: State University of New York Press, 2003.

Part II
Indigenous women's leadership

2. Guthadjaka and Garŋgulkpuy: Indigenous women leaders in Yolngu, Australia-wide and international contexts

Gwenda Baker,[1] Joanne Garŋgulkpuy[2] and
Kathy Guthadjaka[3]

This chapter explores the extraordinary growth in political leadership over the past 30 years among Indigenous women from a remote community. It is representative of a wider Australian phenomenon: the intense participation in democratic affairs by Indigenous women. These are two women from among many more: there are others who are participating at a similar level in this and other communities in the Northern Territory and elsewhere within Australia.

Guthadjaka and Garŋgulkpuy are two Yolngu women leaders from Elcho Island in the Northern Territory, a small island 500 km north-east of Darwin. Geographically isolated, they occupy a difficult space in leadership and democratic action due to their position between two worlds: the Yolngu world and the mainstream Australian world. They have to remain true to their connections to clan and country while working with the wider political and intellectual worlds within Australia and overseas.

Jackie Huggins explains that for an Indigenous leader, '[l]eadership means that you need to respect differences of views and start from where people are at— not where you would want them to be. The trick is to listen, listen, listen, and then act.'[4] Both Guthadjaka and Garŋgulkpuy refer frequently with their elders, raising each individual issue before a consensus is reached. They speak for the community, not themselves. Their leadership is different in the ways that Amanda Sinclair identifies as less ego-driven, more spiritual, with different sources of power and responsibility.[5] Ego is often set aside to respect others and their relationships. The work of Guthadjaka and Garŋgulkpuy as community leaders involves extraordinary intellectual and spiritual demands.

---

1   Monash University.
2   Yalu Marŋgithinyaraw Indigenous Corporation.
3   Charles Darwin University.
4   Jackie Huggins, 'Indigenous Women and Leadership—A Personal Reflection', *Indigenous Law Bulletin* 6(1) (2004): 3.
5   Amanda Sinclair, *Leadership for the Disillusioned: Moving Beyond Myths and Heroes to Leading that Liberates* (Sydney: Allen & Unwin, 2007), 145–68.

Relationships with white powerbrokers are often quite fraught and problematic. Guthadjaka explained to Gwenda that within Yolngu groups, differences of opinion are managed through meetings and consensus. Problems are often triggered in public meetings by white people in control of town services when they select Yolngu leaders to speak, rather than ensuring all participants are empowered to voice their opinions. This can cause animosity between those chosen and those who feel they are denied the opportunity of participating.[6]

Guthadjaka and Garŋgulkpuy are constantly engaged in the processes necessary to reach a culturally acceptable position; and their job as leaders is to both suggest new directions and enact the decisions of the community. As Yolngu women working within both Yolngu and white cultural worlds, Guthadjaka and Garŋgulkpuy must decode and decipher *what* the Western world is saying and doing, examine it in relation to the epistemology of the Yolngu world and consult with their elders for direction. They must then explain it to the rest of the community and discuss its implications. Finally, they will argue an agreed Yolngu position to other Australians and the world.

In their leadership there are two clear spiritual sources: the Yolngu world and Christian teachings brought by the missionaries. Guthadjaka and Garŋgulkpuy operate within the influence of both these traditions. In this chapter, Guthadjaka is more specific about how her Christian beliefs underpin her leadership and work. Garngulkpuy is concerned more with establishing the importance of the spiritual connections to the land and between people in the Yolngu world. Both see themselves as operating with the direction of spiritually based interconnections between people, land and belief systems.

Guthadjaka and Garŋgulkpuy have been pivotal in promoting a wider level of political inquiry and activity within their communities. The two questions on governance they articulate relate to the past, present and future of these communities: how did we get to this point, and what are we going to do about the future of our children? This is a theme that is echoed in the wide range of interviews Gwenda and Garngulkpuy recently completed at Galiwin'ku. They also ask: 'How do we get people to listen to us?'

This chapter explores the leadership of Guthadjaka and Garŋgulkpuy as they seek to answer these questions. It will follow their personal dreams and enterprises, their local, national and international connections. Guthadjaka and Garŋgulkpuy have made significant changes in their lives to follow their vision, to develop plans that will benefit the education and welfare of children.

---

6   Private conversations between Gwenda and Guthadjaka, 2011 and 2012.

Guthadjaka and Garŋgulkpuy

Guthadjaka and Garŋgulkpuy trained and worked as teachers within the NT school system before setting out to pursue their dreams for a better life for the children. Both have interacted with university-orientated teaching and learning systems, participated in numerous research activities and promoted Yolngu leadership and value systems.

Both women were chosen by their fathers to become leaders in their clans. The recruitment of daughters to fulfil these roles is a relatively new development over the past 30 years. Women have grown in the belief in their personal powers and have taken up education opportunities and leadership roles within their communities. The fathers have recognised this growth and come slowly to the decision that women may be the best people to take over clan leadership roles. At first, they had to decide if their daughters were knowledgeable in clan matters and committed to carrying out these roles. Garngulkpuy talked to me about how she questioned her father about clan matters and he asked her about her understanding of important ideas and concepts. Gradually, as he decided that she was perceptive and keen to learn, he taught her important knowledge about origins, storylines and processes. Both women have developed the skills to successfully lead and mediate between clans. They seek and receive counsel and guidance from *their* elders and participate fully in the processes of living a Yolngu life.

All clans have connections to other clans and other people. These are fundamental to the storylines of the Yolngu and all Indigenous people. Kathy Guthadjaka is Warramirri; Joanne Garŋgulkpuy is Wangurri. Warramirri and Wangurri are particularly close clans. Both clans need each other to carry out functions within the Yolngu world, to make relationships and society strong. Garŋgulkpuy explained the relationship in this way: 'Warramirri plants the seeds which Wangurri water to make the seeds grow.'[7] Guthadjaka also talks about planting and growing seed.

Warramirri and Wangurri are both Yirritja, one of the two groups or moieties that complement each other in the Yolngu world. The other moiety is Dhuwa. The members of each moiety have roles and responsibilities in society, and people marry across these two moieties. Guthadjaka is Mari or grandmother to Garŋgulkpuy in relationship terms. Mari is the most important person within the groups of people who surround the individual in relationships within the clan system. Mari nurtures, gives advice, makes decisions and guides.

---

7   Private conversation between Gwenda and Guthadjaka, 11 October 2011.

Guthadjaka and Garngulkpuy through similar processes are shaping a Yolngu version of leadership in society. Their concentration is on Yolngu processes and what it means to be a Yolngu woman leader. We have concentrated on the Yolngu world, the words and the philosophies of the women, not on Western theoretical models.

Both women work to make connections with other women and groups of people within Australia and other societies. They hope there will be wider meanings and applications for Yolngu constructions of leadership and participation in a democratic society.

Kathy Guthadjaka

Kathy Guthadjaka is a Gatjirrk Warramirri woman. She lives at Gäwa, at the northernmost part of Elcho Island. She grew up on the mission on Elcho Island. When Gwenda interviewed her in 2011, Guthadjaka told Gwenda she wanted to be a teacher but she was not particularly interested in school and did not get the grades she needed. After working in several jobs, she began working at the school as a teaching assistant, caught up on her studies and completed an associate diploma in teaching at Batchelor College.[8]

Guthadjaka has spent her life learning in both the Yolngu and the Western worlds, and communicating between the two. Very early in her teaching career, she began reaching out from her tiny remote world to the international world. She travelled to Bali and Java to look at Christian schools, and when she graduated she went as an exchange teacher to Canada to schools in the remote villages in Yellowknife. In her words: 'I didn't know where I was going or what I was doing.'[9] On her return from Canada, Guthadjaka worked at Shepherdson College, the main school on Elcho Island, working up to a grade two teacher. She then taught as a homeland teacher at small outlying settlements.

Guthadjaka's story is also about Gäwa, a Warramirri homeland at the northernmost part of Elcho Island. In 1985 her father, Ngulpurray, made the decision to move his family to Gäwa, in response to the growing problems in the township at Galiwin'ku. Guthadjaka's first trip back to Gäwa with the 'old man' was by boat, as there was otherwise only a bush track. The abundance of wild food—oysters, crayfish and wild honey—was an immediate attraction to

---

8   Kathy Guthadjaka, Interview with Gwenda Baker, Galiwin'ku, 21 June 2011.
9   Ibid.

the place. They surveyed the area of a traditional ceremonial and meeting place and then decided to move slightly east to a bay offering better boat access and living conditions in the wet season.[10]

Ngulpurray asked his daughter Guthadjaka, by this time an experienced teacher, to help lead the people back so the children could live a better life there. Initially a group of 26 men and women and children cut a road to Gäwa by hand, with axes, shovels and fire. Many trips followed, and Guthadjaka began making plans to establish a school at Gäwa.

Guthadjaka said: 'When I went to [the] education [department] to set [it] up I thought it would be easy, because I was qualified.'[11] What Guthadjaka was offered, however, was far from her vision of a school for Gäwa. She was offered a 'Homeland Learning Centre not a proper school. A proper school would get everything and we would get rubbish, maybe tables and chairs left over.'[12] Guthadjaka goes back to the imagery of planting seeds: 'Missionaries were like seed planters, planting a vision. Government has no vision, that's why people are perishing, because there is no common vision for the people.'[13] Guthadjaka believes that '[i]f a child gets a good education in their own place and has a good understanding of their own place they will be successful when they step into the world'.[14]

To obtain funding from the NT Government for a Homeland Learning Centre a community must provide its own buildings and an unpaid teacher for a minimum of six months. If the attendance figures are maintained during that period, it might be recognised as a school. In 1991 Guthadjaka took six months' leave without pay from Shepherdson College to teach full-time at Gäwa, teaching under a tarpaulin, near the beach. The only contribution from the NT Government was for books and pencils, second-hand desks and second-hand chairs (never enough, so most children sat on the ground). In 1992 the NT Government provided $1,500 for a new tarp for the school.

Anthropologist Ian McIntosh graphically described the system of discrimination operating in NT schools. He noted the inequities of the two systems:

> Gäwa and other Homeland Learning Centers were denied any of the $19 million commonwealth government funding for computers, satellite connection, printers and access to distance learning that was to provide

---

10   Ibid. Also Ian McIntosh, 'Build a Future for Our Children: A Case Study of Institutional Discrimination in the Northern Territory of Australia', July 2009, http://www.culturalsurvival.org.au/docs/Case%20Study%20-%20Building%20a%20Future%20for%20our%20children.pdf.
11   Kathy Guthadjaka, Interview, 21 June 2011.
12   Ibid.
13   Ibid.
14   'This is Gotha's Vision' from Gäwa Christian School pamphlet.

for every remote school and 66 cattle stations across Australia. In 2002, ten years after its commencement, the Gäwa Homeland Learning Center had no toilet, running water, power, fax, computer, photocopier or other commonly supplied school equipment.[15]

After one year, Guthadjaka asked for but was refused permission to remain at the Gäwa school as a permanent teacher. She resumed her job at Shepherdson College at Galiwin'ku and became the homeland visiting teacher at Gäwa. From the beginning under Guthadjaka's tutelage, the school was successful. 'Within the first years six students had gone on to successfully complete their HSC [Higher School Certificate].'[16] Despite this success, the residents at Gäwa were no closer to their dream of a locally run, properly resourced school. They built new school buildings with a $15,000 contribution from the NT Government. For 10 years, there were no other funds for infrastructure.

This was a difficult time for Guthadjaka and her vision. After years of petitioning government authorities, Guthadjaka and the community at Gäwa decided to ask the NT Christian School Association to take over the running of the school. For Guthadjaka, to hand over the school was devastating, but there seemed to be no other solution. In 2003 Gäwa was granted independent school status. As McIntosh states: 'The impact of the changed status was immediate and profound ... By becoming an independent school, Gäwa has accessed over 320 times the level of funding for infrastructure that it received as a government remote school, not "special" funding, but "normal" government funding.'[17]

> Guthadjaka proceeded to refashion her relationship to the school and the children she saw as her responsibility. She became the school's cultural advisor, running classes to teach the children Yolngu principles of learning. Bilingual education and two-way learning became the foundation for the new school. Against a background of low attendance at larger schools in larger centres such as Galiwin'ku, at the Gäwa School, attendance rates are high. Of the 50 students on the roll, 80 per cent regularly attend school. This is in comparison with average school attendance rates in Northern Territory Emergency Response (NTER) communities, which fell from 62.1 per cent in November 2009 to 56.5 per cent in November 2010.[18]

In her role as a Yolngu researcher, Guthadjaka has developed strong research, teaching and consultancy links with Charles Darwin University. Guthadjaka's

---

15 McIntosh, 'Build a Future for Our Children'.
16 'This is Gotha's Vision'.
17 Ibid.
18 'Children of the Intervention', UN Conference on the Rights of the Child, www.concernedaustralians. com.au/media/.

teaching leadership role within the wider Australian community and the outside world includes her innovative 'Teaching from Country' classes, which she conducts through Charles Darwin University.[19] Her classes are conducted on Skype from her Gäwa homeland. In December 2011, she visited her classes at Tokyo University with a delegation from Charles Darwin University.

In her role of political advocate for the rights of Yolngu people, Guthadjaka has travelled widely. In October 2011 she presented a report at a UN conference on the rights of the child in Geneva with Yirrkala woman leader Djapirri Mununggirritj. Their talk was simultaneously translated into many languages. Guthadjaka told Gwenda they received strong support from the audience and the UN executive. In contrast, there is not enough support from the Australian population and little interest from Australian governments.

In the 'Children of the Intervention' report, they talked about their fears for the children affected by the intervention legislation in the Northern Territory:

> We fear for their future, for their ability to learn to walk in two worlds, to obtain an education and a job. We fear for their health and their general well-being. But most of all, we fear that these recent changes [NTER legislation] will lead to the loss of our land, our culture and our language.[20]

Conditions of overcrowding and unsafe housing put children's health at risk. High costs for basic foods lead to high rates of malnutrition and illnesses usually seen in Third World countries. Studies have shown that homelands are safer and healthier places for children to live, but the Federal Government plans to reduce financial support to homelands rather than increase it.

Guthadjaka questioned the allocation of teachers to the 45 Homeland Learning Centres in the Northern Territory. 'Why is it', she asked, 'that some children have a qualified teacher for only two or three days each week when all children have a right to a full-time education?' She also expressed concern about the removal of the bilingual education program from NT schools. This, she believes, is the main cause of falling attendance rates.[21] In the past two years, the NT Government has stipulated that there must be four hours of English teaching per day, thus effectively sidelining bilingual teaching. Guthadjaka stated that '[b]ilingual learning programs recognise the importance of gaining competence in the child's first language, before introducing a second language'. She referred to the NT Government's current draft proposal to allow a modified reintroduction

---

19   Guthadjaka's work includes: 'Teaching when nothing is lying around'; and consultancy contributions to gambling and gambling-related harm, sustainable housing, gifted and talented children, maths as a cultural practice, and computers at Gäwa Homeland Centre. See www.cdu.edu.au/yaci.

20   Ibid.

21   Ibid.

of the program to some schools as 'a compromise policy that fails at every level to commit to a successful re-introduction of bilingual learning'. Guthadjaka is a strong advocate for bilingual education and the acknowledgment of the special physical needs of remote settlements.[22]

In her role as a leader in bilingual education advocacy, Guthadjaka has presented at conferences on bilingual education, including the Building Literate Nations National Forum in 2010. She has written and published several Warramirri stories for children. Now she is exploring other means of preserving one of the two Warramirri languages that are at risk of extinction. Her new project will draw on interviews and stories gathered over many years from Warramirri speakers of this dialect.

Guthadjaka sees her life as one of vision and service to her people. For Guthadjaka, it is necessary to have a vision. 'Without a vision we cannot go forward, we can only see a fog that makes us stop.' Guthadjaka's vision makes her 'excited and energetic'.[23] Her leadership and participation in the processes of democratic action in local, territory and international contexts are firmly based in her Yolngu cultural beliefs and processes. To understand her vision and work, we must step outside our Western academic framework and look at the world from a Yolngu epistemology.

When Guthadjaka was talking to Gwenda about the importance of a vision, she referred to a Warramirri story.[24] This story follows the passage over country by some dogs. At one stage they encounter a fog, and the dogs react in different ways. Some are frightened and turn back; some cannot see the way ahead and stay where they are. But there are some who have a vision of what is ahead and keep going.

Guthadjaka reviewed this chapter and she gave us instructions on what to say in this section. She talked about God and His relationship to her work. God existed in Guthadjaka's Yolngu world long before the introduction of Christianity.[25] She acknowledges that to a Western mindset this is not easily understood. Guthadjaka believes God has been fighting for her and her work. She believes God is sending her a message and that people with good heart will see and appreciate the message.

It is the Yolngu way to seek understanding and consensus, not confrontation or fighting. Guthadjaka explained that 'The Children of the Intervention'

---

22 Ibid.

23 Private communication between Gwenda and Guthadjaka, 14 November 2011.

24 Ibid.

25 See also Djiniyini Gondarra, 'Through Similar Journeys Comes Revelation', Generation 3(1) (April 1992): 20–3. Gondarra, Elcho Island leader, theologian and minister, wrote about his grandfather's travels across country and his awareness that there was a greater spirit behind the land and the Dreaming.

document she presented at the United Nations was not an attempt to fight the Government and its Indigenous affairs policies and practices, but to 'put it like a truth' so that they will see. Guthadjaka respects the Government and its position in Australian society. She says, '[i]t is not my part to challenge the government', only to put the issues on the table for people to see.[26]

Joanne Garŋgulkpuy

Joanne Garŋgulkpuy is a Go Golpa Wangurri elder, an experienced teacher and social researcher. She lives at the main township on Elcho Island, Galiwin'ku, where she was born, grew up and went to school. She went to secondary school at Nhulumbuy and later to Batchelor College, where she graduated with a certificate in teaching. Later she went on to complete a graduate diploma in teaching and a graduate certificate in education administration.

Garŋgulkpuy taught at Shepherdson College and as a homeland centre teacher. She rose to the position of executive teacher, administration, and worked in the administration of the homeland schools. Her work overlapped with Guthadjaka's when she visited Gäwa for one or two days a week and assisted her in the development of stories for the children. By 2000 she was becoming worried about the future of the children, and the way in which they were being taught at the college. She saw the need for foundational work at a younger level, a need to explore Yolngu ways of teaching and learning and the need for these processes to be reinvigorated in the community.

With the establishment of the Yalu Marnggithinyaraw Centre at Galiwin'ku, Garŋgulkpuy saw a new role and direction for her work. In 2001 she resigned from the school and was appointed supervisor of the Yalu Marnggithinyaraw project and chief investigator of the Cooperative Research Centre for Aboriginal and Tropical Health (CRCATH) funded project 'Yolngu Theories of Transformation: The Yalu' Story'. For many years she has been the co-coordinator of the centre. The Yalu Marnggithinyaraw Centre is a foundational women's centre in the revival of Yolngu nurturing and learning in the community. *'Yalu Marnggithinyaraw'* means a nest or womb, a nurturing place that starts at the beginning of life, so that all Yolngu children know who they are and who they relate to: the roles and responsibilities that all Yolngu share from birth to the grave.

Garŋgulkpuy has guided and mentored numerous research projects, all with links to the centre and its work. She was associate investigator of the Psychosocial Impact Indicators SCRIF funded project.[27] She helped develop the

---

26   Private communication, 14 November 2011.
27   States/Commonwealth Research Issues Forum (SCRIF).

Yothu Yindi school curriculum for the local primary school, and was involved in collaborations with the Collaborative Research Centre (CRC) for Aboriginal and Tropical Health, the Menzies School of Health Research and the Northern Territory University.

Garŋgulkpuy's clan leadership can be seen in her commitment to learn about and document Wangurri stories. In her chapter 'Garmak Gularriwuy, Gularri Water' based on an interview with her father, Buthimaŋ, Garŋgulkpuy explains the water story that is fundamental to Wangurri roles and responsibilities in Yolngu society.[28] The story traces the source of the water through its pathway to the sea. The Wangurri water source is at a place on Dhalinybuy, in North-East Arnhem Land, about 1.5 hours' south-west of Nhulunbuy. The source contains the 'learning and teaching methodology, confidence research … that is its home'.

> When the water wells up inside Wangurri country, it starts to flow 'and it talks—'gapu dhä-rirrakaymirri'—water with sound in its mouth—'agreeing, negotiating, consulting, stating and empowering'. 'Dhuwandja mayali' ŋunhi yolŋuy dhu marrtji raypirri'yun wäŋa rom larakam dhunupayam'—This means that when Yolŋu advise and admonish each other the land tells the law straight.[29]

As part of her social leadership supporting Territory-wide programs, Garŋgulkpuy has been a member of the Council for Aboriginal Alcohol Program Services Incorporated for many years. In 2007–08 she was chair of the council, and from 2008 to 2011 she was secretary of this organisation. As a member of a study group, Garŋgulkpuy interviewed members of her community who were living on Larrakia land in Darwin. Many of these people were drinkers and the study tried to explain why they were living this way, with the eventual aim of encouraging them to return to their community.[30] This work developed into ongoing programs talking to people, taking them to hospital and encouraging them to return home. There is now an outreach centre in Darwin and two houses for 'long-grass' people in nearby Palmerston. Garŋgulkpuy also ran workshops for leaders from the Tiwi Islands, Groote Eylandt and Maningrida to help them reconnect with 'long-grass' people from their communities. She also worked as a consultant to programs on 'gambling and gambling-related harm' and the 'gifted and talented children' research.

---

28 Timothy Buthimang, talking to his daughter Garngulkpuy and his sister Lisa Walpulay, at the Dingu garden, Galiwin'ku, February 2008, Joanne Garngulkpuy, trans. 'GARMAK GULARRIWUY Gularri Water', Learning Communities: International Journal Of Learning in Social Contexts 2 (2010): 38–47. http://www.cdu.edu.au/centres/spill//journal/LC_Journal_Issue2_2010.pdf.

29 Joanne Garŋgulkpuy, 'GARMAK GULARRIWUY', 39. Joanne's other published chapters include: 'Yolŋu Balandi wataŋumirri'; 'The Yolŋu Child's Pathway'; 'Methodology for Yolŋu Research'; and 'Bundurrpuy', elicited from Wapiriny and 'Teaching from Country—Learning by the Ancient Hearths'.

30 Maypilama, Garngulkpuy, Michael Christie, John Greatorex and Jocelyn Grace, *Yolngu Longrassers on Larrakia Land*, August 2004, http://learnline.cdu.edu.au/yolngustudies/docs/Longgrass_report.pdf.

Garŋgulkpuy's advocacy for the adoption of Yolngu processes of governance has elicited interest and acceptance in academic circles. 'Yolŋu Balandi wataŋumirri' is now used in Australian and North American universities as part of the curriculum and as the basis for workshops on Indigenous governance. It deals with governance within a Yolngu context following Yolngu rules of engagement.[31]

Garŋgulkpuy also wants government and political circles to think about, see and support Yolngu ideas on governance. The Government needs to see where Yolngu are coming from; this would help them to understand the people. There should be less of, in her words, 'visits, visits, visits', and more talking, to help them understand the actual processes of Yolngu governance; to try to work out things that can operate and help support Yolngu governance. The Government needs to accept that

> Yolngu are human, people with different governance who have something to teach them. If they learn some of the inside part, what are some of the ways of governance, then Yolngu and government can work together to develop more plans and programs which will support Yolngu governance.[32]

This would lead to better governance and better outcomes for programs for the people and the Government.

Gwenda and Garŋgulkpuy worked together in 2010–11 on an Australian Institute of Aboriginal and Torres Strait Islander Studies (AIATSIS) Research Grant project called 'Remembering Mission Time'. Gwenda was impressed by her strong commitment to exploring the past with the aim of educating the children on what the Yolngu could, and did, do in mission times; and seeking guidance for how things could be done in the future. When they presented papers at conferences in Canberra and Melbourne in 2011, Garngulkpuy spoke strongly about the situation on the island then and now:

> When I was growing up in the Yolngu rom [law] I was feeling strong and I had strong belief and values and there was encouragement and support from my own people. I was loved by all of them. I had a lot of discipline from my whole integrated family. This made me go to school every day to learn about western knowledge. I was motivated because it was a new thing. In mission times there was everyone supporting the children, now days it's only the mother and father.

---

31 Joanne Garŋgulkpuy, 'Yolŋu Balandi wataŋumirri', 32–37.
32 Private conversations between Gwenda and Garngulkpuy, 2012.

I need to know why children are not going to school today, why children are getting worse and [I wonder] what is the difference between the introduction of western knowledge in mission times and what teachers are teaching today. What has changed and why? Is it the parents or is it the government or is it the curriculum? What were the parents doing in the mission times? They said school was important. There are roles and responsibilities being taken away today.

In mission times the fire was in the middle and we were all around the fire feeling good, talking about things. Today the fire is going out, I am feeling cold and isolated. People are fighting with each other and bad is good and good is bad.[33]

On her return to Galiwin'ku, Garŋgulkpuy used her knowledge from the project to run two workshops, illustrating how the lessons from the past could be used in the present. The photographs and films from the time were used to show the work the Yolngu did in the mission time: the operation of the gardens, which supplied good, fresh food to the people, the fishermen and women who supplied fish for the community, the builders and roadworkers. There were discussions on the work ethic of the Yolngu and how this contributed to feelings of meaning and self-worth.

At Galiwin'ku, Garŋgulkpuy is heavily involved in community activities. She is often called upon to represent the Wangurri clan with her father and respected elder, Buthimaŋ. She sees it as her duty to uphold Yolngu values and responsibilities and to teach and encourage others to do the same. Garŋgulkpuy is clear-thinking and positive, allowing for all clan representatives to have their say and trying to gain consensus amongst them about important processes.

Garŋgulkpuy works as an administrator and teacher in the programs the Yalu Centre now runs: Family as First Teachers (with the Red Cross), including a significant component of teaching using Yolngu methodology, a Community Development Employment Projects (CDEP) teaching program and a chronic diseases program (with the Menzies School of Health). All the programs are short term, and negotiations are continually required to maintain and introduce new programs. Garŋgulkpuy is always looking for new enterprises, ways of reaching out to the community, running programs for children and adults, and educating the wider Australian community beyond the confines of the island. There is an urgent need for a new building for the centre, which has been housed in a small discarded school portable since its inception.

---

33 Joanne Garŋgulkpuy, AIATSIS Conference Canberra, 19 September 2011; and OHHA Conference, Melbourne, 8 October 2011.

Guthadjaka and Garŋgulkpuy are strong leaders who take their roles in the democratic processes in their communities and the wider Australian society very seriously. As good leaders, they are concerned to encourage and mentor others to become leaders and take over duties when required. As Huggins notes: 'It's a very Aboriginal thing to do, to give younger people greater responsibilities within the community as they become able to take those responsibilities on.' Often on Elcho Island there is an overlap between civic and clan leadership and succession plans. This ensures that both clan and civic responsibilities are developed. Guthadjaka took her granddaughter to Geneva with her; Garŋgulkpuy is encouraging a close relative to take on more responsibilities at the Yalu Centre. Women from other clans who show interest and dedication are also being nurtured at the centre. While the future of the children on Elcho Island is still precarious, Indigenous women's leadership in democratic processes seems assured.

References

Buthimang, Timothy. Talking to his daughter Garngulkpuy and his sister Lisa Walpulay, at the Dingu garden, Galiwin'ku, February 2008, Joanne Garngulkpuy, trans. 'GARMAK GULARRIWUY Gularri Water', *Learning Communities: International Journal Of Learning in Social Contexts* 2 (2010): 38–47. http://www.cdu.edu.au/centres/spill//journal/LC_Journal_Issue2_2010.pdf.

'Children of the Intervention.' UN Conference on the Rights of the Child. www.concernedaustralians.com.au/media/.

'Computers at Gäwa Homeland Centre.' http://www.cdu.edu.au/centres/aflf/.

Gondarra, Djiniyini. 'Through Similar Journeys Comes Revelation.' *Generation* 3(1) (April 1992): 20–3.

Garngulkpuy, Joanne. 'GARMAK GULARRIWUY' (2010): 38–47. *Learning Communities: International Journal Of Learning in Social Contexts* 2. http://www.cdu.edu.au/centres/spill//journal/LC_Journal_Issue2_2010.pdf.

Garŋgulkpuy, Joanne. 'Yolŋu Balandi wataŋumirri', (2010): 32–37. *Learning Communities: International Journal Of Learning in Social Contexts* 2. http://www.cdu.edu.au/centres/spill//journal/LC_Journal_Issue2_2010.pdf.

Huggins, Jackie. 'Indigenous Women and Leadership—A Personal Reflection.' *Indigenous Law Bulletin* 6(1) (2005): 5–7.

McIntosh, Ian. 'Build a Future for Our Children: A Case Study of Institutional Discrimination in the Northern Territory of Australia.' 2009. http://www.culturalsurvival.org.au/docs/Case%20Study%20-%20Building%20a%20 Future%20for%20our%20children.pdf.

Maypilama, Garngulkpuy, Michael Christie, John Greatorex and Jocelyn Grace. *Yolngu Longrassers on Larrakia Land*, August 2004. http://learnline.cdu.edu. au/yolngustudies/docs/Longgrass_report.pdf.

Sinclair, Amanda. *Leadership for the Disillusioned: Moving Beyond Myths and Heroes to Leading that Liberates*. Sydney: Allen & Unwin, 2007.

3. Aunty Pearl Gibbs: Leading for Aboriginal rights

Rachel Standfield,[1] Ray Peckham[2] and John Nolan

This chapter explores the work of Pearl Gibbs throughout her exemplary career as an activist and tireless campaigner for Aboriginal rights and democracy in Australia from the 1930s until her death in 1983. Pearl's activism on a national level is well documented in the historiography of Aboriginal politics and campaigns for Aboriginal rights, because of her role as a member of the 1930s Aboriginal campaigns for rights and as a member of the Aborigines Progressive Association and their 'Day of Mourning' campaign for Aboriginal citizenship in 1938,[3] as well as her later roles within women's organisations and working with other women campaigners like Faith Bandler, Joan Strack and Jessie Street.[4] Pearl Gibbs is, however, also remembered in other contexts, and for other reasons, and she is particularly fondly loved and respected by the Aboriginal community in Dubbo, NSW, where she lived for many years, both as a young woman and later in her life.

While she was equally at home in Aboriginal or non-Aboriginal leadership circles, Pearl, we feel, embodied Aboriginal models of leadership. Jackie Huggins' reflections on her own leadership and that of other Aboriginal women offer important insights into the distinctive characteristics of leadership for Aboriginal women. She identifies a leader as one who 'truly' has 'the interests of our community at heart', and when writing of 'our women leaders' recognises that many work behind the scenes and without recognition but for the interests of Aboriginal communities.[5] And, as Huggins also writes, and as we will also

---

1   Monash University.

2   Elder, Dubbo Community.

3   See, for example, Stephanie Gilbert, '"Never Forgotten": Pearl Gibbs (Gambanyi)', in *Uncommon Ground: White Women in Aboriginal History*, eds Anna Cole and Victoria Haskins (Canberra: Aboriginal Studies Press, 2005), 107–26; Sue Taffe, *Black & White Together: FCAATSI, the Federal Council for the Advancement of Aborigines and Torres Strait Islanders, 1958–1973* (Brisbane: University of Queensland Press, 2005).

4   Marilyn Lake, 'Citizenship as Non-Discrimination: Acceptance or Assimilationism? Political Logic and Emotional Investment in Campaigns for Aboriginal Rights in Australia, 1940 to 1970', *Gender & History* 13(3) (November 2001): 566–92; Victoria Haskins, '"Lovable Natives" and "Tribal Sisters": Feminism, Maternalism, and the Campaign for Aboriginal Citizenship in New South Wales in the Late 1930s', *Hecate* 24(2) (1998): 8–21; Victoria Haskins, '"& so we are 'Slave owners'!": Employers and the NSW Aborigines Protection Board Trust Funds', *Labour History* 88 (May 2005): 147–64.

5   Jackie Huggins, 'Indigenous Women and Leadership: A Personal Reflection', *Indigenous Law Bulletin* 6(1) (2004): 1.

explore through this chapter by considering the relationship of Pearl Gibbs and Ray Peckham, Aboriginal leadership styles often prioritise the intergenerational transfer of both knowledge and responsibility:

> It's a very Aboriginal thing to do, to give younger people greater responsibility within the community as they become able to take those responsibilities on. It is a culturally appropriate model that involves respect in both directions—from the younger to the older and the older to the younger.[6]

As Amanda Sinclair notes in this volume, it is vital for feminist scholars of leadership to 'draw attention to the power and privilege reproduced in leadership and leadership research ... They need to continue to fearlessly redirect attention to the ways dominant forms of leadership reinforce the power of a narrow white male elite'.[7] This is a point that scholars of Aboriginal women's leadership such as Huggins, Larissa Behrendt, Pat O'Shane and Aileen Moreton-Robinson make strongly, but they simultaneously draw attention to the fact that it is the action not only of white men, leaders or otherwise who oppress Aboriginal people, but also of white women. As Behrendt states: 'Aboriginal women have been oppressed by white women ... White women can be as racist as white men. White women have benefitted economically from the dispossession of Aboriginal people.'[8] Thus, as these Aboriginal women leaders outline, and as Pearl Gibbs' activism shows, Aboriginal women have fought tirelessly against racism, and stress the 'inter-relationship of racism and sexism' for Aboriginal women.[9]

Pearl Gibbs had an incredibly long career of activism and working for democracy. Her activism began when she advocated on behalf of Aboriginal women working as domestic servants in Sydney, where she also worked as a domestic servant from 1917.[10] She was heavily involved in the Aborigines Progressive Association and was active in the Day of Mourning activities in the sesquicentenary of white settlement in 1938.[11] She was the first woman to serve

---

6   Ibid., 4.
7   Amanda Sinclair, Chapter 1, in this volume.
8   Larissa Behrendt, 'Aboriginal Women and the White Lies of the Feminist Movement: Implications for Aboriginal Women in Rights Discourse', *The Australian Feminist Law Journal* 1 (1993): 31. See also Aileen Moreton-Robinson, 'Tiddas Speakin' Strong: Indigenous Women's Self-Presentation within White Australian feminism', in *Talkin' Up to the White Woman: Indigenous Women and Feminism* (Brisbane: University of Queensland Press, 2000), 40, 73; Huggins, 'Indigenous Women and Leadership'; and Pat O'Shane, 'Is There Any Relevance in the Women's Movement for Aboriginal Women?', *Refractory Girl—A Journal of Radical Feminist Thought* 12 (September 1976): 33.
9   Behrendt, 'Aboriginal Women and the White Lies of the Feminist Movement'; Moreton-Robinson, 'Tiddas Speakin' Strong', 73; Huggins, 'Indigenous Women and Leadership'; and O'Shane, 'Is There Any Relevance in the Women's Movement for Aboriginal Women?', 33.
10   Gilbert, '"Never Forgotten"', 108; Jack Horner, 'Pearl Gibbs: A Biographical Tribute', *Aboriginal History* 7(1) (1983): 12.
11   Gilbert, '"Never Forgotten"', 108; Horner, 'Pearl Gibbs', 14.

on the NSW Aborigines Welfare Board, from 1954 to 1957.[12] She was founding vice-president of the Aboriginal-Australian Fellowship from 1956, and this organisation was incredibly active in petitioning government for constitutional change for Aboriginal people, culminating in the 1967 referendum.[13] She was instrumental in reviving the Aborigines Progressive Association in 1963 as an Aboriginal-controlled organisation which drew on the experiences of Aboriginal communities outside Sydney.[14] She was also an excellent networker and mentor and made use of the media as a channel to both appeal to and remind non-Aboriginal people of their responsibilities to extend the benefits of Australian democracy and living standards to Aboriginal people.[15] Her campaigning, and particularly her speaking and media work, to demand Aboriginal rights was based on bringing the experiences of Aboriginal communities to light on the national stage, to make non-Aboriginal people focus on the real conditions Aboriginal people faced in New South Wales and to compel non-Aboriginal people to act to change those circumstances.[16]

In this chapter, we wish to document and explore the significance of Pearl's work in Aboriginal communities in general, but particularly in Dubbo, through a combination of the memories of two people particularly close to Pearl: Ray Peckham, Dubbo elder and himself an important campaigner for Aboriginal rights from the 1950s, and John Nolan, who knew Pearl from his childhood and later went on to work with her at the first Aboriginal hostel in Dubbo, as well as her legacy for the Dubbo Aboriginal community. This chapter has developed from a presentation given by John and Ray to the elders meeting at the Centre for Aboriginal Studies at Charles Sturt University (CSU) in 2011, which celebrated Pearl's life and her place as a member of the Aboriginal community in Dubbo, which Rachel Standfield attended in her capacity as a lecturer at CSU.[17] John and Ray spoke with love and respect about their relationships with Aunty Pearl, who lived in Dubbo for long periods of her life and during her later life until her death in 1983, and worked with members of the Dubbo Aboriginal community.

This presentation prompted the three of us to work together to consider Pearl's role and to undertake additional research amongst Pearl Gibbs' papers at the Mitchell Library in Sydney, and from there to present as a panel to the Women

---

12 Sue Taffe, 'Pearl Gibbs', Collaborating for Aboriginal Rights website (Canberra: National Museum of Australia, 2008), http://Aboriginalrights.net.au/person.asp?pID=966.

13 Sue Taffe, 'Aboriginal–Australian Fellowship', in ibid., http://Aboriginalrights.net.au/organisation. asp?oID=1.

14 Sue Taffe, 'Aborigines Progressive Association', in ibid., http://Aboriginalrights.net.au/organisation. asp?oID=30.

15 Pearl presented the first radio broadcast by an Aboriginal woman, on Sydney radio station 2GB in 1941. A transcript is included in Kevin J. Gilbert, *Because a White Man'll Never Do It* (Sydney: Angus & Robertson, 1973), 13–17.

16 Pearl's papers include both her own media work and clippings relating to Aboriginal issues in general.

17 Rachel wishes to extend her sincere thanks to John and Ray for their support, their patience and their friendship.

in Democracy conference. In this chapter, we bring together Rachel's research carried out within Pearl's papers with the memories of Ray and John. We aim to provide a sense of the way Pearl's advocacy for Aboriginal rights and democracy was informed by knowledge of, and work with, Aboriginal communities, and to outline how she inspired and challenged other people, both Aboriginal and non-Aboriginal, to be active for Aboriginal rights, to campaign for and support civil rights and rights as Aboriginal peoples. We consider the way Pearl worked to bridge the gap between Aboriginal communities and the non-Aboriginal public, first through the provision of information to Aboriginal communities and the wider non-Aboriginal community through the collection of information and strategic use of the media to publicise Aboriginal issues. We also wish to explore the way Pearl worked to bring positive changes for the Dubbo community and to create new generations of Aboriginal activists by remembering Pearl's role shaping Ray Peckham's activism, and the way she worked with non-Aboriginal campaigners while at the same time keeping them 'honest' in their role.

In looking at the way Pearl connected with communities, we are following a point made by Marilyn Lake about the need to look at the community basis of movements for change, including of course the women's movement and campaigns for Aboriginal rights, which 'have been', Lake writes, 'community based, drawing their strengths from a very diverse range of ordinary people in ordinary communities'.[18] Other papers regarding Aboriginal women's leadership delivered at the Women, Leadership and Democracy conference made similar points, with Pat Dudgeon stressing that 'Aboriginal women's leadership is concerned about community', Gwenda Baker writing about Aboriginal women's community leadership and Noah Riseman providing insight into Sue Gordon's work for her own WA communities.[19] Pearl's own diverse experiences in Aboriginal communities in Sydney and in country New South Wales informed her activism and allowed her to provide a particularly powerful, and grounded, realism to her calls to action.

Pearl worked tirelessly for the Aboriginal community in Dubbo, working with and for local community members in their struggle for rights. Pearl was connected to Aboriginal communities in western New South Wales and particularly to Dubbo for significant periods of her life. Dubbo was the home of William Ferguson, with whom Pearl had a close relationship in their work with the Aborigines Progressive Association, and meetings had been held there. Pearl's connection with Dubbo and her work for the Dubbo Aboriginal communities continued when she returned to Dubbo to live later in life, moving there with her sister and mother in the late 1940s. She became caretaker and a

---

18   Marilyn Lake, 'Founding Fathers, Dutiful Wives and Rebellious Daughters, 2001 Eldershaw Memorial Lecture', *THRA Papers and Proceedings* 48(4) (December 2001): 268–79.
19   See Gwenda Baker, Joanne Garŋgulkpuy and Kathy Guthadjaka, Chapter 2, this volume.

leader, a 'grandmother-type figure' to the many Aboriginal people who would come to stay from out west at the Dubbo Aboriginal Hostel, which she had been instrumental in establishing in 1958.

John had the opportunity to meet Pearl after the Aboriginal Hostel in Bembrose Lane, North Dubbo, was built and opened in the latter part of the 1950s. Eva Shipp was the first caretaker followed by Eric Mason, a regional officer employed by the Aborigines Welfare Board, and then Pearl Gibbs. Pearl's role was caretaker of the premises and she lived rent-free until the land was transferred to the NSW Aboriginal Lands Trust in 1975. John's employment with the NSW Aboriginal Land Trust connected him to Pearl as her landlord, which meant he became the collector of the rent Pearl was now expected to pay, and was in charge of all maintenance and care of the building and grounds. Pearl was a formidable lady, and readers might well imagine the difficulties John faced explaining to Pearl the reason she had to now start paying rent. It took John seven and a half years to finally convince Pearl why she had to pay rent, even though he tried repeatedly and insistently over the years to convince the Aboriginal Lands Trust that this special lady should be treated with much respect and be offered rent-free accommodation as caretaker.

Pearl's papers: Building and remembering activism

Pearl's trunks full of papers—which are now housed in the Mitchell Library—were important artefacts in Pearl's work. Pearl collected newspaper articles about Aboriginal issues, including articles in which the work of Aboriginal campaigners including herself was reported, along with other memorabilia, and she used this collection to bring Aboriginal issues to the attention of people she encountered, to encourage others to also work to promote Aboriginal rights and to relive histories of activism, including her own. They became the basis not only of activism but also of memory; those who knew Pearl in Dubbo had been taken through these papers, regaled with stories of the history of Aboriginal activism, and encouraged to engage with the struggle. These trunks are central to John's memories of Pearl and hours spent in her company; the hostel where Pearl lived was also her 'live-in library', and her old tin trunks full of paper also included clippings and documents from her involvement with the Aborigines Welfare Board and many other organisations with which she had an association. For more than seven years, as Pearl's landlord, John spent many long hours sitting with her as she would direct him to go to a certain trunk under one of the beds, select certain clippings and read an article in its entirety. John remembers this as a very rewarding part of his job as rent collector. There were numerous articles showing photographs that he had never seen before and some were very telling; he remembers clearly photographs of Aboriginal tribal men in chains, and, on the periphery, Aboriginal trackers adorned in a type of police uniform but never being seen as 'the real deal'.

These papers constituted an important part of the struggle for Aboriginal rights in Pearl's work. Heather Goodall relates how Pearl used media information to keep Aboriginal communities abreast of campaigning for Aboriginal rights and as a catalyst to collect more evidence to be used in that struggle. Pearl returned to Brewarrina Station, where she had grown up and had relatives living, for the Christmas period in 1937, taking with her

> the clippings from the Aboriginal movement's successful press campaign in October and the newspapers were secretly passed so eagerly from person to person on the station that they disintegrated from handling while Pearl was there. Intending to gain further evidence for the Select Committee, Pearl spoke mainly with the women, who talked of the poor food, the sexual abuse of the dormitory girls and the insanitary conditions of the treatment room.[20]

In Pearl's speech to the Aborigines conference of the 1938 Day of Mourning, this evidence from the people living on Brewarrina Station became part of the campaign. She had taken the media reports of Aboriginal campaigns to Brewarrina, using it to collect more information, which became further evidence for the citizenship campaign:

> At Brewarrina the children are taught by a man who is not a qualified teacher. Two old men on that station, one blind, the other a cripple, are left by themselves in a half-starved state. The manager of the Station and others get milk from five cows, but the old men get only condensed milk. I spoke to these old men, and when they told me how badly they were treated it made me cry, and pray that this movement will be a success.[21]

Pearl's invocation of this emotionally touching scene of elderly men on the station at Brewarrina typified her role in the actions of the Aborigines Progressive Association, in which she was an outspoken speaker on what were considered 'women's issues'. Her words invoked the emotions of her listeners to relive her experiences with people on the Brewarrina Station to appeal for citizenship rights.

---

20 Heather Goodall, *Invasion to Embassy: Land in Aboriginal Politics in New South Wales, 1770–1972* (Sydney: Allen & Unwin, 1996), 212–13.
21 'Our Historic Day of Mourning and Protest: Aborigines Conference', *The Abo Call*, April 1938: 2, http://www.aiatsis.gov.au/collections/exhibitions/dayofmourning/images/pdf/a334816_s04_m.pdf.

These old men are absolutely neglected. Though on the Reserve, I know that no manager visited them for ten days ... I explained the meaning of full citizenship rights to these old men, and they knew that they would be better off with full citizenship rights than under the Protection Board, because they would get Old Age Pension and proper medical attention.[22]

When Ray Peckham came to work with her in Sydney, Pearl sent him to Central Station every morning to get newspapers from all over the State, and to scour them for information about Aboriginal issues, cutting, pasting and labelling the articles into scrapbooks of clippings. An example of her use of her trunks full of papers to document the struggle for Aboriginal rights was provided in *New Dawn* when the editor met with Pearl in Dubbo as he travelled into western New South Wales. Pearl sat him down and took him through her papers:

With a shock, I realized, as I turned the pages, that the dates on these cuttings were 1938, 1939. I wasn't even born then. In the days when Aborigines kept quiet on reserves and rarely spoke up, Pearl Gibbs was already speaking at public functions about the conditions under which her people were living. As she talked, she showed, indirectly, how the frustration built up in her over the years. Yes, there was progress, she admits, but how slow, how slow. I picked up the book of Human Rights and read out the sonorous, beautiful words, slowly: 'All human beings are born free and equal in dignity and rights. They are endowed with reason and conscience and should act towards one another in a spirit of brotherhood.'

Pearl, a quarter-caste, laughs. 'You wonder what I've got that for, eh? Don't you see? I *have* to be interested in citizenship rights. I'm not quite white enough to be able to ignore them.'[23]

Pearl Gibbs: Bringing Aboriginal communities to the attention of the non-Aboriginal public

Pearl's own diverse experiences in Aboriginal communities in Sydney and throughout New South Wales informed her activism and allowed her to provide a particularly powerful, and grounded, realism to her calls to action. Pearl was an expert public speaker and made excellent use of the media, and especially women's media, to create empathy towards and action for Aboriginal people. In agitating for this change, Pearl explicitly expressed her role in both white and Aboriginal worlds. For example, in a letter to the *Nowra Leader* in 1940, written

---

22   Ibid.
23   'Stopping off at Dubbo on the Track West...', *New Dawn*, January 1971, 7.

when she was living on the NSW South Coast,[24] and in which she took on the manager of the Brewarrina Reserve about conditions faced by Aboriginal people there, Pearl set out her speaking position thus: 'as a person of aboriginal blood, I have a knowledge of our customs, laws and traditions; also a white person's outlook to the questions.'

But she stressed that she spoke as someone who was connected to communities throughout New South Wales:

> I know La Perouse, Roseby Park, Wreck Bay, Wallaga Lakes, and various other aborigine stations, she said. I also know Brewarrina very well. The bad housing, water supply, appalling sanitary conditions, lack of proper education, lack of food, along with unsympathetic managers, make life not worth living for my unfortunate race … Our men fought for democracy and Christianity in 1914–1918, and are doing the same today. Oh, no, Mr Paul, the A.P.B. [Aborigines Protection Board] is not doing the fine job you would have the public believe.[25]

Pearl bridged the gap between the lives of those people who themselves did not have enough power or a voice to be able to fight for rights and the wider community. As Pearl herself recounted to Heather Goodall later in her life in relation to her advocacy for Aboriginal girls in domestic service in Sydney homes: 'A lot of them were helpless and intimidated: they weren't allowed to be responsible.' And Pearl took it upon herself to use her confidence, her voice and her anger at the conditions Aboriginal people were subjected to, to advocate on behalf of people who couldn't advocate for themselves.[26] This was a world into which she invited the media, and, through the media, the non-Aboriginal public to share the experiences of Aboriginal people, to understand the situation of Aboriginal people and to work to extend citizenship rights to the whole community.

In April 1938, Pearl penned a letter to the editor of the *Woman Today* in which she called on her 'white sisters' to become a part of campaigns for Aboriginal rights. 'I am appealing to you', she wrote,

> on behalf of my people to raise your voices with ours and help us to a better deal in life … Surely you are not so callous to ignore our plea. Those of my people living in the more civilised parts of Australia are

---

24 'Newsworthy', *Woman*, 16 June 1941, Scrapbook of newscuttings, c. 1938–1946, MS6922/3X item 1, CY4043, frame 40, Pearl Gibbs Papers, Mitchell Library, Sydney [hereinafter Gibbs Papers].

25 Letter from Pearl Gibbs, 'Case for the Aborigine', to Mr Norman Paul, Aborigine Station, Brewarrina, *Nowra Leader*, 21 June 1940, Scrapbook of newscuttings, c. 1938–1946, MS6922/3X item 1, CY4043, frame 37, Gibbs Papers.

26 Heather Goodall, 'Three Tributes to Pearl Gibbs (1901–1983)—Pearl Gibbs: Aboriginal Patriot', *Aboriginal History* 7(1) (1983): 21.

not asking for the stone of anthropology—but for practical humanity, for the opportunity to feed our children properly, to educate them; in a word, to grant them all the rights and responsibilities of democracy.[27]

And in response the *Woman Today* sent a reporter to talk to Pearl as she waited at Parliament House as part of an Aborigines Progressive Association delegation to talk to parliamentarians about citizenship rights. They did so, as they said, because 'from the letters we receive, we know there are many more women suffering the effects of unjust social conditions, whom we should interview, that we may aid them by giving publicity to their wrongs'. Pearl's heartfelt letter had worked: *Woman Today* came to ask Pearl to outline the discrimination faced by Aboriginal people. She talked about the lack of unemployment benefits, outlining Aboriginal hunger on the missions, the lack of access women had to the baby bonus and, of course, the constant fear women had that their children would be removed—all from the perspective of people she knew personally. The interviewer stressed that she had 'never had the opportunity of talking to anyone as closely related with the Aborigines as you are'.[28]

Twenty years later, as Pearl came to work with the Aborigines Welfare Board, her papers contain another significant interview Pearl conducted, for the union magazine *Our Woman* in 1956. The interview took a different style, but still with the same underlying approach of bringing non-Aboriginal women into the lives of Aboriginal people, to call for action on the basis of common humanity and to bridge the gap between the two communities. As Pearl stated in the beginning of the interview, '[m]y people do not ask for sympathy … we have had that since Captain Cook landed. What we want is justice.'[29] And in the search for justice Pearl took the reporter into another of her communities, that of La Perouse. Pearl conducted the reporter to the home of a young mother and her family, and then took the reporter to a concert of performances by young people.

The reporter, Mary Rafferty, expressed her excitement at being able to engage with Aboriginal people: 'I had not met many Aborigine people, and certainly not seen them "at home". Besides, Mrs Gibbs is the only Aborigine Member of the NSW Aborigines' Welfare Board … Seeing an Aborigines Settlement in her company would be something different.'[30]

The experience had a significant impact on Rafferty, who wrote the following when meeting a young couple, Linda and Roy, and their baby girl Muriel:

27 Pearl Gibbs, 'An Aboriginal Woman Asks for Justice', [Letter], *Woman Today*, April 1938, Scrapbook of newscuttings, c. 1938–1946, MS6922/3X item 1, CY4043, frame 16, Gibbs Papers.

28 Sally Bannister, 'Our Aboriginal Sisters: Appeal for Justice for their Unhappy Race', *Woman Today*, May 1938, Scrapbook of newscuttings, c. 1938–1946, MS6922/3X item 1, CY4043, frame 21, Gibbs Papers.

29 'Justice, Not Sympathy', *Our Women*, March–May 1956, 4, newspaper cutting, Gibbs Papers.

30 'Binya', *Our Women*, March–May 1956, 18, newspaper cutting, Gibbs Papers.

[W]hat a lovely young mother she was! She gave me the baby. Holding her close, stroking the thick black hair, and admiring the dainty little features, I wanted to stay longer and go on talking to the family ... they were so friendly, made me feel right at home ... Pearl of course was an old friend, but I felt even had she not been there I would not have felt any less at ease.[31]

Ray Peckham and Pearl Gibbs: Mentoring and activism

Ray Peckham became an activist for Aboriginal rights because of the encouragement and energy of Pearl Gibbs.[32] He first met her when he was about four or five years of age at the old Talbragar mission about 5 km north of Dubbo, never realising then that one day he would be working with her. Ray was living in Sydney when he was approached by Pearl Gibbs to attend the Berlin Youth Festival. When Ray decided to move to Sydney, where Pearl was also living, she was his only contact in the city. On his arrival, Pearl greeted him and declared: 'I've been waiting for one of you bastards to come down here and give me a hand.' Pearl took Ray to Trades Hall the next day—his first introduction to trade unions. Ray became a builder's labourer, and worked with Jack Mundey, known for introducing the green bans on the Sydney Harbour foreshore.

When Ray arrived in Sydney, the only Aboriginal organisation was the Aboriginal-Australian Fellowship. Pearl had worked with Faith Bandler to establish this organisation four years before, but was conscious that the fellowship was based in Sydney and had limited contact with Aboriginal people outside the metropolitan area. Pearl's work as the only Aboriginal representative and the first Aboriginal woman on the 12-member Aborigines Welfare Board, serving a three-year term from 1954 to 1957, had made her frustrated at having any progressive suggestions overruled. As she described to the 1961 conference of the Aboriginal-Australian Fellowship: 'I am the only woman who has represented the Aborigines on the Welfare Board, and it was a very difficult job trying to stand up against those men who are so well educated and have high positions.'[33] An example of the gulf between the situation of the white men on the Welfare Board and the circumstances faced by Pearl as an Aboriginal woman are outlined in a story related by Pearl to Heather Goodall:

---

31 Ibid.
32 Ray's presentation to the women and democracy conference, where he presented on his relationship to Pearl, was recorded. This recording is available via the Museum of Australian Democracy.
33 Aboriginal-Australian Fellowship, Records, 1956–1978, Mitchell library MLMSS 4057, Box 3, 'Aborigines and Ourselves' conference 1961 convened by the Aboriginal–Australian Fellowship, Reports and discussion, 15.

[Pearl] enjoyed telling the story of the first Christmas of her term, in 1954, in which the white Board members, all senior male bureaucrats or academics, invited her to 'share some frivolities'. Pearl was very aware of the tensions of the situation, and waited until the Board members offered her a Christmas drink. Then she pointed out to them: 'I don't have an exemption certificate, and as you've heard repeatedly, it's only low down white men that give grog to black women'.[34]

A major problem during her time on the Welfare Broad, in her quest to continue connecting with communities, was the restrictions placed on her travel. She was restricted to just two tickets a year, and on one occasion was invited to tour some reserves with the secretary of the board—a trip that would ensure she only saw the best of reserve conditions and could not speak frankly with Aboriginal people about their lives.[35] These restrictions of course meant she could not engage with communities and understand their concerns; they were a key way the board sought to limit her effectiveness and constrain her in her role.

Her work with the Welfare Board and the Aboriginal-Australian Fellowship had thus convinced her of the need to re-establish an Aboriginal-controlled organisation and she emphasised to Ray that the 'first thing we have to do is reintroduce the old Aborigines Progressive Association', to 'get back over the mountain' where people were 'screaming out' for help and leadership. Ray and Pearl made trips to Aboriginal communities west of Sydney to revive the association.

Pearl's influence was central to Ray's activism, through her choice of him as an Aboriginal delegate to attend the Berlin Youth Festival in 1951. The World Federation of Democratic Youth had called for delegates, with Pearl interviewing Aboriginal candidates, but knocking back a number who were keen to take their girlfriends or spouses with them because the costs had to be paid up-front and reimbursed later. About a fortnight before the ship sailed, Ray and Pearl were at a fundraising dance in Sydney. Pearl was becoming anxious as to who would attend the festival after having received a cable asking her to name the delegate. She looked around and at Ray and asked 'would you go?' She was pleased when he replied, 'I wouldn't go anywhere unless I went home to Dubbo to ask Mum', and she sent him on the midnight train to Dubbo to ask permission, and was waiting on the platform when he returned 24 hours later. Ray was lucky his mother knew a Russian woman who assured her that he would be treated well when he travelled behind the Iron Curtain, and his mother gave him permission

---

34   Heather Goodall, '"Assimilation begins in the Home": The State and Aboriginal Women's Work as Mothers in NSW, 1900 to 1960s', *Labour History* (69) (November 1995): 75.
35   Letter from M. H. Saxby, Superintendent of the Aborigines Welfare, to Pearl Gibbs, Aborigines Welfare Board, Sydney, 27 September 1954, Letters and Cards received 1953–1983, MLMSS 6922, Box 1, Gibbs Papers.

to go. The trip almost didn't happen when Ray's passport was not processed in time. On 2 June 1951, Ray was on board the ship waiting to go but still without a passport, until the trade unions—the Waterside Workers, the Building Workers Industrial Union, the Builders' Labourers and the Maritime Workers' Union—refused to let the ship leave Sydney Harbour without Ray, or any other ships leave harbours around Australia. The ship was delayed for four hours until the passport was provided and Ray could travel to the festival.

Ray attended with 95 other young Australians from around the country. He and Brian Thomas were the Aboriginal delegates, and Faith Bandler also attended. They sailed from Fremantle to their first stop in Colombo, Ceylon (Sri Lanka), where, as in all ports they would subsequently stop, they were met and hosted by local young people and shown sites of interest. Ray celebrated his twenty-first birthday between Colombo and their next stop of Bombay, and the ship then sailed through the Suez Canal to London, and they then travelled across Europe, and Ray remembers fondly travelling through Italy before the festival. After the festival he travelled with other delegates in the USSR.

This was a formative experience in Ray's life, which he can now look at as being like a huge tree that started with the planting of a seed by William Ferguson in Dubbo when Ray was only a very small boy, and from then to now the tree has grown, and has blossomed. Ray considered the results of this work are shown by the number of Aboriginal students currently enrolled at Charles Sturt University, where Ray continues to work, in particular working closely with elders locally and from across the nation.

Pearl and non-Aboriginal activists

Pearl worked to build community between Aboriginal and non-Aboriginal people as she did through her media and speaking work, but she was very careful to ensure that this community was one which suited Aboriginal people, and in which Aboriginal people spoke for themselves. Her media and speaking work may have tried to create new non-Aboriginal activists on behalf of Aboriginal causes, but once those people were committed, Pearl was staunch in her insistence that non-Aboriginal activists work for Aboriginal people; she insisted that Aboriginal concerns and views were always central. When she was interviewed in the *New Dawn* in the early 1970s and the interviewer wrote somewhat sarcastically that Pearl had 'educated' him, non-Aboriginal activists Len Fox and Jack Horner both wrote letters to the paper applauding her work and remembering the way she had also 'educated' them. Fox wrote about a meeting with her in 1950:

Pearl started, 'it's all your fault you know', she said, 'it's you whites who are to blame' … She hammered 'you whites' for the whole half hour til the others arrived and I just had to sit there and take it.

It seemed a bit tough that I was the only white in Sydney who had come along to do something about it and here I was getting the blame. But I knew Pearl's stirring record of fighting for her people day in and day out, year after year, and although I took a lot of abuse that night it remains a happy memory. I've never lost my respect for Pearl and her tireless struggle for the dignity of her people.[36]

Horner wrote in a similar vein:

I see that you have been educated by Pearl Gibbs. We were all educated by Pearl at one time or another … When I was active in Sydney years ago, Pearl was one of the koories who kept a watchful eye to make sure that I did not get away with any white man's humbug. At the slightest sign of it, or of pushing a line that was not the way the kooris saw it, I was *jumped* on. Then it was explained to me, that I was expected to write my letters and make my protests exactly as they wanted.[37]

Pearl insisted that non-Aboriginal activism for Aboriginal causes was not about non-Aboriginal people themselves, but always about, and for, the Aboriginal community. In doing so she placed Aboriginal experiences at the forefront and demanded that non-Aboriginal activists accede to the needs of Aboriginal communities, ensuring they recognise their own complicity in Aboriginal disadvantage.

In this sense, as in her other work, Pearl may have been an important national figure, but she was always clear whom she worked for, and she made sure others were clear on this too. Pearl's activism attempted to connect Aboriginal and non-Aboriginal people, bringing the real circumstances faced by Aboriginal communities into the consciousness of non-Aboriginal Australia to agitate for citizenship, democracy and Aboriginal rights. Her work for communities was tireless and she is truly a woman who exemplifies leadership for democracy in this country.

---

36 Len Fox, 'Letter to the Editor', *New Dawn*, June 1971: 15.
37 Jack Horner, 'Letter to the Editor', *New Dawn*, June 1971: 15.

References

Aboriginal-Australian Fellowship. Records 1956–1978. MLMSS 4057, Mitchell Library, Sydney.

Behrendt, Larissa. 'Aboriginal Women and the White Lies of the Feminist Movement: Implications for Aboriginal Women in Rights Discourse.' *The Australian Feminist Law Journal* 1 (1993): 27–44.

Fox, Len. 'Letter to the Editor.' *New Dawn*, June 1971: 15.

Gibbs, Pearl. Papers. MS 6922/3X, Mitchell Library, Sydney.

Gilbert, Kevin J. *Because a White Man'll Never Do It*. Sydney: Angus & Robertson, 1973.

Gilbert, Kevin. 'Three Tributes to Pearl Gibbs (1901–1983)—Pearl Gibbs: Aboriginal Patriot.' *Aboriginal History* 7(1) (1983): 5–9.

Gilbert, Stephanie. '"Never Forgotten": Pearl Gibbs (Gambanyi).' In *Uncommon Ground: White Women in Aboriginal History*, edited by Anna Cole and Victoria Haskins, 107–26. Canberra: Aboriginal Studies Press, 2005.

Goodall, Heather. 'Three Tributes to Pearl Gibbs (1901–1983)—Pearl Gibbs: Aboriginal Patriot.' *Aboriginal History* 7(1) (1983): 20–2.

Goodall, Heather. '"Assimilation begins in the Home": The State and Aboriginal Women's Work as Mothers in NSW, 1900 to 1960s.' *Labour History* 69 (November 1995): 75–101.

Goodall, Heather. *Invasion to Embassy: Land in Aboriginal Politics in New South Wales, 1770–1972*. Sydney: Allen & Unwin, 1996.

Haskins, Victoria. '"Lovable Natives" and "Tribal Sisters": Feminism, Maternalism, and the Campaign for Aboriginal Citizenship in New South Wales in the Late 1930s.' *Hecate* 24(2) (1998): 8–21.

Haskins, Victoria. '"& so we are 'Slave owners'!": Employers and the NSW Aborigines Protection Board Trust Funds.' *Labour History* 88 (May 2005): 147–64.

Horner, Jack. 'Letter to the Editor.' *New Dawn*, June 1971: 15.

Horner, Jack. 'Pearl Gibbs: A Biographical Tribute.' *Aboriginal History* 7(1) (1983): 10–20.

Huggins, Jackie. 'Indigenous Women and Leadership: A Personal Reflection.' *Indigenous Law Bulletin* 6(1) (2004): 5–7.

Lake, Marilyn. 'Citizenship as Non-Discrimination: Acceptance or Assimilationism? Political Logic and Emotional Investment in Campaigns for Aboriginal Rights in Australia, 1940 to 1970.' *Gender & History* 13(3) (November 2001): 566–92.

Lake, Marilyn. 'Founding Fathers, Dutiful Wives and Rebellious Daughters, 2001 Eldershaw Memorial Lecture.' *THRA Papers and Proceedings* 48(4) (December 2001): 268–79.

Moreton-Robinson, Aileen. 'Tiddas Speakin' Strong: Indigenous Women's Self-Presentation within White Australian Feminism.' In *Talkin' Up to the White Woman: Indigenous Women and Feminism*, 150–78. Brisbane: University of Queensland Press, 2000.

O'Shane, Pat. 'Is There Any Relevance in the Women's Movement for Aboriginal Women?' *Refractory Girl—A Journal of Radical Feminist Thought* 12 (September 1976): 31–4.

'Our Historic Day of Mourning and Protest: Aborigines Conference.' *The Abo Call*, April 1938: 2. http://www.aiatsis.gov.au/collections/exhibitions/dayofmourning/images/pdf/a334816_s04_m.pdf.

Peckham, Ray. Presentation to the Women, Leadership and Democracy in Australia Conference, Museum of Australian Democracy, Old Parliament House, Canberra, 1–2 December 2011.

'Stopping off at Dubbo on the Track West...' *New Dawn*, January 1971: 7.

Taffe, Sue. *Black & White Together: FCAATSI, the Federal Council for the Advancement of Aborigines and Torres Strait Islanders, 1958–1973*. Brisbane: University of Queensland Press, 2005.

Taffe, Sue. Collaborating for Aboriginal Rights website. Canberra: National Museum of Australia, 2008. http://indigenousrights.net.au/default.asp.

Part III
Local and global politics

4. Women's International leadership

Marilyn Lake[1]

Leading the world

Internationalism as both ideal and practice exerted a powerful appeal for Australian women activists in the twentieth century even as they moved to the forefront of world history in winning full political rights at the national and State levels at home. These developments were interrelated. Australian women initially presented themselves to international audiences—and were received— as leaders of the world's women, as pioneers of democratic rights, able to report on their unique experience as politically empowered women and show the way forward.[2]

In 1893, Catherine Spence and Margaret Windeyer joined hundreds of American and European women gathered at the astonishingly large Congress of Women, held in the Woman's Building at the World's Columbian Exposition (or World Fair) in Chicago, where Spence gave a talk on 'Effective Voting' (or proportional representation). She also attended the International Conference on Charities and Corrections, as a representative of the SA State Children's Council. Her visit was part of an American lecture tour during which she addressed hundreds of audiences across the United States and made many new friends.

'To that celebrated journalist, poetess and economic writer, Charlotte Perkins Stetson [Gilman], who was a cultured Bostonian, living in San Francisco', Spence wrote in her autobiography, 'I owed one of the best women's meetings I ever addressed. The subject was "State Children and the compulsory clauses in our Education Act" and everywhere in the States people were interested in the splendid work of our State Children's department and educational methods.'[3] Margaret Windeyer, a commissioner to the Chicago Exposition, also attended

1   The University of Melbourne.
2   Marilyn Lake, 'Between Old Worlds and New: Feminist Citizenship, Nation and Race, the Destabilization of Identity', in *Suffrage and Beyond*, eds Caroline Daley and Melanie Nolan (Auckland: Auckland University Press, 1994), 277–94; Marilyn Lake, 'Between Old World "Barbarism" and Stone Age "Primitivism": The Double Difference of the White Australian Feminist', in *Australian Women: Contemporary Feminist Thought*, eds Norma Grieve and Ailsa Burns (Melbourne: Oxford University Press, 1994), 80–91; Angela Woollacott, 'Inventing Commonwealth and Pan-Pacific Feminisms: Australian Women's International Activism in the 1920s–1930s', *Gender and History* 10 (1998).
3   Susan Magarey, ed., *Ever Yours: CH Spence: Catherine Spence's 'An Autobiography' (1825–1910), Diary (1894) and Some Correspondence (1894–1910)* (Adelaide: Wakefield Press, 2005), 147.

the second world congress of the International Council of Women, and on her return home, helped form the first Australian National Council of Women in New South Wales, the sixth in the world, in 1896.

In 1902, Vida Goldstein travelled from Melbourne to the United States to attend the inaugural International Woman Suffrage Conference in Washington, DC, when she was granted an audience with the US President, Theodore Roosevelt, who was keen to meet this representative of the only nation that had extended full political rights to women: the right to vote and to stand for the national parliament.[4] She toured the United States presenting lectures to a wide variety of audiences. As American suffragist Alice Stone Blackwell wrote in Goldstein's autograph book:

> She has a stirring tale to tell,
> And modestly, yet undismayed,
> With facts and figures well arrayed,
> She tells her tale to folks intent,
> From Congressmen to President.[5]

In the United States, Australian women's achievement was hailed as an 'object lesson', as one feminist called it, in helping 'the cause of human liberty throughout the earth'.[6] 'While the principles of democracy were first enunciated in the United States', noted suffragist leader Carrie Chapman Catt, 'Australia has carried them furthest to their logical conclusion'.[7]

Before World War I, Australian feminists took to the international stage as self-conscious international leaders. Vida Goldstein saw her role as a teacher who could offer the lessons of experience and precedent, which she set out in her publication *Woman Suffrage in Australia*, commissioned by the International Woman Suffrage Alliance in 1908 and published as number two in their series on women's suffrage.[8] As an international leader and self-styled ambassador, Goldstein was pleased to address audiences across the United States on the effect of women's enfranchisement in Australia in advancing the interests of women and children.

In international feminist debates over 'equality' and 'difference'—over the question of whether feminists should promote the distinctive interests of women

---

4   Clare Wright, '"A Splendid Object Lesson": A Transnational Perspective on the Birth of a Nation', *Journal of Women's History* (forthcoming).
5   Blackwell verse in 'Autograph Book', in Vida Goldstein, Papers, Women's Library, London, previously the Fawcett Library, now relocated to London School of Economics [hereinafter Goldstein Papers].
6   Josephine Henry, *Commercial Tribune*, 20 July 1902.
7   'Proceedings 36th Annual Convention, 11–17 February 1904', in National American Woman Suffrage Association, Papers, 324.06 v.36, Schlesinger Library, Harvard University, Boston.
8   Vida Goldstein, *Woman Suffrage in Australia* (New York: International Woman Suffrage Alliance, 1908; reprinted Melbourne: Victorian Women's Trust, 2008).

or pursue the same rights as men—Australian feminists initially advocated the cause of 'difference', emphasising distinctive women's values and interests, as mothers and wives and their exploitation as 'creatures of sex'.[9] These interests were what Goldstein emphasised in the United States in 1902—priorities shared by the leaders of the National American Woman Suffrage Association (NAWSA), who sponsored her speaking tour. In farewelling Goldstein, Alice Blackwell of the NAWSA hailed Australian women's international leadership:

> Australia had led the way
> Our land will follow some glad day.
> When that occurs, or soon or late,
> Come back and help us celebrate![10]

In the early years of the twentieth century, Australian women were recognised as international leaders in advancing women's political rights.

Gendered internationalisms

In 1909, Carrie Chapman Catt, who had hosted Goldstein's visit to the United States, referred to the prevalent 'spirit of the 20th century the world calls Internationalism'.[11] As Leila Rupp pointed out in her path-breaking book *Worlds of Women: The Making of an International Women's Movement*, in many ways the years between the two world wars were the 'high tide of internationalism' for women.[12] With the International Council of Women (ICW), the International Alliance of Women for Suffrage and Equal Citizenship (later the International Women's Suffrage Alliance) and Women's International League for Peace and Freedom (WILPF) all active across the world, it was common for feminists to speak of their era as 'the century of internationalism'.[13] By 1920, when the newly formed League of Nations issued a handbook of international organisations, 500 groups, almost all new, claimed that identification in their title. Many of them were women's organisations.

Like women activists from other countries, Australian women looked to the international domain for solidarity, empowerment, respect and validation and to secure the support that would augment local campaigns for full equality as citizens, mothers, workers and individuals, or, as the International Alliance for

---

9   Marilyn Lake, *Getting Equal: The History of Australian Feminism* (Sydney: Allen & Unwin, 1999), 49–86.
10   Goldstein Papers. For further examples, see Marilyn Lake, 'Stirring Tales: Australian Feminism and National Identity, 1900–40', in *The Politics of Identity in Australia*, ed. Geoff Stokes (Melbourne: Cambridge University Press, 1997), 80–4.
11   Leila Rupp, *Worlds of Women: The Making of an International Women's Movement* (Princeton, NJ: Princeton University Press, 1997), 108.
12   Ibid., 34.
13   Ibid., 108.

Suffrage and Equal Citizenship put it in 1920, 'a real equality of liberties, status, and opportunities between men and women'.[14] Women of all backgrounds were inspired by the turn to internationalism and looked to the international domain to advance their rights.

Australian men, for the most part, concentrated on seeking and retaining power in the national domain, in federal and State politics, whether on the side of capital or labour, manufacturers or farmers, city or country, or in non-parliamentary, but powerful civil society organisations such as churches, trade unions and the Returned Sailors' and Soldiers' Imperial League of Australia (RSSILA; later the Returned Services League, RSL). They weren't so theoretically and practically engaged with the idea of internationalism, even though after World War I, national delegations (all male) attended meetings of the League of Nations and the International Labour Organisation (ILO) in Geneva and many men took leadership positions in the League of Nations Union in Australia.[15]

The labour movement sent representatives to the ILO as part of the national delegations, but they tended to see such activity as internationalism in the national interest, a means of raising global working conditions to match those of white Australia, thus keeping the threat of international forces at bay.[16] A number of women interested in labour issues—Muriel Heagney, Ethel Osborne, Eleanor Hinder and Mary Bennett—engaged with the ILO on an informal level. In later decades women joined delegations to the ILO as advisers or secretaries, but an Australian woman was not appointed as a full delegate to the ILO until 1980.

There is a gendered dimension to the history of Australian internationalism. For women in this period, their international engagements arose from their work in civil society and reform organisations, such as the Young Women's Christian Association (YWCA), whereas for men such as former prime minister Stanley Melbourne Bruce and Labor leader H. V. Evatt, participation in the international domain tended to be an extension of their formal positions and roles in national politics.[17] Women's experience of international activism produced convinced internationalists, such as Eleanor Hinder, Constance Duncan and Jessie Street.

---

14   Ibid., 23.

15   Nicholas Brown, 'Enacting the International: R. G. Watt and the League of Nations Union', in *Transnational Ties*, eds Desley Deacon, Penny Russell and Angela Woollacott (Canberra: ANU E Press, 2008), 75–94.

16   James Cotton, 'Australia in the League of Nations: Role, Debates, Presence', in *Australia and the United Nations*, eds James Cotton and David Lee (Canberra: Department of Foreign Affairs and Trade/Longueville, 2012); Marilyn Lake, 'The ILO, Australia and the Asia-Pacific Region: New Solidarities or Internationalism in the National Interest?', in *West Meets East: The ILO from Geneva to the Pacific Rim*, eds Jill Jensen and Nelson Lichtenstein (New York: Palgrave, 2014 [in press]).

17   David Lee, *Stanley Melbourne Bruce: Australian Internationalist* (New York: Continuum, 2010); Neville Meaney, 'Dr HV Evatt and the United Nations: The Problem of Collective Security and Liberal Internationalism', in *Australia and the United Nations*, eds James Cotton and David Lee (Canberra: Department of Foreign Affairs and Trade/Longueville, 2012).

Australian science graduate and reformer Eleanor Hinder was, as Sarah Paddle, Sophie Loy-Wilson and Fiona Paisley have pointed out, at the forefront of 'International Action' in the service of political and industrial reform, in her work in China from the 1920s.[18] As director of the Industrial and Social Division of the Shanghai International Government, Hinder worked with about 50 Chinese colleagues to create a system of factory inspection, health and safety regulation and wage regulation. In the YWCA newsletter, *Threads*, she mused self-consciously on the novelty of her political work:

> International Action is remarkably new to all of us and the first casting of small threads across the spaces that divide us may seem as futile as the spider's filament. But watch them by degrees strengthen into unbreakable bonds. A weaving has started that cannot easily be stopped ... Slogans and posters and handbills, in terms people can understand, distributed broadcast at such times, have led to common thinking and engendered a group mind.[19]

Common thinking and collective action might not always have produced a group mind, but certainly such activism was central to the cause of labour reform and the international women's movement, and offered Australian and other women the opportunity to exercise leadership in reform organisations at the international level, which was mostly unavailable at home.

Although granted the right to vote and stand for election to the National Parliament in 1902, no Australian woman was successful in gaining a seat in the House of Representatives or the Senate until 1943, when Enid Lyons was elected to the House of Representatives as Member for the Tasmanian seat of Darwin (later Braddon) and Dorothy Tangney entered the Senate on the WA Labor ticket. Moreover, no Australian women were elected to leadership positions in trade unions, business organisations or churches in these decades.

Formally equal citizens in the new Commonwealth of Australia from 1902, women were yet marginalised politically at the national level for several decades. They also remained subordinate to men in terms of pay, conditions and opportunities in the workforce, as well as in matters of the custody of children, divorce, domicile and nationality rights until the decades after World War II. Paradoxically, Australian women, the first in the world to win full political rights

---

18 Sarah Paddle, 'For the China of the Future: Western Feminists, Colonisation and International Citizenship in China in the Inter-War Years', *Australian Feminist Studies* 16(36) (2001); Fiona Paisley, 'Cultivating Modernity: Culture and Internationalism in Australia Feminism's Pacific Age', *Journal of Women's History* 14(3) (2002); Fiona Paisley, *Glamour in the Pacific: Cultural Internationalism and Race Politics in the Women's Pan-Pacific* (Honolulu: University of Hawai'i Press, 2009); Sophie Loy-Wilson, '"Liberating Asia": Strikes and Protest in Sydney and Shanghai, 1920–39', *History Workshop Journal* 72(1) (2011).

19 Quoted in Paddle, 'For the China of the Future', 327–8.

at the national level, were more likely to feel at home when abroad, and to find opportunities to exercise political influence and leadership in the international domain.

In studying the history of Australian women's leadership and, in particular, women's political leadership, we need to understand the conditions and contexts that both enabled and constrained women's exercise of leadership, such as the development of the two-party system in Australia and men's investment in securing and maintaining national power. Given the constraints of word length, this chapter focuses on the first half of the twentieth century, when Australian women's international engagement reached a high point, but when the women's movement also changed in its goals and aspirations, moving to more fully embrace the goals of equality and equal opportunity, as enunciated by new organisations such as Open Door International (ODI) and Equal Rights International (ERI), which advocated an end to all sex-based distinctions in employment. Sydney-based feminist Linda Littlejohn was a leading member of ODI, whose founding conference she had attended in Berlin in 1929, while Jessie Street became vice-president of ERI in 1930.[20] Street later became vice-president of the Commission on the Status of Women at the United Nations.

International action on behalf of women and children

In the first decades of women's internationalism, women such as Catherine Spence, Eleanor Hinder, Harriet Newcomb, Eleanor Moore, Bessie Rischbieth, Mary Bennett and Jessie Street took the opportunity to exercise leadership in international civil society organisations working on behalf of women and children. Such transnational activism was facilitated by the common understanding that the interests and needs of 'women' and 'children' were universal in nature, transcending national borders, just as women's paradigmatic exploitation as 'creatures of sex' or 'sex slaves' also crossed borders and boundaries—an understanding encoded in the League of Nations Convention for the Suppression of the Traffic in Women and Children, in 1921.

The 'mother' like the 'woman' was seen as a universal figure, whose needs and rights crossed the boundaries of nation, race and class. As Vida Goldstein stated in opposition to the racial exclusions of the Maternity Allowance 1912:

---

20   Marilyn Lake, 'From Self-Determination via Protection to Equality via Non-Discrimination: Defining Women's Rights at the League of Nations and the United Nations', in *Women's Rights and Human Rights: International Historical Perspectives*, eds Patricia Grimshaw, Katie Holmes and Marilyn Lake (London: Palgrave, 2001), 254–71.

'Maternity is maternity whatever the race.'[21] The 'spirit of motherhood' was invoked by feminist activists across the world as a collective transnational force.[22] In Australia and London, Aboriginal women's rights as mothers—in particular in relation to the guardianship of their children—were prioritised by some feminist advocates, such as Mary Bennett and Constance Ternente Cook, who worked with the League of Nations, the ILO and the British Commonwealth League to seek recognition of Aboriginal women's human rights.[23]

And it was as mothers—as life-givers—that women were called upon to oppose world war in 1914. As early as 7 August 1914, Goldstein's Women's Political Association (WPA) invoked the assumed universality of women's interests when she declared:

> This Association hopes that women everywhere, the life givers of the world will work henceforth with one mind to destroy the perverted sense of national honour and demand that international disputes shall be adjusted by arbitration. This Association resolves to cable to the President of the International Women's Suffrage Alliance, asking that women of all nations be urged to support the actions of President Wilson and lead for immediate arbitration.[24]

In 1915, antiwar activists in Melbourne formed the Women's Peace Army and Sisterhood of International Peace, which affiliated with the International Committee of Women for Permanent Peace in The Hague, later renamed the Women's International League for Peace and Freedom—a long-lived organisation, soon to celebrate its centenary in Australia in the same month and year as the centenary of the landing at Gallipoli. Activists such as Eleanor Moore were inspired by the internationalism of this new organisation, which she hoped would serve to prevent another world war.

A postwar congress held in Zurich in 1919 was attended by three Australians, Goldstein, Cecilia John and Moore, who became the secretary of WILPF in Australia and author of its history, *The Quest for Peace, as I Have Known it in Australia*.[25] That year a conference was also organised by socialist feminists in Melbourne to applaud the 'growth of Internationalism', which they defined as a kind of 'cosmopolitanism'. They called for an end to xenophobia and

---

21 Lake, *Getting Equal*, 76.

22 Seth Koven and Sonya Michel, eds, *Mothers of a New World: Maternalist Politics and the Origins of Welfare States* (New York: Routledge, 1993).

23 Fiona Paisley, 'Citizens of their World: Australian Feminism and Indigenous Rights in the International Context, 1920s and 1930s', *Feminist Review* 58 (1998); Lake, *Getting Equal*, 116–25; Fiona Paisley, *Loving Protection? Australian Feminism and Aboriginal Women's Rights 1919–1939* (Melbourne: Melbourne University Press, 2000).

24 Lake, *Getting Equal*, 63.

25 Eleanor Moore, *The Quest for Peace as I Have Known it in Australia* (Melbourne, 1948).

isolationism and questioned the wisdom of the White Australia Policy. 'Is Internationalism only a word', asked the writer Mary Fullerton, 'or is it a fact?' 'Does not Australia pride herself on being the land of experiments', asked schoolteacher Clara Weekes. 'Why fear the experiment of admitting Asiatics?'[26] Internationally oriented women—such as Goldstein, Hinder and Duncan—led campaigns to end racial discrimination in immigration.

The League of Nations, the pan-Pacific conference and the United Nations

International women's organisations mostly met in Europe or the United States. The Australian Federation of Women's Voters delegations, led by Bessie Rischbieth, attended the triennial congresses of the International Alliance for Suffrage and Equal Citizenship in Rome in 1923, in Paris in 1926 and in Berlin in 1929. But it was Geneva, as Rischbieth explained in a radio broadcast called 'The League of Nations and World Motherhood', which was the 'focussing point for [women's] efforts for peace and social humanitarian work'.[27] Australian women went to the League of Nations as alternate delegates from 1922. The third delegate, Melbourne journalist Stella Allen, returned feeling completely elated. 'In no other place in which she had been', she declared, 'were women and men on such equal terms as in Geneva. The mental attitude was one of absolute equality.'[28] This was the promise of the new international order.

The League of Nations also offered exciting opportunities for networking, socialising and celebrity spotting, as evident from E. C. McDonnell's breathless, but vivid account to Rischbieth in 1928, written from the Hotel de la Paix. She also referred to her efforts—amidst all the socialising—to address issues of sexual morality:

> There is so much to tell you this week I hardly know where to begin. The Assembly has been meeting all this week and on the whole the proceedings have been rather dull. Everyone reads set speeches whether in French or English and then when it has been read especially if in French, there is generally a big exodus and much chatter and movement so that it is rather difficult to follow the translation, added to which the Salle de la Reformation is stuffy to a degree, dreadfully badly ventilated.

---

26 *Woman Voter*, 3 July 1919. See Lake, '"Stirring Tales"', 86.
27 'The League of Nations and World Motherhood', Radio broadcast, in Bessie Mabel Rischbieth, 'Papers and objects 1900–1967', Manuscript Collection, MS2004, National Library of Australia, Canberra [hereinafter Rischbieth Papers].
28 Lake, *Getting Equal*, 159.

… My Commission has sat three times and I have had remarks to make in support of the proposal that the Joint Standing Committee of Women's International Organizations should have a representative on the International Cinematographic Institution which is being set up in Rome … [I] made a prepared speech on the questions of licensed houses, age of consent, and marriage and women police.

… I met Sir Eric and Lady Drummond, Lord Lytton and his wife, Lady Duff Cooper (the famous beauty, formerly Diana Mainwairing), a prince of Siam, a most enlightened person who spoke English with an Oxford accent, Monsieur Benes, Mr Mackenzie King etc I also had a little talk with Dame Edith Lyttleton whom I like very much. Dr Georgina Sweet gave a little luncheon party. I sat next to Princess Radziwill, a very able woman belonging to the Secretariat … The Joint Standing Committee of Women's International Organizations gave a little dinner at which I made a little speech and the ICW gave a reception. I have been to several little informal luncheons and have seen a lot of the Scandinavian women delegates whom I like exceedingly. Madame Appouyi of Hungary is rather a dear too. To-day Senator Mc Lachlan is giving a lunch to the Empire delegation and on Friday I go to a Danish Delegation Dinner.[29]

'It may seem a lot of festivity', she concluded somewhat apologetically to Rischbieth, 'but there is plenty of hard work'. She then listed all the committee reports and newspapers she had to read.

Reading and research were considered prerequisites to international activism, which at one level was thought of as an educative process necessary to the exercise of leadership in the vital work of promoting cross-cultural understanding. At the founding pan-Pacific conference of women in Honolulu, in 1928, delegates were asked to study key questions with reference to prescribed texts and prepared papers. Dr Georgina Sweet reminded E. C. McDonnell, who had been so busy in Geneva, that only papers of 'outstanding merit' were called for.[30] Sweet, a University of Melbourne research scientist, elected international president of the Pan-Pacific Women's Association in 1930, was an ardent reformer, whose leadership in urging women to join together in overcoming national and racial prejudices inspired others to join her crusade in 'cultural internationalism'.[31]

In 1932, delegates were asked to consider 'National Policies Affecting International Relations' and in particular the following questions:

---

29   'McDonnell to Rischbieth', 12 September 1928, 2004/9/120, Rischbieth Papers.
30   'Sweet to McDonnell', 30 April 1929, 2004/6/22, Rischbieth Papers.
31   Paisley, *Glamour in the Pacific*, 52–7.

> Is national control of immigration, especially any exclusion policy, liable to endanger world peace or at least to create political, social, racial and economic complications ... Does your country exclude or limit the immigration of any racial or national type. If so, what justifications are given? What reactions have resulted among the people so treated?[32]

By the 1930s, Australian feminists were well aware of the resentments caused by the White Australia Policy in their region, which were clearly an impediment to true internationalism. Vida Goldstein told an annual meeting of the Australian Federation of Women Voters (AFWV) that our 'Eastern neighbours' deplored Australia's 'arrogant discrimination against them'.[33] Criticising the Australian tendency to identify exclusively with European nations, Eleanor Hinder sent a circular letter to her friends:

> We are, as you know, very isolated with a population 98 per cent British in origin: we have a national religion—the White Australia policy, every organisation looks in affiliation to international groupings which centre in Europe. For the majority of the women in Australia, the women of Oriental countries simply do not exist.[34]

The pan-Pacific conferences showcased a very different and more diverse women's movement.

Muriel Heagney, representing labour women in Honolulu in 1928, reported to her friend Martha Mutt in Geneva: 'It was a great experience and a very fine conference.'

> The oriental women—particularly the Chinese—were charming and remarkably able. I went as a delegate of the Labor Women's Committee endorsed by the Trade Unions of Victoria and NSW. It is the first time a woman delegate has been sent abroad like that to a conference so we are slowly making progress ... The industry section was first class—many of its members you know—Mary Anderson, Elizabeth Christman, Jo Coffin and Mrs Katherine Edson of USA—Miss Bae-tsing Kyong of China (YWCA) made a fine contribution and Miss Yoshi Shoda—lecturer in Sociology—Japan Women's University—Tokyo was also good.[35]

Heagney regretted she was not able to go to the next pan-Pacific conference in 1930, because of the deteriorating economic situation in Australia: 'things

---

32 'National Policies Affecting International Relations', *Bulletin of the Pan-Pacific Union* 154 (1932), quoted in Lake, *Getting Equal*, 162.
33 Ibid., 163.
34 Hinder, 'Circular letter', 12 February 1930, 2004/4/17, Rischbieth Papers.
35 'Muriel Heagney to Martha Muntt 28 December 1928', in International Labour Organisation Archives, WN 12/4/1, Geneva [hereinafter ILO Archives].

are too bad here and the expense so great that it was impossible to get away.'[36] International activism could be expensive and was dependent on independent means, professional incomes or community fundraising. No women were paid by the Australian Government to attend these women's conferences.

Heagney was pleased that Dr Ethel Osborne, an expert in industrial health, was able to attend the 1930 conference and would report back to labour women. Osborne also represented Australia the following year as an alternate delegate at the League of Nations. As Paisley has pointed out, many Australian women saw themselves as perfectly placed—in geographical and historical terms— to mediate between the women of the West and those of the East.[37] Delegates challenged the racial exclusions that underpinned the White Australia Policy at home, even as their pan-Pacific activism often reinscribed the assumed dichotomy between 'advanced' and 'backward' women, between white women and natives.

White women also discovered that what they thought of as 'internationalism' might be understood by colonised peoples as a new form of 'imperialism'. Thus Hinder was challenged by the leader of the Chinese delegation in 1928, medical doctor Mei Iung Ting, who told Western women that if a conference were to be planned for China, it should be Chinese women who should make that decision, but she thought they had more pressing national priorities.[38] As the director of the Pan-Pacific Union reminded Georgina Sweet, they must 'go slowly and gently with [their] Oriental companions … in Japan and China … they resent any forceful leadership of the Occidental'.[39]

Another leading internationalist, active in the peace movement between the wars and secretary of the Victorian branch of the League of Nations Union and of the Bureau of Social and International affairs, was Constance Duncan, who, like Hinder, first went to Asia as a 'missionary' for the YWCA, living, working and learning the language in Japan in the 1920s. Her knowledge of Japanese culture and politics led her to become an expert in the emergent masculine field of 'international relations' and to join delegations to high-level conferences on the Asia-Pacific region. In 1936, she was Victorian delegate to the Institute of Pacific Relations conference in California, and on her return toured Japan and China on behalf of the Bureau of Social and International Affairs and the Australian Broadcasting Commission (ABC). Her task was to gather and disseminate information that would make 'Australians better informed and

36   Ibid.; 'Heagney to Muntt', 31 July 1930, in ibid.
37   Paisley, 'Cultivating Modernity', 105–6.
38   M. I. Ting, 'Report of Chinese delegation', 2004/6/37, Rischbieth Papers; Paddle, 'For the China of the Future'.
39   'Director Pan-Pacific Union to Sweet', 15 January 1929, 2004/6/66, Rischbieth Papers.

more curious about our neighbours in the Orient'. An enlightened public was considered essential since 'Australia is destined to be closely associated with the Orient, which to us is not the Far East but the Near North'.[40]

The rights of women as human beings

Australian women also played a leadership role in turning to the international domain to secure recognition of Aboriginal rights. They were founding members of the British Commonwealth League (BCL), formed in London in 1925, one of whose major goals was the advancement of indigenous rights across the Empire. As a delegate to the founding conference put it in 1925: 'Liberty must go beyond the boundaries of race and sex.'[41] Imperial-minded Mary Bennett was active at the BCL, but also saw the possibilities of internationalism in the conventions promulgated by the ILO, the League of Nations and the United Nations.

In these conventions, she identified novel ways of addressing and ending the multiple oppressions suffered by Aboriginal Australians: their forced labour, their removal from country, the sexual slavery of the women, the removal of their children.[42] Bennett's approach to reform depended on extensive research, but with a small independent income she was able to work without the support of an academic institution. An indefatigable researcher and archivist, she was assiduous in gathering relevant and up-to-date information, in all its detail, and in documenting, always with footnotes, every letter, submission to the authorities and the books she wrote on behalf of Indigenous people from the 1920s through to the 1960s.

Austere in manner, Bennett eschewed the soirees and dinners that characterised the season in Geneva, but forged solidarities with like-minded women reformers such as Ada Bromham, Constance Cooke and Edith Jones. Both her books, *The Australian Aboriginal as a Human Being*, published in 1930, and *Human Rights for Australian Aborigines*, published in 1957, pointed to the new possibilities for gaining recognition of Aboriginal human rights through working with international organisations. 'The founding of a just relation of the white and the dark races is not our problem alone', Bennett wrote in *The Australian Aboriginal as a Human Being*. 'It is a world problem. It is described as the most important business of the century.'[43]

---

40   Hilary Summy, 'From Missionary to Ministerial Adviser: Constance Duncan and Australian–Japan Relations 1922–47', *Australian Journal of Politics and History* 54(1) (2008).

41   Report of Conference, 'The Citizen Rights of Women within the British Empire', in British Commonwealth League Papers, 2160/box Y 792, 37, Mitchell Library, Sydney.

42   Marilyn Lake, 'Colonised and Colonising: The White Australian Feminist Subject', *Women's History Review* 2(3) (1993).

43   Mary Bennett, *The Australian Aboriginal as a Human Being* (London: Alson Rivers, 1930), 11.

In 1930, Bennett addressed the BCL in London on the treatment of Aborigines in Australia and invoked in her speech, as she did in her book, the 1926 Convention on Slavery, which defined slavery as 'the status or condition of a person over whom any or all of the powers attaching to the right of ownership are exercised' and the slave trade as 'all acts involved in the capture, acquisition or disposal of a person with intent to reduce him to slavery'. When the Convention on Slavery was broadened to include forced or compulsory labour in 1930, with the passage of ILO Convention 29, which defined forced labour as 'all work or service which is exacted from any person under the menace of any penalty and for which the said person has not offered himself voluntarily', Bennett immediately brought these provisions to the notice of the Australian authorities. In speeches in London, she charged the Federal Government, which was responsible for the administration of the Northern Territory, with breaking Convention 29 in three ways: employers were using forced labour on private property, they were refusing to pay wages to working natives and they were removing natives from their tribes and families to work in Darwin.

The news story in the *Manchester Guardian* based on Bennett's claims was reprinted in Perth by the *Dawn*, the journal of Rischbieth's Women's Service Guild, which declared that 'never in history' had the welfare of Aboriginal peoples received such publicity as at that moment, at the very heart of the Empire.[44] (It is ironic and poignant that feminists always had such an eye to history, when it would prove to be so uninterested in them.) In the same year in which Bennett addressed the BCL in London, her friend SA feminist Constance Ternente Cooke presented a paper on 'The Status of Aboriginal Women in Australia' to the Pan-Pacific Women's Conference in Honolulu. Cooke explained the position of Aboriginal women historically, providing an early version of what would later be called 'black armband history'. The settlement of Australia, wrote Cooke, was characterised by two great wrongs: first, the settlers took the land, then they took the women.[45]

The first great wrong, she wrote, was when

> the original inhabitants were deprived of all their lands by the legal device of declaring them the property of the Crown. Women as well as men were relegated thus to the position of serfs … The second great wrong to the race has been the interference of the white man with the native women.[46]

---

44   *Dawn*, 16 July 1930, quoted in Lake, *Getting Equal*, 115.
45   Constance Ternente Cooke, 'The Status of Aboriginal Women in Australia', in Anti-Slavery Papers, Br. Emp. S22, G 378, Rhodes House, Oxford.
46   Ibid.

This radical critique voiced by a feminist in an international forum was so threatening to the Australian Government that the Minister for Home Affairs demanded a right of reply and that two papers prepared by his department in response be published along with Cooke's in *The Report of the Proceedings of the Conference.*

The Australian Government also swiftly moved to ratify the 1930 Convention on Forced Labour, the first convention it chose to ratify after many years of delay with regard to others. In order to demonstrate that Australia was an 'advanced' country in the face of allegations of barbarous treatment of Aboriginal workers, as might occur in a 'backward' country, the Federal Government decided to ratify the Forced Labour Convention immediately. In 1931 the Department of Home Affairs wrote to the prime minister: 'As there is no forced labour in the Northern Territory, it is recommended that the Prime Minister's Department be advised that it is desired that the Convention be ratified.'[47] By 1932, the ratification was in place, but little changed in Aboriginal employment conditions. In response to lobbying, the ILO stated that Convention 29 was not the remedy needed by women activists, writing to Travers Buxton at the Anti-Slavery Society in London: 'they are ill advised to concentrate on securing international intervention, for which there is hardly sufficient basis, when so much could be done in Australia itself.'[48]

Campaigns for Aboriginal rights continued to look to the international domain for support. In 1938, writing as general secretary of the Aborigines' Progressive Association, Pearl Gibbs, hoping the League of Nations' mandate system extended to jurisdiction over Indigenous people in the Northern Territory, wrote to the president, enclosing the

> full report of the general Annual Meeting of the Aborigines Progressive Association that was held at Dubbo on 30 June last. There were present about fifty persons of Aboriginal blood who represented a large portion of NSW. Owing to the ill treatment of the aborigines throughout Australia in the past and the recent happenings in Darwin and knowing that the League of Nations has a mandate over the Northern Territory we appeal to you in the interest of the downtrodden natives to exercise your mandated authority in the cause of justice.[49]

The enclosed report of the meeting noted that most of the misdeeds committed by 'detribalized and demoralized aborigines' were caused by 'the brutal and stupid treatment of the aborigines by the white man for the last one hundred

---

47 Department of Home Affairs, 'Memorandum to Prime Minister's Department', 7 October 1931, A1 1931/7727, National Archives of Australia, Canberra. My thanks to Julia Martinez for this reference.
48 'CWH Weaver, ILO to Travers Buxton', 9 August 1931, 206/1/4/0, ILO Archives.
49 'Gibbs to President, League of Nations', 4 July 1938, Political Section 1/34895, ILO Archives.

and fifty years'. Australia's treatment of Aborigines, they said, was incurring 'the contempt of the civilized nations of the world'. The League of Nations official who received Gibbs' plea was not sympathetic, noting on the file: 'I don't think any action is possible or desirable.'[50]

Jessie Street took up the campaign for Aboriginal rights in London in the 1950s, seeking to invoke the human rights set out in the UN Charter and the Universal Declaration of Human Rights in 1948. As vice-president of the Status of Women Commission, she had earlier worked with Bodil Begtrup, the Danish president of the commission, to secure women-friendly amendments to the Draft Declaration. They had to fight hard even to be allowed to participate in discussions. 'It is obvious', Street wrote,

> that some of the members of the Economic and Social Council are not sympathetic with the work of the Status of Women Commission and are trying to belittle it and narrow it down. The Canadian delegate, Mr Smith indulged in various irresponsible and inaccurate witticisms which were rewarded with considerable mirth at our expense.[51]

Five days later, Street wrote to Begtrup again:

> One of the amendments made by the Economic and Social Council to our Report was that office bearers of our Committee should be present only when they discuss particular rights of women. (Canada—Mr Smith again—suggested that we might want to answer something about the rights of nursing mothers which wd give you an [idea] of the thinking of some of them). The intention of our Committee was that the recognition of the rights of women as human beings had been conspicuously absent in the past, for instance in respect of the right to vote, the right to work and own her own earnings, the right to property, the right to guardianship of her own children etc Consequently we believe all phases of the Bill of Human Rights would affect women and think we should be present during the whole of the discussion on the Bill of Human Rights.[52]

As Street left to return to Australia, she wrote again: 'Do what you can dear Bodil to see that our Commission is not slighted. If we assert ourselves this time they will not try again to discriminate against us. I am sending you a cable tonight. Love from Jessie Street.'[53]

---

50   Ibid.
51   Jessie Street to Bodil Begtrup, 2 April 1947, Street Papers, 2683/5/56, National Library of Australia (NLA), Canberra quoted in Lake, 'From Self-Determination via Protection to Equality via Non-Discrimination', 226.
52   Jessie Street to Bodil Begtrup, 7 April 1947, Street Papers, 2683/5/56, NLA, Canberra quoted in ibid.
53   Jessie Street to Bodil Begtrup, 4 June 1947, Street Papers, 2683/5/62, NLA, Canberra quoted in ibid.

Begtrup and Street were successful in securing passage of some amendments, with regard to pronouns and nouns, but defeated in more substantial ones, notably their attempt to change the status of mothers so they would no longer be thought of as a group in need of protection, but recognised as rights-bearing subjects with rights to custody of their children, as well as economic and social rights. 'I think it would be wise', wrote Begtrup, 'in the future to talk about the special conditions we want for motherhood as "the rights of motherhood" … and it will be a help to cut these rights free from "protection" which always gives a sense of inferiority that it will be sound to avoid'. They were defeated. Article 25 specified mothers and children as groups in 'need of care and assistance'.[54]

By the late 1940s, Street was prevented from resuming her position as vice-president of the Status of Women Commission because of political pressure at home, where she was increasingly depicted, including by rival feminists, as a communist or communist fellow traveller. In exile in London in the 1950s, Street followed in the footsteps of Constance Cooke, Edith Jones and Mary Bennett by working with the Anti-Slavery Society, to achieve recognition of the human rights of Aboriginal Australians by invoking the Universal Declaration of Human Rights. Invited to join the executive committee in 1953, she suggested that the Anti-Slavery Society take a case about the denial of Aboriginal rights to the Human Rights Commission, but after much discussion they were persuaded that an Australian organisation should do this to avoid the charge of interference with the internal affairs of another country.

Street then wrote to her contacts in Australia to suggest the various State organisations come together to form a national body which could approach the United Nations. 'I believe', she wrote to H. G. Clements, the WA secretary of the Australian Peace Council, in January 1956,

> and this is my personal opinion, that it would be easier to deal with the question of Aborigines satisfactorily if there was a Commonwealth wide body concerned with the development of full citizenship for Aboriginals … Would it be possible to call an all-Australian Conference on the subject … You have sent me Shirley Andrews' address and I know Mollie Bayne who is President of the Council for Aboriginal Rights.[55]

Andrews wrote back in August 1956, conveying the Victorian Council of Aboriginal Rights' full support for the idea.[56]

Street was also in touch with Pearl Gibbs, who had joined Faith Bandler that year in forming the Aboriginal-Australian Fellowship in Sydney. The following

---

54 Lake, *Getting Equal*, 205.
55 Ibid.
56 Marilyn Lake, *FAITH: Faith Bandler Gentle Activist* (Sydney: Allen & Unwin, 2002).

year another international development, the passage by the ILO of Convention 107, laid the basis for recognition of tribal identities and indigenous claims to land. As usual, Bennett saw the implications immediately, obtained a copy of ILO Convention 107 from Thomas Fox-Pitt at the Anti-Slavery Society and passed it on to Shirley Andrews on the Council of Aboriginal Rights. It became a key document for campaigns for land rights later undertaken by the newly formed Federal Council for Aboriginal Advancement, which had been formed at Street's behest in 1958. ILO Convention 107 was discussed at their annual conference in 1959.

Conclusion

One of the main political achievements of women's international activism aimed at securing Aboriginal rights was to embarrass Australian governments into taking action, or more commonly, claiming to take action. 'How terrified Australians are of criticism', wrote Mary Bennett to Fox-Pitt at the Anti-Slavery Society, 'when an uneasy conscience knows it to be true'.[57] Whether our focus as historians is on Aboriginal rights, equal opportunity, the repeal of discriminatory immigration laws or the achievement of equal pay and affirmative action, an understanding of the dynamics of these campaigns must embrace the international as well as the national domains and the interconnection and intertwining of the two. In engaging with international organisations and committees, international covenants and conventions, Australian women activists showed unprecedented historic leadership in introducing their fellow citizens to a new political order of possibility. More research needs to be done on the ways in which the national and international domains were intertwined in campaigns for sexual and racial equality and the ways in which human rights extended citizenship rights.

These very diverse women reformers were not simply leaders among Australian women. They also played a leadership role when considered in the context of Australian political history, pointing to the importance of the new international domain of the twentieth century, with its solidarities, networks and conferences, its institutions, conventions and covenants as instruments that could be used to end racial and sexual discrimination and secure recognition of all people's equal opportunities and human rights.

---

57 'Bennett to Fox-Pitt', November 1958, S22, Br. Emp. G953a, Anti-Slavery Society Papers.

References

Anti-Slavery Papers. Br. Emp. S22, G 378. Rhodes House, Oxford.

Bennett, Mary. *The Australian Aboriginal as a Human Being*. London: Alson Rivers, 1930.

British Commonwealth League. Papers, 2160. Mitchell Library, Sydney.

Brown, Nicholas. 'Enacting the International: R. G. Watt and the League of Nations Union.' In *Transnational Ties*, edited by Desley Deacon, Penny Russell and Angela Woollacott. Canberra: ANU E Press, 2008.

Cotton, James. 'Australia in the League of Nations: Role, Debates, Presence.' In *Australia and the United Nations*, edited by James Cotton and David Lee, 1–33. Canberra: Department of Foreign Affairs and Trade/Longueville, 2012.

Department of Home Affairs. 'Memorandum to Prime Minister's Department', 7 October 1931. A1 1931/7727. National Archives of Australia, Canberra.

Goldstein, Vida. Papers. Women's Library, London, previously the Fawcett Library, now relocated to London School of Economics.

Goldstein, Vida. *Woman Suffrage in Australia*. New York: International Woman Suffrage Alliance, 1908. [Reprinted Melbourne: Victorian Women's Trust, 2008.]

Henry, Josephine. *Commercial Tribune*, 20 July 1902.

International Labour Organisation Archives. WN 12/4/1. Geneva.

Koven, Seth and Sonya Michel, eds. *Mothers of a New World: Maternalist Politics and the Origins of Welfare States*. New York: Routledge, 1993.

Lake, Marilyn. 'Colonised and Colonising: The White Australian Feminist Subject.' *Women's History Review* 2(3) (1993): 377–86.

Lake, Marilyn. 'Between Old Worlds and New: Feminist Citizenship, Nation and Race, the Destabilization of Identity.' In *Suffrage and Beyond*, edited by Caroline Daley and Melanie Nolan, 277–94. Auckland: Auckland University Press, 1994.

Lake, Marilyn. 'Between Old World "Barbarism" and Stone Age "Primitivism": The Double Difference of the White Australian Feminist.' In *Australian Women: Contemporary Feminist Thought*, edited by Norma Grieve and Ailsa Burns, 80–91. Melbourne: Oxford University Press, 1994.

Lake, Marilyn. 'Stirring Tales: Australian Feminism and National Identity, 1900–40.' In *The Politics of Identity in Australia*, edited by Geoff Stokes, 79–81. Melbourne: Cambridge University Press, 1997.

Lake, Marilyn. *Getting Equal: The History of Australian Feminism*. Sydney: Allen & Unwin, 1999.

Lake, Marilyn. 'From Self-Determination via Protection to Equality via Non-Discrimination: Defining Women's Rights at the League of Nations and the United Nations.' In *Women's Rights and Human Rights: International Historical Perspectives*, edited by Patricia Grimshaw, Katie Holmes and Marilyn Lake, 254–71. London: Palgrave, 2001.

Lake, Marilyn. *FAITH: Faith Bandler Gentle Activist*. Sydney: Allen & Unwin, 2002.

Lake, Marilyn. 'The ILO, Australia and the Asia-Pacific Region: New Solidarities or Internationalism in the National Interest?' In *West Meets East: The ILO from Geneva to the Pacific Rim*, edited by Jill Jensen and Nelson Lichtenstein. New York: Palgrave, 2014 [in press].League of Nations Archives. Political Section, 1/34895. Geneva.

Lee, David. *Stanley Melbourne Bruce: Australian Internationalist*. New York: Continuum, 2010.

Loy-Wilson, Sophie. '"Liberating Asia": Strikes and Protest in Sydney and Shanghai, 1920–39.' *History Workshop Journal* 72(1) (2011): 74–102.

Magarey, Susan, ed. *Ever Yours: CH Spence: Catherine Spence's 'An Autobiography' (1825–1910), Diary (1894) and Some Correspondence (1894–1910)*. Adelaide: Wakefield Press, 2005.

Meaney, Neville. 'Dr HV Evatt and the United Nations: The Problem of Collective Security and Liberal Internationalism.' In *Australia and the United Nations*, edited by James Cotton and David Lee, 34–65. Canberra: Department of Foreign Affairs and Trade/Longueville, 2012.

Moore, Eleanor. *The Quest for Peace as I Have Known it in Australia*. Melbourne, 1948.

National American Woman Suffrage Association. Papers, 324.06. Schlesinger Library, Harvard University, Boston.

Paddle, Sarah. 'For the China of the Future: Western Feminists, Colonisation and International Citizenship in China in the Inter-War Years.' *Australian Feminist Studies* 16(36) (2001): 325–41.

Paisley, Fiona. 'Citizens of their World: Australian Feminism and Indigenous Rights in the International Context, 1920s and 1930s.' *Feminist Review* 58 (1998): 66–84.

Paisley, Fiona. *Loving Protection? Australian Feminism and Aboriginal Women's Rights 1919–1939*. Melbourne: Melbourne University Press, 2000.

Paisley, Fiona. 'Cultivating Modernity: Culture and Internationalism in Australia Feminism's Pacific Age.' *Journal of Women's History* 14(3) (2002): 105–32.

Paisley, Fiona. *Glamour in the Pacific: Cultural Internationalism and Race Politics in the Women's Pan-Pacific*. Honolulu: University of Hawai'i Press, 2009.

Rischbieth, Bessie Mabel. 'Papers and objects 1900–1967.' MS2004. Manuscript Collection. National Library of Australia, Canberra.

Rupp, Leila. *Worlds of Women: The Making of an International Women's Movement*. Princeton, NJ: Princeton University Press, 1997.

Summy, Hilary. 'From Missionary to Ministerial Adviser: Constance Duncan and Australian–Japan Relations 1922–47.' *Australian Journal of Politics and History* 54(1) (2008): 28–43. *Woman Voter*, 3 July 1919.

Woollacott, Angela. 'Inventing Commonwealth and Pan-Pacific Feminisms: Australian Women's International Activism in the 1920s–1930s.' *Gender and History* 10(3) (November 1998): 425–48.

Wright, Clare. '"A Splendid Object Lesson": A Transnational Perspective on the Birth of a Nation.' *Journal of Women's History* (forthcoming).

5. The big stage: Australian women leading global change

Susan Harris Rimmer[1]

I am absolutely providing leadership when I provide a space for others to speak.

— Caroline Lambert

The founding mother of the Australian feminist internationalist movement must be Jessie Street (1889–1970). Street was a role model for all those who came after her, due to the way she saw the possibilities of using the international system in the fight against discrimination. A founder of the UN Commission for the Status of Women, amongst many other achievements, she had infinite energy as a campaigner.

This chapter assesses some of the contributions of Australian women who have been successful in promoting social change using international forums in the 30 years after Jessie Street's work, particularly at the United Nations. Their contribution has been profound, and often undervalued in broader Australian public life. Drawing on previous oral history interviews as well as new interviews (with Elizabeth Evatt,[2] Hilary Charlesworth[3] and Caroline Lambert[4]), I describe the different ways these women have displayed leadership for women's rights on the world stage. I ask how this social change agenda has benefited the Australian women's movement and affected the quality of Australian democracy.

This leads to the question of whether social change in Australia can and should be pursued through international processes, and/or whether international progress for gender equality without reform in Australia can be a goal in its own right. What is the measure of successful leadership in the international sphere? How can successful leadership translate into a contribution to Australian democracy?

---

1   The Australian National University. I am grateful for research assistance provided by Gillian Evans and for comments and leadership provided by Marian Sawer.
2   National Library of Australia Oral History, 'Interview of Elizabeth Evatt by Daniel Connell for the Law in Australia Project, 13 September 1996' (Canberra: National Library of Australia, Canberra).
3   National Library of Australia Oral History, 'Interview of Hilary Charlesworth by Susan Harris Rimmer for the Women's Leadership in a Century of Australian Democracy Project, 22 July 2011' (Canberra: National Library of Australia).
4   National Library of Australia Oral History, 'Interview of Caroline Lambert by Susan Harris Rimmer for the Women's Leadership in a Century of Australian Democracy Project, 11 November 2011' (Canberra: National Library of Australia).

The United Nations is based on progressive ideals of peace, equality and human rights but it is as hierarchical and patriarchal as its constituent member states,[5] and its processes can move at a glacial pace. Sometimes progressive ideas succumb to the lowest common denominator when consensus is required. Entry points and paths to influence are often difficult to detect. It is a space for global diplomacy, but is still dominated by highly educated, well-trained and usually male members of the foreign services.

The role most Australian women leaders have claimed in the international space has been that of 'expert' or a 'thought-leader'. In their chapter in this volume, Marian Sawer and Merrindahl Andrew explore the discomfort felt by feminists with traditional forms of leadership associated with hierarchy and the subordination of women. To influence international affairs is in many ways an elite sport, even as a representative of a non-governmental organisation (NGO). Deliberations in Geneva or New York feature extremely formal and often technical discussions and very clear hierarchies, with politicians and diplomats at the top. How can an international feminist exercise 'shared leadership' emphasising 'democratic process and consensus decision-making' in this context? Who is the constituency? Despite the elite character of multilateral work, in practice the women I studied usually worked in coalition, with a focus on inclusive process and a shared belief in the transformative power of gender equality across national boundaries.

What, then, is the relationship between international advocacy and the quality of Australian democracy? My argument is that domestic reform and engagement with the UN system or other international forums can be a mutually enriching experience. Like Jessie Street, these women have been innovative in their use of the international system or have created new ideas about international law and practice. Their experience has some common themes: the need for both patience and determination; the key role of good gender analysis as opposed to general gender awareness; and the importance of strategic thinking. The last can range from improving decision-making machinery in the interests of women to changing the way the reform agenda is formulated.

These stories of leadership at the international level need to be told, especially as the feminist movement in Australia undergoes generational change. Australian advocates for women's rights should consider using international processes as one of their tools but with full knowledge of the limits to achieving transformative change in this way. These experiences also need to be documented lest they be lost to history.

---

5   See further Hilary Charlesworth and Christine Chinkin, *The Boundaries of International Law* (Manchester: Manchester University Press, 2000).

The Hon. Elizabeth Evatt AC, AO: The judge

Elizabeth Evatt has had a stellar career combining international and domestic work in pursuit of human rights, especially women's rights.[6] Evatt was in some ways born into public life. She is the niece of H. V. Evatt, deputy prime minister and president of the UN General Assembly in 1948. Her father, Clive Evatt, was made a King's Counsel at the age of thirty-five. Elizabeth was brilliant, too, and a prodigy, becoming the youngest student to study law and the first woman to win the Law Medal at the University of Sydney, before completing her masters at Harvard University in the United States. Evatt was appointed deputy president of the Australian Industrial Relations Commission in the 1970s, before becoming the first chief justice of the Family Court of Australia. Her term as chief justice was turbulent, and often dangerous, with attacks on judges and the court itself.[7]

From 1988 to 1993, she was president of the Australian Law Reform Commission and then chancellor of the University of Newcastle. Notably, she chaired the Royal Commission on Human Relations from 1974 to 1977, which dealt with a wide variety of sensitive social issues, such as abortion, contraception, sex education, family law and violence against women. The royal commission broadened official definitions of domestic violence to include emotional and verbal as well as physical abuse.[8]

In 1984, soon after the Commonwealth *Sex Discrimination Act* finally made it through parliament, Evatt was elected as an expert to the Committee on the Elimination of Discrimination against Women, the treaty body for the Convention for the Elimination of All forms of Discrimination against Women (CEDAW).[9] Reportedly, when Anne Summers called Evatt to ask if she accepted the Government's support for her nomination, she was surprised and asked if the CEDAW Committee did anything 'useful'. Summers replied that the Government was nominating her precisely because they wanted CEDAW to do something useful.[10] And so it came to pass. Between 1984 and 1992, Evatt was a member of the committee, serving as its chair from 1989 to 1991. She was then elected a member of the UN Human Rights Committee, from 1993 to 2000, which she

---

6   See further Susan Harris Rimmer, 'Raising Women Up: Analysing Australian Advocacy for Women's Rights under International and Domestic Law', in *Sex Discrimination in Uncertain Times*, ed. Margaret Thornton (Canberra: ANU E Press, 2011).

7   Ruth Newsbury, 'A Battle-Scarred Judge Fights', *The Advertiser* [Adelaide], 10 June 1986: 29.

8   See further Marian Sawer, *Making Women Count: A History of the Women's Electoral Lobby in Australia* (Sydney: UNSW Press, 2008), 48.

9   *United Nations Convention on the Elimination of All forms of Discrimination against Women*, GA res. 34/180, 34 UN GAOR Supp. (No. 46) at 193, UN Doc. A/34/46; 1249 UNTS 13; 19 ILM 33 (New York: United Nations, 1980).

10   Peter Thomson, 'Elizabeth Evatt: Integrating Women's Issues in the United Nations Human Rights System', in *Australians at the United Nations*, Unpublished ms (Canberra: Department of Foreign Affairs and Trade [on file with author], 1996), 4.

combined with a role as a part-time commissioner of the Australian Human Rights and Equal Opportunity Commission (now the Australian Human Rights Commission), from 1995 to 1998. These simultaneous appointments exemplify Evatt's capacity to connect the international and the domestic spheres.

During her long terms with both the CEDAW and the human rights committees, Evatt embarked on a tireless agenda of procedural reform and succeeded, together with a group of like-minded committee members, in improving the quality of analysis of general comments, the structure and length of meetings, the reporting procedures and the breadth of subject matter of the committees.[11] Such procedural reforms led to many substantive outcomes for women's rights, especially in the general recommendations on sexual stereotyping, incompatible reservations to the convention on the grounds of culture and religion, and female circumcision. The document she is best known for—General Recommendation 19, drafted in 1992—found that violence against women constituted discrimination.[12]

This was important because, notwithstanding the numerous strengths of CEDAW—including its extension to private actors and its aim to eliminate harmful customary practices[13]—one of its most glaring shortcomings is the omission of violence from its terms. Under Evatt's direction, the CEDAW Committee endeavoured to rectify this deficiency through Recommendation 19, which specifies gender-based violence as a form of discrimination prohibited by the treaty.[14] The adoption of the Declaration for the Elimination of All forms of Violence against Women by the UN General Assembly in 1993 also responded to this deficiency.[15] This work has been the foundation of many global policies and much jurisprudence. Recommendation 19 and the declaration provide the conceptual basis for 'Outcome 5' of the 2009 report of the National Council to Reduce Violence against Women and their Children.[16] This outcome encompasses strategies to strengthen legal responses to domestic violence, which sit within a wider social response—for example: Strategy 5.1, improve access to justice for women and their children; Strategy 5.2, strengthen leadership across justice systems; and Strategy 5.3, justice systems work better together and with other systems.

---

11   Ibid., 8–10.

12   Committee on the Elimination of All forms of Discrimination against Women, *General Comment 19 on Article 16 (and Article 5), Violence Against Women*, 29/01/92, A/47/38 (New York: United Nations).

13   See Articles 2 and 5. Traditionally, human rights law has only provided protection against governments rather than private actors.

14   Committee on the Elimination of All forms of Discrimination against Women, *General Comment 19 on Article 16 (and Article 5)*.

15   United Nations General Assembly, *Resolution 48/104 of 20 December 1993* (New York: United Nations, 1993).

16   National Council to Reduce Violence against Women and their Children, *Time for Action: National Council's Plan for Australia to Reduce Violence against Women and Children 2009–2021* (Canberra, 2009).

Evatt's work with the Human Rights Committee was equally groundbreaking—working again on the compatibility of reservations to the International Covenant on Civil and Political Rights (ICCPR), contributing to drafting the controversial General Comments on Article 18 (freedom of religion)[17] and drafting Article 25 (free elections and universal suffrage).[18] She worked hard to realise the 'scope and potential' of the ICCPR's emphasis on the right to equality to be a 'powerful tool' to protect the rights of women in all fields, but found it a struggle.[19] Many of her interventions on violence against women, rights in marriage and gendered forms of persecution in asylum claims appear, however, in the revised General Comment on Article 3 (equal rights of men and women) on which she worked closely with Professor Cecilia Medina of Chile. It was issued in March 2000.[20]

Elizabeth Evatt's vision of human rights is ultimately a unifying one. Her particular genius is the ability to look beyond artificial legal boundaries and examine legal instruments from the standpoint of the holistic and lived experience of an affected person, and then to translate this view into impeccably logical, analytically rigorous and technically accurate legal discourse. She sees life in all its messiness, but renders it in judicial prose. When you read the general recommendations and comments she drafted, they sound so much like shining good sense, it is hard to remember how groundbreaking and controversial they were at the time, and how much Evatt had to invest in procedural reform for long periods to realise the opportunity to produce the documents in a collective and empowering manner.

Evatt's work for human rights certainly did not end with her time at the United Nations,[21] but my argument is that just as her international work was influenced by her domestic experience, so too has that international dimension added richness and weight to domestic advocacy—her own and that of the many of us influenced by her. Evatt sees her work as a form of activism,[22] and she is

---

17   Human Rights Committee, *General Comment 22, Article 18 (Forty-Eighth Session, 1993)*, UN Doc. CCPR/C/21/Rev. 1/Add. 4 (1993), Reprinted in *Compilation of General Comments and General Recommendations Adopted by Human Rights Treaty Bodies*, UN Doc. HRI/GEN/1/Rev 6 (New York: United Nations, 2003), 155.

18   Human Rights Committee, *General Comment 25, The Right to Participate in Public Affairs, Voting Rights and the Right of Equal Access to Public Service (Article 25), (Fifty-Seventh Session, 1996)*, UN Doc. CCPR/C/21/Rev. 1/Add. 7 (1996), Reprinted in *Compilation of General Comments and General Recommendations Adopted by Human Rights Treaty Bodies* (New York: United Nations, 2003), 168.

19   Thomson, 'Elizabeth Evatt', 19.

20   Human Rights Committee, *General Comment 28, Equality of Rights between Men and Women (Article 3), (Sixty-Eighth Session, 2000)*, UN Doc. CCPR/C/21/Rev. 1/Add. 10 (2000), Reprinted in *Compilation of General Comments and General Recommendations Adopted by Human Rights Treaty Bodies* (New York: United Nations, 2003), 179.

21   Evatt was a judge of the World Bank Administrative Tribunal, a visiting professor at the University of New South Wales and chair of the board of the Public Interest Advocacy Centre in Sydney. She has for many years been a member of the Australian section of the International Commission of Jurists and was elected as a commissioner in April 2003. She has made valuable contributions to the public debate in recent years on sedition laws, the treatment of asylum-seekers and the need for an Australian Human Rights Act.

22   Kay O'Sullivan, *Trailblazers: The Road to Equality* (Melbourne: Australia Postal Corporation, 2011), 32.

passionate about holding the United Nations to account for upholding human rights and gender equality.[23] Her distinctive brand of leadership may stem from the fact that she often sounds like simply the smartest and most decent person in the room. Professor Hilary Charlesworth, discussed below, describes her as a role model in three words: 'brilliance, energy and commitment.'

Evatt has won the Human Rights Medal amongst many other accolades, and last year was captured as an 'Australian Legend' on a postage stamp. When asked about her theory of leadership, however, she snorted down the phone: 'I just get on with it!' She is very modest about her own role and achievements. Despite, or perhaps because of, her illustrious career, she is today often despondent and critical about human rights issues in Australia and around the globe.[24]

Professor Hilary Charlesworth: The academic/activist

Hilary Charlesworth has achieved global renown for her academic work on feminist approaches to international law. She has been a commissioner for the Australian Law Reform Commission, and was appointed by Australia as a judge to the International Court of Justice for the whaling case in 2011. As a member of a large Melbourne academic family, Hilary, like Elizabeth Evatt, excelled at the University of Melbourne and undertook her doctorate at Harvard University. Professor Charlesworth was given a chair at the University of Adelaide Law School at age thirty-eight. She then came to The Australian National University and has built an international reputation as a jurist.

In 2013, Charlesworth was professor and director of the Centre for International Governance and Justice in the Regulatory Institutions Network at The Australian National University and also holds an appointment as Professor of International Law and Human Rights. She has held visiting appointments at US and European universities. She held an Australian Research Council (ARC) Federation Fellowship from 2005 to 2010 and then an ARC Laureate Fellowship. She was president of the Australian and New Zealand Society of International Law (1997–2001). She is on the editorial boards of a number of international law journals and served as co-editor of the *Australian Yearbook of International Law* from 1996 to 2006 and a member of the Board of Editors of the *American Journal of International Law*, 1999–2009. She was joint winner of the American

23   Rosemary West, 'Judging Women's Place in the World', *The Age*, 10 May 1995, 21.
24   Elizabeth Evatt, 'Falling Short on Women's Rights: Mis-Matches between SDA and the International Regime', in *Human Rights 2004: The Year in Review*, ed. Marius Smith (Melbourne: Castan Centre for Human Rights Law, Monash University, 2005).

Society of International Law's 2006 Goler T. Butcher Medal in recognition of 'outstanding contributions to the development or effective realization of international human rights law'.[25]

Professor Charlesworth has a strong activist streak combined with academic achievement. She led a group of international lawyers to write a public letter in February 2004 challenging the legality of the invasion of Iraq under international law.[26] She has worked with various non-governmental human rights organisations on ways to implement international human rights standards and was chair of the ACT Government's inquiry into an ACT Bill of Rights, which led to the adoption of the ACT *Human Rights Act 2004*—the first such legislation in Australia. She has been working hard to have economic, social and cultural rights included in the Act, which would also be an Australian first.

Like Evatt, Charlesworth emphasises collegiality and collaboration as important to her success. She gives great weight to the 'wonderful richness' and support of a cohort of female and male colleagues throughout her career, especially her writing partner, Christine Chinkin from the London School of Economics, Mary Wood, Andrew Byrnes and John Braithwaite. She notes how much she has benefited from the generosity of mentors, particularly international lawyers Philip Alston and James Crawford.

Although an acknowledged trailblazer, Charlesworth in her National Library of Australia interview, describes her most seminal article as a partial failure or disappointment, because she hoped the mainstream international law discipline would engage and respond to the arguments, and thus far it has not.[27] She celebrates the fact, however, that this work did create space for feminist inquiry. She looks back with most pride on her teaching career and the progress of her students.

When asked to describe women's leadership and social change in the international space, Charlesworth nominates Elizabeth Evatt; Jessie Street; the head of UN Women (2010–13), Michelle Bachelet from Chile, who was once a refugee in Australia; Penny Wensley, Australia's Ambassador to the United Nations and Governor of Queensland from 2008; and Erika Feller, Assistant High Commissioner of the UN Refugee Agency. Of Feller, Charlesworth notes she is a gifted diplomat who will often speak plainly and with strength—excellent Australian characteristics.

---

25 See: American Society of International Law, Awards and Honours. http://www.asil.org/about/awards-and-honors.

26 Hilary Charlesworth, 'Saddam Hussein: My Part in His Downfall', *Wisconsin International Law Journal* 23 (2005): 127–43.

27 Hilary Charlesworth, 'Talking to Ourselves? Feminist Scholarship in International Law', in *Feminist Perspectives on Contemporary International Law*, eds Sari Kouva and Zoe Pearson (Oxford: Hart Publishing, 2011), 17–32.

Charlesworth identified the following values in a leader: resilience, graciousness, humanity, integrity and inspiration. She felt the most admirable women leaders of her experience had certain common methods: they were consultative and approachable, they found consensus if possible, they did not shirk from taking decisions and acting firmly, they weathered scrutiny and criticism, and they had a rich life outside work. She felt senior women leaders were scrutinised more closely, especially for any sign of excess emotion. In opposition, a 'lone wolf' hyper-masculinist style, sometimes adopted by women, meant taking a position and crashing through. This may lead to a reputation for being strong, but meant a leader was unable to deepen their vision and learn. Above all, Professor Charlesworth's style of leadership is by elegant example.

Charlesworth and Evatt as judges and academic experts work within a hierarchy and leave a clear paper trail of their work, even if their own humility and belief in collaboration mean that certain aspects of their leadership may go unrecorded. But what happens if a leader in international reforms for gender equality chooses to work from a civil society position?

Dr Caroline Lambert: The civil society champion

Caroline Lambert has been an advocate for women's economic and social rights at the United Nations, a leader in the Australian women's sector heading many shadow reporting processes for UN treaties[28] and, from 2007, the executive director of the YWCA Australia. Over a 25-year period, she has been involved in a range of community organisations and co-founded (with Barbara Palmer) the Women's Rights Action Network Australia in 1998. She was involved with Amnesty International for many years, and is a past chair of Women's Housing Limited in Victoria. Lambert has a PhD on women, trade, human rights and liberal economic and political theory. She is the co-author of *Critical Chatter: Women and Human Rights Activism in South East Asia* and co-edited *Global Issues, Women and Justice* with Sharon Pickering. She was awarded a Women's Electoral Lobby Vida Goldstein Award for Human Rights in 2002. Of the research subjects, Dr Lambert was the youngest and has a thoughtful view of a feminist leadership style when pursuing national and global change, which takes a deliberate capacity-building approach.

Lambert says she is 'interested in ensuring that the voices of women in Australia, in particular young women's voices, are integrated in the policy process—so that policy can meet their needs and enable girls and young women in Australia to thrive and meet their full potential'. She works with a range of policy tools,

---

28 YWCA Australia and Women's Legal Services Australia, *Australian NGO Shadow Report on the Implementation of CEDAW* (2009).

with a particular expertise in using the UN Human Rights Treaty System, to achieve domestic political change. The CEDAW requires participating countries, including Australia, to put in place legal, policy and financial measures to protect women from discrimination and to uphold their rights. Participating countries must also report to the UN CEDAW Committee about their actions. Australia was last reviewed in July 2010, and before that in 2006.

From 2008 to 2011, YWCA Australia was the lead agency on an Australian Government contract to develop a *CEDAW Shadow Report*, an *Aboriginal and Torres Strait Islander Women's CEDAW Shadow Report*, and follow-up materials. YWCA Australia under Lambert's direction worked with Women's Legal Services New South Wales and Kingsford Legal Centre on the project. In 2012, YWCA Australia developed and launched the CEDAW Action Plan for Women in Australia. The CEDAW Action Plan highlights 15 points that the Australian Government, and State and Territory governments, must work towards in responding to the international community's concerns about the human rights of Australian women. The CEDAW Committee conducted an interim review of Australia in 2012, and a periodic review in 2014.

The approach taken by Lambert to the creation of shadow reports on the Beijing Platform for Action has been one of 'community development'. She believes it is important for feminist activists to challenge hierarchies, making the case that community voices are just as valid as 'expert' voices. She believes that bringing local stories and a community activist approach can have significant impacts on conversations in Geneva and New York—using examples of the Optional Protocol to CEDAW, or having kinship language included at the Commission for the Status of Women, or having women's housing recognised by the then Commission on Human Rights.

She describes herself as 'not an up-front power person'; she tries to exercise mindful leadership through inquiry and collaboration. Her style is based on inquiry, moderation and questioning; she thinks this was initially due partly to lack of confidence in her own voice, but partly to ideological commitment to questioning power and hierarchy. Her style has not necessarily changed but her confidence has grown since becoming the executive director of the YWCA in 2006. She celebrates the history of the YWCA—its brand and traditions are strong.

When asked about the disadvantages of this type of intentional feminist leadership style, she nominated invisibility. She noted that media is fundamentally about conflict and a 'name'. Many feminist spokespeople like Germaine Greer are known for controversy and a highly individualistic style. If an organisation does not heavily promote a front person, good work can be hidden from a wider audience. A flat structure and commitment to consultation can mean the organisation is slower off the mark in responding to media or that it chooses to refer media and opportunities to other women's groups. Lambert believes that to achieve social change, it is better to be in collaboration with government as a constructive or critical friend, but be prepared to name where governments are falling short of their obligations. Media, on the other hand, is fundamentally about conflict. She has been learning to step into conflict, and to trust that hard conversations can lead to better outcomes. She states, however, that 'I am absolutely providing leadership when I provide a space for others to speak'.

When asked who her leadership role models were, she nominated a collective group of inspiring figures, which makes sense for someone who prizes a collective style. The group includes members of Lambert's family, Desmond Tutu and Nelson Mandela, Kate Gilmore from Amnesty International, Ann Walker from the Tribune Centre in New York, colleagues from the Women's Rights Action Network of Australia (WRANA) and YWCA colleagues, as well as collaborators Edwina McDonald and Emily Chew.

She admired Mary Robinson but finds her stature overwhelming, as international figures 'live at a speed' she chooses not to. She also identified Australian Labor Party (ALP) politicians Tanya Plibersek, Claire Moore and Margaret Reynolds for being willing to stand up to the system and make space for others and support their voice.

In many ways the distinctions I have made between these three women are exaggerated. Dr Lambert is also an expert author and the head of a substantial organisation, so the lines between my three subjects are blurry.

Lessons learnt

I implore feminist leaders not to confuse humility with obscurity. The next generation of women needs to know stories of reform and progress and career paths to follow, so please document and share (with due modesty if you must). There are other Australian women leaders on the world stage who deserve whole books to themselves, or whole shelves of books. I would nominate Erika Feller, top UN leader; Helen Caldicott, antinuclear activist;[29] Stella Cornelius, champion of peace and conflict resolution; and Elizabeth Reid, international development pioneer. There is not enough on the record about Australian political figures who have used their role as parliamentarians to further social change for women in the international sphere, such as Margaret Reynolds, Janelle Saffin, Meredith Burgmann and Claire Moore.

---

29   See further Helen Caldicott, *A Passionate Life* (Sydney: Random House, 1996).

There are several other lessons that might be learned from looking closely at leadership in the international context. If Australians are to continue to have an impact on the world stage they need government support but also to remain independent and respected at home for their expertise. Generally speaking, most of the advocates I have researched have not seen their international and domestic work as disconnected, but instead as mutually reinforcing.

Second, collaboration between political leaders and advisers with gender expertise can be a winning combination for women's rights at both domestic and international levels, and this is a rare commodity. Helen L'Orange and Neville Wran, Anne Summers, Geoffrey Yeend and Paul Keating, Susan Ryan and Mike Codd, Margaret Reynolds and Bob Hawke, Gough Whitlam and Elizabeth Reid, and Hilary Charlesworth and Jon Stanhope are all good examples of leadership in different roles that respected the expertise involved in good gender analysis. These collaborations have led to Australian leadership in the international sphere, and better policy at home.[30] In this way Australian political leaders have opened up democratic space for the female half of the population under-represented in almost all key decision-making areas of public life.

We need to have this expertise and leadership represented overseas in international forums where possible in order to help women in other societies and receive insights that can benefit women in Australia. The biographical lens employed in this chapter underscores that necessity. At the Commission for the Status of Women in 2009, Australia finally provided financial support for a representative of Indigenous women in its official delegation, Lesley Slalem. Australia was successful in nominating lawyer Megan Davis for election to the Permanent Forum of Indigenous Peoples in 2011. Australia did not, however, nominate a candidate in 2010 for the CEDAW Committee, despite the noted international expertise of several Australians, not least Andrew Byrnes, Dianne Otto and Hilary Charlesworth.

Leadership must come from many levels for international engagement to strengthen Australian democracy. Government support for Australian NGOs to engage with the UN human rights system is extremely limited and ad hoc. Learning the complex procedures of the UN system takes training, financial support and patience. Often the rewards come after many years of intricate drafting and procedural discussions. Australian NGOs could have that expertise, but usually it resides in one or two individuals like Caroline Lambert, often with little capacity or support for reporting back on international developments. A more systematic and long-term approach for NGO representation based on

---

30   Anne Summers notes that the 'femocrats had to fight and wheedle just like any other bureaucrat, even if their political masters were perhaps at times more sympathetic than other political leaders at different times'. Personal communication with author, 24 February 2010.

a community engagement approach like that displayed by the YWCA would improve the overall quality of Australia's engagement with the United Nations.[31] Another such group the Government should support is Women With Disabilities Australia (WWDA).[32]

Third, procedural reform is important and fundamental to substantive gains. Process matters to gender outcomes. General human rights machinery is still not in place, therefore women's rights always require an extra struggle. The uneven history of Australia's ratification of CEDAW and its Optional Protocol, considered alongside the rocky passage of the *Sex Discrimination Act*, is testament to this fact.

Elizabeth Evatt would say we still have much further to travel in making the rights of women part of the central project of protecting human rights in Australia, and simply achieving a Human Rights Act will also not be enough, if her experience with the ICCPR is any guide.[33] Many other current issues speak of lack of motivation and commitment, a partial and narrow national imagination and a paucity of use of existing evidence for gender analysis when it comes to really valuing Australian women, recognising their dignity and fulfilling their rights.

If we take Evatt's human rights test of whether Australia is committed to 'raise from the lowest level those whose needs are greatest', I am not convinced Australia's parliamentary legislative process, bureaucratic machinery, political debate or data and evaluation methods are designed with that aim in mind. The United Nations has often been more resistant to reform than it should be according to its own charter. The experience of our heroines in this story of raising women up shows that progress will be slow, but possible. It just takes brilliance, energy and commitment. And getting on with it.

---

31 Australian women engaging with the United Nations include: Carolyn Hannan, Pene Mathew, Jane McAdam, Linda Bartolomei, Margaret Bearlin, Quentin Bryce, Gabrielle Cullen, Megan Davis, Anne-Marie Devereux, Alice Edwards, Louise Hand, Ellen Hansen, Lee Kerr, Caroline Lambert, Eve Lester, Libby Lloyd, Caroline Millar, Robyn Moody, Annie Petit, Margaret Reynolds, Ariane Rummery, Eileen Pittaway, Carole Shaw, Leanne Smith, Rosalind Strong, Irene Watson, Felicity Hill, Pera Wells, Penny Wensley, Margaret Callahan, Janet Hunt, Donelle Wheeler, Natasha Yacoub, Sarah McCosker, Letitia Anderson, Kirsten Hagon, Pene Mathew, Miranda Sisson and many more.

32 See further Marian Sawer: 'At the international level, WWDA was able to take part in the decade of negotiations over the UN Convention on the Rights of Persons with Disabilities along with representatives of other disability peaks. Thanks to this presence on the ground, WWDA contributed to the historic achievement of Article 6, which addressed the multiple discrimination experienced by women and girls with disabilities and Article 16, which recognised and required policy and legislative responses to the gender-based aspects of violence and abuse. This achievement was despite the opposition of the Australian government to the inclusion of an article on women in the Convention.' Marian Sawer and Merrindahl Andrew 'Hiding in Plain Sight', in *The Women's Movement in Protest, Institutions and the Internet: Australia in Transnational Perspective* eds Sarah Maddison and Marian Sawer (New York: Routledge, 2013), 78.

33 The Rudd Government rejected the recommendation for federal human rights legislation in April 2010 and said the decision would not be reviewed until 2014.

References

Australian Human Rights Commission and the Australian Government Office for Women. *Women of the World: Know Your International Human Rights*. Canberra: Government of Australia, 2008.

Caldicott, Helen. *A Passionate Life*. Sydney: Random House, 1996.

Committee on the Elimination of All forms of Discrimination against Women. *General Comment 19 on Article 16 (and Article 5). Violence Against Women*. 29/01/92, A/47/38. New York: United Nations.

Committee on the Elimination of All forms of Discrimination against Women. *Consideration of Australia's Combined 4th and 5th Report*. New York: United Nations, 2006.

Committee on the Elimination of All forms of Discrimination against Women. *Consideration of Reports Submitted by States Parties under Article 18 of the Convention on the Elimination of All forms of Discrimination against Women*. Combined Sixth and Seventh Periodic Reports of States Parties: Australia, CEDAW/C/AUL/7. New York: United Nations, 9 March 2009.

Committee on the Elimination of Discrimination against Women. *Forty-Sixth Session Summary Record of the 935th Meeting. New York, on Tuesday, 20 July 2010, at 10 a.m.* CEDAW/C/SR.935. New York: United Nations, 2010.

Charlesworth, Hilary. 'Australia's Relations with the United Nations in the Post Cold War Environment.' Australian Federal Parliament, Joint Standing Committee on Foreign Affairs, Defence and Trade. *Joint Committee Hansard*, 21 March 2001, 429.

Charlesworth, Hilary. 'International Law: A Discipline of Crisis.' *Modern Law Review* 65 (2002): 377.

Charlesworth, Hilary. 'Saddam Hussein: My Part in His Downfall.' *Wisconsin International Law Journal* 23 (2005): 127–43.

Charlesworth, Hilary. 'Inside/Outside: Feminist International Legal Studies and Thirty Years of the CEDAW Convention.' Paper delivered at the Asian Society of International Law Conference, Tokyo, August 2009.

Charlesworth, Hilary. 'Talking to Ourselves? Feminist Scholarship in International Law.' In *Feminist Perspectives on Contemporary International Law*, edited by Sari Kouva and Zoe Pearson, 17–32. Oxford: Hart Publishing, 2011.

Charlesworth, Hilary and Sara Charlesworth. 'The Sex Discrimination Act and International Law.' *University of New South Wales Law Journal* 27 (2004): 858.

Charlesworth, Hilary and Christine Chinkin. *The Boundaries of International Law*. Manchester: Manchester University Press, 2000.

Charlesworth, Hilary, Madeline Chiam, Devika Hovell and George Williams. *No Country is an Island: Australia and International Law*. Sydney: UNSW Press, 2006.

Cusack, Simone. 'Discrimination against Women: Combating its Compounded and Systemic Forms.' *Alternative Law Journal* 34(2) (2009): 86.

Declaration on the Elimination of All forms of Violence against Women. A/RES/48/104. New York: United Nations.

Downer, Alexander, Daryl Williams and Phillip Ruddock. 'Improving the Effectiveness of United Nations Committees.' Joint media release, Parliament House, Canberra, 29 August 2000.

Edwards, Alice. 'Violence against Women as Sex Discrimination: Judging the Jurisprudence of the United Nations Human Rights Treaty Bodies.' *Texas Journal of Women & the Law* 18 (2008): 1.

Evatt, Elizabeth. 'Falling Short on Women's Rights: Mis-Matches between SDA and the International Regime.' In *Human Rights 2004: The Year in Review*, edited by Marius Smith. Melbourne: Castan Centre for Human Rights Law, Monash University, 2005.

Gardam, Judith and Michelle Jarvis. *Women, Armed Conflict and International Law*. The Hague: Kluwer Law International, 2001.

Harris Rimmer, Susan. 'Grand Plans.' In *Capturing the Year 2009: Writings from the ANU College of Asia and the Pacific*, edited by Barbara Nelson and Andrew MacIntyre. Canberra: The Australian National University, 2009.

Harris Rimmer, Susan. 'Raising Women Up: Analysing Australian Advocacy for Women's Rights under International and Domestic Law.' In *Sex Discrimination in Uncertain Times*, edited by Margaret Thornton. Canberra: ANU E Press, 2011.

Human Rights Committee. *General Comment 22, Article 18 (Forty-Eighth Session, 1993)*. UN Doc. CCPR/C/21/Rev. 1/Add. 4 (1993). Reprinted in *Compilation of General Comments and General Recommendations Adopted by Human Rights Treaty Bodies*. UN Doc. HRI/GEN/1/Rev. 6 at 155. New York: United Nations, 2003.

Human Rights Committee. *General Comment 25, The Right to Participate in Public Affairs, Voting Rights and the Right of Equal Access to Public Service (Art 25) (Fifty-Seventh Session, 1996)*. UN Doc. CCPR/C/21/Rev. 1/Add. 7 (1996). Reprinted in *Compilation of General Comments and General Recommendations Adopted by Human Rights Treaty Bodies*. UN Doc. HRI/GEN/1/Rev. 6 at 168. New York: United Nations, 2003.

Human Rights Committee. *General Comment 28, Equality of Rights between Men and Women (Article 3) (Sixty-Eighth Session, 2000)*. UN Doc. CCPR/C/21/Rev. 1/Add. 10 (2000). Reprinted in *Compilation of General Comments and General Recommendations Adopted by Human Rights Treaty Bodies*. UN Doc. HRI/GEN/1/Rev. 6 at 179. New York: United Nations, 2003.

Lambert, Caroline. 'Reproducing Discrimination: Promoting the Equal Sharing of Caring Work in CEDAW, at the ILO and in the SDA.' In *Sex Discrimination in Uncertain Times*, edited by Margaret Thornton. Canberra: ANU E Press, 2011.

Lambert, Caroline, Sharon Pickering and Christine Adler. *Critical Chatter: Women and Human Rights Activism in South East Asia*. Durham, NC: Carolina Academic Press, 2003.

L'Orange, Helen. 'Statement of Helen L'Orange, Leader of the Australian Delegation to the 33rd Session of the Commission for the Status of Women.' Vienna, March–April 1989.

National Council to Reduce Violence against Women and their Children. *Time for Action: National Council's Plan for Australia to Reduce Violence against Women and Children 2009–2021*. Canberra, 2009.

National Library of Australia Oral History. 'Interview of Elizabeth Evatt by Daniel Connell for the Law in Australia Project, 13 September 1996.' Canberra: National Library of Australia.

National Library of Australia Oral History. 'Interview of Hilary Charlesworth by Susan Harris Rimmer for the Women's Leadership in a Century of Australian Democracy Project, 22 July 2011.' Canberra: National Library of Australia.

National Library of Australia Oral History. 'Interview of Caroline Lambert by Susan Harris Rimmer for the Women's Leadership in a Century of Australian Democracy Project, 11 November 2011.' Canberra: National Library of Australia.

Newsbury, Ruth. 'A Battle-Scarred Judge Fights.' *The Advertiser* [Adelaide], 10 June 1986: 29.

New South Wales Task Force on Domestic Violence. *Report of New South Wales Task Force on Domestic Violence to Hon N K Wran QC, MP Premier of New South Wales*. Sydney, July 1981, and follow-up report, 1985.

Optional Protocol to the Convention on the Elimination of All forms of Discrimination against Women. A/RES/54/4. New York: United Nations, 2000.

O'Sullivan, Kay. *Trailblazers: The Road to Equality*. Melbourne: Australia Postal Corporation, 2011. Pickering, Sharon and Caroline Lambert, eds. *Global Issues, Women and Justice*. Sydney: Sydney Institute of Criminology Series, 2004.

Ramsay, Janet. 'The Making of Domestic Violence Policy by the Australian Commonwealth Government and the Government of the State of New South Wales between 1970 and 1985: An Analytical Narrative of Feminist Policy Activism.' PhD dissertation, University of Sydney, 2006.

Sawer, Marian. 'The Long March through the Institutions: Women's Affairs under Fraser and Hawke.' Paper presented at the Australasian Political Studies Association 28th Annual Conference, Brisbane, 27–29 August 1986.

Sawer, Marian. *Sisters in Suits*. Sydney: Allen & Unwin, 1990.

Sawer, Marian. *Femocrats and Ecorats: Women's Policy Machinery in Australia, Canada and New Zealand*. Geneva: United Nations Research Institute for Social Development, 1996.

Sawer, Marian. 'Disappearing Tricks.' *Dialogue: Academy of the Social Sciences in Australia* 27(3) (2008): 4.

Sawer, Marian. *Making Women Count: A History of the Women's Electoral Lobby in Australia*. Sydney: UNSW Press, 2008.

Sawer, Marian and Merrindahl Andrew. 'Hiding in Plain Sight.' In *The Women's Movement in Protest, Institutions and the Internet: Australia in Transnational Perspective,* edited by Sarah Maddison and Marian Sawer, 70–86. New York: Routledge, 2013.

Thomson, Peter. 'Elizabeth Evatt: Integrating Women's Issues in the United Nations Human Rights System.' In *Australians at the United Nations*, Unpublished ms. Canberra: Department of Foreign Affairs and Trade, [on file with the author], 1996.

Thornton, Margaret. 'Auditing the Sex Discrimination Act.' In *Human Rights 2004: The Year in Review*, edited by Marius Smith. Melbourne: Castan Centre for Human Rights Law, Monash University, 2005.

Thornton, Margaret. 'Feminism and the Changing State: The Case of Sex Discrimination.' *Australian Feminist Studies* 21(50) (2006): 151–172. http://www.informaworld.com/.

United Nations Beijing Conference on Women. *Platform for Action and Final Report.* New York: United Nations, 1995. http://www.un.org/womenwatch/confer/beijing/reports/.

United Nations General Assembly. *Resolution 48/104 of 20 December 1993.* New York: United Nations, 1993.

United Nations Nairobi Conference on Women. *Final Report.* New York: United Nations, 1985. http://www.un.org/womenwatch/daw/beijing/otherconferences/Nairobi/Nairobi%20Full%20Optimized.pdf.

United Nations Convention on the Elimination of All forms of Discrimination against Women. GA res. 34/180, 34 UN GAOR Supp. (No. 46) at 193, UN Doc. A/34/46; 1249 UNTS 13; 19 ILM 33. New York: United Nations, 1980.

West, Rosemary. 'Judging Women's Place in the World.' *The Age*, 10 May 1995: 21.

Women's Rights Action Network of Australia (WRANA). *Australian NGO Shadow Report on the Implementation of CEDAW.* 2005.

YWCA Australia. 'CEDAW National Action Plan.' 2011. http://ywca.org.au/advocacy-policy/our-united-nations-work.

YWCA Australia and Women's Legal Services Australia. *Australian NGO Shadow Report on the Implementation of CEDAW.* 2009.

6. 'All our strength, all our kindness and our love': Bertha McNamara, bookseller, socialist, feminist and parliamentary aspirant

Michael Richards[1]

In the foyer of Trades Hall, Sydney, there is a brass plaque with an image of a woman. The inscription on it reads:

Bertha McNamara

kindly and gracious in her splendid way

She knew no nationhood

And her religion each and every day

Was that of doing good.

Jammed up against it when I last visited was a fire hose reel.

Who was Bertha McNamara? A memorial notice printed after her death in 1931 called her 'The Mother of the Australian Labor Movement' and Labor's 'Grand Old Lady', mentioned that she was the mother-in-law of Jack Lang and Henry Lawson, and that she had a faith in socialism, which she was accustomed to proclaim at Labor Party conferences. She is still around on the edge of public memory. There is an entry in the *Australian Dictionary of Biography*, and once there was a hostel named after her in Sydney. A few people have written about her and a search on Google turns up a handful of hits. She has a stub on *Wikipedia*.

There should be more. In her militant challenges to parliamentary Labor, in her work as a radical bookseller and proprietor of a socialist reading room, and in her own political writing, she was one of the early shapers of the Australian labour movement. And if she had succeeded in winning Australian Labor Party (ALP) preselection for the Senate in New South Wales in 1928, she might have become the first woman in the Australian Commonwealth Parliament.[2] When

---

1   The Museum of Australian Democracy at Old Parliament House.
2   And she might have won, if she had been in the top three on the ALP ticket. After a strong campaign in New South Wales, Labor won all three senate seats up for election at the 1928 half-senate election in that State, defeating two incumbent opponents. Overall, the Nationalists and the Country Party easily maintained

she stood for preselection, a year after parliament moved to Canberra and the building now known as Old Parliament House, women had won the right to sit in parliament in only 11 nations in the world but nine of them had already elected women.[3] Although 26 Australian women had stood for election between their national enfranchisement in 1903 and 1943, when the first women were elected, none of them was endorsed by a major party. McNamara was to be no exception.[4]

Indeed, McNamara's path exemplifies much of the Australian feminist experience in the nineteenth and early twentieth centuries. An immigrant who encountered hard times and who for some years could only focus on personal and family survival, she developed as a leader within Australian socialism in the roles of writer, facilitator and networker. Her leadership was as one who influences others, both directly, through her own views, and indirectly, making the views of other change-makers available to men and women with little access through other means to a world of radical alternatives. Her trajectory reminds us that although the early Australian labour movement was strongly characterised by masculine privilege, activist women were vital to its success— but at lower levels in the hierarchy. Late in her life, when she advocated an avowedly feminist claim to parliamentary leadership, she was soundly rejected by her party. Although this was a defeat, followed quickly by her death, an appreciation of her life should acknowledge that she was one of the pioneers for the achievements of Australian women leaders in later years.

The broad facts of Bertha McNamara's life can be gleaned from Verity Burgmann's entry for her in the *Australian Dictionary of Biography*. To paraphrase: Matilda Emilie Bertha Kalkstein (1853–1931) was born at Posen, then part of Prussia. She immigrated to Victoria in 1869 after economic difficulties broke up the family home. There she lived at Bairnsdale, working as governess for an aunt, and in 1872 married Peter Hermann Bredt, a Prussian-born accountant who was the shire secretary. They had six children who lived, and three who died in infancy. In 1888 Bredt died; Bertha was left almost penniless. She moved to Melbourne and worked as a travelling saleswoman, selling jewellery and sewing machines. In 1892 she married William Henry McNamara, who had in 1887 been one of the founders of the Australian Socialist League but who had left it the year before in protest against its decision to support the new Labor Electoral League

control of the 36-member senate, and the Bruce–Page conservative government was returned to office, but Labor's strong result in New South Wales heralded Scullin's landslide win in the House of Representatives election the following year.

3   Government of Australia, *Women in the Senate*, Senate Brief 3 (Canberra: Department of the Senate, April 2014), 6, http://www.aph.gov.au/About_Parliament/Senate/Powers_practice_n_procedures/Senate_Briefs/Brief03.

4   I gratefully acknowledge the warm courtesy of Bertha McNamara's granddaughter, Margaret Bertha McNamara Henry, and her daughter, Lyndal Gaines, both of Brisbane, in providing invaluable assistance in telling this story.

and reformist state socialism. A powerful orator and experienced political organiser, four years younger than his wife, he was Australian born and had been politically active since the mid 1880s. In 1893 the McNamaras opened a bookshop in Castlereagh Street, Sydney, where Bertha also ran a boarding house and to which was adjoined the Socialist Reading Room. In the 1890s she was a leading member of the Social Democratic Federation of Australasia and of the Womanhood Suffrage League of New South Wales. She was a founding member of the Labor Women's Central Organising Committee and a frequent delegate to State Labor conferences. After William's death in 1906, she ran the bookshop on her own, maintaining it in various locations until 1929. The shop was a crucial meeting place for Sydney's left for all of its history. In the 1890s, Verity Burgmann records:

> The back room and the reading room above the shop were scenes of almost constant activity and discussion by socialists, feminists, anarchists, rationalists, Laborites and literary Bohemians ... During World War I the shop was more than ever in demand as an organizing centre for radical activity. Bertha assisted in many ways, especially by selling banned anti-militarist literature.

She died in 1931, after catching a chill in the Sydney Domain, where she had gone to speak against her one-time friend Adela Pankhurst. The former suffragette and socialist had turned in recent years against the causes she and Bertha had once held dear. Now an advocate of industrial peace and fiercely anti-communist, Adela Pankhurst was simply the latest in a long line of deserters from the working-class movement that Bertha McNamara believed in, and against whom she battled for 40 years.[5]

What can we find of Bertha McNamara beyond this? She was a prolific letter writer, writing dozens of letters to the labour press, especially *Labor Daily* in the 1920s. She wrote several pamphlets herself, one of them probably the first published work on Australian socialism by a woman. The bookshop she and her husband ran, along with its Socialist Reading Room, is mentioned in some ephemeral material. There is anecdotal evidence relating to her in accounts of the great names she was associated with, especially Jack Lang, who was said to be terrified of her, especially when she led a delegation of Labor women to the premier's office. There are family papers in the State Library of New South Wales, and a small collection of letters and other manuscripts in H. V. 'Doc' Evatt's papers, held by Flinders University Library in Adelaide. These

---

5   Verity Burgmann, 'McNamara, Matilda Emilie Bertha (1853–1931)', in *Australian Dictionary of Biography Online* (Canberra: National Centre of Biography, The Australian National University), http://adb.anu.edu.au/biography/mcnamara-matilda-emilie-bertha-7431/text12935, and 'McNamara, William Henry (1857–1906)', in *Australian Dictionary of Biography Online* (Canberra: National Centre of Biography, The Australian National University), http://adb.anu.edu.au/biography/mcnamara-william-henry-7432/text12937.

two folders of scorched, fire-damaged papers include also a few papers of her husband's, and letters to both of them, along with a tally of letters to the press by her published in the 1920s.[6] In what follows I draw primarily on these two folders, which I encountered when researching a National Library of Australia exhibition in the early 1990s.

The letters are strong evidence of her role as a networker. For example, in 1927 Mary Hoolahan of Orange, to the west of Bathurst in New South Wales, wrote to her:

> You see, I am cut off from Orange + Molong chiefly by my children, + like to be <u>in it</u> all the same when the class war is on. G. K Chesterton says looking after one child 'is an all-time job'—Bernard Shaw responds 'What about six?' Well I have 7 and no school for them + no help. My neighbour has 1 only and a trained nurse for it, a servant, a cool house and 2 cars, etc. etc., etc. All of us have a small tin shack, or not much better. Well, they are kind to us—but why should moneyed people <u>usurp</u> the joys of giving along with most other things? Even affection is wrested from the poor, for love cannot flourish in dirt and want and with harried tempers—ugliness bred of being overtaxed for generations. Greed and dishonesty and hatred and uncouthness batten on the feelings of the poor … If people think that slavery went out with the traders they are blind. The chief difference is that, whereas in past days slaves + their families had to be fed + clothed + housed, at the present time they are free only <u>to leave</u>—then they must provide for themselves + their <u>numerous</u> families …
>
> If you know where I can procure the writings of the late Louisa Lawson I would be so grateful if you let me know as I am most anxious to get hold of some of them.
>
> Yours in all sisterly feelings, dear Comrade, Mary Hoolahan.[7]

Testimony to the importance of McNamara as both bookseller and political correspondent to her clients, such letters show she was a key point of contact with the world of ideas and books for some of like mind in rural Australia.[8]

---

6   It is possible Evatt was planning a book, some posthumous memorial or collection of her writings, which was never completed. He was at school with her youngest son, William, who was active in the Socialisation Movement in the NSW Labor Party in the late 1920s, and perhaps the son acted as a conduit for the papers: the McNamara and Evatt families remained close friends for many years. Personal communication from Margaret Henry, Bertha's granddaughter, 2011.

7   'Mary Hoolahan to Bertha McNamara', 19 March 1927, Evatt Collection, Special Collections, Flinders University Library, Adelaide [hereinafter Evatt Collection].

8   This letter was written at the time of a struggle for control of the upper house of the NSW legislature, the Legislative Council, at a time when that body was appointed by the governor and not elected. Mary Hoolahan

An earlier group of letters reflects the rivalries of the tiny socialist groups of the period. These are from A. R. Jutson to both Bertha and William McNamara, written in the 1890s from Bourke, in the far north-west of New South Wales. Jutson had been an ally in the Australian Socialist League, but had left it.[9] He worked as a station schoolmaster, and McNamara's bookshop clearly was his lifeline to a world of ideas and books. Writing in 1891 about the Australian Socialist League, he urges:

> As regards the League, I say come out from it: have nothing to do with the unclean thing. Gather a nucleus of real earnest genuine socialists, with brains in their heads; and honesty and truth-feelings in their hearts, and so start afresh in our sacred cause … Recollect, that we are men, brave men and not cowards, fleeing before a revolution, but leaders, guides, redeemers and benefactors, and so let us charge cheerfully and undaunted by all shams and semblances and advance spiritedly on hypocrisy and ignorance, on chaos and the dark.[10]

And in 1894:

> The mad ways of the Trades-unions have disgusted me, and I am losing the faith I once had in their being of use, when we should need them in the fateful hour which is to come … Knaves win in the political struggle; and the honest and just man is defeated. Society seems to be delivered over from the hands of one set of criminals into the hands of another set of criminals as often as the government is changed … Politics is worth earnest study and earnest endeavour, provided that we mean the word to stand for what it once stood for—an application of the principles on which all our social and political action should be founded: namely the great principles of Justice, Truth, and Catholicity, aided by the great truths of what we now call Social Science … Politics has come to mean the crafty management of a political party by caucuses, and all sorts of trickery and finesse in the contests for political power and emolument.[11]

In 1892 the McNamaras too left the Australian Socialist League[12] to found the Social Democratic Federation of Australasia (SDF). In terms strongly reminiscent of Bertha's writing, its 1895 manifesto proclaimed:

---

is remembered by her daughter-in-law as a friend of Mary Gilmore and a committed supporter of Jack Lang. She was widowed later that year, left the land (she and her husband had sharefarmed), returned to Sydney and later taught. Personal correspondence with the Hoolahan family, 1998.

9   Jutson was close enough to the McNamaras that they named their son Bill (William Morris Jutson McNamara 1893–?) after him as well as William Morris. They had two children, Bill and Alice, and Bertha brought six children to the family from her first marriage, including Bertha and Hilda.

10   'A. R. Jutson to W. H. McNamara', 28 December 1891, Evatt Collection.

11   'A. R. Jutson to W. H. & B. McNamara', 8 August 1894, Evatt Collection.

12   The tiny Australian Socialist League struggled with the problem of what to do about the purity of socialist thought in the face of the modest electoral success of the Labor Electoral Leagues and the growing interest a

> The concentration of wealth in the hands of a few non-producers, and the alarming increase of poverty among the workers in every civilised country, is the problem of the age … The workers of bankrupt, tax-ridden countries are only held in check by the bayonet and artillery controlled by nation-pillagers who masquerade as financiers and statesmen … In Australia the worker is economically reduced to a condition of serfdom … The increase of labour-displacing machinery renders the obsolete methods of trade unionism powerless to cope with the power of organised capitalism, and the strike as a means of attack (unless universal) ends in the starvation of those who engage in it.

The federation was launched at the second of two inter-colonial congresses of Australian socialists at Leigh House in Sydney in November 1893, which called for 'the complete abolition of the private ownership of the means of production, distribution, and exchange', and it represented itself as the face of Australian socialism at the Zurich Socialist and Labour Congress of 1893, the third congress of the Second International.[13]

In Australia in these years, the parliamentary Labor movement was going through with its first split, which followed the dramatic emergence of political Labor as a parliamentary force in New South Wales in 1891 and which reflected the ebb and flow of opinion among Australian socialists of the time about the role of parliament. Not all Labor MPs were socialists, and many socialists were dubious of the new Labor parties. The refusal by most of the original 35 Labor parliamentarians to accept caucus control of their votes and a tightened pledge demonstrates how completely they accepted the concept of representative democracy, at least after winning their seats in parliament. Jutson and the McNamaras were not alone in denouncing them as rats. For them, the breakthrough of 1891—hailed in 1991 as the birth of a century-old tradition of Labor in politics—was simply the beginning of another failure, to be set alongside the failure of the unions in the strikes of 1890 and 1891.

---

number of socialist leaders therefore had in the parliamentary process throughout the 1890s. Initially, 'quarter philosophical anarchist, quarter physical-force anarchist, quarter state socialist, and quarter laborite', in the words of one of its founders, T. Batho, the anarchists had left by 1890 and the Labor parliamentarians, among them W. M Hughes and W. A. Holman, by 1897. In that year the league adopted a new manifesto and decided to run its own candidates at future elections, and in 1898 it required its members to resign from any other political organisation, long before Labor introduced the same principal. Ian Turner argues that the ambivalence evident in the ASL's history in the 1890s was common to every socialist group active in Australian politics. How could revolutionary ideals and dreams be reconciled with the desperate need for reforms that were perhaps achievable through parliament, at least in part? Ian Turner, *Industrial Labor and Politics* (Canberra: ANU Press, 1965), 28–9.

13 W. H. Mellor [Secretary], *Manifesto of the Social Democratic Federation of Australasia* (Sydney: The Federation, 1895), MS 9547, Box 1268/5, State Library of Victoria, Melbourne, http://www.reasoninrevolt. net.au/biogs/E000042b.htm.

As has been well documented, labour activist responses were many.[14] Some, including William Lane and Mary Gilmore, took refuge in foreign utopianism, attempting to establish a cooperative settlement in Paraguay. E. J. Banfield retreated within Australia, finding a refuge from political disillusion in a life as an island beachcomber, gardener and writer on Dunk Island, in far north Queensland. Others sought ideological purity within the tiny splinter parties and movements of the left, or opted to stay within the Labor Party and attempt to keep alive the principles of socialism within an increasingly non-socialist party. Bertha McNamara was in the end one of these. By the end of the first decade of the twentieth century she was a socialist activist within the Labor Party, suspicious of its parliamentary members but, almost at the end of her life, herself a candidate for the Australian Senate. Untangling her political trajectory in the 1890s and then after the formation of the SDF is at times a difficult task. One way of doing it is through her writing.

The pamphlet *Home Talk on Socialism and the Redemption of the World's Labourers*, published in Hobart in 1891 under the anonymous authorship of 'A Woman', was her first known publication. It was also one of the very first books or pamphlets espousing socialism to be published in Australia, and was published soon after she had become actively involved in radical politics. Only one copy is known to survive in a public collection, in the Mitchell Library in Sydney. In this, as in so many other respects, McNamara's fragile documentary record epitomises the vulnerability and near-invisibility of so much feminist history. In 20 years of searching, I have never found another copy: if not for this library copy, the nature of her first-known publication might have been lost forever.

The pamphlet is short, only nine pages, and written in a terse, direct style. 'The misery of our social life', she begins, 'who can see, hear and read about it, and not be moved to use their utmost endeavours to aid in a reform for the better'.[15] She tells of a mansion close by: 'Even from where I am writing I can see a grand palatial residence, the beautiful grounds whereon it stands are sloping right down to a lovely river bank, with the mild autumn sun shining upon it—Eden itself could scarce have looked fairer.'[16] But:

> [T]he mansion is shut up, no one remains but a caretaker and a gardener somewhere located in the back premises. Its owner has gone to live in another beautiful mansion near a large city, where he and his family can enjoy the gaiety of the winter season. He soweth not, neither

---

14   See, for example, Verity Burgmann, *'In Our Time': Socialism and the Rise of Labor, 1885–1905* (Sydney: George Allen & Unwin, 1985).
15   [Bertha McNamara], *Home Talk on Socialism, and the Redemption of the World's Labourers* (Hobart: Calder, Bowden & Co., 1891), 1.
16   Ibid., 6–7.

does he reap, neither does he make himself otherwise useful, he is an independent gentleman of a large fortune. Only a short distance from this beautiful mansion, are a number of small cottages, more or less in preservation, mostly less, here the labourers live with their families, the men who toil, who sow, and who reap, to provide the rich man and his kindred with bread; the men who, to the best of their strength and ability, do their share of life's labour. Here they live, with wife and children, huddled together in a few small rooms, and even these are the rich man's property.[17]

She writes of the shearers' strike in Queensland, where working men 'after trying in vain all means of peaceful cohesion … have gone out on strike to take back by force and open warfare what others have taken from them and are keeping from them, by stealth and stratagem'. However:

> Government under the control of Capital has, under the plea of keeping law and order, sent out its soldiery to aid one section of the community against the other … [and] comes the shameful report, which, if true, must make every patriotic Australian blush. We, who have so recently been shocked, and protested against half-civilized Russia's cruel treatment of its prisoners; we, who read with shudders of the atrocities committed in the penal regime of Van Dieman's Land—we read, in our year of grace, that the Shearer's Union strike leaders are chained to each other, to prevent escape, on their way to prison. Once again, who would not be a Socialist, and help with might and strength to build a social structure where strife and fighting would cease.[18]

McNamara cites Edward Bellamy's novel *Looking Backward* twice in this 1891 pamphlet, once as an example of a 'perfected human society' and once as a warning that under capitalism even the rich are not exempt from the prospect of loss and pain. Bellamy's utopian socialist novel, first published in the United States in 1888, had a wide influence on Australian radical thought. McNamara may have read the edition published by E. W. Cole in Australia in 1888 or 1889 or read the version serialised by William Lane in *The Worker* in 1890.[19] Bellamy's portrait of a society in which human goodness is allowed to flourish and such traits as crime and aggression disappear simply because there is no need for them once inequality and poverty have been overcome is strongly reminiscent of the tone of McNamara's pamphlet.[20]

---

17 Ibid., 7.
18 Ibid., 8.
19 *Looking Backward* was published again in Melbourne by Cole in 1920, by Andrade's Bookshop in the 1920s, in a braille edition in 1925 and in Sydney in 1932 by the socialist activist E. E. Judd, who reissued it in 1942 and 1943 under the imprimatur of the Socialist Labor Party of Australia, along with its sequel, *Equality*.
20 Bellamy's influence on working-class readers in Australia is further attested to by T. A. Coghlan, writing in 1918: '[In Australia] the workers are a reading class and Bellamy's solution of the problem of living, his

An unpublished short story by McNamara turns on another socialist classic of the times, and was perhaps written in the mid or late 1890s. Arthur Richmond begins work in an English textile factory when he is twelve. He invents a device that improved the machines: being too poor to patent it himself, he trusts his employer with the idea, and has it stolen from him. But it does result in a transfer to the engineering workshop, where he can explore his mechanical genius. He invents another device, which will automate part of the weaving process, but decides to keep it to himself. And he has fallen in love with the girl next door: she will not have to slave as his parents had, once his invention is completed. Then a stranger comes to town and holds a great meeting in the market square. This is his message:

> Machinery is everywhere replacing human labour, in the workshops, in the fields, in the factories. The workers are told they must go, there is no work for them and strong men look aghast and tired weary women look white with fear and the little children are crying for bread. And where do they go to these starving unfortunates, to the slums of the big cities, to the gaols, to the lunatic asylums. Those that once had happy, though frugal, homes. And they and their children degenerate into criminals, into the human drift which parades our streets and cries to you 'a penny sir, for god's sake a penny, to buy shelter or bread.'[21]

Arthur Richmond is transfixed:

> He did not stop to listen for any more it was as if an arrow had pierced his heart and his brain. Oh for mercy sakes, here in his hand he held the fate [of] … thousands of thousands, for work or to beg rob or steal or worse of all starve. These harmless, still little screws and wires, they could make thousands weep. What for? To enrich himself and a few manufacturers … Who would be able to enjoy the fresh air, who would be able to improve their homes, their persons and minds, whilst his machine was doing all the work? … …The picture in his mind almost

combination of socialism and individual liberty, won the enthusiastic assent of all. The book was read and discussed in workshop and on station, in the mining camp and amongst the timber getters, in fact, wherever a few workers were gathered together, there Bellamy was discussed and approved.' Coghlan, quoted in John Sendy, *Melbourne's Radical Bookshops: History, People, Appreciation* (Melbourne: International Bookshop, 1983), in which there is also an interesting discussion of Andrade's Bookshop and E. W. Cole. For Cole, see also: Ted Turnley, *Cole of the Book Arcade* (Melbourne: Cole Publications, 1974). Enthusiasm for Bellamy's influence was not unanimous. Another of the McNamaras' correspondents, socialist journalist A. G. Yewen, wrote in 1890 from the *Boomerang* office in Brisbane: 'I have seen Mabbott, Casey, Seymour & Lane. They are all well. They are making the A. L. F. [Australian Labor Federation] "hum". The Bellamy gang I have not yet seen, but from what I can gather it is nothing better than a bunch of cranks. They meet and spin cobwebs & inextricably wind themselves up in the meshes of their own idiocy. Bellamy's book has undoubtedly done good, but if it resulted in nothing better than in the formation of Bellamy societies—Then heaven help us for the Bellamyites won't.' 'A. G. Yewen to W. H. McNamara', 28 December 1890, Evatt Collection.

21   Bertha McNamara, 'For the Good Time Coming', date unknown, unpublished ms, 4, Evatt Collection.

crushed him to the ground. He reached his work-room, he hardly knew how. Here he beheld his wondrous little machine the offspring of long hours of patient study, the result of long hours of toil … But it was no good to him, he could never use it. Thou (sic) he thought [of] his sweetheart, the pretty home he had pictured as the result of his labour but every note in the prospective [?] was a vail [sic] of human suffering, every thread in the pretty dresses he was going to buy for her to wear was made up of wasted limbs and starved human beings.[22]

Brooding on the choice he has to make, he is visited by his sweetheart, who tells him her brother has given her a book bought at the same rally, Robert Blatchford's *Merrie England*:

It's such a curious little book and makes it as clear as daylight that we ought not to be poor, not any one of us, and moreover it says, that the Government, or the State, or the people, I don't know which, should own the machinery and the land and all the rest, and give everybody according to his needs, and that everybody should work according to his ability, and that the hours of labour should be regulated according to those labour-saving machines. This is balm to Gilead, my sweetheart he said. We will read it together and learn a great deal of what we ought to know. Even while he was speaking, he had resolved, that his machine should await completion until the conditions where [sic] so altered, that it would become a blessing instead as [sic] a curse to his fellow-creatures.[23]

McNamara concludes with a plea: 'And now how long my kind readers will he and we have to wait, how long oh people how long? Let us gather together all our strength, all our kindness and our love and work for the good time coming.'[24]

Again, it is one of the bestsellers of late nineteenth-century socialism that McNamara urges upon her readers. Blatchford's *Merrie England* was published in England in 1893. Its impact was immediate, both in Britain and elsewhere in the English-speaking world, and it sold more than a million copies. William Morris, lecturing to the Hammersmith Socialist Society in 1895, attested to the book's importance in Britain:

The thousands who have read that book must if they have done so carefully have found out that something better is possible to be thought of than the life of a prosperous mill-hand … Self-respect, happy and fit

---

22   Ibid., 5–6.
23   Ibid., 11–12.
24   Ibid., 18.

work, leisure, beautiful surroundings, in a word, the earth our own and the fullness thereof, and nobody really dares to assert that this good life can be attained till we are essentially and practically Socialized.[25]

Although there appears not to have been an Australian edition of *Merrie England*, Blatchford joined Bellamy to become one of the two socialist classics to be found in thousands of Australian homes, often alongside a work of the previous decade, Edward Carpenter's prose poem *Towards Democracy* (1883). I suspect they were read rather more than the works of Marx and Engels. Blatchford and Morris (especially his novel *News from Nowhere*, published in 1890) have sometimes been interpreted as backward-looking yearnings for a mythical pastoral golden age—symptoms of dislocation and despair rather than agents of change[26]—but here, in the political writings of an Australian socialist and bookseller, Blatchford's book sits alongside Bellamy's as campaigning weapons, as models for a better and fairer society.

Edward Bellamy was not terribly clear on how the transition to the socialist United States of the twenty-first century was to be achieved: it is not revolution he writes about so much as its results. McNamara was clearer, with a consistent line of argument in support of equal suffrage, which begins in the 1891 pamphlet and which continues throughout her political life. In 1891 she supported industrial militancy but not forceful violent revolution.[27] 'How can each and all of us help to undo the evils of the past and present', she concluded in 1891:

By the ballot-box certainly. By only giving votes to such men, who with a strong voice and hand will abolish plural voting, which gives our large proprietors an undue advantage over the poor man. By only voting men to our Councils of Government, who, with a strong voice and hand put down children's labour, and who instead will give work to the broad-shouldered, able unemployed men and the strong young women. To men, who, instead of the factory, will give our children leisure to grow, and our youth, one and all of them an equal liberal education. Neither must we mind rewarding such men liberally, so that their whole time and energy may be devoted to their stupendous work. And, moreover, that fit men will be chosen from the midst of the working classes, who themselves have practically endured the present hardships and unjust treatment of a working man's life.[28]

---

25 Quoted in E. P. Thompson, *William Morris* (London: Merlin, 1977), 622.
26 See, for example: Jan Marsh, *Back to the Land: The Pastoral Impulse in Victorian England* (London: Quartet Books, 1982).
27 For the strike, see: Stuart Svensen, *The Shearers' War* (Brisbane: University of Queensland Press, 1989).
28 McNamara, *Home Talk on Socialism*, 8.

McNamara's advocacy of an effective parliamentary role for working-class representatives (men and elected only by men) was, however, becoming more guarded. Many socialists argued that parliament was only useful as a forum for revolutionary propaganda. The political course adopted by the various Australian labour groups of using their small but useful voting power as a lever for immediate reforms—the tactic denounced by Jutson in his letters to William McNamara—was anathema to such revolutionaries as well.[29] Social Democracy, as launched by the federation at Sydney Trades Hall on May Day in 1895, brought together in the Second International democratic-socialist and labour thinking that still distrusted Labor parliamentarians but could find a role for them.[30] McNamara's acceptance of parliamentary activism became more and more conditional, as, for example, in her 1894 pamphlet *Commercialism and Distribution of the Nineteenth Century*. This advocated

> a decentralized form of socialism, where working-class people would create a better society by assuming control of their immediate environment, as producers and as consumers. Only when socialism had already been built up from below would it be safe to direct the state to nationalize the means of production, distribution and exchange—Labor politicians could not be trusted.[31]

In her next published work, the 1908 pamphlet *How to Become Rich beyond the Dreams of Avarice in the Shortest Possible Time*, published by herself and dedicated to the memory of 'My Dear Husband, William Henry McNamara, who died May 12 '05, and whose life and health were spent in the cause for the emancipation of the world's workers', she continued to urge working-class participation in parliamentary politics. Her main concern, however, was the need for Labor's leaders to return to their socialist roots:

> Now surely we ... are not going to perpetuate the Old Order under a new name by substituting desperate struggles between Laborites and Socialists, thus keeping the working class once more asunder, following this or that leader, knowing not whither they are going. Surely it is time for us to take heed of the lessons that history teaches, and, to our utmost ability, prevent the mistakes of our predecessors, for we can hardly plead their ignorance. It is time that with all our might we prevent so dire a calamity as a political struggle between the workers again. It is the people, the poor people, who suffer and are eagerly awaiting the Dawn of the Millennium.[32]

---

29 See Ian Turner, *Industrial Labour and Politics* (Canberra: ANU Press, 1965), 21.
30 The ALP today is still a member of the Second International's descendant, the Socialist International.
31 Burgmann, 'McNamara, Matilda Emilie Bertha (1853–1931)', 350.
32 Bertha McNamara, *How to Become Rich beyond the Dreams of Avarice; or, Labor & Socialism* (Sydney: [B. McNamara], 1908), 4.

For the rest of her life, she remained militant both in her views and in the books she sold.[33] In 1928, campaigning for senate preselection, she argued:

> I have from my earliest recollection held the strong conviction that it is little use to patch up this hideous social system called Capitalism, and there is little use in patching it with small reforms which chiefly consists (sic) of robbing Peter to pay Paul and makes the rent more hideous still. Financial Reform Abolition of Interest paying and borrowing is the centre from which we have to start, all other things required and desired being around it such as proper housing, proper food, proper medical attendance and proper Education.[34]

'If all our Labor Traitors had been true to the cause' in parliament, she asked in 1924, including her erstwhile customer Billy Hughes,

> how much further we would be to Social Reconstruction by now. How much misery there would have been saved in the world. Even the capitalistic World-War would never have taken place. Labor, Socialism and Communism has no time or place for Wars [in] its objects of Co-operation and Justice for all men. 60,000 young Australians would now be enriching their beloved land instead of nurturing the soil of Europe and elsewhere with their dead bodies and mountains of heartbreaks and oceans of tears would have been spared to the loved ones of home. Think of this you Judas Iscariots what you have got to answer for … Well will it be if they [the working classes] will not be deluded by the Capitalist orators and press. The lambs to lie down with the Lion. Well they ought to know by this what the Lion has done with the Workers for thousands of years, made slaves of them and will ever do so if they may, wether [sic] it be chattel slaves or wage slaves.[35]

So should we take much notice of Bertha McNamara? Much in her political rhetoric was common to the era. Is she simply an interesting example of a politically motivated immigrant who overcame the difficulty of her poverty, published some interesting pamphlets and was a conduit to a world of ideas and activism for her circle? I would argue that she matters, in part because of her commitment to women's rights and women's leadership. This is clearly articulated in a 1928 address at the Pyrmont Workers Centre:

---

33 McNamara's bookshop in Castlereagh Street was mentioned in the *Sydney Sun* in 1922, at a time when it was about to be demolished. It was described then as 'The Bookshop of Isms! It is a familiar resort in Castlereagh-street, this depot of terrific literature. All sorts of cheerful foreign gentlemen and amiable conspirators have stalked in and out of its little, narrow door in the years when anarchy was a hobby of much the same calibre as chess or dominoes.' *Sydney Sun*, 29 December 1922. I am indebted to the late John Holroyd for this pre-Trove reference.

34 Bertha McNamara, 'Preselection circular to ALP members', 1928, unpublished ms, Evatt Collection.

35 'Letter to *Labour Daily*', c. 1924, unpublished ms, Evatt Collection.

That women should receive an equal chance with men in the Councils of Social Welfare, they as well as the men have to live under the law are responsible to the law and have to bear the burden equally with the men and especially as concerns the workers wives often more so, industrially as well as in personal home affairs. Therefore they should equally share in the making of laws.[36]

And in her *Manifesto to All Laborites* seeking senate preselection, also of 1928, she was unequivocal in her demand that women should be elected to parliament, based on their equal share in the struggle for social justice:

As the *unanimously* chosen representative of the Labor women of this State, I appeal to you, both men and women, particularly Unionists, to remember that whatever standards of relative comfort you have today are the result not only of the fight, politically *and* industrially, of our men, but also of *our women*. Woman has shown, not only as an active Unionist in those callings to which capitalist economics has forced her; not only as a *militant propagandist* in local A. L. P. branches and at elections, but also as a fellow-sufferer and fellow-fighter during the strikes and lock-outs that have been forced on Labor, that she *must share the burden* of the battle for a better system.

If that is so, how can you then deny woman a share in the administrative and executive work of Labor?

To do so is to ask of woman all, and to concede her—nothing; nothing but the toil and moil; it is to look upon her not as a help-mate and comrade, but as a drudge and slave.[37]

It was not her own history of loyalty to the party that should count with preselectors, she argued, but rather '[t]he duty that you as Unionists and Laborites owe to your women-folk; to your mothers, your wives, your sisters, your fellow-sharers of the privations of the battle for a better social system ... *A Vote for WOMAN is a Vote for PROGRESS'*.[38]

She was appealing to deaf ears: it was not until 1943 that a Labor woman entered the Senate, when Dorothy Tangney won endorsement high enough up the ballot paper to be elected from Western Australia. Instead, McNamara was marginalised to the safe role of 'Mother of the Movement'.

---

36 Bertha McNamara, 'Pyrmont Centre of Workers', 1928, Unpublished ms, Evatt collection.

37 Bertha McNamara, 'Manifesto to all Laborites/Particularly All Unionists of N.S.W. from Mrs. Bertha McNamara (Sydney: Labor Daily, 1928)', one-page ephemeron, emphasis original, Evatt Collection.

38 Ibid.

I have discussed Bertha McNamara as a bookseller, a socialist and as a feminist. What was she like as a person? That she was a forceful speaker and writer is clear. Here, for example, is a brief passage entitled 'Crucified Again', denouncing the diplomatic representatives at the Hague Convention of 1907: 'This lickspittle Royalist, Lawyer, Usurer crew who pretend they want to promote peace, whilst at the same time they are upholding and defending the pernicious … Kingcraft, Priestcraft, Usury, the Worship of the Golden Calf all of which leads to strife and makes war almost a necessity.'[39] But she had a gentler side. In a loving reminiscence of her, Clarice McNamara, one of her daughters-in-law, spoke of her first visits to McNamara's bookshop:

> No picture in my memory could be clearer than those overcrowded shelves bulging with lively books and journals, and behind the counter the compelling personality of the little proprietress. No-one who did not know her would have guessed, from her sparkling periwinkle-blue eyes, her beautiful skin and soft white hair and her general air of maternal tenderness mixed with a lovely sense of fun, that this was one of the most dogged fighters for human rights and social justice in the history of Australian politics.[40]

And in a letter to her husband, William McNamara, written in 1894, something of the indomitable spirit of Bertha McNamara can be glimpsed. He was in prison, serving a six-month term for selling a newspaper, *Hard Cash*, which had libelled a financial corporation during the great bank crashes of the 1890s that wiped out the savings of thousands of Australian families:

> My dear Willy I can see you are anything but happy, make your mind easy, eat, drink, sleep and be merry so as to be strong and well when you come home to work for us and the dear baby … I was watching all last this week for a possible chance to send you some books but not one occured so ? I will send Hilda next week and send books and the other few articles you mention. Its impossible for me to carry baby and the parcels or else you should not have to wait for them. It is equally

---

39 Bertha McNamara, 'Crucified Again', 1907, unpublished ms, Evatt Collection.
40 Clarice McNamara was herself a life-long activist. A public schoolteacher, she discovered she had been sent to the countryside by the Education Department at the beginning of her career to get her away from radical associations. She wrote for *Workers Weekly* as Ann Scarlitt and was active in the Militant Women's Group (associated with the Communist Party of Australia) in the 1920s. She later refused an offer of secret membership of the party and with her husband, William (Bill) McNamara, took the Labor side in the disputes of the 1930s and later, 'owing to my complete disillusionment about the Soviet dictatorship with its subsequent terrible purges and trials and killings of dissidents, together with my reading of Trotsky's moving autobiography'. She was also active in the New Education Fellowship, a progressive educational reform movement founded in the United Kingdom in 1921, and was a close friend of Mary Alice Evatt. Clarice McNamara, 'Trailing the Twentieth Century', Unpublished autobiography in the McNamara family papers, courtesy of Margaret Bertha McNamara Henry, 133. See also Audrey Johnson, *Bread and Roses* (Sydney: Left Book Club, 1990), 9–27.

impossible to leave him at home when I do come as it takes the best part of a day and he is so mischievous it takes just all of us to mind him, excepting while he sleeps and that is not much … Your father wrote another very kind letter … and said he would forward some assistance later on. We received some money which had been collected on the Yarra. Don't fret or trouble about going into the other Gaol you may rest assured that this will not happen while there is anyone to help.[41]

I have sketched Bertha McNamara's career, and discussed her political views, as expressed in surviving manuscripts and rare pamphlets. I have suggested the importance of literary inspiration to her in modelling alternatives to the misery and despair she encountered, in both the poverty that dogged her own life at every turn and in the larger poverty of economic depression. Political views formed in the 1880s and 1890s, through the worst depression and political turmoil known to white Australia up to that time, remained the source of her hope for the future when the country again encountered despair and economic recession in the late 1920s. As a bookseller, as a gatekeeper for radical thought in Sydney and beyond, from the 1890s to the late 1920s, she is a figure of significance in Australian political history, and one who contributed to the growth of new models of feminist leadership.

The Museum of Australian Democracy entered into the 'Women and Leadership' project in order to learn more about how to approach the task of telling the story of women in Australian democracy, and in order to support the collection of the material evidence of women's leadership. Although some have criticised the museum for an apparent focus on 'the displacement of the politics of redistribution by the politics of recognition'[42] in our exhibitions, it is surely the case that the extension of political rights to women is an important story per se. The challenge in a museum is to tell a story that is anchored in holdings and displays of relevant material culture. As my colleague Libby Stewart has shown, the museum has been more successful in doing this with regard to the British suffrage experience than that of Australia. The material culture is fugitive, ephemeral and scarce. As yet there is little of it in the collection, although it is a high priority.

In an insightful keynote address to the Museums Australia Conference in Perth in 2011, Ross Gibson suggested that a museum might be a keeping place for feelings as well as meanings, a place where the systems of feelings that motivate people, and the key shifts in their shape, could be explored.[43] How could we

---

41   'Bertha McNamara to William McNamara', 27 April 1894, Evatt Collection.
42   Marian Sawer and Peter Brent, 'Equality and Australian Democracy', *Democratic Audit Discussion Paper*, October 2011, 28, http://democraticaudit.org.au/wp-content/uploads/2009/03/sawer_brent2011.pdf.
43   Ross Gibson, 'Systems of Feeling', Keynote address to the Museums Australia Conference, Perth, 18 November 2011.

create a 'sense of readiness' among museum visitors to experience the huge shift in thinking of people like Bertha McNamara a century and more ago as they demanded the apparently impossible: a place in the parliament, at the heart of the governing of Australia? Is material culture from the past enough, especially when the material evidence of political life is so ephemeral?

Professor Gibson asked how we might bring aesthetics into interplay with the semantic, a theme addressed also by Andrea Witcomb in interrogating memorials.[44] I have sometimes wondered whether a possible starting point might be to introduce a group of women into King's Hall as partners in a conversation with the bronze bas-reliefs of the parliamentary 'Founding Fathers' who have gazed from its columns since 1927. They could also mirror and challenge George V, who has also been there since 1927. This is what our highly successful museum theatre project for the Centenary of Federation, 'The King's Hall 9', did in 2001. This brought Catherine Helen Spence, Muriel Matters and Jessie Street (also an unsuccessful Labor candidate for a seat in this House) into King's Hall and the Chambers.

I think (and this is purely a personal view and has no endorsement by the museum) representation of the women who first stood for Federal Parliament, and some of those who first tried to break the barriers into *this* building, whether endorsed by their party or not, could also help bridge the gap between Australian political history before 1927 and the heritage significance of Old Parliament House. Thus visitors would meet Mary Moore-Bentley, one of the four women who stood for parliament in 1903, who won the largest number of votes for a female candidate in New South Wales—18,924—and who wrote a feminist science fiction novel, *A Woman of Mars; or, Australia's Enfranchised Woman*.[45] They would meet Vida Goldstein, who openly spoke of an ambition to be prime minister, who won 51,497 votes in Victoria in 1903, and who stood again four more times between 1910 and 1917.[46] With her would stand Nellie Martel, advocate for equal pay, who won the support of 18,502 voters for the Senate in 1903;[47] and Selina Anderson, trade unionist and the first woman to

44   Andrea Witcomb, 'Using Immersive and Interactive Approaches to Interpreting Traumatic Experiences', Keynote address to the Museums Australia Conference, Perth, 17 November 2011.

45   Mary Moore-Bentley, *A Woman of Mars; or, Australia's Enfranchised Woman* (Sydney: Edwards, Dunlop, 1901). See also entry for 'Mary Ling' (her married name), in Margaret Bettison, 'Ling, Mary (1865–1953)', in *Australian Dictionary of Biography Online* (Canberra: National Centre of Biography, The Australian National University), http://adb.anu.edu.au/biography/ling-mary-13048/text23595.

46   Janice N. Brownfoot, 'Goldstein, Vida Jane (1869–1949)', in *Australian Dictionary of Biography Online* (Canberra: National Centre of Biography, The Australian National University), http://adb.anu.edu.au/biography/goldstein-vida-jane-6418/text10975.

47   Margaret Bettison, 'Martel, Ellen Alma (Nellie) (1855–1940)', in *Australian Dictionary of Biography Online* (Canberra: National Centre of Biography, The Australian National University), http://adb.anu.edu.au/biography/martel-ellen-alma-nellie-13081/text23663.

stand for the House of Representatives, who secured 18 per cent of the vote in Dalley and who in 1908 (as Selina Siggins) was one of the first women to stand for the SA Legislative Assembly. And they might also meet Bertha McNamara.

The Museum of Australian Democracy embraced this Australian Research Council project because the museum saw it as being about helping it and other like institutions to devise better ways of interpreting the story of women and leadership for visitors, onsite and online, as well as being about improving understanding of what museums can and should collect to represent that theme. What could museums do to better explore it, in ways that are historically sound and fiscally prudent, but also imaginative, creative and able to speak to a wide range of visitors, many of whom know nothing of the background? This too will need 'all our strength, all our kindness and our love'.

References

Bettison, Margaret. 'Ling, Mary (1865–1953).' In *Australian Dictionary of Biography Online*. Canberra: National Centre of Biography, The Australian National University. http://adb.anu.edu.au/biography/ling-mary-13048/text23595.

Bettison, Margaret. 'Martel, Ellen Alma (Nellie) (1855–1940).' In *Australian Dictionary of Biography Online*. Canberra: National Centre of Biography, The Australian National University. http://adb.anu.edu.au/biography/martel-ellen-alma-nellie-13081/text23663.

Brownfoot, Janice N. 'Goldstein, Vida Jane (1869–1949).' In *Australian Dictionary of Biography Online*. Canberra: National Centre of Biography, The Australian National University. http://adb.anu.edu.au/biography/goldstein-vida-jane-6418/text10975.

Burgmann, Verity. *'In Our Time': Socialism and the Rise of Labor, 1885–1905.* Sydney: George Allen & Unwin, 1985.

Burgmann, Verity. 'McNamara, Matilda Emilie Bertha (1853–1931).' In *Australian Dictionary of Biography Online*. Canberra: National Centre of Biography, The Australian National University. http://adb.anu.edu.au/biography/mcnamara-matilda-emilie-bertha-7431/text12935.

Burgmann, Verity. 'McNamara, William Henry (1857–1906).' In *Australian Dictionary of Biography Online*. Canberra: National Centre of Biography, The Australian National University. http://adb.anu.edu.au/biography/mcnamara-william-henry-7432/text12937.

Burgmann, Verity. *'In Our Time': Socialism and the Rise of Labor, 1885–1905*. Sydney: George Allen & Unwin, 1985.

Evatt Collection. Special Collections. Flinders University Library, Adelaide.

Gibson, Ross. 'Systems of Feeling.' Keynote address to the Museums Australia Conference, Perth, 18 November 2011.

Government of Australia. *Women in the Senate*. Senate Brief 3. Canberra: Department of the Senate, April 2014.

Johnson, Audrey. *Bread and Roses*. Sydney: Left Book Club, 1990.

McNamara, Bertha. *How to Become Rich beyond the Dreams of Avarice; or, Labor & Socialism*. Sydney: [B. McNamara], 1908.

[McNamara, Bertha]. *Home Talk on Socialism, and the Redemption of the World's Labourers*. Hobart: Calder, Bowden & Co., 1891.

McNamara, Clarice. 'Trailing the Twentieth Century.' Unpublished autobiography in the McNamara family papers, courtesy of Margaret Bertha McNamara Henry.

Marsh, Jan. *Back to the Land: The Pastoral Impulse in Victorian England*. London: Quartet Books, 1982.

Mellor, W. H. *Manifesto of the Social Democratic Federation of Australasia*. Sydney: The Federation, 1895. MS 9547, Box 1268/5, State Library of Victoria, Melbourne. http://www.reasoninrevolt.net.au/biogs/E000042b.htm.

Moore-Bentley, Mary. *A Woman of Mars; or, Australia's Enfranchised Woman*. Sydney: Edwards, Dunlop, 1901.

Sawer, Marian and Peter Brent. *Equality and Australian Democracy*. Democratic Audit Discussion Paper, October 2011. http://democraticaudit.org.au/wp-content/uploads/2009/03/sawer_brent2011.pdf.

Sendy, John. *Melbourne's Radical Bookshops:History, People, Appreciation*. Melbourne: International Bookshop, 1983.

Svensen, Stuart. *The Shearers' War*. Brisbane: University of Queensland Press, 1989.

Sydney Sun, 29 December 1922.

Thompson, E. P. *William Morris*. London: Merlin, 1977.

Turner, Ian. *Industrial Labor and Politics*. Canberra: ANU Press, 1965.

Turnley, Ted. *Cole of the Book Arcade*. Melbourne: Cole Publications, 1974.

Witcomb, Andrea. 'Using Immersive and Interactive Approaches to Interpreting Traumatic Experiences.' Keynote address to the Museums Australia Conference, Perth, 17 November 2011.

7. Moderate and mainstream: Leadership in the National Council of Women of Australia, 1930s–1970s

Judith Smart[1] and Marian Quartly[2]

A major step in the development of women's activism and civic awareness in Australia was the formation of National Councils of Women in all States between 1896 and 1910, culminating in the emergence of the Federated Councils in 1924–25 and the National Council of Women of Australia (NCWA) in 1931.[3] Linked to the International Council of Women (ICW), and through it first to the League of Nations and later the United Nations, the council movement provided, in the words of one of its early leaders, a conduit for mainstream Australian women's organisations and their members to 'accomplish good, useful, humane work in the best interests of the nation'.[4] It aimed to 'bring together for discussion [and] the forming of public opinion, the workers who are doing the practical work of social education and improvement'.[5] Because the council was conceived as an umbrella structure, existing women's groups of all kinds could gather under its shelter at national and international levels to discuss matters of common interest, to gather information and to learn from each other in order to promote peace and general wellbeing. This structure also ensured that leadership within the council would develop along the lines described by Amanda Sinclair as 'adaptive': 'a process of influence … aimed at mobilising people towards changes … in values, attitudes, approaches, behaviours and ideologies.'[6]

Though the councils included radicals among their affiliates, the feminist face they presented was self-consciously moderate with an emphasis on information, education and cooperation rather than on activism, agitation and opposition. The councils' two founding objectives dedicated constituent members to 'unity of thought, sympathy and purpose' among women 'of all classes, parties and creeds' and, importantly, to the 'the application of the Golden Rule to society, custom and law' in the interests of, as the preamble to the constitution put

---

1 RMIT University and The University of Melbourne.
2 Monash University.
3 The organisation was named the National Council of Women of Australia (NCWA) in 1931, but it became known generally as the Australian National Council of Women (ANCW) before it officially returned to the original NCWA nomenclature in 1970.
4 *Australian Woman's Sphere*, December 1901.
5 'Presidential Address', in National Council of Women of Queensland (NCWQ), *Annual Report 1930/1931*, 7.
6 Amanda Sinclair, Chapter 1, this volume.

it, 'the highest good of the family and the State'.[7] But membership of the ICW also committed the Australian councils to a growing list of policies that reflected a broad liberal equal rights feminist agenda and inevitably involved them in lobbying and policy development, usually through specialist standing committees. Until the mid 1970s, the councils were the major voice of mainstream women's views in government and community forums, and the number of their affiliated organisations enabled NCWA leaders to claim they represented the views of more than a million Australian women. Through its ICW affiliation and its participation in regional conferences and seminars, NCWA was also the strongest non-governmental organisation channel via which Australian women could speak and be heard internationally. In this chapter, we examine the constraints this broad leadership role placed on national presidents from the 1930s to the 1970s and the various means they employed to inform and lead their diverse membership on the issues of equity and justice to which affiliation with the ICW committed them.

The National Councils of Women (NCW) developed in a period when leadership styles available, even in politically radical feminist groups (such as Vida Goldstein's Women's Political Association or Bessie Rischbieth's Australian Federation of Women Voters), generally assumed a masculinist model of power and a hierarchical organisational structure. In the early years of the councils' history into the 1920s, status and class also played important roles in defining leadership qualities, the first presidents in most States being vice-regal wives, with their successors coming from the local social elite, whose wealth enabled them to travel and act as delegates to ICW conferences. From the late 1920s, professionally qualified women—doctors, lawyers, school principals, social workers, university teachers—became more prominent, and the spectrum of expertise grew wider in succeeding decades. It might be thought that such women would assume that, because of their social or expert status, where they led others would automatically follow. But because the councils were coalitions and affiliation was voluntary, status did not always mean power, and constitutional authority had to be adapted to specific circumstances.

From the inception of the ICW, achieving common cause among women meant that formal control by national councils over their members had to be limited and political engagement circumscribed. The version of this principle in a recent National Council of Women Victoria (NCWV) constitution reads:

> The Council is broadly based non party political and non sectarian, bringing together a wide range of community interests. Therefore, an

---

7   *Australian Woman's Sphere*, December 1901.

organisation willing to become affiliated with Council shall remain to all intents and purposes autonomous beyond compliance with the terms of this Constitution.

General adherence to this principle largely accounts for the longevity of the councils in Australia, and, as political scientist Carol Mueller has noted, the 'rule-generating capacity' of such mass-based formal organisations has enabled them to deal more effectively with internal discord than radical collectivist ones.[8] But, because of the restricted constitutional power NCW leaders could exercise over member societies and the looseness of the NCWA's federal structure, presidents and other office-bearers also had to focus on bringing members along with them rather than relying on rules and by-laws. The desirability of consensus in a rule-based context has encouraged flexibility and emphasised the value of networking and holding educational seminars and conferences. Policy has been developed by broadly representative standing committees, even if inevitably a great deal of the final writing work has fallen to a few individuals. Achieving consensus was, however, a slow process, and councils sometimes lagged behind their own more progressive affiliates.

The council movement was founded on the belief that the welfare of home and family was the basis of racial and national fitness, as well as of the ideal international order: a family of nations. Tasmanian president in 1901, Lady Dodds, quoted the ICW's first president, Lady Aberdeen, as saying: 'We hold fast to the belief that woman's first duty must be her home … and that by its home life every country will stand or fall.'[9] In the mid 1920s, Mildred Muscio, newly elected NSW president and soon to be federal council president, elaborated on the public responsibility this entailed for women:

[T]here is no real opposition between women's interests inside the home and her interests outside the home. She must go outside the home in order to be efficient within it; and it is because of her real and important experience within the home that woman ought to go outside to take place in public affairs.[10]

Muscio also clearly recognised the change modern professional and scientific approaches had brought to this work—a process of rationalisation historical sociologist Kerreen Reiger has termed the 'disenchantment of the home'.[11] Doctors, lawyers, teachers and university women in the NCW played a key

---

8   Carol Mueller, 'The Organisational Basis of Conflict in Contemporary Feminism', in *Feminist Organizations: Harvest of the New Women's Movement*, eds Myra Marx Ferree and Patricia Yancey Martin (Philadelphia: Temple University Press, 1995), 263–75.

9   *Mercury* [Hobart], 26 April 1901.

10   National Council of Women New South Wales (NCWNSW), *Biennial Reports for 1926–1928*, 3.

11   After Max Weber. See Kerreen Reiger, *The Disenchantment of the Home: Modernizing the Australian Family 1880–1940* (Melbourne: Oxford University Press, 1985).

role in this development. As Muscio observed, 'the woman who now faces … domestic problems is not the woman who faced them half a century ago: she brings education, science, logic and experience of the outside world to aid her', for domestic problems 'have become national problems … More and more our laws concern themselves with the affairs of the home', and thus, '[i]ndustry, economics, politics, laws are only our own experience written larger'.[12] In effect, the women's movement had conducted a successful assault on the formerly dominant masculinist preoccupations of the public sphere, though its representatives had not achieved the power necessary to direct strategies for redressing the problems they had highlighted. The gendered inequality in the distribution of power was thus assuming greater importance in council deliberations at the time the NCWA was emerging. While suffrage had already been won at the national level in 1902 and in all States by 1908, and the right to stand for federal and State legislatures was also conceded between 1902 and 1924, other issues of equality before the law such as equal and uniform marriage and divorce laws, equal guardianship rights and the right to sit on juries and the bench, were becoming more pressing in council forums. Matters of social and economic equality were also receiving greater consideration: representation on public boards and committees of inquiry, the right of married women to work, and equal pay.

The two issues to be considered in this chapter—uniform and equal national divorce laws and equal pay—put in tension the relationship between family and public life; but both also emphasised what Marilyn Lake has identified as the transition from a primary focus on protection to greater concern for equality.[13] The work of NCWA leaders to bring their varied membership with them in support of change recognised the importance of taking the resulting discomforts and doubts into account. One key means of doing this was to invoke the Australian councils' international commitments to the ICW—also an important part of the leaders' own education and awareness of the transnational nature of many issues they faced.

Divorce law

As early as 1899, the ICW had asked all national councils to consider 'the nature of the laws concerned with the domestic relations which exist in all civilised countries'.[14] In Australia only occasional attention was paid to marriage laws in the early years, such as when Rose Scott's radical plea for marriage as 'a

---

12 NCWNSW, *Biennial Reports for 1926–1928*, 3, 4.
13 Marilyn Lake, 'A History of Feminism in Australia', in *Oxford Companion to Australian Feminism*, ed. Barbara Caine (Melbourne: Oxford University Press, 1998).
14 Ibid., 17.

partnership between equals economically' was met with the response that she had overlooked 'the element of love' that justified 'cheerfully accept[ing] burdens and dependence on that account'.[15] Most councils followed the familiar maternalist path and gave their primary attention to laws affecting children rather than the more confronting issues relating to marital breakdown. Nevertheless, it became increasingly apparent that many of the problems concerning the welfare of women and children were the result of desertion of husbands and fathers. In the Australian context, the problem was compounded by the fact that marriage law was controlled by the States. Even though Section 51 of the Commonwealth *Constitution* empowered the Federal Government to legislate on marriage and divorce from 1901, no national government took up the challenge until 1959. Six different sets of law and jurisdictions made enforcement of court orders across State borders extremely difficult and expensive for a woman, whose legal domicile followed that of her husband. Feminist reformers quickly concluded that uniform federal legislation was necessary, though opponents feared that the most liberal State laws would be imposed on all to the detriment of marriage as an institution.

Of all the possible remedies for women's inequality within marriage, uniform grounds for divorce had the greatest potential to divide the national councils. From the earliest period, the mainstream women's movement was more concerned to preserve marriage than to consider its dissolution. The stigma attached to divorce and fears that easier access would only bring hardship to women and children were widespread, and, given the difficulties of enforcing maintenance orders and the lack of other forms of economic security available to a married woman apart from her husband's income, these fears were well founded. In circumstances where separation or divorce did occur, it was thus important for the woman to be able to prove her respectability by assigning fault to her absent or erstwhile husband. In this context, if the councils were to pursue this issue, careful judgment and leadership skills were required.

While opposition to any measures that could make divorce easier were held by a number of NCW figures, such as Australia's first woman MP, Edith Cowan,[16] radical feminists in both the ICW and the Australian councils stood opposed on principle to the unequal legal status of men and women within marriage, including unequal grounds for divorce. Council leaders had to steer a path between these views. One tactic was to call on the expertise of lawyers to provide information; another was to focus particularly on the protective purpose of reform proposals. As early as 1905, the Victorian council engaged the first Australian woman admitted to the bar, Flos Greig, to address members

---

15   *Daily Telegraph*, 26 June 1901.

16   Judith Allen, *Rose Scott: Vision and Revision in Feminism* (Melbourne: Oxford University Press, 1994), 148.

on anomalies in the divorce law.[17] By 1911, the NSW council was proposing support for uniform federal legislation, and, in 1912, an interstate meeting committed all councils to discuss it with their constituents.[18] During 1913, both Victoria and Queensland suggested federal legislation be considered at the next gathering,[19] but war intervened.

By the 1920s, the increasing numbers of women lawyers, at least in the eastern States, provided a pool of new experts able and willing to advise the councils on the anomalies of divorce law. They typically headed the councils' standing committees on laws and the legal position of women and thus acted as conduits with the ICW. At federal conferences, women lawyers such as New South Wales' Sybil Morrison were now speaking the modern language of equal rights rather than protection. Victoria's Joan Rosanove argued that marriage should be based on 'the idea of partnership and equality', rather than the husband's ownership of the wife. 'Whilst not dealing with the question of whether divorce is a good or bad institution ... there is a set of rules by which a man can divorce his wife, and another set for a woman.'[20] Uniform federal marriage and divorce law, they argued, was the most effective way of tackling this problem and, with the councils' growing commitment to gender equality, divorce reform was becoming less confronting than in previous years. The first meeting of the new federal council in 1925 passed a resolution in favour of uniformity and more extended consideration took place in 1926.[21] In 1927, the councils specifically agreed that the State councils would 'make further endeavours to obtain exact information on desirable amendments to the laws in each State with the object of embodying them in one Federal act'.[22] The 1928 federal conference took a further step in reaffirming the necessity for federal legislation, delegates also stressed including the 'economic independence of wives' in any proposal and the States were asked to consider a model already in place—the Swedish marriage law, which stipulated an equal economic partnership between husband and wife—with a view to the principle being 'embodied in our Federal marriage law'.[23] Rose Scott was thus vindicated, though she had died three years earlier.

---

17   *The Argus* [Melbourne], 26 October 1905.

18   *Sydney Morning Herald*, 31 July 1912.

19   'Executive Minutes', 3 March 1913, and 'Council Minutes', 7 March 1913, both in National Council of Women of Queensland (NCWQ), NCWQ Papers, UQFL402, Minute Book 03, Fryer Library, University of Queensland, Brisbane [hereinafter NCWQ Papers]; *Brisbane Courier*, 10 March 1913.

20   'FCNCWA Conference', July 1926, in National Council of Women of Australia (NCWA) Papers, MS7583, Box 12, 'FCNCWA Minute Book 1924–28', National Library of Australia, Canberra [hereinafter NCWA Papers]; Ada Norris, *Champions of the Impossible: A History of the National Council of Women of Victoria 1902–1977* (Melbourne: Hawthorn Press, 1978), 67–9; *Housewife*, [Victoria], 5 November 1929, 4.

21   'FCNCWA Conference', September 1925, and 'Brisbane', July 1926, NCWA Papers, Box 12.

22   'Report of FCNCWA Conference', in *The Argus* [Melbourne], 17 September 1927.

23   'FCNCWA Conference', July 1928, NCWA Papers, Box 12; National Council of Women of Queensland, *Annual Report 1927/28*, 25, 26.

In the ensuing three decades, the Australian National Council of Women (ANCW) board regularly approached the Federal Government seeking a uniform law; but, partly at least to reassure those who remained concerned about 'easy divorce', this was always pursued in concert with protective domicile and maintenance issues, though these were also in accord with ICW policy.[24] Despite the efforts of individual MPs approached by the Australian councils in the 1930s, little was achieved. In 1944, the Labor government's attorney-general assured the ANCA that its views concerning uniformity of divorce laws and Australian domicile would be considered,[25] but, though another long battle for equal nationality rights for married women was won in Australia in 1946 and confirmed by the 1948 *Nationality and Citizenship Act*,[26] there was no corresponding progress towards uniform marriage and divorce laws. When in May 1950 the NCWA secretary wrote to the new Liberal government requesting 'legislation granting Australia a common domicile and a uniform marriage and divorce law', she noted dryly that '[f]rom the time of the formation of the ANCW, in 1924, we have sent this resolution to the Government in office'[27]—without effect.

In pursuing uniform federal divorce legislation and retaining the support of State councils and their affiliates, NCWA leaders consistently assured members that their actions did not mean support for divorce as such. Their coupling of the matter with the domicile and maintenance issues points to the motivation of many women reformers and the point on which radicals and conservatives could come together: the need to relieve the problems of women whose marriages had irretrievably broken down. The board's actions in approaching the Government late in 1943–44 were stimulated by a motion moved by the first woman elected to the Senate, Labor's Dorothy Tangney. Tangney was primarily concerned with the plight of Australian wives deserted by their US servicemen husbands and was advised by long-term legal affiliate of the Victorian council Anna Brennan. Tangney recalled later that she raised 'the subject of uniform divorce laws' because 'I experienced the greatest difficulty in trying to get justice for the deserted wives due to variations between the different State laws concerning matrimonial causes'.[28] NCWA leaders supported this position, but Tangney remembered that many others did not:

---

24   International Council of Women (ICW), ICW Resolutions, http://www.ncwc.ca/pdf/ICW-CIF_Resolutions. pdf, 114–17. Indeed, the ICW resolution of 1924 enjoined national councils to study the text of laws relating to desertion in their countries and recommend modifications or amendments necessary. They also asked the League of Nations through its Codification of International Law committee to study the question of 'desertion of the family' and, later, to draw up a convention to enforce the payment of alimony, including sanctions against debtors.

25   'ANCW Board Minutes', 16 December 1943, 20 January 1944, 2 February 1944, NCWA Papers, Box 12.

26   M. Page Baldwin, 'Subject to Empire: Married Women and the British Nationality and Status of Aliens Act', *Journal of British Studies* 40(4) (October 2001): 522 ff.

27   'Attorney-General to Secretary ANCW', 20 May 1950, ANCW Correspondence 1936–1971, NCWA Papers, MS 5193/1, Folder 1.

28   *Commonwealth Parliamentary Debates*, Senate, 25 November 1959, 1834.

> I was very broadly criticised throughout Australia by many people who thought my main objective was to make divorce easier. I had to issue a public statement to show that that was not my intention, and that I did not think that if there were divorce laws in Australia any woman should be penalised merely because of geographical situation.[29]

In 1951, the ICW welcomed the enunciation of the principle of equality in marriage in the UN Declaration of Human Rights, and looked forward to a convention stipulating equality between spouses. Within the NCWA, this strengthened the voices of leaders concerned with women's rights in marriage, and the board asked all States to comment on what grounds for divorce should be included in federal legislation.[30] The NCWV was singled out as representing the only State significantly 'out of step'[31]—presumably a reference to the fact that, alone of the States, the Victorian *Matrimonial Causes Act* preserved the old inequitable provisions whereby a husband could divorce his wife for a single act of adultery, while a wife had to prove 'aggravated adultery'. At the same time, Victorian MHR Percy Joske, who had long worked for uniform federal legislation, was asked to advise the national board on drafting a bill, and the NCWA also took the issue to the Women's Jubilee Convention in Canberra, which requested a royal commission concerning marriage and divorce laws.[32] In the ensuing months, Marie Breen, NCWA's international secretary and its main link to the ICW, joined Joske in radio broadcasts promoting reform.[33] In September 1952, the board was told that Joske was almost ready to put the bill before government and that the NCWA's Laws Standing Committee was providing him with further information.[34]

Now that change at last seemed possible, conservatives in the State councils revealed considerable hesitancy. Achieving consensus took delicate negotiation on the part of State presidents and the national president, Ruth Gibson. Council affiliates included organisations based in religious denominations, like the Catholic St Joan's Social and Political Alliance and the Anglican Mothers' Union—both totally opposed to any federal divorce legislation. The St Joan's Alliance feared 'all the grounds of divorce in all the States would be made grounds of divorce under Commonwealth Law'.[35] This proliferation argument was common in the State councils. A meeting of the Queensland council was told 'the allowable grounds for divorce in the various states totalled 23, but that Queensland had only 7 grounds', and that 'to achieve uniformity Queensland

---

29 Ibid.
30 'ANCW Board Minutes', 28 August 1951, NCWA Papers, MS7583, Box 12.
31 'ANCW Board Minutes', 23 October 1951, in ibid.
32 'ANCW Board Minutes', 11 September 1951 and 23 October 1951, in ibid.
33 'ANCW Board Minutes', 11 March 1952 and 13 May 1952, in ibid.
34 'ANCW Board Minutes', 23 September 1952, in ibid.
35 'Statement by St Joan's Alliance, Marriage and Divorce Bill 1947', NAA A432 1956/2207, National Archives of Australia, Canberra [hereinafter NAA].

might have to accept additional grounds which might make divorce easier'. The note-taker even-handedly summed up the mixed feelings: 'Most members were in favour of the principle of uniformity, no one wanted divorce in general made easier, everyone agreed that the first care should be to the happiness of home and family.'[36]

At the 1954 national conference, Ruth Gibson paid due respect to this unstable amalgam of views. While celebrating the fact that 'in the matter of divorce laws … the ANCW has long since taken the lead in urging reforms', she promptly qualified this with a defence of family as 'the very foundation stone of national life'. At the same time, she stood for equality: 'Whatever our views on divorce, the fact remains that marked inequalities exist in law as between men and women and as between States, and it seems only fair and just that these should be removed.' Moreover: 'It does not automatically follow that with uniformity will come easier divorce … the solution may probably lie in a suitable compromise between the existing State laws.' This careful statement proved effective: 'ANCW reaffirmed its belief in the desirability of … uniform divorce laws for Australia' and asked the Federal Government 'to take early action'.[37]

Yet again, the Federal Government procrastinated, though, in 1955, Joske achieved a national domicile for women with the passage of his Matrimonial Causes Bill. But not until 1957 was Joske's wideranging measure for uniform national marriage and divorce laws finally introduced to parliament.[38] Again, NCWA commitment was tested by principled opposition within its own ranks. South Australia, previously strong in support of national legislation,[39] was advised by its legal subcommittee to reject the Joske Bill because it contained no provision for judicial separation. Lawyer Roma Mitchell, State convenor of laws, was both a champion of equal rights and a practising Catholic. She argued that judicial separation on the SA legislative model allowed a dignified alternative to women unwilling to divorce; this provision would disappear if the Joske Bill passed. But the council executive, while thanking Mitchell, minuted: 'General feeling that opposition to the Bill of Mr Joske should not be stirred up, as it is most desirable there should be an Australian Act on Matrimonial Causes.'[40]

---

36   'Minutes of Special Meeting of the National Council of Women of Queensland', 4 November 1953, NCWQ Papers, Minute Book 14, Part b.

37   'ANCW Minutes of Conference, Adelaide', 1954, NCWA Papers, 2, 31.

38   The origins can be traced to 1947 when Evatt appointed Joske and two other lawyers to draft a uniform federal marriage and divorce law. See file, 'Marriage and Divorce Bill 1947', NAA A432 1956/2207, NAA; also Henry Finlay, *To Have But Not to Hold: A History of Attitudes to Marriage and Divorce in Australia 1858–1975* (Sydney: The Federation Press, 2005), 304–07.

39   For example, 'Minutes of Executive', 4 November 1952, National Council of Women of South Australia (NCWSA) Papers, SRG297, State Library of South Australia, Adelaide, Series 1 [hereinafter NCWSA Papers].

40   'Minutes of Executive', 30 July 1957 and 12 September 1957 [insert], in ibid.

In the event, Joske's Bill stalled, and he withdrew it when Prime Minister Robert Menzies promised a 'commensurate' government measure. Attorney-General Garfield Barwick's Matrimonial Causes Bill was in fact much more radical than Joske's. The grounds for divorce were scrupulously non-discriminatory in gender terms, to the extent of expecting a guilty wife to pay children's maintenance.[41] Barwick also included a provision borrowed from the WA Act that allowed divorce after five years' separation—in effect divorce without a guilty party. Members from both sides of parliament condemned this clause, Labor's Dorothy Tangney on the grounds that 'in nine cases out of ten, in Western Australia, it is the women who suffer under this provision', 'dumped for some bright young thing' after years of childbearing and rearing and providing support for their husbands.[42]

One might expect to find this kind of opposition in the NCW but this is not the case. In the consistently conservative Queensland council, for example, there was no support for the request of a representative of the Association for the Defence of the Family to sign a petition to the Queen protesting the no-fault clause.[43] But nor was there overt rejoicing at the passage of the legislation in most States, probably reflecting council leaders' understanding that many members viewed uniform divorce legislation as an unfortunate necessity in a federated nation. Though the Victorian laws convener was 'delighted' that 'at last' an Australian law existed, national president Thelma Metcalfe, in her presidential address to the 1960 conference, merely noted the passage of the legislation without making any further comment.[44] The councils now turned their attention to continuing maintenance problems, a minimum marriage age and removal of the marriage bar for women in the public service.

Equal pay

One of the subjects on the agenda at the 1899 ICW congress in London was equal pay for equal work, though no resolution was passed. The Australian councils gave consideration to equal pay almost from their beginnings in New South Wales in 1896, but, despite the clear advocacy of some of the more radical affiliates, leaders decided then and over the ensuing decade that 'the time had not arrived for its consideration', recognising the dangers of forcing the issue before most members were ready. Again the sticking point was the preservation

41   'Marriage and Divorce Bill 1947', NAA A432 1956/2207, NAA.
42   *Commonwealth Parliamentary Debates*, Senate, 25 November 1959, 1835.
43   'Minutes of General Meeting of NCWQ', 24 August 1960, NCWQ Papers, Minute Book 15, Part a.
44   National Council of Women of Victoria, *Annual Report 1959*, 18; National Council of Women of Australia, *ANCW Report and Minutes of the Biennial Conference, Canberra, A.C.T., 29th October – 4th November, 1960*, 15.

of the family and women's role as wives and mothers—perceived by some to be threatened by the economic independence equal pay would make possible for women.[45]

From 1909, the Victorian council made tentative steps beyond discussion towards support for equal pay, though less as a matter of principle than as one of justice for a particular group of respectable middle-class women: teachers.[46] The NCWV's leaders judged that, presented in this limited way, equal pay would seem less radical or threatening to the majority of its members. When its affiliate, the Women's Political Association, combined with Labor Party women to call a rally demanding equal pay legislation in July 1913, the NCW did not formally participate, though some of its more radical members, including the Lady Teachers' Association, the women's section of the People's Liberal Party and the Australian Women's Association, did.[47] A year later, however, council representatives did attend a meeting to discuss the Government's refusal to remedy the position of women teachers and supported a resolution for equal pay for equal work as 'fair play'.[48] The momentum was lost in the war years, though the NSW and Queensland councils resolved in 1915 to support equal pay for women taking men's positions, and, when in 1918 Victoria's women teachers revived their campaign, the council passed a resolution of support and asked all affiliated societies to send individual resolutions to the premier.[49] In 1921, NCWV also joined a deputation urging equal pay for equal work in the public service.[50]

At this point, Australia's councils were ahead of the ICW, which had limited its discussion to conditions and pay of women workers and only established its standing committee on Trades and Professions and Employment at the Rome conference of 1914. Signs there that a more political approach was emerging were halted by war and the cessation of meetings and standing committee activities;[51] however, in the immediate postwar years, the ICW moved in advance of the Australian councils. Following Article 427 of the Treaty of

---

45 'NCWNSW Executive', 12 November 1896 and 20 November 1896, NCWNSW Records, Minute Book 1895–1904; and 'NCWNSW Executive', 3 June 1909 and 1 July 1909, NCWNSW Records, Minute Book 1904–1913, Box MLK 03009.

46 'Report National Council of Women', Typescript by Evelyn Gough, NCWV International Secretary, for ICW Toronto Quinquennial Meeting, 1909; Norris, *Champions of the Impossible*, 14.

47 *The Argus* [Melbourne], 1 August 1913.

48 *The Age*, 3 July 1914.

49 'NCWQ Executive Minutes', 30 August 1915, NCWQ Papers, NCWQ Minute Book 04 1913–1915, Part b; Martha Sear, *The National Council of Women of NSW: A Chronology 1896–1996* (Sydney: NCWNSW, 1996); 'Council Minutes', 24 July and 22 August 1918, National Council of Women of Victoria (NCWV) Papers in transit to State Library of Victoria, Melbourne [hereinafter NCWV Papers].

50 Norris, *Champions of the Impossible*, 41.

51 Catherine Jacques and Sylvie Lefebvre, 'The Working Methods of the ICW: From its Creation to the Second World War', in *Women Changing the World: A History of the International Council of Women*, eds Eliane Gubin and Leen van Molle (Brussels: Éditions Racine, 2005), 101–4.

Versailles 'that men and women should receive equal remuneration for work of equal value', an executive meeting at The Hague in 1922 affirmed 'the principle of "equal pay for equal work" which signifies that payment be not influenced by the sex of the worker'. This resolution was strengthened at the full ICW meeting in Washington, DC, in 1925 to read 'that wages should be established on the basis of the occupation and not on the basis of sex'.[52] By this time the international movement, like Australian women's organisations, had come to link economic independence in marriage to the equal pay question.[53] At the preceding conference in Kristiania, Norway, in 1920, the ICW resolved that a wife 'should be legally entitled to a certain just proportion of her husband's income'.[54] In Australia in 1921, Justice Piddington, chairman of the royal commission into the basic wage (1919–20), suggested modification of the family basis of wage fixation to cover only a man and his wife, supplemented with a scheme of child endowment to be paid directly to mothers. NCW leaders, as well as labour movement women, wanted this proposal extended, suggesting substitution of an individual-based wage determination for the family-based one, with additional separate state-provided endowment of mothers as well as children.[55] There could be no grounds in this view for awarding men higher wages than women doing the same work. Support for this principle was a significant step for the Australian NCW, since most women's organisations remained committed to the maternalist view of women's primary duty to home and family, and the responsibility of men as breadwinners. After discussing the 1922 ICW resolution at State council level for more than four years,[56] delegates to the 1926 federal conference resolved both to 'approve of the principle of child endowment by a re-adjustment of the method of payment of wages' and 'to oppose the professional inequality of women, and demand for them equal opportunities and rights within the various employments', including 'equal pay for equal work, which signifies that wages should be established on the basis of the occupation and not on the basis of the sex'.[57]

The councils also took the case for national endowment and an individual basis for wage fixation to the 1927 Royal Commission on Childhood Endowment. One of the commissioners was NCW federal president Mildred Muscio. As Lake and John Murphy have both noted, Muscio wrote the 1929 minority report with

---

52 ICW Resolutions, 176. They seem, however, not to have recognised the significance of using the terms 'payment' and 'wages' rather than the more encompassing 'remuneration' in Article 427 of the treaty.
53 Marilyn Lake, 'The Independence of Women and the Brotherhood of Man: Debates in the Labour Movement over Equal Pay and Motherhood Endowment in the 1920's', *Labour History* (63) (November 1992): 1–24.
54 ICW Resolutions, 115.
55 Lake, 'The Independence of Women and the Brotherhood of Man', 1–24; also Penelope Johnson, 'Gender, Class and Work: The Council of Action for Equal Pay Campaign in Australia during World War II', *Labour History* (50) (May 1986): 134–7.
56 For example, 'NCWQ Council', 13 October 1922, NCWQ Papers, NCWQ Minute Book 06 1919–23, Part c.
57 'FCNCWA Conference', July 1926, in NCWA Papers, 'FCNCWA Minute Book 1924–28'.

John Curtin in support of means-tested government endowment for third and subsequent children. Like the Labor Party women, she was forced into retreat on the breadwinner's wage, based on the needs of parents and two children.[58] She saw this compromise as the best chance of achieving a modicum of economic justice for the most needy women. Child endowment would at least give the poorest mothers some independent maintenance, however inadequate, that was not dependent on what the father or husband deigned or was forced to hand out. The federal endowment scheme that was finally introduced early in 1941 was for second and subsequent children and was not means tested. There was no suggestion that the family basis of wages determination would be altered to underwrite it but it did enable the Menzies Government to negotiate with the Arbitration Court to defer wage increases.[59]

Throughout this period, the councils—held steadfast in part by ICW policy—did not resile from support for equal pay and an individual rather than a family basis for wage fixation, though they did not campaign actively for this in the depression years and do not seem to have joined other women's organisations in support of Muriel Heagney's Council of Action for Equal Pay, formed in 1937.[60] It is likely the leaders were aware that many affiliates had reservations about demanding equal pay when so many male breadwinners were unemployed. During World War II, however, the executive argued that all women in the fighting services should be awarded equal pay—also all women called up for national service.[61] And, towards the end of the war, the NCWA board supported a call for legislation mandating a minimum female wage rate of 75 per cent of the male standard as a step towards equal pay.[62]

At the Commonwealth Arbitration Court's 1949–50 basic wage inquiry, which set women's basic rate at 75 per cent of a man's, the councils joined many women's organisations in intervening—though in rather tokenistic terms, it being agreed that international secretary Marie Breen should make a statement that equal pay had long been on the platform of Australian councils and the ICW.[63] More serious engagement occurred in the basic wage case of 1952–53 against the employers' request for reduction of the women's rate to 60 per cent. In the intervening period, the International Labour Organisation (ILO)

58   John Murphy, *A Decent Provision: Australian Welfare Policy, 1870–1949* (Farnham, UK, and Burlington, Vt: Ashgate, 2011): 138–49; Lake, 'The Independence of Women and the Brotherhood of Man', 1–24.

59   Murphy, *A Decent Provision*, 203–4.

60   For example, the 1933 NCWA conference supported equal pay and opportunity in the Federal Public Service. Norris, *Champions of the Impossible*, 64. Resolutions in 1935 affirmed the ICW position on the right of women, 'married or unmarried', to 'have the same right as a man to keep or obtain paid work' and 'to promote equal conditions of work between men and women'. 'NCWA Annual Meeting, Brisbane', August 1935, NCWA Papers, Box 11.

61   'ANCW Board Minutes', 29 June 1942, NCWA Papers, Box 12; Norris, *Champions of the Impossible*, 85.

62   'ANCW Board Minutes', 28 July 1945, NCWA Papers, Box 12.

63   'ANCW Board Minutes', 28 November 1949, in ibid.

adopted its Equal Remuneration Convention (C100, 1951) in support of 'rates of remuneration established without discrimination based on sex'. The ICW, which had preserved close links with the ILO from the interwar years, 'vigorously' supported the international convention proposal.[64] When the Australian delegation abstained from voting on ILO Convention 100, opting instead for the less binding Recommendation 90, NCWA, conscious of its responsibility as 'part of a vast international organisation such as the I.C.W. with its direct contacts with the United Nations', urged government ratification of the convention.[65] Thus, when the Victorian Chamber of Manufactures requested the Arbitration Court to reduce the women's rate in 1952–53, NCWA moved decisively, joining the Australian Federation of Business and Professional Women in seeking leave to intervene. Molly Kingston, Legal Women's Association president and also NCWV convenor of laws, was briefed as counsel and NCWV partially funded the intervention.[66]

As president of NCWV in 1952 and 1953, Ada Norris was a key instigator of NCWA's decision to intervene, having been approached by the Women Graduates Association and the Legal Women's Association of Victoria. Norris, who deputised for the Australian council president in the case, stressed that their action should be viewed not as an end in itself but as part of 'their progress towards equal pay for equal work'.[67] While acknowledging that the Australian Council of Trade Unions (ACTU) 'carried the burden of the case', Norris judged the action of 'representatives of women's voluntary organisations' as influential and an 'important precedent for similar interventions' in 1969, 1972 and 1974.[68] She must, then, have been particularly galled when, as Australia's delegate to the UN Status of Women Commission in March 1962, she was obliged by the Government to vote against a resolution calling on countries to ratify ILO Convention 100.[69]

Through the 1950s and early 1960s, the Liberal Government and the masculinist ACTU both claimed to support equal pay in general terms, but passed responsibility for doing anything about it to each other and to the Arbitration Court.[70] NCWA was frustrated by the failure of the Liberal Government to take action in light of explicit support for equal pay in the party's platform. In 1961, the board wrote a letter of protest to the four Liberal Party women senators (three of whom had close NCWA connections) when they voted against a Labor

64   'ICW Conference, Athens 1951', in ICW Resolutions, 181.
65   Ruth Gibson's presidential address, in 'ANCW Minutes of Conference, Adelaide, 1954', NCWA Papers, 1.
66   National Council of Women of Victoria, *Annual Report 1953*, 6; Norris, *Champions of the Impossible*, 105.
67   National Council of Women of Victoria, *Annual Report 1953*, 6, 8.
68   Norris, *Champions of the Impossible*, 104–5.
69   Norris was Australia's delegate to CSW for an unprecedented three sessions from 1961 to 1963. On the Australian Government's position, see Tom Sheridan and Pat Stretton, 'Pragmatic Procrastination: Governments, Unions and Equal Pay,' *Labour History* 94 (May 2008): 144.
70   See ibid., 133–56.

Party amendment to the Public Service Bill to provide for equal remuneration within the Commonwealth Public Service. The women senators were sharply reminded that had they voted for Senator Willesee's motion it would have been carried. The letter concluded: 'This protest is in conformity with ANCW's policy on equal pay for women.'[71] A reply came from Agnes Robertson, the senator from Western Australia. She made some effort to defend the political appropriateness of the women's vote—the amendment was a Labor Party 'red herring' to delay the passage of the Bill—but the crucial point was that Menzies himself had declared that the Government would not accept the amendment: 'So you can see that we had no option but to uphold the Government's decision at this particular time.' Robertson made it clear that this was not a decision she approved of: 'I would remind you that I have worked all my life for equal pay for equal work.' She had written to the government leader in the Senate 'asking for information', and she quoted in full his infuriatingly contradictory reply:

> As you know, the official platform of the Liberal Party of Australia includes 'acceptance of the principle of equal remuneration for men and women for work of equal value'. The Government's attitude to this question has been stated on many occasions and was put quite clearly during the recent debates in Parliament on the Public Service Bill. That view is that it is for the Commonwealth Conciliation and Arbitration Commission and its associated tribunals in particular fields to determine the rates of remuneration for both men and women.[72]

Ada Norris was aware that change was a slow process and required patience and education. She believed, as she later wrote, that the Equal Pay Committee the NCWV set up after the 1953 basic wage case, together with the pamphlet it published, helped educate opinion—for '[i]n the long run the decisions of the court reflect the changes in society, and these changes have their origins in the thinking of individual people'.[73] In 1969, as NCWA president, Norris was again a key figure in putting together and presenting the council's case before the Arbitration Court for equal pay in the meat industries and the Commonwealth Public Service. In doing so, she joined with the Australian Federation of Women Voters, the Business and Professional Women's Association and the Union of Australian Women (UAW). The court's favourable decision would have variable repercussions for other women workers, flowing to some but not others, with actual numbers 'hard to estimate', as Norris reported. Her clear and concise summation, including a list of Commonwealth and Victorian awards and determinations attracting equal pay, was later used in preparation for the case presented to the Arbitration Court for the NCWA by Shirley Horne in November

---

71 'ANCW Board Minutes', 27 February 1961, NCWA Papers, Box 13.
72 'Agnes Robertson to ANCW', 10 March 1961, NCWA Papers, ANCW Correspondence, MS5193, Box 7.
73 Norris, *Champions of the Impossible*, 141–2.

1972,[74] and was influential in the court's decision, alongside the presentations by the UAW and Women's Liberation. By 1972, the council pointed out, 'it was estimated that only 18.24 per cent of the women in the work force now receive equal pay', and, calling on international precedent and example once more, Horne showed that the 1969 limited decision was 'out of phase with the principles enunciated by the United Nations and its associated organisation, the International Labour Organisation'. The NCWA case, prepared again by the Victorians, also pointed to recent legislation in New Zealand and to the fact that community attitudes to women's work, including that of married women, had changed—in part, they might have added, as a result of their own work amongst their affiliates and the wider community.[75]

All these arguments were used by Mr Justice Moore to justify the court's decision to support the new—for Australia—principle enunciated more than two decades earlier by the ILO of 'equal pay for work of equal value'. But the decision explicitly rejected the request of the NCWA and other women's groups to apply the male minimum wage to women workers and thus finally abandon the family basis of wage fixation.[76] As Norris had commented of the 1969 decision, Australia could not ratify the 1951 ILO convention until its terms 'exist in law and practice throughout Australia',[77] and the 1972 decision still left mandated equal pay incomplete. A single adult minimum wage was not conceded until 1974, when the NCWA again intervened, along with the UAW and the Women's Electoral Lobby. At last, in December of that year, Australia ratified ILO Convention 100.[78]

Conclusion

Impatience with the slow processes and conventional procedures of the NCW partly accounted for the appeal to a younger generation of second-wave feminism. But young women's rejection of the councils as old-fashioned and conservative failed to recognise how much their 'adaptive leadership' had in fact achieved. The broad acceptance within the wider women's movement of the need for legal equality in marriage (and divorce) and in employment can be credited at least in part to the gentle pressure of the leaders of the national councils. And the reluctant adoption by government of 'women's issues' like uniform divorce

---

74   Ada Norris, 'Equal Pay Review (Victoria & Commonwealth)', in Shirley Horne's equal pay file, NCWV Papers [hereinafter Horne File].
75   'Statement Made on behalf of the National Council of Women of Australia in the Commonwealth Conciliation and Arbitration Commission in Intervening in the Equal Pay Case, 3rd November 1972', Horne File.
76   'National Wage and Equal Pay Cases 1972—Statement by Mr Justice Moore', Sydney, 15 December 1972, Horne File.
77   Norris, 'Equal Pay Review'.
78   Norris, *Champions of the Impossible*, 140–1, 145.

law and equal pay came only when that gentle pressure—and other social and cultural changes—had established the issues as mainstream, reasonable and politically viable. This was the greatest achievement of the NCWA, and one that was intimately related to the understanding, support, inspiration and sense of responsibility its leaders drew from being part of an international movement.

References

Allen, Judith. *Rose Scott: Vision and Revision in Feminism*. Melbourne: Oxford University Press, 1994.

Australian Woman's Sphere. December 1901.

Baldwin, M. Page. 'Subject to Empire: Married Women and the British Nationality and Status of Aliens Act.' *Journal of British Studies* 40(4) (October 2001): 522–56.

Brisbane Courier, 10 March 1913.

Commonwealth Parliamentary Debates. Senate. 25 November 1959.

Daily Telegraph. 26 June 1901.

Finlay, Henry. *To Have But Not to Hold: A History of Attitudes to Marriage and Divorce in Australia 1858–1975*. Sydney: The Federation Press, 2005.

Housewife [Victoria]. 5 November 1929.

International Council of Women (ICW). ICW Resolutions. http://www.ncwc.ca/pdf/ICW-CIF_Resolutions.pdf.

Jacques, Catherine and Sylvie Lefebvre. 'The Working Methods of the ICW: From its Creation to the Second World War.' In *Women Changing the World: A History of the International Council of Women*, edited by Eliane Gubin and Leen van Molle, 101–4. Brussels: Éditions Racine, 2005.

Johnson, Penelope. 'Gender, Class and Work: The Council of Action for Equal Pay Campaign in Australia during World War II.' *Labour History* 50 (May 1986): 134–7.

Lake, Marilyn. 'The Independence of Women and the Brotherhood of Man: Debates in the Labour Movement over Equal Pay and Motherhood Endowment in the 1920s.' *Labour History* 63 (November 1992): 1–24.

Lake, Marilyn. 'A History of Feminism in Australia.' In *Oxford Companion to Australian Feminism*, edited by Barbara Caine, 132–42. Melbourne: Oxford University Press, 1998.

'Marriage and Divorce Bill 1947.' NAA A432 1956/2207. National Archives of Australia, Canberra.

Mercury [Hobart]. 26 April 1901.

Mueller, Carol. 'The Organisational Basis of Conflict in Contemporary Feminism.' In *Feminist Organizations: Harvest of the New Women's Movement*, edited by Myra Marx Ferree and Patricia Yancey Martin, 263–75. Philadelphia: Temple University Press, 1995.

Murphy, John. *A Decent Provision: Australian Welfare Policy, 1870–1949.* Farnham, UK, and Burlington, Vt: Ashgate, 2011.

National Council of Women of Australia. *ANCW Report and Minutes of the Biennial Conference, Canberra, A.C.T., 29th October – 4th November, 1960.*

National Council of Women of Australia (NCWA) Papers. MS7583 and MS5193. National Library of Australia, Canberra.

National Council of Women of New South Wales (NCWNSW) Records. MS3739. Mitchell Library, Sydney.

National Council of Women of New South Wales. *Biennial Reports for 1926–1928.*

National Council of Women of Queensland (NCWQ). Papers. UQFL402. Fryer Library, University of Queensland, Brisbane.

National Council of Women of Queensland. *Annual Report 1927/28; 1930/1931.*

National Council of Women of South Australia (NCWSA) Papers. SRG297. State Library of South Australia, Adelaide.

National Council of Women of Victoria (NCWV). Papers in transit to State Library of Victoria, Melbourne.

National Council of Women of Victoria. *Annual Report 1953.*

National Council of Women of Victoria. *Annual Report 1959.*

Norris, Ada. *Champions of the Impossible: A History of the National Council of Women of Victoria 1902–1977.* Melbourne: Hawthorn Press, 1978.Reiger, Kerreen. *The Disenchantment of the Home: Modernizing the Australian Family 1880–1940.* Melbourne: Oxford University Press, 1985.

'Report National Council of Women.' Typescript by Evelyn Gough, NCWV International Secretary, for ICW Toronto Quinquennial Meeting, 1909.

Sear, Martha. *The National Council of Women of NSW: A Chronology 1896–1996*. Sydney: NCWNSW, 1996.

Sheridan, Tom and Pat Stretton. 'Pragmatic Procrastination: Governments, Unions and Equal Pay.' *Labour History* 94 (May 2008): 133–56.

'Statement by St Joan's Alliance, Marriage and Divorce Bill 1947.' NAA A432 1956/2207. National Archives of Australia, Canberra.

Sydney Morning Herald. 31 July 1912.

The Age. 3 July 1914.

The Argus [Melbourne]. 26 October 1905; 1 August 1913; 17 September 1927.

8. 'Part of the human condition': Women in the Australian disability rights movement

Nikki Henningham[1]

People with disabilities form the largest minority in Australia and are amongst the nation's most disadvantaged people, with substandard outcomes on most indicators of community participation and *wellbeing*.[2] Despite this, most people tend not to think of disability rights as a political issue, as they do feminism or the struggle for Aboriginal self-determination. Instead, they tend to perceive disability as a personal problem to be overcome. Does this oversight stem from a collective fear of disability since everyone is a candidate for it? As Doris Fleischer and Frieda Zames observe, '"[h]andicapism" … is the only "ism" to which *all* human beings are susceptible'.[3] We are all vulnerable and subject to the vagaries of accident, illness and old age. Yet, despite the likelihood that we will all be potential recipients of their hard-fought gains, the struggle of disability rights activists against 'handicapism' has failed to capture the imagination of historians.

There has been very little historical writing about the Australian disability rights movement (ADRM). The stories of Australian people with disabilities— out of sight and out of mind—have generally been overlooked by historians except where their experience is central to the topic (for example, the impact of war or the rise of the eugenics movement) or when they can be contained within narratives of exceptionalism in stories of people like Alan Marshall 'jumping puddles' or Tilly Aston 'overcoming' her vision impairment.[4] Historians the world over 'have generally treated disability as a personal tragedy to be overcome, not a cultural construct to be questioned'.[5] The individuals who

---

1   The University of Melbourne.

2   Productivity Commission (PC), 'Disability Care and Support', *Productivity Commission Inquiry Report* (54) (31 July 2011); PricewaterhouseCoopers (Australia), *Disability* Expectations: Investing in a Better Life, A Stronger Australia Report (Sydney: PricewaterhouseCoopers, 2011), http://www.pwc.com.au/industry/ government/assets/disability-in-australia.pdf.

3   Doris Jame Fleischer and Frieda Zames, *The Disability Rights Movement: From Charity to Confrontation* (Philadelphia: Temple University Press, 2001), xv.

4   See, for example, O. S. Green, 'Aston, Matilda Ann (1873–1947)', *Australian Dictionary of Biography Online* (Canberra: National Centre of Biography, The Australian National University), http://adb.anu.edu.au/ biography/aston-matilda-ann-5078/text8471; Eileen E. Ewing, *'Can't I? Just Watch Me!': A Biography of Hazel Bedwin M.B.E* (Melbourne: Landvale Enterprises, 1981); and Alan Marshall, *I Can Jump Puddles* (Sydney: Penguin, 2004) (first published in 1955).

5   Douglas C. Baynton, 'Defectives in the Land: Disability and American Immigration Policy, 1882–1924', *Journal of American Ethnic History* 24(3) (2005): 41.

participated in the ADRM are therefore the ones who have been left with the task of communicating the transformative idea that it is not bodily impairment that disables people but socially constructed physical and attitudinal barriers.[6] Since the movement took shape in the late 1970s, politicising the personal has been central to the task of breaking down these barriers.

Women have taken leadership roles in the struggle for disability rights in Australia. They've directed organisations, run businesses, headed families, assumed political office, played elite sport, published innovative academic research and advocated for their rights. They've done so in the context of a movement that encompasses a wide range of issues and includes activists with many different political perspectives, across the country and across eras: Tilly Aston in the late nineteenth century founded the Victorian Association of Braille Writers and later established the Association for the Advancement of the Blind (now Vision Australia); Elizabeth Hastings was appointed Australia's first Disability Discrimination Commissioner in 1993; Kelly Vincent in 2010 became the youngest woman ever elected to an Australian parliament and the first person with a disability elected to the SA Parliament. The leadership of women with disabilities, in disability activism and beyond, has been important to the development of public recognition and understanding of the issues confronting Australian people with disabilities and the ongoing challenge of eliminating discrimination.[7]

This chapter explores some of the ways in which Australian women have risen to this challenge. It refers to and builds upon their work through an analysis that describes women's leadership in disability activism over the past 30 years. It uses, in the main, oral testimony of activists themselves to highlight the issues they believed were most important, that best defined their styles of leadership and that characterised women's involvement in the movement. The focus will be on the period leading up to and immediately after the International Year of Disabled Persons (IYDP) in 1981 and the period in the early 1980s when a distinctly feminist consciousness began to inform activism. The chapter will explore the ways in which feminism influenced disability politics and will focus on the women who insisted that disability politics needed to be understood as a human rights issue of universal importance.

---

6   Margaret Cooper, 'The Australian Disability Rights Movement: Freeing the Power of Advocacy' (MA thesis, School of Social Work, University of Melbourne, 1999); Margaret Cooper, 'The Disability Rights Movement Lives', *Disability and Society* 14(2) (1999): 217–26; Rhonda Galbally, *Just Passions: The Personal is Political* (Melbourne: Pluto Press, 2004); Joan Hume, 'Disability and History', *Radical Sydney* (2010) http://radicalsydney.blogspot.com.au/p/on-disability-and-history.html; Helen Meekosha, 'The Politics of Representation or the Politics of Presence: The Challenge of Disability', in *Speaking for the People: Representation in Australian Politics*, eds Marian Sawer and Gianni Zappala (Melbourne: Melbourne University Press, 2001).
7   See, for example, 'Kelly Vincent', *The 100 Leaders Project*, http://100leaders.org.au/themes/following-your-dream/kelly-vincent/; Green, 'Aston, Matilda Ann'; 'Obituary: Elizabeth Hastings', *Women With Disabilities Australia News* (15) (1998), http://www.wwda.org.au/issue15.htm.

The chapter does so somewhat arbitrarily; there has been so little written in the area that to condense the complete history of the ADRM into the space provided would be general to the point of meaninglessness. My aim is to provide examples of women's activism as a way of introducing readers to some people who should be better known for the impact they had on improving the lives of people with disabilities. I approach the task cautiously, given the ambivalence most women with disabilities have about the narratives of exceptionalism and 'courageous battles against the odds' that accompany stories of their achievement. Stella Young, editor of *Ramp Up*, a website for news, discussion and opinion about disability in Australia, provides an explanation for this ambivalence. She describes the worst of these representations as a form of 'inspiration porn', designed to make able-bodied people feel better about themselves when they are feeling down. ('Things could be worse, I could be one of *them*'!) Images of unnamed disabled people depicted as objects of inspiration and accompanied by slogans like 'the only disability in life is a bad attitude' exceptionalise and objectify people with disabilities and are premised on the assumption that the disabled people depicted 'have terrible lives, and that it takes some extra pluck to live them'. This isn't the case, and she gets tired of being congratulated for simply existing.[8]

Furthermore, stories of courage against the odds can create a dangerous impression. They can signal that if people with disabilities can't 'defy the odds' to 'overcome their disability' then the social structures that discriminate against them are not to blame; rather it's their attitude. 'It says that if we fail to be happy, to smile and to live lives that make those around us feel good, it's because we're not trying hard enough.'[9] What Young describes here is a form of marginalisation that seems to be singularly owned by the disabled. 'Unlike racial, ethnic, and sexual minorities', says historian Catherine J. Kudlick, 'disabled people experience attacks cloaked in pity accompanied by a widely held perception that no one wishes them ill'.[10] Put-down by pity is an insidious form of discrimination

Young's view has its critics. For some people with disabilities the very act of making it through a day *is* an achievement.[11] Indeed, leading advocates such as Keran Howe, executive director of Women with Disabilities Victoria (WDV), acknowledge that their own stories of success and achievement can provide inspiration for other women with disabilities confronting discrimination in their daily lives. As individuals, they've been able to overcome obstacles, but

---

8 Stella Young, 'We're Not Here for Your Inspiration', *Ramp Up*, ABC Online, 2 July 2012, http://www.abc.net.au/rampup/articles/2012/07/02/3537035.htm.
9 Ibid.
10 Catherine J. Kudlick, 'Why We Need Another "Other"', *The America Historical Review* 108(3) (June 2001): 768.
11 See comments after Young, 'We're Not Here for Your Inspiration'.

they recognise that not everyone has the capacity 'to keeping banging on about the issues' in positional leadership roles.[12] So Howe and others will be role models but they don't want their stories to be used to justify any argument that the social order doesn't need changing. 'One of the most challenging aspects of disability', says Kudlick, 'is to convince non-disabled people that ... disability is not always a tragedy, a hardship or a lack but in fact offers much of value'.[13] One of the challenges of writing the history of disability is recognising and resolving that tension between honouring individual achievement and foregrounding the barriers that make that achievement so remarkable.

With the rise of the ADRM in the 1970s and the accompanying understanding of history as a source of empowerment for marginalised social groups, we have seen scholarship aimed at reconciling that tension by representing people with disabilities as 'more than another Other to add to a list that scholars either indulge or decry as being "politically correct"'.[14] As people with disabilities began to describe how social structures, not their impairment, were the source of their exclusion, theories of disability as a social construct, not a medical problem, provided a platform for approaching disability 'not simply as the variations that exist in human behavior, functioning, sensory acuity, and cognitive processing, but more crucially [in terms of] the meaning we make of these variations'.[15] Helen Meekosha, Christopher Newell, Gerard Goggin and Karen Solditac are internationally recognised Australian academics who have made significant contributions to the emerging field of disability studies. Through critical analyses of disability, they have helped us to understand that there are a variety of ways of understanding disability as a construct with a past that informs the present.[16] They, like other women featured in this chapter, have fought for the recognition of the *value* of disability 'as simply a part of the human condition' and campaigned for the citizenship rights of people who 'do not wish to "be included": they wish ... to be acknowledged that they already belong'.[17]

---

12 Keran Howe interviewed by Nikki Henningham, Melbourne, 24 June 2010, Personal collection [hereinafter Howe Interview].

13 Kudlick, 'Why We Need Another "Other"', 769.

14 Catherine Kudlick, 'Comment: Comparative Observations on Disability in History', *Journal of American Ethnic History* 24(3) (2005): 60.

15 Simi Linton, *Claiming Disability: Knowledge and Identity* (New York: New York University Press, 2001), 2.

16 See, for example, Gerard Goggin and Christopher Newell, *Disability in Australia: Exposing a Social Apartheid* (Sydney: UNSW Press, 2004); Karen Soldatic and Helen Meekosha, 'Disability and Neoliberal State Formations', in *The Routledge Handbook of Disability Studies*, eds Nick Watson, Carol Thomas and Alan Roulstone (London: Routledge, 2012), 195–210.

17 Elizabeth Hastings, 'FounDDAtions: Reflections on the First Five Years of the Disability Discrimination Act in Australia', Australian Human Rights and Equal Opportunity Commission website, http://humanrights. gov.au/disability_rights/hr_disab/found.html.

Women in the early disability rights movement

Space does not permit a comprehensive account of the rise of the disability rights movement in Australia in the 1970s and 1980s. There have been some partial accounts provided by those who participated, but a study comparable with Fleischer and Zames' analysis of the movement in the United States is yet to be written.[18] Lifelong activists such as Margaret Cooper in Victoria and Joan Hume in New South Wales have commented upon the influence of activism from the United States, and the impact of national and international publications. They have also stressed the importance and influence of courageous individuals who showed them that being shut away in institutions, silently accepting exclusion and discrimination, was not the only option available to people with disabilities. People who asserted what little power they had over their lives by questioning the appalling treatment they received had a profound impact upon Cooper, who learned from them that an independent life was possible for people who 'took control and spoke up'.[19] What this meant, in practical terms, was mobilising: a) to create social support networks for people with disabilities so they felt less isolated and discovered strength in numbers; and b) to advocate their rights for social inclusion on their own terms.

Women were prominent in the late 1970s and early 1980s in these efforts to mobilise. The late Lesley Hall, former CEO of the Australian Federation of Disability Organisations (AFDO), the peak body for disability organisations in Australia, was instrumental in establishing Victoria's first Disability Resource Centre (DRC), in Brunswick in 1981.[20] This, according to Margaret Cooper, was 'a radical and a vital step towards enacting what would become a basic priority for the disability rights movement, that there should be "nothing about us without us"'. Set up along the lines of the Independent Living Centres that were being established in the United States, where 'people with disabilities ran their own show', the DRC was not only important as a tool of empowerment and social support. As Cooper points out, it was also important because it was 'a step towards people with disabilities managing their own advocacy on a more formal, funded level'.[21]

---

18   Fleischer and Zames, *The Disability Rights Movement*; Cooper, 'The Disability Rights Movement Lives'; Hume, 'Disability and History'.

19   Margaret Cooper, interviewed by Nikki Henningham in the Women with Disabilities Project, 19 July 2010, National Library of Australia Oral History and Folklore Collection, ORAL TRC 6240/6, National Library of Australia, Canberra [hereinafter Cooper Interview]. See also, Nikki Henningham, 'Margaret Cooper: Feminist and Disability Activist', in *Founders, Firsts and Feminists: Women Leaders in Twentieth-Century Australia*, eds Fiona Davis, Nell Musgrove and Judith Smart (Melbourne: eScholarship Research Centre, University of Melbourne, 2011), http://www.womenaustralia.info/leaders/fff/pdfs/cooper.pdf, 261–73.

20   Lesley Hall, interviewed by Nikki Henningham and Rosemary Francis in the Women with Disabilities Project, 7 June 2010, National Library of Australia Oral History and Folklore Collection, ORAL TRC 6240/2, National Library of Australia, Canberra [hereinafter Hall Interview].

21   Cooper Interview.

The DRC was one of many initiatives that grew roots out of the funding and atmosphere that accompanied the IYDP in 1981. It was 'a crucial year', said Hall, 'for getting everyone to understand that people with disabilities needed to be involved and lead their own projects'.[22] The experience of academic Natalie Tomas is typical of this early experience of group formation. Living in East St Kilda in 1981, Tomas, a history student at Monash University, decided to start a disability action group. Their first meeting was held in her flat; subsequent meetings were held in the St Kilda Municipal Library. 'I had no idea what I was doing', she remembered nearly 30 years later. 'I was just a nineteen year old student who had never organised anything in her life. But I thought it was a good idea.' She met people, they networked and they talked about the things they could do and change.[23] Social support and affirmation were important steps in the activist's journey.

As it did for many women with disabilities, this sort of grassroots activism marked her entry into formal disability activism and politics.[24] Also, as with many women with disabilities, it was not marked by any sort of feminist consciousness. Early grassroots activism focused on advocacy to see that very basic, universal human rights were granted to people with disabilities: rights to education, housing, employment and accessibility, especially to public transport.

Women were at the forefront of many of the public protests about inadequate access to such services in the lead-up to the IYDP, especially protests relating to public transport. Whilst protests happened across the country in all major cities, one of the most publicised was in Sydney, because it was captured on film. In 1979, at the opening of the Eastern Suburbs Railway at Bondi Junction, a state-of-the-art transport hub designed to be replicated in other locations, a small group of protestors in wheelchairs and their supporters, including Joan Hume and filmmaker Genni Batterham, were jostled, spat at, told that they were 'spoiling the view' and that they 'should go home to their nursing homes'.[25] The behaviour is graphically captured in the internationally acclaimed documentary film *Pins and Needles*, about Batterham's coming to grips with her own disability.[26] Premier Neville Wran, who officiated, was deeply embarrassed as he proclaimed

---

22 Hall Interview.

23 Natalie Tomas, interviewed by Nikki Henningham and Rosemary Francis in the Women with Disabilities Project, 18 June 2010, National Library of Australia Oral History and Folklore Collection, ORAL TRC 6240/3, National Library of Australia, Canberra [hereinafter Thomas Interview].

24 Ibid.; Cooper Interview; Hall Interview. See also Cooper, 'The Australian Disability Rights Movement'; and Hume, 'Disability and History'.

25 Hume, 'Disability and History'.

26 Barbara Chobocky, dir., *Pins and Needles*, [film] (Sydney: AFI Distribution, 1980).

the station to be 'open to many'.[27] He acknowledged later, when announcing the establishment of the NSW wheelchair taxi subsidy program as one of a raft of IYDP programs in 1981, that his experience at the protest motivated him.

For women with disabilities like Hume and Batterham, mobilising support for basic human rights for all people with disabilities was an important first stage in their activism. 'From little things, big things grow', said Hume, as she reflected on the journey from Bondi Junction in 1979 to the passage of the Commonwealth *Disability Discrimination Act* in 1992.[28]

Women and the International Year of Disabled Persons, 1981

Early in 1980 award-winning advertising executive Phillip Adams met with three consultants to get advice on an important government-funded project. Adams had just been appointed by a Commonwealth Government ministerial committee to devise the media campaign to accompany 1981's United Nation's International Year of Disabled Persons. His brief was to educate the Australian public and to help them to 'see ability within disability', and he believed he had the strategy sorted within 10 minutes of being awarded the contract. Filmed portraits of Stephen Hawking, Franklin Delano Roosevelt—'any of the mighty afflicted', he said—'would be grist to my media mill'. The approach was ratified by the ministerial committee with satisfaction and speed.[29]

The consultants he met were three women with disabilities. When Elizabeth Hastings, Edith Hall and Rhonda Galbally came through the door using their wheelchairs and crutches, Adams knew he was dealing with people who would persevere until their message sunk in. Their presence 'was testament', said Adams, 'to their determination, given that our building ... ha[d] no disabled access'.[30] At the meeting, the three women explained to Adams, politely, that he was 'a buffoon', and that his campaign involving 'super crips' (Elizabeth Hastings' words) like Hawking and Roosevelt would do nothing for 'the tens of thousands of ordinary human beings who suffered everything from the fears and stigmatising of the "the able-bodied" to a comprehensive apartheid'. This year people with disabilities would claim the right to speak for themselves; 1981 had to be 'the year of disabled people, not the year for them'.[31]

---

27 Personal Correspondence with Joan Hume, 18 December 2012.

28 Hume, 'Disability and History'.

29 Chris Hosking and Phillip Adams, 'Brave, Sensual, Feisty, Warrior: The Passionate Spirit, the Enquiring Vigorous Mind, and the Steadfast Love, Our Friend and Colleague, Elizabeth Hastings Born 21.1.1949 – Dies 13.10.1998', *Australian and New Zealand Psychodrama Association Journal* 7 (December 1998): 17.

30 Ibid., 1.

31 Ibid.

Adams required no convincing but was obliged to advise the ministerial committee of the change in tack. The members took some persuading to adopt the new, assertive slogan 'Break Down the Barriers'. Said Adams: 'They could see a campaign leading to demands for new legislation.'[32] But he prevailed and 'the Government's hopes for a sweet year of sloganism came to naught'.[33] Adams, accompanied by Galbally, Hall or Hastings, travelled the country, taping interviews with hundreds of ordinary people with disabilities. Their stories formed the platform of an advertising campaign that won the 1982 Golden Lion Award at Cannes for the best advertising campaign in the world.[34] It was the first time advertising had been used as an effective tool to fight for the rights of people with disabilities. 'With Phillip's ads, and with our media and speaking campaigns', said Rhonda Galbally, 'we put disability rights on to the agenda and helped break down the institutional walls'.[35] Importantly, remembers Adams, 'by the end of the year, the disabled people of Australia had joined [Elizabeth, Edith and Rhonda] in speaking out for themselves'.[36]

To say that Hastings, Hall and Galbally influenced Adams' thinking on how to understand disability is understating the extent of their impact. He claims that no-one taught him more about human rights than they did.[37] 'They made me realise that they [human rights] weren't merely an issue in Burma or Afghanistan', he said. 'They were missing here every time our bigotry, our buildings or our institutions placed a barrier in a disabled person's path.'[38] Indeed, one of the most important outcomes of the IYPD was the impact on communities of people with disabilities and those who were 'not yet disabled (NYD)'[39] of hearing people with disabilities taking control of events and speaking for themselves. Those in the former group were inspired to join the campaign for their rights; those in the latter began the slow process of transforming their understanding of the 'problem' of disability from a medical concern to a social problem.

Not everyone was as quick as Philip Adams to comprehend disability within the framework of human rights. But after a year of exposure to the advertising campaign there were many more 'NYD' people starting to make that transformative journey. The leadership role taken by women at this time was crucial in creating the platform to successfully advocate for important structural changes and legislative measures that would follow, such as the

---

32 Ibid.
33 Galbally, *Just Passions*, 16.
34 Hosking and Adams, 'Brave, Sensual, Feisty, Warrior', 18.
35 Galbally, *Just Passions*, 16.
36 Hosking and Adams, 'Brave, Sensual, Feisty, Warrior', 18.
37 Ibid.
38 Ibid.
39 NYD was a label used by Elizabeth Hastings to described the 'able-bodied' population in Mark Ragg, 'The Quiet Enabler: Elizabeth Hasting, Australia's First Disability Discrimination Commissioner', *The Bulletin*, 15 March 1994: 42.

1981 survey of people with disabilities conducted by the Australian Bureau of Statistics (ABS), the 1983 Commonwealth Review of Handicapped Persons and the establishment of the Disability Advisory Council of Australia (DACA), also in 1983. A decade later, in 1992, the *Commonwealth Disability Discrimination Act* was passed, paving the way for the establishment of the office of the Disability Discrimination Commissioner.[40] It wasn't until there seemed to be real action on some of these basic human mechanisms to protect the rights of all people with disabilities that women in the movement began to form a view that disability politics' interactions with gender politics led to women with disabilities being 'doubly disadvantaged'.[41]

'Doubly disadvantaged': Disability and feminism intersect

While there were some important advances and responses from government and the community at large throughout the 1980s, there were still some significant blind spots. Many women with disabilities came to see that some of the worst of these related to the special issues they confronted. Some related to basic socioeconomics. Compared with men with disabilities, women were more likely to be poorly educated, unemployed, in institutional care and without access to adequate rehabilitation and health services.[42]

Additionally, many activists began to express concerns that there were aspects of gendered discrimination that lay, quite literally, in the bodies of women with disabilities. They battled the pervasive and discriminatory notion that they had imperfect, unattractive, asexual bodies, which, in Hall's words, 'excluded them from society's norm'.[43] The fact that women with disabilities had a right to a sex life, the shape and boundaries of which should be determined by them, was a taboo subject that was taken on with candour and passion by the young New South Welshwoman Genni Batterham in *Pins and Needles*.[44] Diagnosed with multiple sclerosis (MS) at the age of twenty-three, Batterham and her husband documented her life with MS in a series of films over eight years.[45] Sex and

---

40   For a comprehensive list of legislative measures, see Mary Lindsay, *Commonwealth Disability Policy 1983–1995*, Background Paper 2 (Canberra: Australian Parliamentary Library, 1995–96), http://www.aph.gov.au/library/pubs/bp/1995-96/96bp06.htm.

41   Tomas Interview. See also Natalie Tomas, *'Double Disadvantage': Barriers Facing Women with Disabilities in Accessing Employment, Education and Training Opportunities—A Discussion Paper* (Disability Employment Action Centre, Melbourne, 1991).

42   Ibid.

43   Hall Interview.

44   Chobocky, *Pins and Needles*.

45   See also Hugh Piper, dir., *Riding the Gale*, [film] (Canberra, Ronin Films, Independent Productions International & Stormbringer Films); *Where's the Give and Take?* [film] (Sydney: Stormbringer Film Productions, Creative Development Branch, Australian Film Commission, NSW Department of Youth and Community Services, 1981).

sexuality were documentary focal points that, as one reviewer suggested, 'forced the viewer to reassess attitudes about the disabled and challenge historical value judgements about their needs'.[46]

The idea that women with disabilities had bodies that they were entitled to manage in ways they saw fit was confronting. That the reviewer acknowledged the NYD community's need to respond to this by adjusting *their* thinking indicates that some people were starting to understand that although impairment is real, it is how we respond to it that makes it disabling. In other words, they were beginning to see the plasticity of disability as a social and cultural construction. Helen Meekosha has unpacked the social and cultural constructions of disability in Australia, and the complex web of meanings and relationships embedded in those constructions in order to underline the centrality of the politics of representation to the disability rights movement and to the women within that movement. She has argued that understandings of disability are fluid and no more fixed in biology than understandings of gender and race, and points to the historical dimensions of that constructedness, noting that almost from its foundations Australia preferred to lock disabled people away in institutions, preventing the 'pollution' of the wider population with 'defective' genes.[47] In the Australian colonial context, where development of a new society relied on the labour of the strong and the fit, where physical prowess became a measure of manhood while beauty and fitness to bear children were the cultural markers of femininity, the bodies of people with disabilities were regarded as defective and 'valueless'.[48]

Women with disabilities, however, had been highlighting the relationship between real bodies and the warped meanings attached to them as a central plank of their feminist activism several years before Meekosha articulated this theory. Hall, for instance, became increasingly frustrated by the way traditional, patriarchal, gender hierarchies were played out in disability organisations and the apparent lack of concern for the needs of women with disabilities in the

---

46 'Review of Pins and Needles', *The Age*, 23 June 1988, 14; See also Chobocky, *Pins and Needles*.

47 Helen Meekosha, 'A Feminist/Gendered Critique of the Intersections of Race and Disability: The Australian Experience', Paper presented to the Faculty of Education and the Department of Educational Studies, University of British Columbia, Vancouver, 23 June 2005, http://www.wwda.org.au/gendis2001.htm, 5; Carolyn Frohmader and Helen Meekosha, 'Recognition, Respect and Rights: Women with Disabilities in a Globalised World', in *Disability and Social Theory: New Developments and Directions*, eds Dan Goodley, Bill Hughes and Lennard Davis (Hampshire: Palgrave Macmillan, 2012), 287–307; Helen Meekosha, 'Contextualizing Disability: Developing Southern/Global Theory', Keynote paper presented at the Fourth Disability Studies Conference, Lancaster University, Bailrigg, 2–4 September 2008, http://www.wwda.org.au/meekosha2008.htm, 9.

48 Baynton ('Defectives in the Land') and Kudlick ('Why We Need Another "Other"') have both explored these themes in the North American context. Jane Sherwin has argued that this understanding of disability still governs many contemporary attitudes towards people with disabilities. See Jane Sherwin, 'Leadership for Social Inclusion in the Lives of People with Disabilities', *The International Journal of Leadership in Public Services* 6 (Supplement) (September 2010): 84–93.

feminist movement. She was a founding member of the Women with Disabilities Feminist Collective (WDFC) that formed in Victoria in response. The WDFC was a social support organisation that engaged in overt political action. One of its earliest and best-known actions was its opposition to the Miss Australia quest, a beauty contest that raised funds for what was then called the Spastic Society, a charity that raised money on behalf of people with cerebral palsy. Hall and her group challenged the concept of the quest as a particularly objectionable form of fundraiser for people with disabilities, given its focus on physical perfection 'as the norm all must attain if they are to be fully accepted into society'.[49]

Feminist activists and lobby groups for people with disabilities protested outside the national finals throughout the 1970s. The IYDP in 1981 provided the catalyst for sustained opposition to the quest. Hall was among a group of feminists and disability activists who managed to gain access to the Melbourne Town Hall, where the event was being held, and reach the stage—a challenging act in itself given her restricted mobility. The protests received significant press coverage and provoked a range of responses, from strong support from people within the Spastic Society and other disability charities to criticism from conservative people with disabilities, who believed the protestors were 'ungrateful spoilsports'. This was an attitude that angered activists even further, due to the patronising 'charity model of victimhood' it represented.[50] In Sydney in 1983, Hume and her colleagues found it particularly galling when there was not a single person with cerebral palsy in sight during the red carpet arrival to the event—an event that women with disabilities themselves were not encouraged or permitted to enter. Says Hume, 'They were not considered beautiful or socially acceptable enough'.[51] These protests were, arguably, the first public acts to place disability as a feminist issue on the agenda.

Attitudes towards the bodies of women with disabilities began to drive the activism of many women in the ADRM as they began to understand the extent of the human rights abuses that were committed because of them. The forced sterilisations, child removals and appallingly high rates of physical and sexual violence were problems that were barely acknowledged, and remain at the heart of much activism today.[52] On the one hand, women with disabilities were represented as asexual beings who weren't expected to form loving relationships, bear children of their own or establish families. On the other, their sexuality was

---

49   Hall Interview.
50   Ibid.; Hume, 'Disability and History'.
51   Hume, 'Disability and History'.
52   For a summary, see Frohmader and Meekosha, 'Recognition, Respect and Rights'. Also, Carolyn Frohmader, *There is No Justice—THERE'S Just US. The Status of Women with Disabilities in Australia* (Canberra: Women With Disabilities Australia, 2002).

recognised and exploited by the hundreds of people who abused them at rates substantially higher than those experienced by women in the community at large.

Women disability activists began talking about these problems in public forums and felt that their voices on these important human rights issues were being ignored by men in the disability rights movement and many women in the feminist movement. Cooper experienced the hard edge of this ignorance from both quarters in the mid 1980s. The first time came at an international meeting of Disabled People's International (DPI) in the Bahamas in 1985. It took a threat from all the women delegates to withdraw from the organisation for the men to take them seriously. The second time came at the hands of the feminist movement. In 1985 Cooper returned from the euphoria of the moment in the Bahamas to attend a National Agenda for Women Conference in Canberra. Broken promises over funding saw her at odds with some of the 'mainstream' feminist organisations. The constant glossing over of the issues confronted by Indigenous women, migrant and refugee women and women with disabilities promoted discussion and coalition amongst those marginalised groups.[53]

In response, a formal Women's Network was established within the DPI. This translated into the formation of the National Women's Network (NWN) within the DPI in Australia in 1985. Cooper, Tomas and Hastings were all early members of the network, and they found that they had much in common with several members of the WDFC, like Hall, especially with regard to prioritising the problems of access to women's health services and domestic violence. Working as an unfunded network with little support from the male-dominated leadership of DPI(A), these women decided in the mid 1990s that they would be better off going it alone. In 1995, the network incorporated and changed its name to Women With Disabilities Australia (WWDA), a new organisation with the aim of providing a 'national voice for the needs and rights of women with disabilities and a national force to improve the lives and life chances of women with disabilities'.[54] As the peak organisation for women with disabilities in Australia, WWDA's establishment marked an important phase in the evolution of women's leadership within the ADRM. The politics of representation was always a central feature of disability activism, and throughout the 1990s its feminist edge solidified as women insisted that it was not enough for men to speak out on their behalf. 'Nothing about us Without Us' was a gendered mantra.[55]

---

53   Cooper Interview; and Cooper, 'The Australian Disability Rights Movement'.
54   Women With Disabilities Australia, Webpage, http://www.wwda.org.au/background.htm.
55   Sue Salthouse refers to the use of the phrase as a slogan by people with disabilities in 'Brave New World: Is the Convention on the Rights of Persons with Disabilities a Blueprint for Utopia?', Paper presented at the Australian Federation of Disability Organisations Conference, Melbourne, May 2009, www.wwda.org.au/afdopapermay09.doc.

Over the past two decades the organisation has developed from one concerned primarily with building individual confidence and self-esteem to an internationally recognised human rights organisation. WWDA leaders continue to reinforce the message that disability is not a medical problem but a human rights issue, so the work of WWDA is grounded in a rights-based framework that links gender and disability issues to the full range of civil, political, economic, social and cultural rights.[56] WWDA has taken a leading role in creating this framework at an international level, a prime example being its work to ensure that a specific article on women (Article 6) was included in the UN Convention on the Rights of Persons with Disabilities, a treaty ratified by Australia in 2008.[57]

Conclusion: Activism in the twenty-first century

Cooper has been involved with the ADRM since she was living in hostels in the 1960s and has had plenty of opportunity to watch it evolve over the past 40 years. From gaining inspiration from courageous individuals who refused to be patronised and infantilised, and supporting others through conversation and coffee to mobilising direct action, lobbying those in power with the capacity to make changes and working to establish organisations to give people with disabilities a voice—all this while managing work, study, relationship and other family obligations—Cooper has seen people and ideas come and go but she has never lost sight of what, for her, is the most important thing a leader must have: a passion for the issues.[58]

Add to that a mechanism by which people can formulate ideas and communicate their passion and you get a sense of how Cooper understood effective leadership amongst women in the ADRM. She maintains that it was the feminist collective model of leadership that WWDA insisted upon that made it successful. She enjoyed participating in feminist organisations that were structured in ways that enabled information to be shared. They were 'circular' in shape rather than hierarchical, with leaders more like 'spokes in a wheel' who facilitated communication than figures sitting on high disseminating information as they saw fit. 'We did some amazing things', she says, 'acknowledging each other's point of view ... listening to everyone's opinion ... practising consensus decision making, thinking up ways by which other women could receive assistance to

56 Women With Disabilities Australia (WWDA), *Annual Report 2009–2010* (Hobart: Women With Disabilities Australia, 2010), http://www.wwda.org.au/wwdarepts.htm.

57 Sue Salthouse interviewed by Nikki Henningham in the Women and Leadership in a Century of Australian Democracy Oral History Project, 20 May 2011, National Library of Australia, Canberra, http://nla. gov.au/nla.oh-vn5197761 [hereinafter Salthouse Interview]. For an account of the successes of WWDA at an international level, see also Frohmader and Meekosha, 'Recognition, Respect and Rights', 298–303.

58 Cooper Interview.

reach their goals'. Of course, this leadership model was time-consuming and very hard work, but, as Cooper indicates, it was 'infinitely more empowering than the old ways'.[59]

Likewise, Sue Salthouse, WWDA president 2009–12, believes the effectiveness of WWDA nationally and abroad has come about not because of a focus on individuals but because individuals were, by and large, able to put their egos to one side for the sake of the group.[60] This has made interviews with women recognised by their peers to be leaders in the movement a challenging but interesting exercise. Most are reluctant to talk about themselves as leaders, except in the context of how they worked within a group to influence change. Understanding what constitutes good leadership matters, it matters enormously, but not as a position so much as a process resulting in change. What it achieves and how it does so are what count.

This is not to say that as individuals, these women don't recognise what it is they bring to the table. They rate themselves highly on their commitment, their strategic vision, their ability to share knowledge effectively and their use of networks to maximise their efficiency as facilitators. But what they are insistent upon is the importance of a leadership model that allows for a form of 'sharing'. They stress that it is impossible for any one person to carry all the traits required to be an effective leader, so the context in which they operate is all important. They almost always describe what they do in relation to how they connect with the group, with the issues and with the fight for social justice and human rights, without a hint of the 'heroic model' informing their processes. They conceptualise leadership within the 'hub and spokes' model of the collective, where knowledge is shared and the leader is the person who facilitates that sharing, within and beyond the organisation. A leader knows when to call in expertise from people at the rim of the wheel when required, and when to allow someone else to be added as an additional spoke. But, according to Sue Salthouse, she also knows when to rely on her own good judgment. 'While needing to be inclusive and consultative, prepared and hard-working', she says, 'you can't be self-effacing. A good leader has to have presence.'[61]

A good leader also has to be present. Says Salthouse, 'they must have a seat at the table', not only because it is vital that the voices of women with disabilities be heard but also because there is enormous symbolic importance attached to women with disabilities being seen to be leaders. They need to be able to demonstrate to themselves and the able-bodied people around them 'I look

---

59   Ibid.; Margaret Cooper, *Empowerment and Women with Disabilities* (Hobart: Women With Disabilities Australia, 1995), http://www.wwda.org.au/empow.htm.
60   Salthouse Interview.
61   Ibid.

like you, only sitting down'.[62] Then, as Hastings hoped, we may proceed to a position where it is fully acknowledged that women with disabilities don't need to be included because they 'already belong'.[63]

References

Baynton, Douglas C. 'Defectives in the Land: Disability and American Immigration Policy, 1882–1924.' Journal of American Ethnic History 24(3) (2005): 31–44.

Chobocky, Barbara, dir. *Pins and Needles*, [film]. Sydney: AFI Distribution, 1980.

Cooper, Margaret. *Empowerment and Women with Disabilities*. Hobart: Women With Disabilities Australia, 1995. http://www.wwda.org.au/empow.htm.

Cooper, Margaret. 'The Australian Disability Rights Movement: Freeing the Power of Advocacy.' MA thesis, School of Social Work, University of Melbourne, 1999.

Cooper, Margaret. 'The Disability Rights Movement Lives.' *Disability and Society* 14(2) (1999): 217–26.

Cooper, Margaret. Interviewed by Nikki Henningham in the Women with Disabilities Project, 19 July 2010. National Library of Australia Oral History and Folklore Collection, ORAL TRC 6240/6. National Library of Australia, Canberra.

Ewing, Eileen E. *'Can't I? Just Watch Me!': A Biography of Hazel Bedwin MBE*. Melbourne: Landvale Enterprises, 1981.

Fleischer, Doris Jame and Frieda Zames. *The Disability Rights Movement: From Charity to Confrontation*. Philadelphia: Temple University Press, 2001.

Frohmader, Carolyn. *There is No Justice—THERE'S Just US. The Status of Women with Disabilities in Australia*. Canberra: Women With Disabilities Australia, 2002.

Frohmader, Carolyn and Helen Meekosha. 'Recognition, Respect and Rights: Women with Disabilities in a Globalised World.' In *Disability and Social Theory: New Developments and Directions*, edited by Dan Goodley, Bill Hughes and Lennard Davis, 287–307. Hampshire: Palgrave Macmillan, 2012.

---

62 Ibid.
63 Hastings, 'FounDDAtions'.

Galbally, Rhonda. *Just Passions: The Personal is Political*. Melbourne: Pluto Press, 2004.

Goggin, Gerard and Christopher Newell. *Disability in Australia: Exposing a Social Apartheid*. Sydney: UNSW Press, 2004.

Green, O. S. 'Aston, Matilda Ann (1873–1947).' *Australian Dictionary of Biography Online*. Canberra: National Centre of Biography, The Australian National University. http://adb.anu.edu.au/biography/aston-matilda-ann-5078/text8471.

Hall, Lesley. Interviewed by Nikki Henningham and Rosemary Francis in the Women with Disabilities Project, 7 June 2010. National Library of Australia Oral History and Folklore Collection, ORAL TRC 6240/2. National Library of Australia, Canberra.

Hastings, Elizabeth. 'FounDDAtions: Reflections on the First Five Years of the Disability Discrimination Act in Australia.' Australian Human Rights and Equal Opportunity Commission website. http://humanrights.gov.au/disability_rights/hr_disab/found.html.

Henningham, Nikki. 'Margaret Cooper: Feminist and Disability Activist.' In *Founders, Firsts and Feminists: Women Leaders in Twentieth-Century Australia*, edited by Fiona Davis, Nell Musgrove and Judith Smart, 261–73. Melbourne: eScholarship Research Centre, University of Melbourne, 2011. http://www.womenaustralia.info/leaders/fff/pdfs/cooper.pdf.

Hosking, Chris and Phillip Adams. 'Brave, Sensual, Feisty, Warrior: The Passionate Spirit, the Enquiring Vigorous Mind, and the Steadfast Love, Our Friend and Colleague, Elizabeth Hastings Born 21.1.1949 – Dies 13.10.1998.' *Australian and New Zealand Psychodrama Association Journal* 7 (December 1998): 4–19.

Howe, Keran. Interviewed by Nikki Henningham, Melbourne, 24 June 2010. Personal Collection.

Hume, Joan. 'Disability and History.' *Radical Sydney* (2010). http://radicalsydney.blogspot.com.au/p/on-disability-and-history.html.

'Kelly Vincent.' *The 100 Leaders Project*. http://100leaders.org.au/themes/following-your-dream/kelly-vincent/.

Kudlick, Catherine. 'Comment: Comparative Observations on Disability in History.' *Journal of American Ethnic History* 24(3) (2005): 59–62.

Kudlick, Catherine J. 'Why We Need Another "Other".' *The America Historical Review* 108(3) (June 2001): 763–93.

Lindsay, Mary. *Commonwealth Disability Policy 1983–1995*. Background Paper 2. Canberra: Australian Parliamentary Library, 1995–96.

Linton, Simi. *Claiming Disability: Knowledge and Identity*. New York: New York University Press, 2001.

Marshall, Alan. *I Can Jump Puddles*. Sydney: Penguin, 2004.

Meekosha, Helen. 'A Feminist/Gendered Critique of the Intersections of Race and Disability: The Australian Experience.' Paper presented to the Faculty of Education and the Department of Educational Studies, University of British Columbia, Vancouver, 23 June 2005. http://www.wwda.org.au/gendis2001.htm.

Meekosha, Helen. 'The Politics of Representation or the Politics of Presence: The Challenge of Disability.' In *Speaking for the People: Representation in Australian Politics*, edited by Marian Sawer and Gianni Zappala. Melbourne: Melbourne University Press, 2001.

Meekosha, Helen. 'Contextualizing Disability: Developing Southern/Global Theory.' Keynote paper presented at the Fourth Disability Studies Conference, Lancaster University, Bailrigg, 2–4 September 2008. http://www.wwda.org.au/meekosha2008.htm.

'Obituary: Elizabeth Hastings.' *Women With Disabilities Australia News* (15) (1998). http://www.wwda.org.au/issue15.htm.

Piper, Hugh, dir. *Riding the Gale*, [film]. Canberra: Ronin Films, Independent Productions International & Stormbringer Films.

PricewaterhouseCoopers (Australia). *Disability Expectations: Investing in a Better Life, A Stronger Australia Report*. Sydney: PricewaterhouseCoopers, 2011. http://www.pwc.com.au/industry/government/assets/disability-in-australia.pdf.

Productivity Commission. 'Disability Care and Support.' *Productivity Commission Inquiry Report* 54 (31 July 2011).

Ragg, Mark. 'The Quiet Enabler: Elizabeth Hasting, Australia's First Disability Discrimination Commissioner.' *The Bulletin*, 15 March 1994: 42.

'Review of Pins and Needles.' *The Age*, 23 June 1988: 14.

Salthouse, Sue. Interviewed by Nikki Henningham in the Women and Leadership in a Century of Australian Democracy Oral History Project, 20 May 2011. National Library of Australia, Canberra. http://nla.gov.au/nla.oh-vn5197761.

Salthouse, Sue. 'Brave New World: Is the Convention on the Rights of Persons with Disabilities a Blueprint for Utopia?' Paper presented at the Australian Federation of Disability Organisations Conference, Melbourne, May 2009. www.wwda.org.au/afdopapermay09.doc .

Sherwin, Jane. 'Leadership for Social Inclusion in the Lives of People with Disabilities.' *The International Journal of Leadership in Public Services* 6 (Supplement) (September 2010): 84–93.

Soldatic, Karen and Helen Meekosha. 'Disability and Neoliberal State Formations.' In *The Routledge Handbook of Disability Studies*, edited by Nick Watson, Carol Thomas and Alan Roulstone, 195–210. London: Routledge, 2012.

Tomas, Natalie. *'Double Disadvantage': Barriers Facing Women with Disabilities in Accessing Employment, Education and Training Opportunities—A Discussion Paper*. Disability Employment Action Centre, Melbourne, 1991.

Tomas, Natalie. Interviewed by Nikki Henningham and Rosemary Francis in the Women with Disabilities Project, 18 June 2010. National Library of Australia Oral History and Folklore Collection, ORAL TRC 6240/3. National Library of Australia, Canberra.

Where's the Give and Take? [film] Sydney: Stormbringer Film Productions, Creative Development Branch, Australian Film Commission, NSW Department of Youth and Community Services, 1981.

Women With Disabilities Australia (WWDA). *Annual Report 2009–2010*. Hobart: Women With Disabilities Australia, 2010. http://www.wwda.org. au/wwdarepts.htm.

Women With Disabilities Australia. Webpage. http://www.wwda.org.au/ background.htm.

Young, Stella. 'We're Not Here for Your Inspiration.' *Ramp Up*, ABC Online, 2 July 2012. http://www.abc.net.au/rampup/articles/2012/07/02/3537035. htm.

Part IV
Leadership and the professions

9. Female factory inspectors and leadership in early twentieth-century Australia

Joy Damousi[1]

In her memoirs published in 1921, the British factory inspector Adelaide Anderson recalled what drew her to the 'calling' of inspection. The 'idealizing powers of youth … embarking on a calling that involved conduct of legal proceedings and much other technical knowledge of an entirely novel kind for women of that day, counted for much', she recalled. There were also the 'authority and powers to enquire into and enforce remedies for wrong conditions, or to persuade sympathetic employers to provide amenities that the law could not enforce', which were other appealing aspects of the role. It was unusual for a woman to assume the position, and the appearance of a female inspector immediately drew surprise and comment.[2]

In the context of the rapidly shifting industrial and urban landscapes of the late nineteenth and early twentieth centuries, the role of the female factory inspector invites an analysis of the concept of 'leadership' within the framework of administrative leadership. Some of the women who occupied these roles viewed their position as an opportunity to radicalise the workplace and bring about drastic social change through their activities, while others believed the task of the female inspector was a more modest and reformist one. A contrast in styles could be seen in the work and careers of three Australian female factory inspectors—Agnes Milne, Margaret Cuthbertson and Annie Duncan—all of whom worked as factory inspectors when the position was in its infancy. All of them expressed a vision for better industrial conditions for women and demonstrated considerable administrative flair in attempting to achieve it. Although Duncan and Cuthbertson did not see themselves as leading working-class women or as spokeswomen on their behalf—unlike Milne—they were effective in advocating an improvement to their conditions. In doing so, they were raising concerns about the appalling industrial conditions of working-class women that men within the union movement did so ineffectually in the early decades of the twentieth century. In this regard, however militant or otherwise their application of the law, the female factory inspectors were advocating measures to support women's involvement in waged work, changes

---

1   The University of Melbourne.
2   Adelaide Mary Anderson, *Woman in the Factory: An Administrative Adventure 1893–1921* (London: John Murray, 1921), 1.

to which the male-dominated union movement was indifferent, or paid only lip-service; some unionists feared the competition of lower-paid women workers. In the absence of male unionists' effective intervention, state-supported female factory inspectors were in a unique position to take a particularly constructive role in improving women's working conditions.[3]

By adopting the perspective of administrative leadership embedded within an organisational structure, this chapter argues that the position of the factory inspector points to how leadership can be understood within a bureaucratic framework. While my focus is on particular factory inspectors, the chief aim is to examine how they *administered* the *Factory Acts* as a form of leadership. This approach follows recent literature that considers the interplay of processes within administrative structures, and explores how influence within these structures is exercised.[4]

This chapter also aims to position the meaning of leadership within a specific historical context. While the literature on women and leadership is now voluminous, little of it considers notions of leadership historically, or as a category that changes in meaning over time with respect to how specific historical circumstances shaped, defined and contested that meaning. This is especially the case in relation to women, for whom the leadership literature stresses contemporary strategies of management, diverse models of effective leadership, attempts to elevate women into leadership positions and how women leaders can effectively implement workplace change.[5] As some historians have noted, leadership defined exclusively by traditional notions of power within hierarchical organisations is not a useful model when considering women's historical role and participation in society. In order to capture the diversity and complexity of women's roles in a range of activities in the past, a historically grounded definition that takes into account the opportunities available to women, the diversity of activities they undertook and a more flexible definition of leadership is more appropriate to understanding the role of women in attempting to bring about social change. Equally, while broader definitions of leadership have emerged in the leadership literature, historians continue to define and understand leadership in more conventional terms, largely in relation

---

3   See Raelene Frances, *The Politics of Work: Gender and Labour in Victoria, 1880–1939* (Cambridge: Cambridge University Press, 1993); Patricia Grimshaw, 'The "Equals and Comrades of Men"? Tocsin and "the Woman Question"', in *Debutante Nation: Feminism Contests the 1890s*, eds Susan Magarey, Sue Rowley and Susan Sheridan (Sydney: Allen & Unwin, 1993), 100–13.

4   See Amanda Sinclair's essay in this volume; Mary Uhl-Bien, Russ Marion and Bill McKelvey, 'Complexity Leadership Theory: Shifting Leadership from the Industrial Age to the Knowledge Era', in *Leadership, Gender, and Organisation: Issues in Business Ethics*, eds P. H. Werhane and M. Painter-Moralnd (London: Springer, 2011), 128–31.

5   See, for instance, Barbara Kellerman and Deborah L. Rhode, eds, *Women and Leadership: The State of Play and Strategies for Change* (San Francisco: Wiley, 2007); Jean Lau Chin, Bernice Lott and Janis Sanchez-Hucles, *Women and Leadership: Transforming Visions and Diverse Voices* (Oxford: Blackwell, 2007); Dayle Smith, *Women at Work: Leadership for the Next Century* (New Jersey: Prentice Hall, 2000).

to political leaders and leaders of institutions or social movements. These studies capture a vital part of Australia's political history, but women who were not engaged in overtly public acts of leadership are often rendered invisible in such historical accounts.[6]

Framing the history of female factory inspectors in this way offers a further departure point from the historiography of factory inspectors. This work has largely focused on the relationship of female inspectors to the women's movement and cross-class encounters[7] and to their role in anti-sweating reform.[8] While these perspectives offer key insights into the way in which the role was undertaken in Britain and New Zealand, the Australian context of female factory inspection provides fertile material for considering the diversity of approaches adopted by different factory inspectors as well as an opportunity to explore the historically specific definition of 'leadership' at the turn of the twentieth century.

I will briefly sketch out what factory inspection involved and then turn to how three pioneer women factory inspectors sought to adopt different approaches to their obligations as leading administrators.

The origins of factory inspection

Factory inspectors were appointed by State governments between the late nineteenth and early twentieth centuries, often as a response to investigations that exposed the abysmal working conditions and subsistence wages of workers in factories and workshops in cities around Australia. Their role was to inspect these places of work and report on the conditions therein. In many cases inspectors had broad powers and were expected to enforce the various State acts governing factories and working conditions. Given the reports of factory inspectors often formed the basis of investigations into working conditions, especially those of working women, there is scope to explore the role they played in representing working-class experience.

There are three significant shifts in this history that took place during the nineteenth and early twentieth centuries. The first was the early Victorian

---

6 For recent works that look at women in prominent politics, see Deborah Brennan and Louise Chappell, eds, 'No Fit Place for Women?' Women in NSW Politics, 1856–2006 (Sydney: UNSW Press, 2006); Madeline Grey, Challenging Women: Towards Equality in the Parliament of Victoria (Melbourne: Australian Scholarly Publishing, 2009); Marian Sawer and Gail Radford, Making Women Count: A History of the Women's Electoral Lobby in Australia (Sydney: UNSW Press, 2009).

7 Ruth Livesey, 'The Politics of Work: Feminism, Professionalisation and Women Inspectors of Factories and Workshops', Women's History Review 13(2) (2004): 233–62.

8 Barbara Harrison and Melanie Nolan, 'Reflections in Colonial Glass? Women Factory Inspectors in Britain and New Zealand 1893–1921', Women's History Review 13(2) (2004): 263–88.

legislation in Britain that was established during the 1830s to 1860s and that included inspectorates of factories, prisons, schools, mines and railways. Arising out of a need for social reform to address the problems of industrialisation and urbanisation, this legislation established a mechanism whereby inspectors could intervene in certain activities to ensure a range of requirements was being met.[9]

The second aspect of inspection—that of factory legislation within Australia— was established about 50 years later. During the 1880s and 1890s, pressure was exerted from predominately the Protestant churches and the emerging labour movement to appoint factory inspectors to allow them to enter premises and provide a reporting mechanism.[10] In both Britain and Australia these legislative reforms were designed to protect women and children from the horrors of industrial exploitation.

Finally, from 1905, the federal system of arbitration that was established in Australia ensured that not only women and children were protected, but also all workers. In South Australia, the Industrial Court retained powers of enforcement for inspectors and was responsible for administering laws relating to industrial issues.[11] Broad powers of inspection remained a central aspect of the court's jurisdiction as inspectors could 'enter any place, or premises … wherein … any industry is carried on … and inspect and view any work, material, machinery, article, matter, or thing whatsoever … and interrogate any person … in respect of … any matter or thing of which the Court has cognisance'.[12]

The trend of appointing public female factory inspectors emerged at a remarkable time.

First, at the turn of the twentieth century, factory inspection was part of the growth of state bureaucracy and public administration. As Hacking has argued, when new kinds of people came to be counted during the nineteenth century, factory inspectorates in England and Wales 'created … the official form of the class structure of industrial societies'.[13] Counting created new ways for 'people to be'. It was not the case that people

> spontaneously come to fit their categories. When factory inspectors in England and Wales went to the mills, they found … people … loosely

---

9   Gerald Rhodes, *Inspectorates in British Government: Law Enforcement and Standards of Efficiency* (Sydney: Allen & Unwin, 1981), 1–3; Arthur J. Taylor, *Laissez-Faire and State Intervention in Nineteenth-Century Britain* (London: Macmillan, 1972), 56.

10   Wilfrid Prest, Kerrie Round and Carol Fort, eds, *The Wakefield Companion to South Australian History* (Adelaide: Wakefield Press, 2001), 526–7.

11   George Anderson, *Fixation of Wages in Australia* (Melbourne: Macmillan/Melbourne University Press, 1929), 98–9.

12   Ibid., 100.

13   Ian Hacking, 'How Should We Do the History of Statistics?', in *The Foucault Effect*, eds G. Burchett, C. Gordon and P. Miller (Chicago: Chicago University Press, 1991), 183.

sorted according to tasks and wages. But when they had finished their reports, mill-hands had precise ways in which to work, and the owner has a clear set of concepts about how to employ workers according to the ways in which he was obliged to classify them.[14]

Second, in the period between 1890 and 1914, women's place in the industrial world underwent a dramatic shift. As manufacturing increased so too did women's place within it. During this time, the opportunities for women in the paid workforce had expanded considerably. In 1913, together with Henrietta McGowan, Cuthbertson published a woman's guide to employment opportunities and working conditions. In *Woman's Work*, the authors aimed to 'set before the prospective worker the ways and means by which she can earn an honest livelihood, together with some idea of remuneration she may expect to receive as a return for her investment of time, study, work and money'.[15] The growth of the factory system in the 1880s and 1890s saw increasing numbers of women enter into the system, especially single women. Low wages, long hours and poor working conditions characterised labour in these factories.[16] 'Sweating' became an increasing problem in these years, and inspectors were particularly vigilant in attempting to eradicate it. Women's entry into the factory system increased dramatically during the federation period, as the belief that only a woman could attend to the needs of female workers gained currency.[17] The increased incidence of sweating further strengthened the case to specifically employ a female inspector.[18]

Third, the role of female factory inspector offered an opportunity for women to develop a career in a new profession that was evolving. Prior to this, women had been active in 'inspecting' in other ways. Inspection by women dates back to the early part of the nineteenth century in Britain when upper-class and middle-class female reformers 'inspected' the workhouses of the poor, and assisted them with charity, philanthropy and 'rescue work'.[19] Social reformers such as Henry Mayhew and others began the scientific approach to such inspection through their reports and in documenting their findings.[20] Philanthropy and charity amongst middle-class women were mirrored in Australia and were particularly

---

14   Ian Hacking, 'Making Up People', in *Reconstructing Individualism: Autonomy, Individuality, and the Self in Western Thought*, eds T. C. Heller, M. Sosna and D. E. Wellbery (Stanford: Stanford University Press, 1986), 223.

15   Henrietta C. McGowan and Margaret Cuthbertson, *Woman's Work* (Melbourne: Thomas C. Lothian, 1913).

16   Frances, *The Politics of Work*, 17–20.

17   Harrison Ord, 'Chief Inspector of Factories, to Under Secretary', 24 January 1894, VPRS 3992, Unit 787, Item X 94/5122, Public Records Office, Melbourne.

18   *Victorian Government Gazette*, 3rd Supplement (13) (1920), 107.

19   Olive Banks, *Faces of Feminism: A Study of Feminism as a Social Movement* (Oxford: Martin Robertson, 1981–82), 15–19; Barbara Caine, *Victorian Feminists* (Oxford: Oxford University Press, 1992–93), 105–8.

20   Judith R. Walkowitz, *City of Dreadful Delight: Narratives of Sexual Danger in Late-Victorian London* (London: Virago, 1992), 19.

evident from the mid nineteenth century. Ladies' benevolent societies attempted to assist the poor, particularly by visiting districts.[21] 'Inspecting' was deemed to be an appropriate form of political and public activity for middle-class female reformers involved in charity work during the nineteenth century. 'Lady supervisors' assumed considerable power in their supervisorial role, and the reformers perceived of their role as akin to professionals such as medical officers and official inspectors.[22] The systematic inspection of prisons was a procedure that was actively promoted by female reformers such as Elizabeth Fry.[23] Factory 'inspecting' derived from this tradition, for whilst it signified an important entree of women into the industrial field, it did so in terms similar to that of the premise of earlier female 'inspectors': that they would bring a feminine quality to a social problem concerning women. There developed a close relationship between factory inspection and philanthropy. The professionalisation of the practice of inspection was part of the growth of government during the nineteenth century. It came into being to regulate the increasing numbers of people in the factories, or enterprises, which had expanded. While its origins date back to the eighteenth century, it was not until the mid to late nineteenth century that it was implemented systematically.[24]

In occupying these positions, female factory inspectors were unusual given the paucity of women in public positions of responsibility and embarking on a career within the embryonic structure of public administration. Margaret Cuthbertson, whose background was in government bureaucracy, saw her role as a social reformer. She brought a feminist sensibility to it, coming from a background of agitating for women's reforms. Agnes Milne used the information-gathering exercise and observation techniques to actively and overtly agitate for social reforms. She took the additional step of interpreting workers' experiences and so exposed herself to accusations of bias, inadvertently entering into what became a battlefield of interpretation between opponents of sweating and those who did not believe it existed. Annie Duncan was neither a proclaimed labour activist nor a feminist; she prided herself on what she saw as a professional undertaking her duties as an inspector, which did not involve adopting an overt political position. But while she did not declare a commitment to an ideological label, Duncan nevertheless was a staunch advocate of change to women's working conditions. Within the administrative structures in which they operated, each of these women was part of a process that aimed to better the conditions for women workers through their regular visits to factories and the reports and

---

21 Penny Russell, *'A Wish of Distinction': Colonial Gentility and Femininity* (Melbourne: Melbourne University Press, 1994), 192.

22 Jane Finnis, 'Louisa Twining and the Workhouse Visiting Society' (MA thesis, Department of History, University of Melbourne, 1995), 39–40.

23 See Elizabeth Gurney Fry, *Observations on the Visiting, Superintendence, and Government of Female Prisoners* (London: 1827).

24 Rhodes, *Inspectorates in British Government*, 2.

recommendations they documented. Leadership was demonstrated, I argue, through administering the *Factory Acts* in ways that aimed to improve women's working conditions and highlight areas where improvement was necessary. I will now turn to explore how Cuthbertson, Milne and Duncan achieved this within the administrative structures in which they worked.

Margaret Cuthbertson was appointed as female factory inspector in 1894—the first woman to be appointed to the position in Australia. Cuthbertson was born in 1864. She had worked in the factory system before entering the Victorian Public Service in July 1888 as a telephone switchboard attendant in the postmaster's general department. She joined the public service at the age of twenty-four, earning a salary of £66 per annum.[25] With the introduction of the *Factories and Shops Act* in 1885 and its application a year later, factory inspectors were appointed for the first time.[26] Victoria was the first to appoint a female inspector. Other States soon followed, when Augusta Zadow was appointed in South Australia in 1895, and Annie Duncan in New South Wales in 1897.[27]

Defining the work in Victoria

Cuthbertson brought the organisational skills she had acquired as an active feminist to her job as factory inspector. Cuthbertson's experience in the public service led to a long association with the Victorian Women's Public Servants' Association. Cuthbertson had a longstanding commitment to feminist issues. As a member of the executive of the National Council of Women (NCW), she was active in various subcommittees. The work Cuthbertson undertook on many of these subcommittees involved a form of 'inspection'. One such subcommittee lobbied for the appointment of police 'matrons' in city and suburban lockups.[28]

The report of the subcommittee to appoint female police recommended that the conditions at the lockups be improved, and that bail be refused for prostitutes to keep them off the streets from 7 am to 7 pm.[29] The need to 'protect' women echoes Cuthbertson's other occupation—that of the protection of women in industry.[30] 'Inspecting' thus became a central role of the organisation and of Cuthbertson's

---

25 'Report of the Chief Inspector of Factories, Work-Rooms and Shops' [hereinafter CIF], *Victorian Parliamentary Papers* [hereinafter VPP], 3rd Supplement (17) (1894), 105.

26 Raelene Frances, 'Ord, Harrison (1862–1910)', *Australian Dictionary of Biography. Volume 11* (Canberra: National Centre of Biography, The Australian National University, 1988), 90.

27 Christine Finnimore, *A Woman of Difference: Augusta Zadow and the 1894 Factories Act* (Adelaide: Workcover, 1995), 19; Kay Daniels, 'Duncan, Annie Jane (1858–1943)', *Australian Dictionary of Biography. Volume 8* (Canberra: National Centre of Biography, The Australian National University, 1981), 366.

28 *Woman's Sphere*, 10 May 1903: 301.

29 Ada Norris, *Champions of the Impossible: A History of the National Council of Women of Victoria 1902–1977* (Melbourne: The Hawthorn Press, 1978), 12.

30 See ibid., 301–3.

activities. As well as practising it themselves, they advocated the appointment of more inspectors in various areas. In 1904, the NCW argued for the need for the appointment of women inspectors to monitor child welfare, and two years later, supported the *Infant Life Protection Act* to maximise protection.[31] The NCW agitated for the appointment of inspectors. In 1909, it was reported that a 'deputation waited on the Chief Secretary to ask that, when new inspectors are appointed to visit boarded-out children, they shall be trained nurses, and especially qualified'.[32] In regards to education, a letter was sent in 1913 'asking for the appointment of women inspectors in that department'.[33]

Cuthbertson's approach was gradual and pragmatic, working within the administrative process. Her aim was social change, but she endeavoured to implement it within the confines of her position. That is not to say that she was not committed to reform on a variety of issues. Cuthbertson protected the rights of women workers and attempted to defend their conditions. The situation of women being retrenched once they reached a certain age was an injustice she highlighted in her reports.

> If a girl knows that her wages depend on gaining experience, adaptability and expertness at her trade she will endeavour to acquire them … but if she knows that when she attains a certain age she must go because her wages must be increased—Well! why should she get old before there is any absolute necessity to do so?[34]

That women were being paid according to age, rather than experience, was problematic.[35]

Low wages was another major concern. Dressmakers came in for particular scrutiny. 'Employers are always complaining of the dearth of good workers', Cuthbertson reported, 'but the low wages paid should be sufficient reason to deter any girl who required to earn her living from going into it'.[36] Many employers she found complied with the regulations, 'but there are others who take the fullest advantage possible of the fact that they are not protected by the Act to work them long hours, and refuse to give them a half-holiday'.[37]

Cuthbertson saw the benefit of work, when it came to training character, and she was at times sanctimonious when judging her charges.

---

31 Helen E. Gillan, *A Brief History of the National Council of Women of Victoria, 1900–1945* (Melbourne: NCW, 1944), 13–14.
32 Ibid., 16.
33 Ibid., 19.
34 CIF, year ended 31 December 1901, *VPP* 2 (1902), 22.
35 CIF, year ended 31 December 1909, *VPP* 2 (1910), 14.
36 CIF, year ended 31 December 1903, *VPP* 2 (1904), 16.
37 CIF, year ended 31 December 1904, *VPP* 3 (1905), 42.

In the absence of home training and discipline which, unfortunately, so many girls are entirely without, the uniform hours, restraint under which they are placed, regularity of work, and association with older steadier girls, have a decidedly improving effect upon young girls coming into factories, and tend to the formation of a character at once self-restrained and industrious.[38]

She was also critical of other girls, and expressed her frustration with them. Dressmakers, she claimed, 'had neither ambition nor incentive to improve they have been made to understand that as the rate of pay prescribed is progressive with years of service at the trade, they must progress accordingly and make themselves worth the money if they are to be retained'.[39] The argument that women were replacing men was a constant cry during this time, and Cuthbertson is at pains to impress that this is not the case. After commenting on the 'increase of women in the various trades under the Acts' in 1906, she emphasised that it 'has been contended that because of the greater increase of women and girls in registered factories, they are taking the place of men, but I do not think these figures bear out this statement'.[40] For Cuthbertson, leadership entailed administering the *Factory Acts* in ways that aimed to bring about effective and significant social change.

A radical agenda

Agnes Milne agreed with this objective but her style was a very different one, which reflected an alternative way of bringing about change. Milne redefined the parameters of factory inspection by infusing the role with a radical agenda. Milne politicised the position of factory inspection by acting as a trade union advocate and radical social reformer in her capacity as inspector. She did this through her individual inspector's reports, which could be highly influential in provoking debate and awareness of industrial issues. Milne attempted to exert considerable individual power in the way she represented the conditions of the working classes, and used the information she gathered through her work to promote radical causes. By repeatedly raising the problem of sweating in her reports and in strenuously arguing for this working experience to be fully documented, Milne used her position to advance the rights of the woman worker. Milne was an inspector turned working-class advocate, who used the opportunities available to her within an administrative structure to attempt to directly influence social change.

---

38 CIF, year ended 31 December 1895, *VPP* 2 (1896), 7.
39 CIF, year ended 31 December 1905, *VPP* 2 (1906), 19.
40 CIF, year ended 31 December 1906, *VPP* 2 (1907), 53.

Agnes Milne was appointed female factory inspector on 22 July 1896. During the 1890s, sweating became a central concern for feminist and labour activists throughout Australia. It involved usually female labourers undertaking work in their own homes; thus employers saved on overheads and did not have to comply with State regulations governing wages and conditions. The prevalence of sweating provided the motivation for legislation to regulate the labour market.[41]

In a series of articles written in 1899 and published in the *Journal of Agriculture and Industry*, Milne called for the end of sweating through regulation and the *Factory Act*s and for work to be performed in factories rather than workshops and homes where they could not be regulated. It was through 'judicious legislation' that she believed 'the toiling masses, both male and female', would be emancipated.[42] Milne ensured that employers conformed to the conditions laid out in the *Factory Act*s. Her reports indicate a meticulous and scrupulous approach to ensuring that employers conformed to government regulations of 'hours of work, cleanliness, sanitary facilities, ventilation and light in workshops and factories'.[43] In addition, however, she also agitated against, publicised and politicised the cause of sweating. Taking such an overt political and at times militant stance was unusual for a factory inspector at this time. Unlike Cuthbertson, Milne came through working-class ranks and radical politics. She used her position to promote alternative political programs and workers' rights in ways Cuthbertson would have deemed inappropriate.

Milne had no interest in providing a female sensibility to the inspector's job—in fact, she at times accused women workers of indifference and of being complicit in their own oppression. How did she view her position from a so-called 'woman's standpoint'? The real enemies of women workers were the women themselves, she argued.

> So long as there are women (married or unmarried) eager and able to take work to their homes, and do it in the intervals of another business, domestic service, or home duties, the true workers will never disentangle themselves from the vicious circle in which low wages tend to bad work, and bad work compels low wages.[44]

---

41 Stuart Macintyre, *Winners and Losers: The Pursuit of Social Justice in Australian History* (Sydney: Allen & Unwin, 1985), 43.

42 Agnes Milne, 'Woman's Work and Wages', *Journal of Agriculture and Industry* (October 1899): 343.

43 Helen Jones, *In Her Own Name: A History of Women in South Australia from 1836* (Adelaide: Wakefield Press, 1986), 71.

44 Agnes Milne, 'Working of the Factory Act', *Journal of Agriculture and Industry* ii(4) (November 1898): 387.

She was disappointed with the indifference of the workers she was protecting: 'I am of [the] opinion that it is in a great measure the fault of the workers themselves, who clamor for cheap bargains, not caring how little their fellow workers get for their labour.'[45]

What Milne brought to inspection as an activist in an official position with labour sympathies marked her out from her middle-class counterparts. This was most apparent in the way in which the category of 'outdoor worker' was especially discussed through Milne's reports. She did not invent the category, but her discussion of it within her inspection reports provided the framework from which she argued for reform. The various activities she identified to be within this category and her views of this assumed a form of representation that, as we shall see, offended others. What were represented as 'facts' and 'interpretation' became blurred in Milne's reports. Although inspection was meant to be a *subjective* activity of reportage, she used it to construct knowledge in a particular way about health and safety and working conditions, which promoted her cause. As Gerald Rhodes observes, inspection in the late nineteenth century involved 'persuasion rather than prosecution, and ... prevention of breaches of the law rather than their detection'. But Milne saw it as her role not only to scrutinise and assess working conditions and to 'promote the underlying purposes of the legislation',[46] but also to 'emancipate' the workers.

Milne's crusading zeal to extend the parameters of her inspection reflected her belief that the aim of her work was to have 'all wrongs righted, as far as it is in the power of inspectors to do so'. Inevitably there was growing disquiet that Milne was taking matters into her own hands and conducting inspection business beyond her position.[47]

Milne interpreted her administrative role in terms that attempted to push the boundaries of her position as factory inspector. She endeavoured to administer the *Factory Acts* in ways that demonstrated a forceful and highly politicised process of leadership. In this regard, her style of operating within her position was in dramatic contrast with that of Annie Duncan, who eschewed political ideology and defined her role in striking and contrasting terms.

New female professionalism

Annie Duncan came from a background that did not overtly include any desire to serve other causes. For her, it was through her professional identity that she sought to offer a form of 'leadership': a 'pioneer career woman'. It was within

---

45 'Reports of Inspectors of Factories', *Proceedings of the Parliament South Australia* 2(i)(54) (1897).
46 Rhodes, *Inspectorates in British Government*, 64–5.
47 'CIF to the Minister of Industry', 7 January 1897, vol. 1, State Records of South Australia, Adelaide.

this identity, and in promoting the case of how a single, professional women could bring about social change within an administrative structure, that we could see evidence of a factory inspector administering and monitoring the law within the rules and regulations of the position of factory inspector in professional, rather than necessarily overtly political, terms.

Born in 1858 in Port Adelaide, Duncan inherited a small amount of money from her physician father, who died in 1878. The depression of the 1890s had an impact on her fortunes, and she travelled to London, where she met Lucy Deane, one of the first factory inspectors. There she discovered a network of kindred spirits and connected with the leading factory reformers of the day: Rose Squire, Adelaide Anderson and Beatrice and Sidney Webb. She undertook courses with the National Health Society and the Sanitary Institute. In April 1894, she passed the examination for inspector of nuisances and was appointed to the South Kensington district. Her appointment was not renewed and she then returned to Australia.

Duncan was appointed factory inspector in February 1897 in the labour and industry branch of the NSW Department of Public Instruction under the *Factories and Shops Act* of 1896. In 1912, she was promoted to inspector, a position she occupied until she retired in 1918.

Her background was not in the labour or women's movements, but sprang instead from a Christian conviction for social justice. A committed Anglican, Duncan was a member of the Women's Auxiliary of the Australian Board of Missions and the Girls' Friendly Society. She was a founder of the Business and Professional Women's Club of Sydney and a member of the Women's Club. After travelling in Australia and overseas during the 1920s, she lived in Adelaide in 1930, where she joined several societies and clubs: the Adelaide Music Salon, the Alliance Française, the Victoria League and the Lyceum Club. Duncan died in 1943.[48]

Duncan's leadership as a factory inspector encompassed the values of fairness, equity and transparency, rather than radical upheaval, but she could be firm and assertive in her application of the industrial laws she was expected to administer and apply to a range of issues and circumstances. The examples below demonstrate a form of leadership that embraced advocating social change within the bureaucracy.

The issue of pay for both male and female workers alerted the need for reform:

> Is it not clearly wrong that any girl, or any growing boy, however strong, can legally be called upon to work such excessive hours … Payment

---

48   Daniels, 'Duncan, Annie Jane (1858–1943)'.

of overtime is very frequently held over, in some instances for weeks, and in the majority of cases no allowance either by way of advance or addition is made for tea money. This is rather hard on girls and boys drawing low wages, who have little or no money in their pockets to meet emergencies.[49]

Duncan staunchly opposed the view that women were taking men's jobs and argued that the factory system had in fact created a system of deskilling that meant women were often more adept at factory tasks. As long as they were paid less than men, they would be favoured by employers. Women were also entitled to earn a living respectfully, and not rely on men or the degradation of the factory system. 'I trust that the day will come', she wrote in *The Public Service Journal* in 1904, 'when the women who do not marry will still be able to support themselves with dignity and success, but in ways better suited to their womanly powers and constitution'.[50]

Forming a constant theme in her reports were the dirty, unhygienic and overcrowded working conditions in Sydney's factories. In 1902, Duncan observed how one employer did not recognise the danger of heat in the bakehouse, where women were working directly above the ovens, which made the areas very hot and dangerous. This 'abnormal heat', she observed, should be regarded as 'unsuitable for young growing girls'.[51] Working conditions that Duncan identified were in need of urgent attention included the close proximity of stables to shops and workrooms; that pure and cold drinking water be made available for drinking purposes; and that adequate wash basins be installed. These conditions, Duncan asserted, could be addressed through 'common sense' on the part of the employers and 'discipline' on that of the employees. In the case of the latter, the issue of washbasins in otherwise 'well-ordered factories' was that workers waste time at the basins and that it presents an issue of hygiene.[52]

Furthermore, Duncan addressed the issue of seating arrangements for workers, especially for shop assistants. There was resistance to this, as in 'some cases seats have been put in and then removed when it was supposed that the vigilance of the inspector was relaxing'.[53] On this issue, she argued that employers were resistant and so pointed to the need for the inspector to have a wider role:

[I]f this provision is to be effectively enforced, that the sections dealing with the matter should be so amended as to give the visiting inspectors,

---

49   Ibid., 11.
50   Annie Duncan, 'Woman's Place in the Industrial World', *The Public Service Journal* 10 (November 1904).
51   'Report on the Working of the Factories and Shops Act', *NSW Votes and Proceedings* 3 (1903), 12.
52   Ibid.
53   Ibid., 13.

and not the employer or employee the right to determine what form of seat shall be considered satisfactory, and what position such seat shall occupy, so as to be really available for the use of the shop assistants.

Duncan believed that whatever the apparent statements of the employers, there was an expectation that shop assistants would stand the entire time. She undertook her own investigations into this matter:

> In a shop in which seats are provided, I heard girls complain of the fatigue to which their tired faces gave testimony, and when, my identity being unknown, I asked them why they did not sit down for a few minutes if they had seats, they laughed at the idea of supposing that they would thus venture to bring down upon themselves the remark of the powers that be.[54]

Duncan's reports are a detailed chronicle of social change in the workplace and especially in manufacturing. In 1904, she argued that major shifts in manufacturing were in fact in the introduction of technologies: 'Much has lately been said on the supposed displacement of men by women, but I venture to think that no such generalization should hastily be made, and that the statistical returns and the experience of this Department do not so far bear out this theory.'

This was because men and women mainly undertook separate tasks. In the tailoring trade, Duncan astutely noticed:

> The real conflict of interests, the true comparison, lies between the hand-worker and the power machine, and in proportion as real factory work increases, so will power machinists increase in number and the hand-workers decrease; and so will comparatively larger numbers of women and children at lower wages be employed, because of the many and minutely sub-divided processes which ensue.[55]

She concluded that 'the increase in occupation for women is chiefly found to be growing; firstly, in those industries which are their proper domain, and next in those trades in which power machinery is causing a redistribution of labour'. The introduction of machinery and new technologies was demanding new responsibilities of employers, many of whom were not taking these seriously. This was apparent in the case of accidents: 'The employer, then, has everything to gain and little to lose, except in cases of flagrant neglect, by the use of machinery; while the workman has little to gain, and stands to lose.'[56]

---

54 Ibid.
55 'Report on the Working of the Factories and Shops Act', *NSW Votes and Proceedings* 4 (1904), 11.
56 Ibid., 12.

Another issue Duncan investigated through her administrative role was that of child labour. Duncan investigated the case of children under fourteen years of age. Children regularly went on their own initiative to make an application at a factory. Parents were often 'easy-going' in their attitude towards children working in factories instead of attending school. Why were children so eager to work in the factories?

The point that came out prominently in the matter was the fact that the rejected children were all below par in some way, in health, education or discipline, and that they preferred the 'go' and excitement of factory life, with its comparative emancipation and the pride of wage-earning, to the individual mental effort of school life and its strict discipline. There was very little evidence that parents as a whole were anxious to curtail the period of school attendance, but a good deal of general 'slackness' was apparent.[57]

The issue of children workers was also discussed in the context of the employment of underaged children as fruit pickers. In the past, permission had been given for children between the ages of thirteen and fourteen, but those under thirteen had also slipped into the system. The danger Duncan identified was that

> when tired of stoning fruit, [they would] slip away to an older friend or companion, and try their hand on some simple machine that looks easy to work and interesting to experiment upon, and when the factory is working at high pressure, foremen and forewomen are apt to lose sight of the small people.[58]

This was an inappropriate workplace for children:

> In any case, a factory working at full pressure is no place for children, and the latest award, which raises their pay out of all proportion to their value, has now the desired effect of shutting them out from this particular occupation. Elderly women now do the work of fruit-picking, and their employers consider the results more satisfactory.[59]

The official appointment to factories of medical women was another area in which Duncan agitated. After an incident involving an injury to the hand of a young woman, Duncan believed there should be 'a medical woman officially appointed for work in the factories'. 'For the sake of themselves and of their offspring, our working girls have a right to the very best expert advice that can be brought to bear upon their working conditions.' In time, she argued,

---

57   'Report on the Working of the Factories and Shops Act', *NSW Votes and Proceedings* 2 (1909), 19.
58   'Report on the Working of the Factories and Shops Act', *NSW Votes and Proceedings* 5 (1914–15), 25.
59   Ibid.

the public conscience will be roused to insist that the conditions of women's work shall in every avenue of public life be established on a basis better fitted to their own natural constitution, instead of being fitted into the gaps left in the pattern, and originally cut out for men.[60]

Duncan joined social reformers of the day who argued against the factory system in relation to healthy motherhood:

[I]t was much to be desired that this State should give its cordial and strong support to the principle of securing to women, the future mothers of Australian people, the unbroken rest which is so essential to prevent breakdown of bodily strength and nervous constitution ... For the working woman whose energies are by the nature of things devoted to the making of a hard living and to whom ... luxuries are forbidden, there remain broken health and lowered vitality, and all the other conditions which tell against happy and healthy motherhood.[61]

It was Duncan's pride in her professionalism as an administrator that she brought to the role that she emphasised when she finally left the position:

Whether from temperamental or physical causes, we all have our limitations, and I can only say that at least I have tried to do my duty conscientiously and without favour. It remains for those who are younger and more vigorous to carry on the work in the light of modern ideas and knowledge.[62]

Duncan's administrative reports illuminate the working conditions of women workers and more generally the condition of industrial workers at a time of dramatic social and industrial changes within the Australian workplace. These reports reflect an administrator implementing social change through her activities, which involved identifying and acting on improving the conditions of working-class women. Undertaking and performing these tasks represent a form of leadership, as they were influential acts advocating for and resulting in social and industrial change.

Conclusion

In this chapter I have argued that through an examination of the activities of three female factory inspectors the notion of women's administrative leadership can be explored historically. Duncan, Cuthbertson and Milne were all appointed

---

60   Ibid., 28.

61   'Report on the Working of the Factories and Shops Act', *NSW Votes and Proceedings* 1908 2 (2nd Session), 22.

62   'Report on the Working of the Factories and Shops Act', *NSW Votes and Proceedings* 1918 3, 20.

to their jobs as factory inspectors at a time of rapid changes of industrialisation and urbanisation. The position came with considerable responsibility and direct influence, for administering the *Factory Acts* could have a major impact on highlighting and improving the conditions of working women. The three women discussed in this chapter administered the role in different ways, but all aimed to improve women's working conditions, which was not always a high priority within the male-dominated unions. Milne's approach could be characterised as one of a radical crusade to use the position to politicise working-class women. Cuthbertson was inspired by a feminist commitment to the improvement of women's position in society more generally. This was not a sentiment she shared with Duncan, who was not politically motivated but who believed her role was to administer the *Acts* as professionally as she could. For Duncan, it was the pioneering role she believed she was playing in paving the way for the independent career woman and making a distinctive contribution to women's place in society.

The history of female factory inspectors not only points to an example of women assuming positions of authority and responsibility. It also suggests ways that they exercised leadership by promoting an improvement of industrial conditions for women within a bureaucratic and administrative framework. In doing so, it argues for a more flexible and historically grounded understanding of leadership, which encompasses the opportunities available to women at a given time, the diversity of activities they undertook and the positions they adopted within their roles towards bringing about social change.

References

Anderson, Adelaide Mary. *Woman in the Factory: An Administrative Adventure 1893–1921*. London: John Murray, 1921.

Anderson, George. *Fixation of Wages in Australia*. Melbourne: Macmillan/Melbourne University Press, 1929.

Banks, Olive. *Faces of Feminism: A Study of Feminism as a Social Movement*. Oxford: Martin Robertson, 1981–82.

Brennan, Deborah and Louise Chappell, eds. *'No Fit Place for Women?' Women in NSW Politics, 1856–2006*. Sydney: UNSW Press, 2006.

Caine, Barbara. *Victorian Feminists*. Oxford: Oxford University Press, 1992–93.

Chin, Jean Lau, Bernice Lott and Janis Sanchez-Hucles. *Women and Leadership: Transforming Visions and Diverse Voices*. Oxford: Blackwell, 2007.

'CIF to the Minister of Industry'. 7 January 1897, vol. 1. State Records of South Australia, Adelaide.

Daniels, Kay. 'Duncan, Annie Jane (1858–1943).' *Australian Dictionary of Biography, Volume 8*. Canberra: National Centre of Biography, The Australian National University, 1981.

Duncan, Annie. 'Woman's Place in the Industrial World.' *The Public Service Journal* 10 (November 1904): 13–14.

Finnimore, Christine. *A Woman of Difference: Augusta Zadow and the 1894 Factories Act*. Adelaide: Workcover, 1995.

Finnis, Jane. 'Louisa Twining and the Workhouse Visiting Society.' MA thesis, Department of History, University of Melbourne, 1995.

Frances, Raelene. 'Ord, Harrison (1862–1910).' *Australian Dictionary of Biography*. *Volume 11*. Canberra: National Centre of Biography, The Australian National University, 1988.

Frances, Raelene. *The Politics of Work: Gender and Labour in Victoria, 1880–1939*. Cambridge: Cambridge University Press, 1993.

Gillan, Helen E. *A Brief History of the National Council of Women of Victoria, 1900–1945*. Melbourne: NCW, 1944.

Grey, Madeline. *Challenging Women: Towards Equality in the Parliament of Victoria*. Melbourne: Australian Scholarly Publishing, 2009.

Grimshaw, Patricia. 'The "Equals and Comrades of Men"? Tocsin and "the Woman Question".' In *Debutante Nation: Feminism Contests the 1890s*, edited by Susan Magarey, Sue Rowley and Susan Sheridan, 100–13. Sydney: Allen & Unwin, 1993.

Gurney Fry, Elizabeth. *Observations on the Visiting, Superintendence, and Government of Female Prisoners*. London: J and A. Arch, 1827.

Hacking, Ian. 'Making Up People.' In *Reconstructing Individualism: Autonomy, Individuality, and the Self in Western Thought*, edited by T. C. Heller, M. Sosna and D. E. Wellbery, 222–36. Stanford: Stanford University Press, 1986.

Hacking, Ian. 'How Should We Do the History of Statistics?' In *The Foucault Effect*, edited by G. Burchett, C. Gordon and P. Miller, 181–195. Chicago: Chicago University Press, 1991.

Harrison, Barbara and Melanie Nolan. 'Reflections in Colonial Glass? Women Factory Inspectors in Britain and New Zealand 1893–1921.' *Women's History Review* 13(2) (2004): 263–88.

Jones, Helen. *In Her Own Name: A History of Women in South Australia from 1836*. Adelaide: Wakefield Press, 1986.

Kellerman, Barbara and Deborah L. Rhode, eds. *Women and Leadership: The State of Play and Strategies for Change*. San Francisco: Wiley, 2007.

Livesey, Ruth. 'The Politics of Work: Feminism, Professionalisation and Women Inspectors of Factories and Workshops.' *Women's History Review* 13(2) (2004): 233–62.

McGowan, Henrietta C. and Margaret Cuthbertson. *Woman's Work*. Melbourne: Thomas C. Lothian, 1913.

Macintyre, Stuart. *Winners and Losers: The Pursuit of Social Justice in Australian History*. Sydney: Allen & Unwin, 1985.

Milne, Agnes. 'Working of the Factory Act.' *Journal of Agriculture and Industry* ii(4) (November 1898): 386–7.

Milne, Agnes. 'Woman's Work and Wages.' *Journal of Agriculture and Industry* iii(3) (October 1899): 342–3.

Norris, Ada. *Champions of the Impossible: A History of the National Council of Women of Victoria 1902–1977*. Melbourne: The Hawthorn Press, 1978.

Ord, Harrison. 'Chief Inspector of Factories, to Under Secretary.' 24 January 1894, VPRS 3992, Unit 787, Item X 94/5122. Public Records Office, Melbourne.

Prest, Wilfrid, Kerrie Round and Carol Fort, eds. *The Wakefield Companion to South Australian History*. Adelaide: Wakefield Press, 2001.

'Report of the Chief Inspector of Factories, Work-Rooms and Shops.' *Victorian Parliamentary Papers*, 1896–1910.

'Reports of Inspectors of Factories.' *Proceedings of the Parliament South Australia* 2 (54) (1897).

'Report on the Working of the Factories and Shops Act.' *NSW Votes and Proceedings* 3 (1903); 4 (1904); 2 (2nd Session) (1908); 5 (1914–15); 3 (1918).

Rhodes, Gerald. *Inspectorates in British Government: Law Enforcement and Standards of Efficiency*. London: Allen & Unwin, 1981.

Russell, Penny. *'A Wish of Distinction': Colonial Gentility and Femininity*. Melbourne: Melbourne University Press, 1994.

Sawer, Marian and Gail Radford. *Making Women Count: A History of the Women's Electoral Lobby in Australia*. Sydney: UNSW Press, 2009.

Smith, Dayle. *Women at Work: Leadership for the Next Century*. New Jersey: Prentice Hall, 2000.

Taylor, Arthur J. *Laissez-Faire and State Intervention in Nineteenth-Century Britain*. London: Macmillan, 1972.

Uhl-Bien, Mary, Russ Marion and Bill McKelvey. 'Complexity Leadership Theory: Shifting Leadership from the Industrial Age to the Knowledge Era.' In *Leadership, Gender, and Organisation: Issues in Business Ethics*, edited by P. H. Werhane and M. Painter-Moralnd, 128–31. London: Springer, 2011.

Victorian Government Gazette, 3rd Supplement (13) (1920).

Walkowitz, Judith R. *City of Dreadful Delight: Narratives of Sexual Danger in Late-Victorian London*. London: Virago, 1992.

Woman's Sphere, 10 May 1903.

10. From philanthropy to social entrepreneurship

Shurlee Swain[1]

If leadership, as Amanda Sinclair argues in this volume, is to be defined in terms of the ability to influence and change the public agenda and improve the life experiences of people both in the present and in the future then philanthropy provides an excellent field in which to explore its application to women. Philanthropy, in its nineteenth-century usage, encompassed both the giving of money and the giving of time in the service of others. While women seldom commanded large fortunes, they were able to give of their time both to the administration of charitable institutions and to the provision of direct services. Philanthropy was a responsibility and an assertion of class and provided an avenue through which women could develop and display their leadership abilities. This chapter studies the ways in which women's philanthropy was transformed during the twentieth century. It argues that rising levels of education opened professional careers to women who traditionally would have been involved in philanthropy, not least the new profession of social work, which took control of many of the spheres previously the domain of charity. These same forces, however, also increased the number of women in control of substantial fortunes, and these women, influenced by second-wave feminism, were leaders in shaping new forms of philanthropy that seek to move beyond amelioration and to promote social change.

Nineteenth-century philanthropy

'Denied access to political participation and barred from remunerative occupations', Kathleen McCarthy has argued, 'middle-class women donors, volunteers and organisational entrepreneurs … [used] philanthropic contributions of time, money and possessions … to carve out a public niche for themselves'.[2] When, in 1905, a Melbourne newspaper acclaimed the city's 10 leading citizens, the only two women who made the list were there by virtue of their philanthropy.[3] In the 15 months from August 1909 to November 1910,

---

1   Australian Catholic University.
2   Kathleen McCarthy, 'Women and Philanthropy', *Voluntas: International Journal of Voluntary and Non-Profit Organisations* 7(4) (1996): 332.

3   The two women named were Janet, Lady Clarke, and Selina Sutherland. *Herald*, 31 May 1905, cited in Annette Lewis, 'Janet Lady Clarke (1851–1909). Leader in the Good Work', PhD thesis, Deakin University, Melbourne, 2010, 26.

Australia lost both of these women, plus three others who had been stalwarts of nineteenth-century philanthropy. Their lives epitomised McCarthy's argument for the efficacy of philanthropy as an avenue to power at a time when woman's place was traditionally constrained within the bounds of family and home. Yet the diversity of their experiences also illustrates that the philanthropic pathway was a varied one, suggesting, at the beginning of the twentieth century, the multiple ways in which 'doing good' would provide opportunities for leadership for women over the coming decades.

The lives of Elizabeth Austin and Janet, Lady Clarke, modelled an older notion of philanthropy, a form of *noblesse oblige* that tarnished the term until quite late in the new century. Proclaimed on her death in November 1910 as 'a thoroughly good philanthropic woman',[4] Austin was the widow of a wealthy pastoralist. Although she had engaged in the charitable activities expected of a woman of her class throughout her marriage, in her widowhood she moved to philanthropy on a larger scale, initially anonymously, using a son-in-law to speak on her behalf, but later more openly, always taking an interest in the management of the institutions she had funded.[5] As the wife of Victoria's richest man, and Australia's only hereditary baronet, Janet, Lady Clarke, enthusiastically embraced the philanthropic responsibilities that came with her position. Carefully schooled in her new role by Lady Bowen, the wife of the Victorian governor, she accepted invitations to join the committees of most Melbourne charities concerned with the welfare of women and children, although as a young mother with a growing family, and later a society hostess with a range of other responsibilities, she was not always assiduous in her attendance. When Clarke died in November 1909, *The Argus* declared '[a]ny movement that had for its aim the welfare of the community, in the uplifting of humanity, found in her a ready, willing, and able ally'.[6] Many of the recipients of her beneficence lined the streets for her funeral procession—one of the most impressive Melbourne had seen to that time.[7] Clarke's most recent biographer has defended her against accusations that her philanthropic activity was 'simply a public demonstration of the *noblesse oblige* idea', arguing instead that her religious faith inspired 'a genuine commitment to improve living standards for the underprivileged in society', and a desire to 'bring permanent changes' in their lives.[8] Certainly, she

---

4   'Obituary', *Kilmore Free Press* [Victoria], 8 September 1910: 2, http://nla.gov.au/nla.news-article58275711.
5   Shurlee Swain, 'Perhaps to Spite Her Children: The Philanthropy of Elizabeth Austin', *Australian Philanthropy* (30) (1996): 10–15.
6   'Janet Lady Clarke. Her Death Announced', *The Argus* [Melbourne], 29 April 1909: 6, http://nla.gov.au/nla.news-article10708702.
7   'Janet Lady Clarke. An Impressive Funeral', *The Argus* [Melbourne], 30 April 1909: 4, http://nla.gov.au/nla.news-article10681512.
8   Lewis, 'Janet Lady Clarke (1851–1909)', 134.

did actively involve herself in management and policy development in relation to the organisations with which she was involved; however, her philanthropy remained an interest rather than a profession.

In this sense, Catherine Helen Spence can be seen as a transitional figure. A single woman with no independent income, she earned a living through writing, building a public profile as a commentator on social issues, initially in South Australia, but later nationally. While her obituary constructed her as an observer of both the transformation of 'the objects and organization of philanthropic and charitable enterprises' and the 'official recognition of the value of women's work upon various Government boards', this disguises the degree to which she was a participant in these interlinked processes.[9] Spence understood herself as 'a new woman ... awakened to a sense of capacity and responsibility, not merely to the family and the household, but to the State'.[10] Although she never took a salary from her work for state children, the prominent role she played laid firm foundations for the women who would make such work a profession in the years following her death.[11] Mary MacKillop (St Mary of the Cross), who died in August 1909, and Selina Sutherland, who died in October 1909, had no independent financial resources and hence were supported through their philanthropic activities, MacKillop through the religious order which she co-founded, and Sutherland through honoraria donated by the supporters of the four separate child-rescue organisations she established during her lifetime. While MacKillop's death passed with little notice in the secular press,[12] Sutherland was acclaimed as a 'great philanthropist',[13] 'a fine figure in the records of Victorian charity, a hard worker, and a woman whose heart was in her work'.[14] In the twentieth century, the path tentatively pioneered by Sutherland and MacKillop would provide professional leadership opportunities to large numbers of women, although the older model of voluntary charity did not entirely disappear.

The women who carried nineteenth-century notions of philanthropy into the twentieth rarely spoke about their motivation. Nor would they have called themselves leaders. Confined within conventional feminine tropes of silence, secrecy and sacrifice, they did not talk publicly about the positions they occupied, leaving it to others to praise them, usually after their deaths, in

---

9 'Honouring a Grand Old Woman', *The Register* [Adelaide], 31 October 1910: 6, http://nla.gov.au/nla.news-article59129722.

10 'Miss Spence, Octogenarian', *The Register* [Adelaide], 31 October 1905: 6, http://nla.gov.au/nla.news-page4423118.

11 Catherine Spence, *State Children in Australia* (Adelaide: Vardon & Sons, 1907).

12 'Personal', *The Advertiser* [Adelaide], 10 August 1909: 6, http://nla.gov.au/nla.news-article5753659.

13 'The Death of Miss Sutherland, the Great Philanthropist', *Fitzroy City Press* [Melbourne], 15 October 1909: 3, http://nla.gov.au/nla.news-article65684211.

14 'Death of Miss Sutherland', *The Argus* [Melbourne], 9 October 1909: 19, http://nla.gov.au/nla.news-article10739458.

ways that sought more to present them as exemplars of the feminine rather than as individuals who were challenging perceptions of women's place. Angela Woollacott has identified World War I as a key point of transition in women's activity in the public sphere.[15] Australia provides an interesting arena in which to study this shift. Its early enfranchisement of women provided alternatives to philanthropy as a way of bringing about change, with activists on both the left and the right now able to exercise power through feminist, industrial or political organisations.[16] First-wave feminism had opened higher education to women, with graduates increasingly able to base their claims to leadership on professional competence rather than moral authority. While several of the prominent early graduates struggled to gain acceptance in their professions, they were able to use their qualifications to take a leadership role in the philanthropic sphere, recasting the work as an obligation that came from their higher education.[17] Compelled by ill health to withdraw from her distinguished academic career, Melbourne scientist Dr Georgina Sweet transferred her talents to the community sphere, rising to international leadership in two organisations promoting the welfare of women. As a single woman, and the sole survivor of her family, she was also a substantial philanthropist both during her life and after her death, focusing her giving on increasing the educational opportunities for women. Another early science graduate, Ada à Beckett, was able to draw on the resources of her barrister husband as well as her own talents to combine paid employment and family life while still pursuing the philanthropic activities expected of a woman of her class, always grounding her decisions in research rather than the moral judgments that had dominated the field in the past.[18]

The gradual construction of a welfare state rendered marginal many activities previously conducted by women; however, a space remained both for women who found themselves in command of a large fortune to make substantial donations to philanthropic causes and for other, often less affluent women to build a career out of what would previously have been seen as purely philanthropic activity. Eliza Hall had been a regular donor throughout her marriage, particularly to charities working with women and children, but it was as a widow that she made her greatest contribution. Childless and the major beneficiary of her mining magnate husband's estate, she established a trust to make regular distributions to religious, financial and educational causes across

---

15   Angela Woollacott, 'From Moral to Professional Authority: Secularism, Social Work and Middle-Class Women's Self Construction in WW1 Britain', *Journal of Women's History* 10(2) (1998): 85.

16   Shurlee Swain, 'Women and Philanthropy in Colonial and Post-Colonial Australia', *Voluntas: International Journal of Voluntary and Non-Profit Organisations* 7(4) (1996): 440.

17   'Women and Universities', *The Register* [Adelaide], 8 June 1925: 5, http://nla.gov.au/nla.news-article54915469.

18   Julie Marginson, 'à Beckett, Ada Mary (1872–1948)', *Australian Dictionary of Biography Online* (Canberra: National Centre of Biography, The Australian National University), http://adb.anu.edu.au/biography/a-beckett-ada-mary-4963/text8235.

the three States in which the fortune had been amassed.[19] Victorian stud breeder Janet Biddlecombe was also a childless widow whose philanthropy was largely hidden until after her death; however, she differed from Hall in that the money she donated was substantially her own, the result of her success in reviving the pastoral holding she controlled after the death of her father.[20] For each of these women, philanthropy bought immortality, Hall's name incorporated into the Walter and Eliza Hall Institute funded from the trust and Biddlecombe's in properties constructed as a result of her donations and bequests.

Melbourne's Edith Onians, described as 'mother to the newsboys', was independently wealthy so did not need to seek paid employment, but she built a career nevertheless, using her position as honorary secretary to the City Newsboys Society as a base from which to build a reputation as an expert in the field of boy rescue, travelling, speaking and writing and, eventually, being appointed to positions on government and non-governmental organisations.[21] In Adelaide, Annie Green, who commenced her career as a volunteer at the City Mission, rose to become its first female superintendent. In the process, the role of the superintendent was reconceptualised from one of managing to one of caring, and hence one appropriately undertaken by a woman, although the essential tasks remained unchanged.[22] Anglican sister Kate Clutterbuck established two of Perth's major children's homes, taking the title first of 'Mum', and later of 'Gran', to the hundreds of children who passed through her care.[23] The use of maternal terms to describe such women is also indicative of the pathway philanthropy offered towards social motherhood—a status that positioned them as superior to the biological mothers of the children they set out to help. Such a positioning had the potential to disempower poor mothers under the guise of assisting their children.

While the organisations that emerged as a medium for women's activism—the National Council of Women, Red Cross, the Country Women's Association and the Young Women's Christian Association—continued to use the language of

---

19   Hazel King, 'Hall, Eliza Rowdon (1847–1916)', *Australian Dictionary of Biography Online* (Canberra: National Centre of Biography, The Australian National University), http://adb.anu.edu.au/biography/hall-eliza-rowdon-7056/text11215.

20   Diane Langmore, 'Biddlecombe, Janet (1866–1954)', *Australian Dictionary of Biography Online* (Canberra: National Centre of Biography, The Australian National University), http://adb.anu.edu.au/biography/biddlecombe-janet-107/text16729.

21   'Miss Edith Onians was "Mother" to the Newsboys', *The Age*, 18 August 1955: 2, http://news.google.com/newspapers?nid=1300&dat=19550818&id=cYYQAAAAIBAJ&sjid=5ZQDAAAAIBAJ&pg=7194,2634283.

22   'The Submerged Tenth', *The Mail* [Adelaide], 17 February 1923: 18, http://nla.gov.au/nla.news-article63779161; Julie-Ann Ellis, 'Green, Anne Syrett (1858–1936)', Australian Dictionary of Biography Online (Canberra: National Centre of Biography, The Australian National University), http://adb.anu.edu.au/biography/green-anne-syrett-12950/text23405.

23   Noël Stewart, 'Clutterbuck, Katherine Mary (1861–1946)', *Australian Dictionary of Biography Online* (Canberra: National Centre of Biography, The Australian National University), http://adb.anu.edu.au/biography/clutterbuck-katherine-mary-5691/text9619.

maternalism, they provided valuable avenues through which women could develop and demonstrate a range of non-maternal leadership skills on the local, national or international stage. The positions on which they chose to take a stand, however, all too often made them appear backward and judgmental compared with the progressive, benevolent, supposedly universalist state—a view that was reinforced by the fact that 'philanthropists were generally in the vanguard of opposition to social change'.[24] Tasmania's Emily Dobson (1842–1934) was described as being involved in every charitable organisation in the State. The wife of the premier, and associated in her own right with a range of conservative political organisations, she argued that her aim was to 'improve all sections of society'. Like most elite philanthropic women, however, she saw that change as taking place 'within the context of existing society'.[25] Zina Cumbrae-Stewart dominated Brisbane's charitable network in a similar way, arguing vigorously for suitably qualified women to be given greater responsibility in public life, while urging other women to resist modernity and to support rather than compete with men. When, during World War I, the Government moved to regulate working conditions for domestic servants, she was strident in her opposition, arguing that 'if servants were given more leisure their mistresses would have less time to devote to charitable works'.[26]

On the committees that still controlled such major charities as hospitals, and aged-care and children's homes, women fought for acceptance where membership had previously been restricted to men, and in turn invited prominent men to join their own organisations, but in both cases, the result, too often, was a confining of women to the more 'domestic' roles, defining leadership in terms of skills more commonly coded male.[27] The result, social work historian R. J. Lawrence concluded, was a 'cleavage' in the administration of welfare:

> On the one hand there was an approach through broad legislative measures, sponsored by political parties and administered by government, largely male, officials; on the other was an approach through numerous small voluntary organizations, catering for individual needs, sponsored by a wide variety of citizen groups or churches, with detailed work largely in the hands of unpaid women in the higher income groups.[28]

---

24 Swain, 'Women and Philanthropy in Colonial and Post-Colonial Australia', 437.

25 Alison Alexander, 'Perceptions of Women's Role in Tasmania, 1803–1914', *Bulletin of the Centre for Tasmanian Historical Studies* 3(2) (1991–92): 96.

26 Jean Stewart, 'Zina Beatrice Selwyn Cumbrae-Stewart: A Powerful Woman', *Journal of the Royal Historical Society of Queensland* 19(1) (February 2005): 610–27.

27 Swain, 'Women and Philanthropy in Colonial and Post-Colonial Australia', 440.

28 Robert Lawrence, *Professional Social Work in Australia* (Canberra: The Australian National University, 1965), 29.

Even where social reform created the opportunity for paid employment in what had been the philanthropic sector, 'a woman supported by her husband, or by a private income was, from a financial viewpoint, the ideal worker for agencies short of funds'.[29]

This is not to argue that there was no place for the older model of elite female philanthropy, nor that it did not continue to offer significant leadership opportunities to elite women. In Victoria, Dame Mabel Brookes reigned over the Queen Victoria Hospital from 1923 until five years before her death in 1975.[30] As president, she waged a long battle to get adequate accommodation for the hospital—a struggle she described in feminist terms as 'a fight by women against prejudice, suspicion and intolerance of women'. When the hospital was finally relocated to the refurbished Melbourne Hospital site, she declared 'there's no finer feeling than winning the supposedly hopeless battle'.[31] Her struggle was not dissimilar to that of Sydney's Dr Lucy Gullett (1876–1949), who, according to early social worker Katharine Ogilvie, 'used her wit, her gift of words, her kindness and her unreasonable optimism to touch the hearts of women in every walk of life and in every part of Sydney, so that they became permanent and ardent supporters' of the Rachel Forster Hospital, which she had founded, as, like the Queen Vic, a hospital in which women could be treated by female doctors.[32] Hospital administration also provided a power base for Melbourne's Dame Elisabeth Murdoch, who, understanding philanthropy as a responsibility attached to wealth, involved herself in a wide range of causes in the early years of her marriage. Widowed in 1952, she began a pattern of substantial donations, and two years later assumed the presidency of the Royal Children's Hospital, a position she occupied for 11 years, during which she oversaw both the fundraising and the organisation involved in rebuilding the hospital on a new site. While she tolerated the socialising that committee membership involved, she came increasingly to advocate direct giving, which, she believed, 'would ease the burden of committees and leave them freer to do necessary work'.[33]

At the local level, philanthropy continued to provide an important way of building community, with groups of women coming together to establish many of the services that would later be taken over by the state. Women who rose to leadership in such local organisations were sent as representatives to State and national organisations such as the Country Women's Association (CWA) and

---

29 Ibid., 28.

30 Laurie O'Brien and Cynthia Turner, 'Hospital Almoning: Portrait of the First Decade', *Australian Social Work* 32(4) (1979): 9.

31 Dame Mabel Brookes (as told to Michael Courtney), 'The Hour I'll Never Forget', *The Argus* [Melbourne], 19 January 1956: 8, http://nla.gov.au/nla.news-article72531074.

32 'Dr Lucy Gullett', *Sydney Morning Herald*, 18 November 1949: 2, http://nla.gov.au/nla.news-article18135727.

33 'Influence of Home', *The Courier-Mail* [Brisbane], 5 August 1939: 1, http://nla.gov.au/nla.news-article40832252.

the National Council of Women (NCW), providing rural and suburban women with the opportunity to influence national debates. Lottie Leal, for example, rose from her base in suburban Thebarton, to lead the SA NCW. She did not embrace feminism, arguing that women 'should command respect not demand it', earning positions of authority through their intelligence rather than being 'thrust forward ... merely to give them equality with men',[34] but she served as an influential role model to younger women, representing women's interests on several State committees. Launceston widow Nellie Dougharty found in philanthropy an occupation to fill the gap in her life after her young husband died during World War I. Although she had few financial resources to donate to her many causes, she developed talents as an organiser and advocate, which saw her recognised as a leader in her local community.[35]

The advent of professional social work

The shift Woollacott has identified was more apparent in the development of the profession of social work in Australia; however, it would be incorrect to position this in opposition to established models of philanthropy. The call for the introduction of professional social work was championed by female philanthropists through conservative women's organisations, and the first women who entered the profession often came from families with long traditions of philanthropic engagement. Brookes, initially, had been sceptical of the need for the new profession, but after visiting several hospitals in England her scepticism changed to enthusiasm. On her return, she convened a meeting to gain support for a local Institute of Almoners.[36] Mrs Kent Hughes, a member of the Melbourne Hospital auxiliary, having seen British almoners at work during a similar trip, persuaded her fellow auxiliary members to raise the money that brought Agnes Macintyre to Melbourne in 1929 to establish the first almoners' training program.[37] Almoners' departments were established in Victorian public hospitals over the next decade but the expectation was that they would continue to be funded by women's voluntary fundraising. In Sydney, the path to professionalisation was forged by an alliance of three women's groups—the NCW, the Young Women's Christian Association (YWCA) and women involved in industrial welfare—who together established the Board of Social Studies and Training in 1928.[38] In order to realise their ambition of having professional

---

34   'National Council News', *The Advertiser* [Adelaide], 17 September 1930: 6, http://nla.gov.au/nla.news-article73824206.

35   Jeanette Roelvink, 'Dougharty, Helen Elizabeth (Nellie) (1886–1968)', *Australian Dictionary of Biography Online* (Canberra: National Centre of Biography, The Australian National University), http://adb.anu.edu.au/biography/dougharty-helen-elizabeth-nellie-12891/text23289.

36   Lawrence, *Professional Social Work in Australia*, 34.

37   Ibid., 35.

38   Damian J. Gleeson, 'Some New Perspectives on Early Australian Social Work', *Australian Social Work* 61(3) (2008): 212; Helen Marchant, 'A Feminist Perspective on the Development of the Social Work Profession

training move from the philanthropic to the university sector, women in both cities were forced to forge alliances with sympathetic men within the academy. This began a pattern in which the leadership opportunities for women inherent in a profession that was and has continued to be female dominated were often seen as a threat to its status.[39]

The early years of professional social work in Australia reflect the cleavage Lawrence has identified in social welfare more generally. The graduates of the new training courses, joined by women who had undertaken courses in the United States, were engaged in a process of defining the new profession; however, opportunities to exercise leadership were constrained both by gender and by their status as employees.[40] The widespread restrictions on the employment of married women meant that only the minority who remained single stayed long enough in the profession to gain substantial expertise, leaving the even smaller group of male graduates with privileged access to senior positions.[41] The first graduates were concentrated in hospitals where they were commonly positioned alongside nurses as providing a service to the male-dominated medical profession.[42] When professional education moved into the universities, male academics delivered the theoretical content, leaving women, working under male direction, to deal with the practical aspects.[43] Although for most of the male academics teaching into the social work course was a sideline to their main responsibilities, women were not seen as eligible to take positions of leadership.[44] Appointed to the University of Sydney in 1945, Norma Parker acted as program director repeatedly over the next 14 years, as male directors came and went, but was never offered the position on a permanent basis.[45] Lawrence, who was later to become Australia's first professor of social work, found this apparent oversight unsurprising. Parker's interest, he claims, 'was not in administration; she was primarily a first-rate practitioner and teacher of social casework'—a claim that seems to ignore her leadership roles outside the academy, as founding president of the Australian Association of Social Workers, a position she held from 1946 to 1953, and the key role she played in the foundation of the Australian Council of Social Services.[46] Parker's experiences were far from unusual. Amy Wheaton, director of the Adelaide course, did

---

in New South Wales', *Australian Social Work* 38(1) (1985): 35.

39   Marchant, 'A Feminist Perspective on the Development of the Social Work Profession in New South Wales', 39.

40   Lawrence, *Professional Social Work in Australia*, ix.

41   Elaine Martin, 'Themes in a History of the Social Work Profession', *International Social Work* 35 (1992): 333.

42   Ibid., 338.

43   Marchant, 'A Feminist Perspective on the Development of the Social Work Profession in New South Wales', 40; Frances Crawford and Sabina Leitmann, 'The Midwifery of Power? Reflections on the Development of Professional Social Work in Western Australia', *Australian Social Work* 54(3) (2001): 47.

44   Lawrence, *Professional Social Work in Australia*, 44.

45   Ibid., 130.

46   Ibid.

most of the teaching, but only after her health broke down was she offered an increase in staff and a 'belated rise in her status'.[47] Appointed to the University of Queensland in 1973, Edna Chamberlain was Australia's first female professor of social work,[48] but well into the 1970s the heads of Australian schools of social work continued to be male, often from overseas, and rarely with substantial practical experience.[49]

Outside the academy the early social workers had to tread a cautious path in order to advance the claims of the new profession without alienating either the philanthropic women who until then had commanded the field or the male professionals and managers on whose support they were dependent.[50] Accounts of the way in which they negotiated this task tend to emphasise qualities coded as female. Sydney social worker Kate Ogilvie, for example, is applauded as a 'forceful leader' and a formidable advocate for her cause, yet her success is ascribed to her 'personal gifts ... and her capacity for relationships and for inspiring confidence'.[51] Norma Parker was described as 'not ambitious', but rather 'she did things because they needed to be done', creating opportunities for 'good people' rather than claiming the credit for herself.[52] In her reminiscences, Parker noted how, during her early days in Melbourne, she came to realise that 'one served quite a long apprenticeship before you earned the right to have anything to say ... It took years to be accepted; when that happy day finally arrived, all was well, but it was a weary process'.[53]

A gendered profession

Although World War II created greater opportunities for female social workers to exercise leadership, particularly through the expansion of the Red Cross,[54] the gender imbalance continued to be seen as a problem for the status of the profession well into the 1960s. Lawrence's 1965 history of social work returns to this theme repeatedly when looking towards the future. The women attracted to the work, he argues, were all too easily dismissed as 'nice girls from nice families', while the single women who 'provided the group's work with continuity and leadership ... were "career women" ... sometimes unkindly described as

---

47   Ibid., 53.

48   Stephanie Green, 'Edna Chamberlain: In Retrospect', *Australian Social Work* 47(3) (1994): 7.

49   Crawford and Leitmann, 'The Midwifery of Power?', 47.

50   S. Greig Smith, 'Three Ladies from England', *Forum* 7(2) (1954): 1–2; O'Brien and Turner, 'Hospital Almoning', 11.

51   Smith, 'Three Ladies from England', 1–2; Norma Parker, 'Katharine Ogilvie', *Australian Social Work* 36(2) (1983): 4.

52   Millie Mills, 'Editorial', *Australian Social Work* 39(2) (1986): 3.

53   Norma Parker, 'Early Social Work in Retrospect', *Australian Social Work* 32(4) (1979): 19.

54   Lawrence, *Professional Social Work in Australia*, 90.

"frustrated spinsters"'.[55] The future of the profession, Lawrence believed, lay in attracting more men, who would display a greater sense of commitment in the early stages of their career, stay longer in the profession and, rather than accept inadequate employment conditions, would insist on independent and equal status with the older established professions. Men, he argued, could move smoothly into positions of leadership. Unhampered by community attitudes to professional women, they could more easily bridge the gaps between government and non-governmental agencies. Equal in importance, however, was his assumption, grounded in contemporary gendered understandings of leadership, that men were implicitly more rounded individuals who relied 'less completely upon their work for social and personal satisfactions because they have a family and home of their own', took a broader view of individual problems and were generally more aware of the 'father's part in life'.[56]

The relaxation of restrictions on married women's employment saw more women remaining or returning to the profession by the 1970s; however, the increase in numbers was not immediately reflected in a rise in the proportion of leadership positions occupied by women. A developing feminist analysis highlighted the 'fundamentally patriarchal assumptions' that functioned to advantage men.[57] Some of these advantages were structural. While ameliorative provisions such as child care and part-time work had been introduced to overcome labour shortages, the underlying assumption remained that mothers were the ones who were responsible for managing the family. The career of the male social worker could proceed unimpeded because he had a wife at home to deal with these responsibilities.[58]

A more significant barrier to progression, however, was identified in the definitions of leadership that operated in the field—definitions that favoured indirect policy or administrative roles over female-dominated casework.[59] This division now came to be understood as indicative of patriarchal oppression, internalised by male and female social workers alike. Caring work was coded female, transferring into the workplace the responsibilities assumed by women in the home. Female social workers were constituted as 'the housewives of society', while leadership status was conferred on those who occupied non-direct practice positions, still effectively coded male.[60] Although the last decades of the twentieth century saw many more women move into positions of

---

55   Ibid., 70.
56   Ibid., 198.
57   Sue Brown, 'A Woman's Profession', in *Gender Reclaimed: Women in Social Work*, eds Helen Marchant and Betsy Wearing (Sydney: Hale & Iremonger, 1986), 225.
58   Ibid., 227.
59   Ibid., 230.
60   Helen Kiel, 'Women in Social Work: Caretakers or Policy Makers?', *Australian Social Work* 36(2) (1983): 9–11.

leadership, they generally did so only by accepting masculinised definitions of what leadership in the profession actually entailed, rather than by challenging the gendered devaluation of care.

Feminist philanthropy

While the profession struggled with such issues, women's philanthropy was being transformed. By the end of the century, women in employment were more likely to give than their male counterparts, and they gave a larger proportion of their taxable income.[61] The desire to make a difference is undoubtedly an important motivation, but philanthropy continues to provide opportunities for female empowerment, establishing and managing their own foundations rather than being subsumed within existing male-dominated structures.[62] Although remnants of the society fundraiser continue,[63] the term philanthropy is increasingly associated with notions of social enterprise or social entrepreneurship, as a new generation of women, influenced by 1970s feminism, seeks to use their inherited or earned wealth for change rather than relief.[64] The focus for this new philanthropy is Melbourne, but it has attracted supporters in other States, coming together as the Women Donors Network, which aims to direct its members to use their donations to address the 'unique circumstances and specific needs of women and girls'.[65]

In her later years, Dame Elisabeth Murdoch was a precursor and a role model for this new generation of philanthropists. While many of her early donations had been anonymous, she came to believe that being publicly identified as a leader was important, not for her personal glory but in the hope that her example would encourage other people. She also argued that philanthropists needed to be actively involved in the work they were assisting. 'The advantage of wealth is that you have an opportunity to do so much good ... it's perfectly easy to give it away and nothing to be particularly proud of but it's being involved and knowing what you are helping' that are important.[66] Murdoch chose the causes she would support, and while her donations to key cultural and charitable

---

61   Margaret Steinberg and Lara Cain, *Putting Paid to Prescribed Roles: A New Era for Australian Women and Philanthropy*, Working Paper No. CPNS16 (Centre of Philanthropy and Nonprofit Studies, Queensland University of Technology, Brisbane, 2003), 8.

62   Ibid.

63   See, for example, the story of Sydney's Lady Mary Fairfax in Michael Gilding, *Secrets of the Super Rich* (Sydney: HarperCollins, 2010), ch. 7.

64   Anne O'Brien, 'Charity and Philanthropy', *Dictionary of Sydney*, http://www.dictionaryofsydney.org/item/251.

65   'Women Donors Investing in Women and Girls', http://www.womendonors.org.au/index.php?option=com_content&view=article&id=38&Itemid=95.

66   Transcript, *Enough Rope*, ABC TV, 23 June 2008, http://www.abc.net.au/tv/enoughrope/transcripts/s2283021.htm.

organisations were substantial, she also supported a drama group for women prisoners and work amongst newly arrived refugees, causes that took her well outside her conservative social circle.[67]

A key leader amongst the new generation of philanthropists is Jill Reichstein, who, radicalised in the protests of the 1960s, was quickly frustrated with the conservative, ameliorative approach taken by her father's foundation, which she joined at the age of twenty-six. Assuming the chair 10 years later, she transformed its approach, influenced by the concept of social change philanthropy.[68] In America, she argues, 'when you have excess wealth it's your responsibility to share it', and social change philanthropy enables her to blend this philosophy with her feminist principles. Her notion of leadership attempts to break down the hierarchy between the 'donor and the donee' through working in partnership with the groups which are funded in order to bring about change.[69] Reichstein believes women's work experience equips them to provide a very different type of philanthropic leadership. Where the men who run foundations traditionally have come from a banking or finance background, the women who move into the sector often bring experience in community-based organisations—a move she describes as shifting roles 'from poacher to gamekeeper'.[70]

Women at the forefront of this movement only accept the label of leader if they are able to redefine it in feminist terms. 'As long as leadership is seen to be acting with passion, or mentoring and helping to effect change through education, then I am comfortable with being called a leader', says Reichstein.[71] Businesswoman Carol Schwartz sees her philanthropy as part of her commitment to negotiating 'the complicated relationship between making money and creating social good'.[72] For Eve Mahlab, co-founder of the Australian Women Donors Network, social change philanthropy represents the third wave of the women's movement: 'The first got us the vote. The second gave us more access to decently paid work rather than the unpaid home duties in which we had previously been trapped. We must now move into policy and decision making roles at all levels.' The challenge for women who have benefited from the first two waves of the movement is to use their advantage for the benefit of other women and their

67   Elizabeth Cham, 'Foreword', *Australian Philanthropy: Honouring the Philanthropy of Dame Elisabeth Murdoch* 51 (2003): 2, http://www.philanthropy.org.au/pdfs/philaus/AustralianPhilanthropy_Issue51.pdf.

68   Briony Goode, 'Change for the Better', *WellBeing* [Mosman, NSW] 126 (2010): 27.

69   'Women of Power and Influence', *Compass*, ABC TV, 25 February 2007, http://www.abc.net.au/compass/s1835941.htm.

70   Jill Reichstein, 'On Women and Philanthropy', *Australian Philanthropy* 71 (2008): 12.

71   Jill Reichstein, Interviewed by Nikki Henningham for the Women and Leadership in a Century of Australian Democracy Oral History Project, in Melbourne, 12 May 2011, National Library of Australia, Canberra, http://nla.gov.au/nla.cat-vn5216522.

72   Carol Schwartz, Interviewed by Nikki Henningham for the Women and Leadership in a Century of Australian Democracy Oral History Project, in Melbourne, 11 May, 22 June and 13 September 2011, National Library of Australia, Canberra, http://nla.gov.au/nla.oh-vn5216518.

families, practising a new type of leadership that involves working alongside rather than for the people they identify as being in need.[73] Mahlab's call has found a receptive audience amongst young successful women determined to use at least some of their private wealth and their professional skills for public rather than personal benefit.[74]

Conclusion

At the end of the twentieth century the bulk of caring work continued to be coded female. With the welfare state in retreat, governments again sought to encourage philanthropy. Advances in women's education had, however, diversified the leadership opportunities that such activity offered, with women increasingly earning and controlling assets in their own right. While it would be unrealistic to overestimate the influence of social change philanthropy on the field as a whole, it does provide evidence that while social workers remain ambivalent about confronting gendered notions of leadership, women in philanthropy have moved from a situation where they used philanthropy as an avenue to leadership and power, to one in which they employ their leadership skills and power in the interests of philanthropy.

References

Alexander, Alison. 'Perceptions of Women's Role in Tasmania, 1803–1914.' *Bulletin of the Centre for Tasmanian Historical Studies* 3(2) (1991–92): 81–98.

Brookes, Dame Mabel (as told to Michael Courtney). 'The Hour I'll Never Forget.' *The Argus* [Melbourne], 19 January 1956: 8. http://nla.gov.au/nla. news-article72531074.

Brown, Sue. 'A Woman's Profession.' In *Gender Reclaimed: Women in Social Work*, edited by Helen Marchant and Betsy Wearing, 223–33. Sydney: Hale & Iremonger, 1986.

Cham, Elizabeth. 'Foreword.' *Australian Philanthropy*: *Honouring the Philanthropy of Dame Elisabeth Murdoch* 51 (2003): 2. http://www.philanthropy.org.au/ pdfs/philaus/AustralianPhilanthropy_Issue51.pdf.

---

73 Eve Mahlab, 'Does Gender Still Matter?', *Australian Philanthropy* 71 (2008): 3.
74 See, for example, Kristi Mansfield, founder of the Greenstone Group—Philanthropy Advisers: http://greenstonegroup.wordpress.com/biography/.

Crawford, Frances and Sabina Leitmann. 'The Midwifery of Power? Reflections on the Development of Professional Social Work in Western Australia.' *Australian Social Work* 54(3) (2001): 43–54.

'Death of Miss Sutherland.' *The Argus* [Melbourne], 9 October 1909: 19. http://nla.gov.au/nla.news-article10739458.

'Dr Lucy Gullett.' *Sydney Morning Herald*, 18 November 1949: 2. http://nla.gov.au/nla.news-article18135727.

Ellis, Julie-Ann. 'Green, Anne Syrett (1858–1936).' *Australian Dictionary of Biography Online*. Canberra: National Centre of Biography, The Australian National University. http://adb.anu.edu.au/biography/green-anne-syrett-12950/text23405.

Gilding, Michael. *Secrets of the Super Rich*. Sydney: HarperCollins, 2010.

Gleeson, Damian J. 'Some New Perspectives on Early Australian Social Work.' *Australian Social Work* 61(3) (2008): 207–25.

Goode, Briony. 'Change for the Better [Jill Reichstein and the social change philanthropy movement].' *WellBeing* [Mosman, NSW] 126 (2010): 26–8.

Green, Stephanie. 'Edna Chamberlain: In Retrospect.' *Australian Social Work* 47(3) (1994): 3–11.

'Honouring a Grand Old Woman.' *The Register* [Adelaide], 31 October 1910: 6. http://nla.gov.au/nla.news-article59129722.

'Influence of Home.' *The Courier-Mail* [Brisbane], 5 August 1939: 1. http://nla.gov.au/nla.news-article40832252.

'Janet Lady Clarke. Her Death Announced.' *The Argus* [Melbourne], 29 April 1909: 6. http://nla.gov.au/nla.news-article10708702.

'Janet Lady Clarke. An Impressive Funeral.' *The Argus* [Melbourne], 30 April 1909: 4. http://nla.gov.au/nla.news-article10681512.

Kiel, Helen. 'Women in Social Work: Caretakers or Policy Makers?' *Australian Social Work* 36(2) (1983): 9–11.

King, Hazel. 'Hall, Eliza Rowdon (1847–1916).' *Australian Dictionary of Biography Online*. Canberra: National Centre of Biography, The Australian National University. http://adb.anu.edu.au/biography/hall-eliza-rowdon-7056/text11215.

Langmore, Diane. 'Biddlecombe, Janet (1866–1954).' *Australian Dictionary of Biography Online*. Canberra: National Centre of Biography, The Australian National University. http://adb.anu.edu.au/biography/biddlecombe-janet-107/text16729.

Lawrence, Robert. *Professional Social Work in Australia*. Canberra: The Australian National University, 1965.

Lewis, Annette. 'Janet Lady Clarke (1851–1909). Leader in the Good Work.' PhD thesis, Deakin University, Melbourne, 2010.

McCarthy, Kathleen. 'Women and Philanthropy.' *Voluntas: International Journal of Voluntary and Non-Profit Organisations* 7(4) (1996): 331–5.

Mahlab, Eve. 'Does Gender Still Matter?' *Australian Philanthropy* 71 (2008): 3.

Marchant, Helen. 'A Feminist Perspective on the Development of the Social Work Profession in New South Wales.' *Australian Social Work* 38(1) (1985): 35–43.

Marginson, Julie. 'à Beckett, Ada Mary (1872–1948).' *Australian Dictionary of Biography Online*. Canberra: National Centre of Biography, The Australian National University. http://adb.anu.edu.au/biography/a-beckett-ada-mary-4963/text8235.

Martin, Elaine. 'Themes in a History of the Social Work Profession.' *International Social Work* 35 (1992): 11–22.

Mills, Millie. 'Editorial.' *Australian Social Work* 39(2) (1986): 2–3.

'Miss Edith Onians was "Mother" to the Newsboys.' *The Age*, 18 August 1955: 2. http://news.google.com/newspapers?nid=1300&dat=19550818&id=cYYQAAAAIBAJ&sjid=5ZQDAAAAIBAJ&pg=7194,2634283.

'Miss Spence, Octogenarian.' *The Register* [Adelaide], 31 October 1905: 6. http://nla.gov.au/nla.news-page4423118.

'National Council News.' *The Advertiser* [Adelaide], 17 September 1930: 6. http://nla.gov.au/nla.news-article73824206.

'Obituary.' *Kilmore Free Press* [Victoria], 8 September 1910: 2. http://nla.gov.au/nla.news-article58275711.

O'Brien, Anne. 'Charity and Philanthropy.' *Dictionary of Sydney*. http://dictionaryofsydney.org/entry/charity_and_philanthropy.

O'Brien, Laurie and Cynthia Turner. 'Hospital Almoning: Portrait of the First Decade.' *Australian Social Work* 32(4) (1979): 7–12.

Parker, Norma. 'Early Social Work in Retrospect.' *Australian Social Work* 32(4) (1979): 13–20.

Parker, Norma. 'Katharine Ogilvie.' *Australian Social Work* 36(2) (1983): 3–8.

'Personal.' *The Advertiser* [Adelaide], 10 August 1909: 6. http://nla.gov.au/nla. news-article5753659.

Reichstein, Jill. 'On Women and Philanthropy.' *Australian Philanthropy* 71 (2008): 71.

Reichstein, Jill. Interviewed by Nikki Henningham for the Women and Leadership in a Century of Australian Democracy Oral History Project, in Melbourne, 12 May 2011. National Library of Australia, Canberra. http:// nla.gov.au/nla.cat-vn5216522.

Roelvink, Jeanette. 'Dougharty, Helen Elizabeth (Nellie) (1886–1968).' *Australian Dictionary of Biography Online*. Canberra: National Centre of Biography, The Australian National University. http://adb.anu.edu.au/biography/ dougharty-helen-elizabeth-nellie-12891/text23289.

Schwartz, Carol. Interviewed by Nikki Henningham for the Women and Leadership in a Century of Australian Democracy Oral History Project, in Melbourne, 11 May, 22 June and 13 September 2011. National Library of Australia, Canberra. http://nla.gov.au/nla.oh-vn5216518.

Smith, S. Greig. 'Three Ladies from England.' *Forum* 7(2) (1954): 1–2.

Spence, Catherine. *State Children in Australia*. Adelaide: Vardon & Sons, 1907.

Steinberg, Margaret and Lara Cain. *Putting Paid to Prescribed Roles: A New Era for Australian Women and Philanthropy*. Working Paper No. CPNS16, Centre of Philanthropy and Nonprofit Studies, Queensland University of Technology, Brisbane, 2003.

Stewart, Jean. 'Zina Beatrice Selwyn Cumbrae-Stewart: A Powerful Woman.' *Journal of the Royal Historical Society of Queensland* 19 (February 2005): 610–27.

Stewart, Noël. 'Clutterbuck, Katherine Mary (1861–1946).' *Australian Dictionary of Biography Online*. Canberra: National Centre of Biography, The Australian National University. http://adb.anu.edu.au/biography/clutterbuck- katherine-mary-5691/text9619.

Swain, Shurlee. 'Perhaps to Spite Her Children: The Philanthropy of Elizabeth Austin.' *Australian Philanthropy* 30 (1996): 10–15.

Swain, Shurlee. 'Women and Philanthropy in Colonial and Post-Colonial Australia.' *Voluntas* 7(4) (1996): 428–43.

'The Death of Miss Sutherland, the Great Philanthropist.' *Fitzroy City Press* [Melbourne], 15 October 1909: 3. http://nla.gov.au/nla.news-article65684211.

'The Submerged Tenth.' *The Mail* [Adelaide], 17 February 1923: 18. http://nla.gov.au/nla.news-article63779161.

Transcript. *Enough Rope*, ABC TV, 23 June 2008. http://www.abc.net.au/tv/enoughrope/transcripts/s2283021.htm.

'Women and Universities.' *The Register* [Adelaide], 8 June 1925: 5. http://nla.gov.au/nla.news-article54915469.

'Women Donors Investing in Women and Girls.' http://www.womendonors.org.au/index.php?option=com_content&view=article&id=38&Itemid=95.

'Women of Power and Influence.' *Compass*, ABC TV, 25 February 2007. http://www.abc.net.au/compass/s1835941.htm.

Woollacott, Angela. 'From Moral to Professional Authority: Secularism, Social Work and Middle-Class Women's Self Construction in WW1 Britain.' *Journal of Women's History* 10(2) (1998): 85–111.

11. Academic women and research leadership in twentieth-century Australia

Patricia Grimshaw[1] and Rosemary Francis[2]

While the focus of analysis of leadership in tertiary institutions is most commonly the capacities of the most senior academic administrators, many academics at less elevated levels in the hierarchy also can exert major influence in their disciplinary areas that has significant impact nationally and internationally. This chapter offers an insight into Australian women's leadership in the academic profession in the twentieth century through the careers of outstanding scholars who from the mid 1950s were elected fellows of the Australian learned academies. Women faced considerable barriers to employment in universities before the expansion of secondary and tertiary education in the postwar years increased their opportunities to gain academic positions and advance the cutting edges of their disciplines. Yet, starting in 1956, when the first woman was elected to a learned academy, talented women were singled out as research leaders through this peer evaluation of their importance. With the social changes in gender expectations that the women's movement inspired and the Australian Labor Party's affirmative action policies of the 1980s, the number of female senior scholars who reached this standing increased markedly—noticeable especially in the humanities and social sciences. First, this chapter considers the careers of the first group of academicians who were elected to the four academies from 1956 to 1976; second, it traces the election of women from the late 1970s to the end of the century, including a few scholars who became leaders of the academies themselves. The story of academic women and research leadership is overall one of progressive change, but also indicates that gender equity has yet to be attained in the academic profession or, consequently, in the learned academies.

In an interview in 1997, the recently retired Professor Mollie Holman, a leading physiologist, who in 1970 had become the third woman elected a fellow of the Australian Academy of Science, recalled with warmth and gratitude her long and satisfying career. But she referred also to the challenges the academic profession presented to its members by the last decade of the twentieth century:

---

1   The University of Melbourne.
2   The University of Melbourne.

> Every academic has got three responsibilities, three jobs in one lifetime: one is to be an administrator, one is to be a teacher and one is to be a researcher. It's virtually impossible to be fully satisfied that you've done well in any of the three areas ... It's an impossible life being an academic.[3]

Recent scholarly studies of women's leadership in academia have focused primarily on those people who have filled the highest positions in academic administration. In Australian universities the appointment of female vice-chancellors and deputy vice-chancellors has been a recent phenomenon and numbers remain relatively few.[4] Yet as the political scientist Amanda Sinclair has suggested, if we view leadership as the exercise of influence, rather than associate it simply with those who fill top executive or administrative positions, we may discern how power resides in people at lower levels in hierarchical systems.[5] This chapter focuses on women's leadership in research in the Australian academic profession, through the experiences of creative scholars elected by their scholarly peers as fellows of the learned academies. The pursuit of curiosity-based research is the distinguishing factor of the work expectations of academics; it is the core area on which entry to, and promotions within, the profession has crucially depended and on which universities themselves have been ranked against each other. Election to a learned academy has provided a marker of excellence in research that has not until very recently existed for teaching and administration. For those at the coalface of academic working life, teaching commitments have often overridden other demands. Yet teaching has been notoriously difficult to assess and remains so, despite such innovations as student questionnaires and staff prizes for outstanding performance. The

---

3   Mollie Holman, Interviewed by Ragbir Bhathal, 1997, National Library of Australia Oral History and Folklore Collection, ORAL TRC 3600, National Library of Australia, Canberra [hereinafter Holman Interview]; see also Ragbir Bhathal, 'Mollie Holman: Physiologist', in *Profiles: Australian Women Scientists*, ed. Ragbir Bhathal (Canberra: National Library of Australia, 1999), 99–106.

4   For a discussion, see: Tanya Fitzgerald, Julie White and Helen M. Gunter, eds, *Hard Labour? Academic Work and the Changing Landscape of Higher Education* (Bingley, UK: Emerald Electronic Resource, 2012); Colleen Chesterman, Anne Ross-Smith and Margaret Peters, 'Changing the Landscape? Women in Academic Leadership in Australia', http://65.54.113.26/Publication/6223987/changing-the-landscape-women-in-academic-leadership-in-australia, 11. See also: Colleen Chesterman, Anne Ross-Smith and Margaret Peters, '"Not Doable Jobs": Exploring Women's Attitudes to Academic Leadership Roles', *Women's Studies International Forum* 28(2) (2005): 163–80; Colleen Chesterman, Anne Ross-Smith and Margaret Peters, 'The Gendered Impact on Organisations of a Critical Mass of Women in Senior Management', *Policy and Society* 24(4) (2005): 69–91.

5   Amanda Sinclair, 'Not Just "Adding Women In": Women Re-Making Leadership', in *Seizing the Initiative: Australian Women Leaders in Politics, Workplaces and Communities*, eds Rosemary Francis, Patricia Grimshaw and Ann Standish (Melbourne: eScholarship Research Centre, University of Melbourne, 2012), 5–36. See also: Amanda Sinclair, *Leadership for the Disillusioned: Moving beyond Myths and Heroes to Leading that Liberates* (Sydney: Allen & Unwin, 2007); Amanda Sinclair, *Doing Leadership Differently: Gender, Power, and Sexuality in a Changing Business Culture* (Melbourne: Melbourne University Press, 1998).

assessment of success in administration has been even more problematic, and again remains anecdotal despite the existence of appraisals and university 'climate surveys'.

Historically there were sharp challenges to talented women's aspirations to academic work embedded in the social structures that shaped women's access to tertiary degrees and advanced research opportunities. After women gained entry to universities and the granting of political citizenship, some women, emboldened by the first women's movement, slowly broke down barriers to entry to professions of high status and generous remuneration. Few women, however, entered the academic profession or rose far up its hierarchy before World War II. They had a more numerous presence following the postwar expansion of the tertiary sector when the second wave of the women's movement stimulated increasing acceptance of women, including married women, in the profession. By the end of the twentieth and the start of the twenty-first centuries, women's place in teaching, research and senior administration in the tertiary sector was secure, if unevenly spread—remarkable given the few decades in which this was achieved.[6] This chapter explores this transition through the example of women's leadership in research. It considers the challenging gender culture of academia that shaped the careers of the first women academicians and their research profiles that led to their election to the learned academies from 1956 to 1976. It then considers the rapid increase in the ranks of female academicians that started in the late 1970s and continued to the end of the century, noting the wider opportunities of these academicians to develop more varied working histories.

The first women in the academies had been educated in tertiary institutions where they had very few female mentors, and had often been among the first women employed in lectureships in their disciplines. They were not usually helped by the nature of entry to the profession. As a form of employment, academic work has been anomalous within the history of other professions in which entry is controlled by formal credentials that may be monitored and revised, but remain foundational. Early in the twentieth century, during the formation of professions, aspirants might have gained entry through an apprenticeship or

---

6   For recent histories of Australian universities, see Julia Horne and Geoff Sherington, *Sydney: The Making of a Public University* (Melbourne: Melbourne University Publishing, 2012); Graeme Davison and Kate Murphy, *University Unlimited: The Monash Story* (Sydney: Allen & Unwin, 2012); Stuart Macintyre and Richard Selleck, *A Short History of the University of Melbourne* (Melbourne: Melbourne University Press, 2003); John Poynter and Carolyn Rasmussen, *A History of the University of Melbourne, 1935–1975* (Melbourne: J. R. Poynter, 1995); Patricia Grimshaw and Lynne Strachan, eds, *The Half-Open Door: Sixteen Modern Australian Women Look at Professional Life and Achievement* (Sydney: Hale & Iremonger, 1982); Bettina Cass, *Why So Few? Women Academics in Australian Universities* (Sydney: University of Sydney Press, 1983); Madge Dawson and Heather Radi, eds, *Against the Odds: Fifteen Professional Women Reflect on their Lives and Careers* (Sydney: Hale & Iremonger, 1984); Patricia Crawford and Myrna Tonkinson, *The Missing Chapters: Women Staff at the University of Western Australia, 1963–1987* (Perth: Centre for Western Australian History, University of Western Australia, 1988).

self-education. Gradually, however, the pathways to acceptance as a legitimate doctor, lawyer, engineer, accountant, architect, dentist, schoolteacher, social worker or nurse became subject to qualifications acquired through post-school training—usually accredited degrees from tertiary institutions. Although in the post World War II years a doctorate in process or completed and some record of scholarly publication became anticipated, academic employment sustained inexact criteria for entry and, once inside, for evaluation of performance. Selection committees might take into consideration alongside the candidate's achievement the standing of the supervisor and the university in which the doctorate was completed. Committees needed to rank the significance of a plethora of papers published in scholarly journals, chapters in scholarly collections and monographs, and the originality of completed research. Even more subjectively, they considered a candidate's potential for cutting-edge discovery across a working lifetime.[7] Then again, there could be considerable discrepancy in how committees evaluated scholarly output against a record of successful performance in teaching. Members of selection panels, in addition, interviewed candidates and rated a scholar's capacity to fit well into a particular academic culture of students and colleagues, or to engage persuasively with various audiences. Conscious and unconscious bias against women could thrive in the fluid circumstances of academic appointments without attracting notice, let alone offering the bases for a female candidate to mount explicit challenges on the basis of gender.[8]

Australian universities were coeducational institutions substantially reliant on government; there was a thin affluent middle class in Australia, and what little wealth was devoted to philanthropy was not commonly funnelled to universities. That was left to governments to do, as was much else. With a numerically much reduced Indigenous people and settler governments hostile to the migration of their Asian neighbours, the country sustained a relatively small and socially provincial population. Given the reliance on primary production and practical, anti-intellectual attitudes, aspirants for tertiary degrees were few. Women students clustered mainly in the humanities or sciences, not usually prepared for, or consciously avoiding, the professional faculties like medicine and law that in any case openly discouraged women.

---

7   See Michele Lamont, *How Professors Think: Inside the Curious World of Academic Judgment* (Cambridge, Mass.: Harvard University Press, 2009); Pierre Bourdieu, *Homo Academicus* (Paris: Editions de Minuit, 1984); Raewyn Connell and June Crawford, 'Mapping the Intellectual Labour Process', *Journal of Sociology* 43(2) (2007): 187–205; Raewyn Connell, 'Core Activity: Reflexive Intellectual Workers and Cultural Crisis', *Journal of Sociology* 42(1) (2006): 5–23; Paul Boreham, Alec Pemberton and Paul Wilson, eds, *The Professions in Australia: A Critical Appraisal* (Brisbane: University of Queensland Press, 1976).

8   Margaret Thornton, 'The Mirage of Merit: Constructing the "Ideal Academic"', Paper presented at the Symposium on Workplace Culture in Higher Education, University of Melbourne, October 2011. See also Anne Witz, *Professions and Patriarchy* (London and New York: Routledge, 1992).

Engagement with sustained research usually relied on academic employment and up to the 1970s women were seldom found in tenured lectureships. The extension of social and political rights to women by 1902 had not counteracted impediments to women's entry to professional employment outside nursing and teaching.[9] Employment in the professions that commanded high status and salaries was strongly embedded in class and gender divisions. Only a select number of women had access to academically oriented secondary educations in fee-paying schools and to expensive university degrees. A woman needed not only to harbour enthusiasm for extended years of education but also to have parents who were prepared to fund them. Moreover, although Australia had a reputation for egalitarianism, a strong gender division of labour blocked most educated married women's access to wage earning; only adult unmarried daughters might be permitted to pursue careers.[10] Marriage bars in place in a number of workplaces obliged women to give up tenured positions on marriage, and in addition social pressure sufficed to dissuade married women from waged work if they had children.

The few women academics appointed to lectureships from the 1900s up to the 1960s needed to survive burdensome workloads in understaffed departments where lecturers had to assume most tasks necessary to protect the credentialling process for student degrees. The universities before the expansion of the postwar period were small institutions where male professors, with a small entourage of staff, undertook the teaching and most administration. The gendered culture of academia and the conscious or unconscious discrimination of the academic culture were leavened by the outstanding liberalism of the few men who encouraged women's research endeavours. Let us look at the example at the University of Melbourne of the botanist Dr Ethel McLennan, who felt she had overestimated her capacities when she applied unsuccessfully in the late 1930s for the advertised professorship. The professor of bacteriology advised the selection committee:

> Of her claims as a Scientist and Research worker there is no doubt. As to her ability to administer the Department and to re-organise it, I feel completely assured ... I believe that if this University is ever to appoint

9   Beverley Kingston, *My Wife, My Daughter, and Poor Mary Ann: Women and Work in Australia* (Melbourne: Thomas Nelson, 1975); Patricia Grimshaw, John Murphy and Belinda Probert, eds, *Double Shift: Working Mothers and Social Change in Australia* (Melbourne: Circa, 2005).

10   Janet McCalman, *Journeyings: The Biography of a Middle-Class Generation 1920–1990* (Melbourne: Melbourne University Press, 1995); Alison Mackinnon, *The New Women: Adelaide's Early Women Graduates* (Adelaide: Wakefield Press, 1986); Alison Mackinnon, *Love and Freedom: Professional Women and the Reshaping of Personal Life* (Melbourne: Cambridge University Press, 1997); Alison Mackinnon, *Women, Love and Learning: The Double Bind* (New York: P. Lang, 2012).

a woman to a Professorial Chair this opportunity should not be missed as we might go a very long time without ever again having so generally capable and fitting a person.[11]

She was passed over nevertheless for a young Englishman of promise. Her publication list would have been further developed, McLennan confessed, had she not had full responsibilities for junior classes three years in a row, because of the recurrent illnesses of the professor and the absence overseas of another colleague. 'Some of my friends encouraged me more than I was inclined to encourage myself', she explained apologetically.[12]

Even as late as the 1950s evidence of gender bias was not hard to find. In 1957 the eminent Sir Keith Hancock, head of the Research School of Social Sciences at The Australian National University, wrote to the vice-chancellor in jocular style offering his estimate of the value of appointing academic women: 'It is no private fad of my own to insist that good professors will not long continue to do their best work unless they are reinforced by charwomen.'[13] And the archives of the University of Melbourne reveal another professor's attitudes that must have deflected all but the hardiest women from academic aspirations. In 1955 Professor John La Nauze was appointed to the second chair of the history school, a position many had expected would go to an associate professor, Kathleen Fitzpatrick, who finally did not apply. Following his appointment, he wrote to assure Fitzpatrick of her continuing value to the school, to the other professor, Max Crawford, and not least to himself:

> Well, instead of being left to your knitting, you will now have a double burden of keeping *two* men sane and charitable and calm. I have never imagined that it would be anything but a partnership of three, in which if two are active in the eyes of the world, the third will often bear burdens but not get applause. I think it will be a pretty sound firm.[14]

Despite such disparagement, Fitzpatrick was in fact to become an inaugural member of the Australian Academy of the Humanities (AAH): her achievements figure below.

---

11 'Prof. Woodruff to the Vice Chancellor', 14 December 1937, McLennan Papers, cited in Jane Carey, 'Departing from their Sphere? Australian Women and Science, 1880–1960' (PhD thesis, University of Melbourne, 2003), 240.

12 Cited in Farley Kelly, *Degrees of Liberation: A Short History of Women in the University of Melbourne* (Melbourne: Women Graduates Centenary Committee, University of Melbourne, 1985). For a fuller discussion, see: Patricia Grimshaw and Jane Carey, 'Foremothers VI: Kathleen Fitzpatrick (1905-1990), Margaret Kiddle (1914–1958) and Australian History after the Second World War', *Gender & History* 13(2) (August 2001): 349–73.

13 Cited in 'ANU Presentation to the Review of the Institute of Advanced Studies 1990', Typescript, 73. We owe this reference to Charles Coppel.

14 'John La Nauze to Kathleen Fitzpatrick', 25 May 1955, in Kathleen Fitzpatrick Collection, Box 1, University of Melbourne Archives, Melbourne [hereinafter Fitzpatrick Collection].

An advanced student and tutor in the history school and later an outstanding historian, Inga Clendinnen gave her opinions in a forum discussing this period: 'We were meant to go on and be the carers, the primary carers, as it were, of the tutorial classes, but as for being groomed for greatness, no.' Professor La Nauze had assured Clendinnen she was the most intelligent student he had ever taught, but he would never recommend her for a scholarship because she 'would simply marry and have babies. He would not recommend a woman for a scholarship'; nor, indeed, would he supervise a woman postgraduate.[15] When a part-time lecturer, June Philipp, a married woman, asked for some time off when she was pregnant, a woman colleague reported:

> As for La Nauze, the things he's saying about part-time lecturers, married female[s], potentialities of, are quite shocking and bode ill for the continuation of the species. He's torn between sadistic delight that June is being forced to fulfil her proper function and despair at the thought of coping with Australian History.[16]

This did not seem hopeful territory for the nurturance of female academicians.

Three of the country's learned academies emerged from committees of leading academics who were involved during World War II and the immediate postwar years in planning for postwar reconstruction.[17] The Australian Academy of Science (AAS) was founded in 1954 by Australian fellows of the Royal Society of London, with Sir Mark Oliphant as its founding president.[18] Prominent academics in the humanities and social sciences set up separate councils, the Humanities Research Council and the Social Sciences Research Council, which converted into the two learned academies: the Australian Academy of the Humanities (AAH), established in 1969,[19] and the Academy of the Social Sciences in Australia (ASSA), which formed in 1971. The fourth learned academy was the Australian Academy of Technological Sciences (ATS), established in 1976 when applied scientists felt the need for a distinct academy separate from the AAS;[20] the ATS eventually incorporated engineers and used the acronym ATSE. The means by which fellows were elected differed slightly between the academies, but basic to it was the promotion of a candidate by several fellows, an initial assessment from the appropriate disciplinary section through a secret ballot

---

15   'Second Discussion Session', in Stuart Macintyre and Peter McPhee eds, *Max Crawford's School of History* (Melbourne: History Department, University of Melbourne, 2000), 75.

16   'Margaret Kiddle to Max Crawford', 29 January 1958, Fitzpatrick Collection, Box 16.

17   See Stuart Macintyre, *The Poor Relation: A History of the Social Sciences in Australia* (Melbourne: Melbourne University Press, 2010).

18   See Frank Fenner, *The Australian Academy of Science: The First Twenty-Five Years* (Canberra: Australian Academy of Science, 1980).

19   Graeme Davison wrote on the inauguration of the AAH in 'Phoenix Rising: The Academy and the Humanities in 1969', *Humanities Australia* 1 (2010): 6–14.

20   See John W. Zillman, *ATSE 1975–2005: The First 30 Years—A Short History of the Origins and Development of the Australian Academy of Technological Sciences and Engineering (ATSE)* (Melbourne: ATSE, 2005).

and, if there was sufficient approval, the confirmation of a candidate through a vote of the entire membership. The AAS had a tight restriction on the number of new fellows elected from each section. While the AAH and the ASSA similarly grouped fellows into disciplinary interest groups, they were more flexible in their evaluations of scholarly achievement. There have of course been numerous excellent scholars who have escaped identification as potential academicians: indeed, some used to assert that one's chances of being nominated for an academy lessened with every mile of distance from Canberra. We can nevertheless say that those who were elected to fellowships were outstanding in research.

Despite an unwelcoming academic climate in the universities in the early decades of the century, some senior male academics stood out for their keenness to nurture the academic aspirations of women, some of whom received institutional support for excellent careers. Fifteen women became fellows of the learned academies between 1956, when the first woman, Dorothy Hill, was elected to the AAS, and 1976, when two women became inaugural fellows of the ATS. Five of the fellows were pure or applied scientists, and 10 were from the humanities and social sciences. Seven of the 15 fellows were born before or during World War I, and the remaining eight were born in the 1920s and 1930s. Three were born outside Australia and almost all, if they undertook doctorates, did so in overseas universities; just one graduated a PhD from an Australian university, but this followed advanced research experience in two northern countries. All travelled on diverse pathways to research prominence, sustained by their families' investment in their educational achievements and by the encouragement of (usually) male university mentors. Their ultimate success, however, was a tribute to their personal talents, ingenuity and determination.[21] Their careers constituted notable achievement in an academic climate generally discouraging of female endeavour. Their leadership lay not only in their innovation in their disciplines but also in their pioneering status, which gave heart and encouragement to other women who followed them. Many of these pioneers, of course, mentored a rising generation of young women scholars.

The fellows elected to the AAS entered tertiary institutions straight from school, proceeded into doctoral studies without a lengthy break and entered tertiary employment with exemplary track records. They were prominent in geology, mathematics and physiology. The first academician, Queensland geologist Dorothy Hill, was elected to the AAS in 1956 at the age of forty-nine. Born in Brisbane in 1907, she undertook a science degree at the University of Queensland, where she graduated in 1928 with first-class honours in geology. She

---

21 For a fuller examination of the careers of the first female academicians, see: Patricia Grimshaw and Rosemary Francis, 'Women Research Leaders in the Australian Learned Academies: 1954–1976', in *Seizing the Initiative: Australian Women Leaders in Politics, Workplaces and Communities*, eds Rosemary Francis, Patricia Grimshaw and Ann Standish (Melbourne: eScholarship Research Centre, University of Melbourne, 2012), 223–46.

then proceeded on a scholarship to Cambridge University, where she completed a doctorate focused on the study of corals that would become her continuing research area. Following short-term fellowships, Hill returned in 1937 to a position at her home university in Brisbane. Despite a career interrupted by years of war work, her publications when she became a fellow reflected a fine research engagement.[22] Among other many later accomplishments, in 1970 Hill held a year's interim position as president of the AAS; it would be 25 years before another woman headed a learned academy.

There was a gap until 1969 when the academy elected the fifty-five-year-old mathematician Hanna Neumann. Like other academics in Australian universities, her education had been entirely gained abroad—in her case, her school education also, during a disturbed period. Born in Berlin in 1914, she graduated from the University of Berlin with distinction in 1936 and began postgraduate research at the University of Gottingen. In 1938 she joined her fiancé, the Jewish refugee and mathematician Bernhard Neumann, who had fled to England. There the couple married; they had five children. While her husband found temporary employment elsewhere, Hanna enrolled as an external student at Oxford University, pursuing doctoral research while living in a caravan with her growing family around her.[23] She graduated DPhil in 1944 and was awarded an Oxford DSc in 1955. After holding academic positions in Britain, in 1962 she was appointed, along with her husband, to The Australian National University, where she was eventually promoted to a professorship. A specialist in group theory and a mathematician of profound originality, she died of a brain aneurism in 1971, two years after her election.

The physiologist Mollie Holman was aged forty when in 1970 she became the third woman elected to the AAS. Born in Launceston in 1930, the daughter of a radiologist, her secondary education was completed at Merton Hall in Melbourne. She proceeded to an undergraduate degree at the University of Melbourne with a BSc in 1952 and an MA in physiology under Professor Douglas Wright in 1955. For her doctorate at Oxford University, she focused

22 'Dr John Cole, Interview with Dorothy Hill', 1981, www.science.org.au/fellows/memoirs.hill.html; K. S. W Campbell and J. S. Jell, 'Dorothy Hill 1907–1997', *Historical Records of Australian Science* 12(2) (1998): 205–28; Tim Sherratt, 'Finding Life in Ancient Corals: Dorothy Hill', *Australasian Science* (Summer 1995), Australian Science Archives Project, www.asap.unimelb.edu.au/bsparcs/exhib/journal/as. See also: http://www.australianwomen.info. For Australian women in science, see: Carey, 'Departing from their Sphere?'; Claire Hooker, *Irresistible Forces: Australian Women in Science* (Melbourne: Melbourne University Press, 2004); Ragbir Bhathal, ed., *Profiles: Australian Women Scientists* (Canberra: National Library of Australia, 1999).
23 Kenneth F. Fowler, 'Neumann, Hanna (1914–1971)', in *Australian Dictionary of Biography. Volume 15* (Melbourne: Melbourne University Press, 2000), 465; Michael Newman and Gordon Wall, 'Hanna Neumann 1914–1971', *Records of the Australian Academy of Science* 3(2) (1975), www.science.org.au/fellows/memoirs. hill.html; G. E. Wall, 'Hanna Neumann', *Journal of the Australian Mathematical Society* 17(1) (1974): 1–28; Rosanne Walker, 'Hanna Neumann (1914–1971)', *Australasian Science* 22(1) (2001): 46; 'Interview by Professor Bob Crompton with Bernard Neumann', 1998, www.science.org.au/scientists/interviews/html.

on the interaction of nerve cells with smooth muscles in the body, which she would continue to develop into what became major research findings. When she returned to a lectureship at the University of Melbourne, she found she had been allocated a laboratory in the university paint shop. She moved quite soon in 1963 to a senior lectureship at Monash University, where in 1970 she received a personal chair, and where she stayed throughout her career.[24]

The AAH appointed four women as inaugural fellows in 1969: two historians, an art historian and a specialist in literary studies. Three were serving members of the Humanities Research Council: Ursula Hoff, Marnie Bassett and Kathleen Fitzpatrick. Ursula Hoff, sixty years of age in 1969, had experienced—as was the case with Neumann—an education disrupted by the rise of Nazism. Born in London in 1909 to German Jewish parents, she graduated from Hamburg University in English literature and art history, but fled with her family to London in 1933 when Hitler came to power. She returned to Hamburg to complete her doctoral thesis on Rembrandt in 1935. She found work in prestigious London museums before migrating to Australia in 1939 to take up a secretarial position at University Women's College in Melbourne. Eventually she worked as keeper of prints and drawings in the National Gallery of Victoria and as lecturer in art history at the University of Melbourne. She was widely esteemed for her significant studies of European and Australian art history and enjoyed a very long and distinguished career until her death in Melbourne in 2005.[25]

The historians Kathleen Fitzpatrick and Marnie Bassett and the literary critic and poet Judith Wright did not hold doctorates: it was their highly respected published writing that had established their scholarly reputations.[26] Fitzpatrick, mentioned above for a new professor's condescending treatment, was sixty-four when she became a foundation member of the AAH, seven years after retiring from the history school at the University of Melbourne.[27] She was born in rural Victoria in 1905, completed a BA honours at the University of Melbourne in 1926 and two years later a second BA, at Oxford University. She returned to

---

24 Holman Interview; Bhathal, *Profiles*, 99–106; 'Interview by Dr Max Blythe', 1998, www.science.org.au/scientists/interviews/html; Bhathal, 'Mollie Holman'. For other studies of women in science, see: Farley Kelly, *On the Edge of Discovery: Australian Women in Science* (Melbourne: Text Publishing, 1993).

25 Jaynie Anderson, 'Ursula Hoff (1909–2005)', http://www.humanities.org.au/Fellowship/Obituaries.aspx; Colin Holden, *The Outsider: A Portrait of Ursula Hoff* (Melbourne: Australian Scholarly Publishing, 2009).

26 Kathleen Fitzpatrick, *Solid Bluestone Foundations and Other Memories of a Melbourne Girlhood 1908–1928* (Melbourne: Macmillan, 1983); Kathleen Fitzpatrick, 'A Cloistered Life', in *The Half-Open Door: Sixteen Modern Australian Women Look at Professional Life and Achievement*, eds Patricia Grimshaw and Lynne Strahan (Sydney: Hale & Iremonger, 1982), 118–33.

27 Alison Patrick, 'Fitzpatrick, Kathleen Elizabeth (1905–1990)', *Australian Dictionary of Biography Online* (Canberra: National Centre of Biography, The Australian National University), http://adb.anu.edu.au/biography/fitzpatrick/kathleen-elizabeth-12500/text22491; Jane Carey and Patricia Grimshaw, *Women Historians and Women's History: Kathleen Fitzpatrick (1905–1990), Margaret Kiddle (1914–1958) and the Melbourne History School* (Melbourne: Department of History, University of Melbourne, 2001); Kathleen Fitzpatrick, *Martin Boyd* (Melbourne: Lansdowne Press, 1963).

Australia to a temporary lecturing appointment but on her marriage to Brian Fitzpatrick in 1932, as was required of married women, she had to resign. Following a divorce, she returned to a lectureship in the history school at Melbourne in 1939. She served in the war as president of the Council for Women in War Work, and was promoted in the school to senior lecturer in 1942 and associate professor in 1948. She acted as head of department in the professor's absences and became celebrated as a gifted teacher. By the time of her admission to the AAH in 1969, Fitzpatrick's publications included biographies of Sir John Franklin and Martin Boyd and a study of Australian explorers.[28] She proceeded to research and publish, including an acclaimed autobiography, *Solid Bluestone Foundations*, until her death in 1990.

The most senior of the first group of academicians, Marnie Bassett, was eighty at her admission to the AAH. Born in Melbourne in 1889 and educated at home by governesses, she was refused permission by her mother to enrol in a degree and instead she worked as a secretary for her academic father. A lover of history, she audited lectures at the University of Melbourne, where Professor Ernest Scott fostered her early research. After war work, she married and postponed ambitions to undertake research as she raised her three children. From 1940, however, she published a steady stream of books that swiftly became classics of Australian history; particularly impressive was her biographical writing on colonial subjects, *The Governor's Lady* (1940) and *The Hentys: A Colonial Tapestry* (1954). Monash University awarded her an honorary DLitt degree in 1968; the University of Melbourne did likewise in 1974.[29] She died in 1980. The fourth of the inaugural fellows was the poet Judith Wright McKinney, better known as Judith Wright. She was born on a pastoral station in northern New South Wales in 1915, was educated at home and attended boarding school for her final secondary years. She began a BA degree at the University of Sydney but could not graduate because she had not matriculated, lacking the required standard in mathematics. Nevertheless, for a period Wright tutored casually in the English Department at the University of Sydney.[30] By 1969, when she was elected to the AAH, her critical literary writing was widely admired, but even more so, her poetry. Her output and reputation continued to grow up to her death in 2000.

The remaining two AAH fellows appointed up to 1976 were the scholar of English Leonie Kramer and the French literary specialist Judith Robinson-Valery. Both

---

28 See Grimshaw and Carey, 'Foremothers VI'.

29 Ann Blainey, 'Bassett, Lady Flora Marjorie (Marnie) (1889–1980)', *Australian Dictionary of Biography Online* (Canberra: National Centre of Biography, The Australian National University), http://adb.anu.edu.au/biography/bassett-lady-flora-marjorie-marnie-9448/text16613.

30 Elizabeth Webby, 'Judith Wright McKinney (1915–2000) Obituary', http://www.humanities.org.au/Fellowship/Obituaries.aspx; Judith Wright, *Half a Lifetime*, ed. Patricia Clarke (Melbourne: Text Publishing, 1999); Veronica Brady, *South of My Days: A Biography of Judith Wright* (Sydney: Angus & Robertson, 1998).

were Australian-born and educated and had undertaken postgraduate work abroad. The Canberra-born (in 1933) French language expert Judith Robinson-Valery completed her doctorate at the Sorbonne in Paris following her first degree at the University of Sydney. Her thesis was published in 1958, while she held a research fellowship at Girton College, Cambridge. For 11 years from 1963, she held a professorship at the University of New South Wales, and was elected to the AAH in 1972 at the age of thirty-nine, cited as a distinguished scholar in French literature. She returned to Paris to live and work in 1974, and died there in 2010.[31] Kramer, a specialist in Australian literature, was elected to the AAH in 1974. She was born Leonie Gibson in Melbourne in 1924 and was educated at the Presbyterian Ladies' College. After her undergraduate degree at the University of Melbourne, she completed a PhD at Oxford University, and returned to Australia to take up a lectureship at the University of New South Wales. She became a professor at the University of Sydney in 1968 where she continued to pursue a productive and influential career that included a period as chancellor of the university.[32]

Unlike the situation in the AAH, there were no female members of the Social Science Research Council when most of the existing members became inaugural fellows of the ASSA in 1971: the outstanding English-born and Cambridge-educated Pacific anthropologist Camilla Wedgwood, who had held a number of posts in Australia, had been a member but died in 1955.[33] Norma McArthur, the notable demographer of the Pacific Islands, was elected as an inaugural fellow. She had moved from her Australian undergraduate degree to undertake research for a PhD at the University of London. No explanation is given for her decision to resign at the end of her first year in the ASSA. Her extensive original, path-breaking research continued to be consulted up to her death in 1984 and beyond.[34]

Several others of the early academicians in the ASSA undertook their doctoral research in the United States rather than the United Kingdom—a choice that, given American prominence in the fast-developing area, would grow in popularity. The sociologist Jean Martin was elected to the ASSA in its first year. Born in Melbourne in 1923, she completed an undergraduate degree at

---

31   Robert Pickering, 'Judith Robinson-Valery 1933–2012', *Australian Journal of French Studies* (September 2010); James Lawler, 'Robinson-Valery, Judith Ogilvie (1933–2010)', www.humanities.org.au/Fellowship/Obituaries.aspx.

32   'Kramer, Leonie Judith', in *The Oxford Companion to Australian History*, eds Graeme Davison, John Hirst and Stuart Macintyre (Melbourne: Oxford University Press, 2000); 'Kramer, Leonie Judith, (1924–)', http://www.womenaustralia.info/biogs/IMP0037b.htm.

33   David Wetherell, 'Wedgwood, Camilla Hildegarde (1901–1955)', *Australian Dictionary of Biography Online* (Canberra: National Centre of Biography, The Australian National University), http://adb.anu.edu.au/biography/wedgwood-camilla-hildegarde-11992/text21503.

34   See 'McArthur, Norma (1921–1984)', *Obituaries Australia Online* (Canberra: National Centre of Biography, The Australian National University), http://oa.anu.edu.au/obituary/mcarthur-norma-677/text678.

the University of Sydney before pursuing research at the London School of Economics and the University of Chicago. She returned to Australia and completed her PhD at The Australian National University. In 1965 she became the inaugural professor of sociology at La Trobe University.[35] She died in 1979, having made a remarkable impact on the development of studies of migration and multicultural Australia. Two further early fellows were the legal scholar Enid Campbell and the sociologist Jacqueline Goodnow. Elected in 1972 at forty years of age, Campbell undertook a PhD at Duke University in North Carolina before taking up an appointment at Monash University; in 1967 she was promoted to a professorship.[36] Campbell, renowned then and now as a gifted scholar of constitutional studies, died in 2012. Goodnow was elected to the ASSA in 1976. Born in Toowoomba, Queensland, she undertook her first degree at the University of Sydney, followed by a PhD from Harvard University; she was appointed a professor at Macquarie University in the year of her election.[37] She was and remains highly influential in her field of the sociology of families, communities and cultures.

Finally, in the ranks of this group of early fellows were two women who figured among the inaugural fellows of the ATS(E) in 1976. Both were employed for most of their working lives in research institutes rather than in universities. The food scientist June Olley was born in London in 1924. She completed a PhD at the University of London and held a research position in Scotland before moving in 1968 to work in the Commonwealth Scientific and Industrial Research Organisation (CSIRO) in Tasmania. Olley was fifty-two years old when she became a fellow in the ATS in 1976 for her notable work as a fish technologist. The animal geneticist Helen Newton Turner was sixty-eight and retired when she was elected to the ATS in 1976. She was by then an internationally recognised world expert on sheep genetics, with research that had a substantial impact on merino sheep breeding.[38] Born in Sydney in 1908, she graduated with a degree

---

35   Katy Richmond, 'Martin, Jean Isobel (1923–1979)', *Australian Dictionary of Biography. Volume 15* (Melbourne: Melbourne University Press, 2000); Wilfred David Borrie, 'Dr Jean Isobel Martin', in *Annual Report of the ASSA 1978–1979*, 10. See also Macintyre, *The Poor Relation*.

36   Matthew Groves (ed.), *Law and Government in Australia: Essays in Honour of Enid Campbell* (Melbourne: Federation Press, 2005); Matthew Groves, 'Obituary: Enid Mona Campbell AC, OBE, 1932–2010', *AIAL Forum* 63 (2009): 1–3.

37   Academy of Social Sciences in Australia, 'Emeritus Professor Jacqueline Goodnow', *Academy Fellows*, http://www.assa.edu.au/fellowship/fellow/116; Jacqueline Goodnow, Interviewed by Nikki Henningham, 2005, National Library of Australia Oral History and Folklore Collection, NLA ORAL TRC 5547, National Library of Australia, Canberra; 'Jacqueline Jarrett Goodnow', in *Women in Psychology: A Biobibliographic Sourcebook*, eds A. N. O'Connell and M. K. Russo (New York: Greenwood Press, 1990), 134–42.

38   Helen Newton Turner, Interviewed by Ann Moyal, 1993, National Library of Australia Oral History and Folklore Collection, NLA ORAL TRC 2902, National Library of Australia, Canberra; Ann Moyal, ed., *Portraits in Science* (Canberra: National Library of Australia, 1994); Nessy Allen, 'Australian Women in Science: Two Unorthodox Careers', *Women's Studies International Forum* 15(5–6) (1992): 551–62; and Nessy Allen, 'Helen Newton Turner and the Wool Industry', *Journal of Australian Studies* 33 (1992): 56–62; Gavan McCarthy, 'Turner, Helen Alma Newton (1908–1995)', in *Encyclopedia of Australian Science*, www.eoas.info/biogs/ P004129b.

in architecture from the University of Sydney, but, unemployed in the 1930s depression, she learned typing and found a job as a secretary to Dr Ian Clunies Ross in the Council for Scientific and Industrial Research (CSIR, later the CSIRO) division of animal health. Curious about the data she typed, she returned to university part-time to undertake statistics subjects. Impressed by her talent, Clunies Ross awarded her overseas leave to work alongside a foremost British statistician. She returned home to the post of senior research scientist in the Division of Animal Genetics, leading the team working on sheep genetics from 1956 to 1973. In 1970 she was awarded the degree of Doctor of Science at the University of Sydney. In retirement, she continued offering practical assistance in science nationally and internationally until her death in 1995.

Of this first group of academicians, Leonie Kramer, Judith Robinson-Valery, Jean Martin and Jacqueline Goodnow embarked on their first jobs as married women with children, and achieved their notable work under complex domestic and work conditions. It was an intimation of things to come, as marriage bars disappeared and new notions of the gender division of labour altered women's perceptions of balancing the work of care with waged work.[39] A postwar economic boom on the back of industrial development and a vigorous immigration policy brought marked changes in the capacity of the Australian workforce to include adult women as workers. Educational opportunities for girls at secondary level expanded along with the establishment of numerous new tertiary institutions. The number of women students in higher education grew and these students diversified their choices of courses to include the professional sector—for example, law and medicine. Significantly for the academic profession, the proportion also rose of women opting for research higher degrees, including the PhD, which was emerging as essential for securing an ongoing lectureship. Not only did more women gain entry-point positions but also through promotion processes women began to hold positions at the upper levels of the academic ladder, including professorships, in increasing numbers.[40]

Beginning in the mid to late 1960s, there was an influx of married women into the waged workforce, including the academic profession, which increased the pool of talent very considerably. A major social movement, based in the labour movement and the separate middle-class women's groups, stimulated changes in attitudes towards women and women's own aspirations.[41] These groups collaborated to undermine the entrenched notion of the family wage that had prioritised male waged work and to unsettle gender divisions within

39   Grimshaw et al., *Double Shift*.
40   Beverley Ward, 'The Female Professor: A Rare Australian Species, the Who and How' (PhD thesis, Murdoch University, Perth, 2003).
41   Marilyn Lake, *Getting Equal: The History of Australian Feminism* (Sydney: Allen & Unwin, 1999).

workplaces.[42] The pace of women's entry into tertiary research quickened considerably with equal opportunity legislation and increasingly included women with children. The movement of aspirant female academics into advanced education, first employment and promotion benefited in the 1980s from the equal employment opportunity legislation seen through Federal Parliament by the Australian Labor Party government under Bob Hawke. The *Sex Discrimination Act* of 1984 outlawed discrimination on the basis of sex in employment and the *Affirmative Action Act* of 1986 made the reporting of statistics on women in the profession mandatory. Universities immediately established units to monitor women's employment and establish targets (not quotas) for the recruitment and promotion of women to the higher levels of the academic hierarchy. These innovations had a remarkable impact on the work situations of women in most tertiary institutions.

The pool of potential female researchers and hence of future academicians enlarged in an impressive fashion. The flow of women into the academies followed accordingly in the 1980s, 1990s and early 2000s. In 1976 the total membership of the AAS after 22 years of operation stood at 194, two of whom were women. In the same year there were 112 fellows of the AAH, five of whom were women, and 150 ASSA fellows—a number that included three women. The total membership of the ATS in its first year of 1976 was 64, including two women. With the increased number of women in a wider range of research degrees, their appearance at the upper levels of the academic ladder became commonplace. Far more potential fellows emerged and the critical mass of female fellows within the academies stimulated further nominations of women. Elections of women, especially in the AAH and the ASSA, edged up in the 1980s and then increased quite rapidly in the 1990s and 2000s.

The rate of increase was most marked in the ASSA. Following on from McArthur, Martin, Campbell and Goodnow in the early 1970s, it elected the anthropologist Marie Reay in 1977 and the geographer Fay Gale in 1979. In the 1980s nine further women were elected: political scientist Carole Pateman, historian Pat Jalland, economist Helen Hughes, Beverley Raphael in social medicine, lawyers Marcia Neave and Alice Tay, and three sociologists, Eva Etzioni-Halevy, Bettina Cass and Jane Marceau. In the 1990s it elected 46 women and in the 2000s, 72; and 10 more women were admitted as fellows in 2011.[43]

There was also a noticeable increase in the elections of women to the AAH. Following Leonie Kramer in 1974, it elected the linguist Luise Hercus in 1978

---

42   Patricia Grimshaw, Nell Musgrove and Shurlee Swain, 'The Australian Labour Movement and Working Mothers in the United Nation's Decade for Women, 1975–1985', in *The Time of their Lives: The Eight Hour Day and Working Life*, eds J. Kimber and P. Love (Melbourne: Australian Society for the Study of Labour History, 2007), 137–52.

43   See information on the ASSA website: www.assa.edu.au.

and archaeologist Isabel McBride in 1979. The 1980s saw the election of nine women: in the arts and art history, Virginia Spate, Margaret Manion, Ann Galbally and Margaret Plant; in history, Dale Kent; in Asian studies, Margaret Kartomi; in archaeology, Sylvia Hallam and Betty Meehan; and Anna Wierzbicka in linguistics. In the 1990s, 30 women were elected and in the 2000s, a further 50.[44]

The increase was also apparent in the two science academies, although the record was less impressive. There were comparatively fewer women in professorial or other senior research posts in science but the science academies also appeared to resist any special efforts to identify and elect women of talent.[45] No further women were elected to the AAS in the 1970s after Holman and in the 1980s just three more were admitted: palaeontologist Elizabeth Truswell, molecular geneticist Suzanne Cory and biologist Jan Anderson. These entry numbers tripled in the 1990s, with nine women elected, and in the first decade of the 2000s a further 20 women were elected. Turning to the ATSE, after its initial appointments in the inaugural year, the academy elected microbiologist Nancy Millis in 1977, followed in the 1980s by plant biologists Elizabeth Dennis and Adrienne Clarke. Seventeen more women were elected in the 1990s. By the end of 2012, just more than one-tenth of the AAS membership and just less than one-tenth of the ATSE were women. In comparison, about one-fifth of the fellows in the AAH and one-quarter in the ASSA were women.[46]

Among the outstanding women elected to the academies in these later years were five who became leaders of the academies themselves when they were elected president. The University of Sydney archaeologist Professor Margaret Clunies Ross was president from 1995 to 1998, and its current president, cultural studies scholar Professor Lesley Johnson, was elected to the post at the end of 2011. Geographer Professor Fay Gale held the presidency of the ASSA from 1998 to 2000 and was succeeded by economist Professor Sue Richardson for a term from 2001 to 2003. The current, and first female, elected president of the AAS is molecular biologist Professor Suzanne Cory, who assumed the presidency in 2010. All bar one of these women were born in the 1940s. Elected to the academies as outstanding researchers, they had all shown a remarkable range of skills in other academic work including administrative leadership.

---

44 See information on the AAH website: www.humanities.org.au.

45 Professor Tom Healy, Personal communication, Melbourne, 24 April 2012.

46 At the end of 2012, the numbers of female and male fellows of the learned academies stood as follows: the AAH had 561 fellows, including overseas and honorary fellows, of whom 102 were women; the ASSA had 535 fellows, including honorary and overseas fellows, of whom 143 were women; the AAS had more than 400 fellows, of whom 42 were women; and the ATSE had more than 800 fellows, of whom 60 were women. Sources: academy websites. At their elections in 2012, the AAH elected 16 new fellows, eight of whom were women (50 per cent); the ASSA elected 17 new fellows, four of whom were women (approximately 25 per cent); the AAS elected 21 new fellows, four of whom were women (19 per cent); and the ATSE elected 38 new fellows, 11 of whom were women (approximately 29 per cent).

All five held doctorates—Clunies Ross and Cory from Oxford University, but Johnson, Gale and Richardson from Australian universities, indicating that outstanding research training was no longer confined exclusively to top northern-hemisphere universities. By the date of their election to their academies and since, they had carried out outstanding research within lecturing positions. Most had raised children alongside their demanding academic work, which had ceased to be anomalous, though the logistics of combining waged work and child care continued to complicate women's lives rather more than men's.[47] They were not only internationally known and respected but also had been able, through cheaper travel and through the Internet, to access materials and sustain networks of allied scholars throughout the world, enabling continual collaboration and sharing of knowledge.

All assumed these leadership positions in the academies after undertaking university administrative leadership, several at very senior levels, demonstrating the practice of Australian universities of encouraging their top researchers into administration. Women first entered leadership positions as heads of departments and schools, deans of faculties and heads of research centres, professional associations and national units such as Australian Research Council (ARC) panels. From the appointment in 1987 of Professor Diane Yerbury as Australia's first female vice-chancellor at Macquarie University in Sydney, a small but growing number of women have become deputy vice-chancellors and vice-chancellors.

Margaret Clunies Ross was elected to the AAH in 1990 for outstanding expertise in Old and Middle English language and literature, and Old Norse (Old Icelandic) language and literature. Born in Adelaide in 1942, her first degree was from the University of Adelaide in English and her doctorate was from Oxford University (Somerville College). She served on the council of the AAH before taking up the presidency. She headed a research centre in her area at the University of Sydney.[48] The second woman appointed as AAH president, Sydney-born Lesley Johnson, was elected to the AAH in 1999 for her scholarly contribution to cultural studies, Australian history and gender studies. Her undergraduate degree was from the University of Sydney; she undertook a Masters of Education at the University of Queensland and a PhD at Monash University. Johnson became pro-vice-chancellor (research) at the University of Technology, Sydney, in 1995, a position she held for nine years; from 2004 to 2009, she was deputy vice-chancellor (research) at Griffith University. Johnson

---

47 See Alexis Coe, 'Being Married Helps Professors Get Ahead, but Only if They're Male', *The Atlantic*, 17 January 2013.
48 For details on Margaret Clunies Ross, see www.humanities.org.au; University of Sydney website: www. sydney.edu.au; Sharon Maree Harrison, 'Clunies Ross, Margaret Beryl', in *The Encyclopedia of Women's Leadership in Twentieth-Century Australia*, eds Judith Smart and Shurlee Swain (Australian Women's Archive Project, 2014), http://www.womenaustralia.info/leaders/biogs/WLE0547b.htm.

also served on various ARC committees and for three years was a member of its council.[49] Professor Anna Haebich and Professor Gillian Whitlock are currently vice-presidents of the AAH—a post several other women have held in the AAH in the past decade: Professors Ros Pesman (2005–06); Anne Freadman (2007); Elizabeth Webby (2007–09); and Kate Burridge (2007–09).

Fay Gale, the second woman to lead an academy and the first to lead the ASSA, was born in Adelaide in 1932, attended the University of Adelaide for her undergraduate and doctoral degrees and was in 1979 elected fellow of the ASSA for her outstanding research that included studies of urban Aborigines. Gale had a distinguished research career, combined with extensive senior administration. In 1978, she became the first woman professor at the University of Adelaide; she was appointed pro-vice-chancellor in 1988 and subsequently became vice-chancellor of the University of Western Australia in 1990. She died in 2008.[50] Sue Richardson, born in Melbourne in 1946, undertook her undergraduate degree at the University of Melbourne and her doctorate at La Trobe University, becoming its first doctoral graduate. Her research has focused on the labour market, and she served for a period as director of the National Institute of Labour Studies at Flinders University of South Australia.[51] The incoming president of the ASSA in 2013, psychologist Professor Deborah Terry, is another academician who has combined a fine research engagement with senior administration; she is currently Deputy Vice-Chancellor of the University of Queensland.

Suzanne Cory, born in Melbourne in 1942, undertook her first degree at the University of Melbourne and her doctorate at Cambridge University, where she worked in the laboratory of the Nobel Prize winner Francis Crick.[52] After postdoctoral research, she returned to Melbourne in 1971 to work at the Walter and Eliza Hall Institute of Medical Research in Melbourne. She served as its director from 1996 to 2009. She was elected a fellow of the AAS in 1986 and in

49   For details on Lesley Johnson, see ASSA website: www.assa.edu.au; Sharon Maree Harrison, 'Johnson, Lesley Ruth', in *The Encyclopedia of Women's Leadership in Twentieth-Century Australia*, eds Judith Smart and Shurlee Swain (Australian Women's Archive Project, 2014), http://www.womenaustralia.info/leaders/biogs/WLE0552b.htm.

50   For details on Fay Gale, see ASSA website: www.assa.edu.au. See also Fay Gale, 'Taking on the Academy', in *Carrying the Banner: Women, Leadership and Activism in Australia*, eds Joan Eveline and Lorraine Hayden (Perth: University of Western Australia Press, 1999), 136–44; Sharon Maree Harrison, 'Gale, Gwendoline Fay', in *The Encyclopedia of Women's Leadership in Twentieth-Century Australia*, eds Judith Smart and Shurlee Swain (Australian Women's Archive Project, 2014), http://www.womenaustralia.info/leaders/biogs/WLE0574b.htm.

51   For details on Sue Richardson, see ASSA website: www.assa.edu.au; Flinders University website: www.flinders.edu.au; Sharon Maree Harrison, 'Richardson, Susan (Sue)', in *The Encyclopedia of Women's Leadership in Twentieth-Century Australia*, eds Judith Smart and Shurlee Swain (Australian Women's Archive Project, 2014), http://www.womenaustralia.info/leaders/biogs/WLE0570b.htm.

52   For details on Suzanne Cory, see http://science.org.au/fellows/council/index.html; Ragbir Bhathal, 'Suzanne Cory: Medical Scientist', in *Profiles: Australian Women Scientists*, ed. Ragbir Bhathal (Canberra: National Library of Australia, 1999), 89–98; Sharon Maree Harrison, 'Cory, Suzanne', in *The Encyclopedia of Women's Leadership in Twentieth-Century Australia*, eds Judith Smart and Shurlee Swain (Australian Women's Archive Project, 2014), http://www.womenaustralia.info/leaders/biogs/WLE0541b.htm.

1992 became a fellow of the Royal Society of London. She has participated in highly important international as well as national research forums and scholarly organisations. Her work as president of the AAS has included advocacy for girls and women in science.

The ATSE has yet to appoint a woman as president, but Professor Mary O'Kane, a computer engineer in speech recognition, is currently vice-president. Born in 1954 in Mount Morgan, Queensland, her first degree in physics and mathematics was from the University of Queensland and her PhD from The Australian National University.[53] She was the first female vice-chancellor of the University of Adelaide, chaired the Research Grants Committee of the ARC and is currently the NSW Chief Scientist and Engineer. She serves an academy that is marked, as is the AAS, by a decided gender imbalance. In 2012, 52 of a total of some 800 members were women.[54] In the AAS in 2012 there were 35 female fellows out of a total of just more than 400, including corresponding fellows.[55] These figures contrasted fairly strongly with the proportions of fellows in the ASSA and the AAH: 140 women out of 524 fellows (including honorary fellows), in the ASSA; and 94 female fellows out of 524 fellows (including honorary fellows), in the AAH.

The marked gender imbalance in the science academies reflects the gender imbalance in senior science positions in the universities, though there are members of these academies who think they could with effort diminish the size of the gap. The ATSE has taken the somewhat unusual step for a learned academy to redress the gender ratio beginning with the academy's adoption in November 2010 of a gender equity policy. The policy 'recognises leadership is needed to address the gender imbalance both within the Academy membership and its activities as well as more broadly in promoting women in senior level in technological sciences and engineering in Australia'.[56] In 2011 the academy alerted fellows to an element of bias in their election process when it instituted a positive discrimination policy to increase the numbers of women fellows. It announced the establishment of a target for the election of women, to constitute one-third of new fellows elected each year.[57]

---

53   Ragbir Bhathal, 'Mary O'Kane: Computer Engineer', in *Profiles: Australian Women Scientists*, ed. Ragbir Bhathal (Canberra: National Library of Australia, 1999), 133–4; Harrison, 'Mary O'Kane'.
54   See information on the ATSE website: www.atse.org.au.
55   See information on the AAS website: www.science.org.au.
56   Australian Academy of Technological Sciences and Engineers (ATSE), 'ATSE Takes Further Gender Equity Steps', Media release, 29 June 2011.
57   Ibid.; Australian Academy of Technological Sciences and Engineers (ATSE). ATSE endorsed the UN Women's Empowerment Principles and the development of a program of action to back ATSE's Gender Equity Policy (including implementing the gender targets for membership) by an ATSE Gender Equity Implementation Group.

We may conclude that women have attained a considerable degree of equity in the tertiary sector in Australia when we look at more than 100 years of participation. We argue that the relative egalitarianism of Australian society has disguised the class and gender biases of access to professional employment: discriminatory access to the upper reaches of secondary education, social conservatism around the family and the strong gender division in workplaces that the countervailing pressure of the women's movement lessened but did not eliminate. This has had considerable implications for women who aspired to or gained work as academics. With the expectation that the state would fund universities, women from the 1920s competed unequally with men for positions in coeducational tertiary institutions. Starting after World War II but with greater frequency from the 1970s, women's increased entry into postgraduate research enabled them a more numerous place in the starting points for tenured positions from which they could be promoted to all levels of the academic hierarchy. Many excelled in research and some assumed academic administrative responsibilities. Fresh challenges to the funding base of universities have once again set in train differing trajectories in academia, given that women's training, entry and ability to sustain a foothold were bound to be comparatively fragile in these circumstances.

Partly because of the uneven spread of women across the disciplines, women in senior administrative positions by the first decade of the twenty-first century were proportionately fewer than men, even at the level of heads of departments, heads of schools and deans of faculties. This gender imbalance was more pronounced at the most senior levels. Universities Australia, the vice-chancellors' organisation, has recently discussed ways of identifying women with future career aspirations in senior administration and working to increase female numbers. Perhaps the very structure and assumptions of the positions are what deter women. Some social scientists in the field of leadership and management studies consider women have a distinctive management style—more consultative and more interested in seeking consensus than men.[58] Many senior women who participated in a research project in 2005 did not perceive themselves as treated equally as academic leaders, and found the pressure on them to sustain business management practices uncongenial. One female vice-chancellor was quoted as saying: 'You have to assert your authority. You're not given authority. You have to take it. Men are given it. It's a very significant difference.' Women were 'still judged more harshly, because they are not seen as legitimate leaders':

> When we look at a male manager going into a job we sit there and expect them to be successful and look for success. In Australia things are exactly the opposite for women. There's still a level at which we all

---

58 See Sinclair, *Doing Leadership Differently*; and 'Not Just "Adding Women In"'.

think at some deep psychological level that the first mistake they make is evidence of the fact that you're waiting for them to fail. I think that the whole issue for women is the amount of time that they've got to get runs on the boards is much less. It's very dangerous for them if there's a major misjudgement of which they're guilty in their reign.[59]

While the research horizons of women rose considerably in the last decades of the twentieth century, analysts of higher education unsettle any tendencies to complacency about the place of women in the new 'enterprise university', querying whether gains women have made would automatically continue.[60] Successive governments have squeezed the allocation of funds to the tertiary sector, and universities have been compelled to expand the sale of teaching and knowledge to continue their own development. The enrolment of full fee-paying Asian students has gone some way to meet the gap, in addition to the imposition of charges for domestic students to access fee-bearing post-first degree courses.[61] These changes have put particular pressure on non-professional areas such as the humanities. At a seminar at the University of Melbourne in October 2011, for example, Queensland researchers Glenda Strachan and Robyn May pointed to a trend towards the feminisation of teaching, its increasing casualisation and its consequent devaluation. Women remain most numerous at the first rungs of the academic hierarchy associated with teaching, as casual tutors and demonstrators and temporary lecturers.[62] Some would deny the claim that women across all levels invest more in teaching than do men, but anecdotally, certainly, women have the reputation of extending more generous attention to individual students and this reduces their involvement in research.

The *Workplace Gender Equality Act* passed by Julia Gillard's Labor Government in 2012 required all universities to report on five 'gender equality indicators', to identify existing problems and encourage improvements. The long, long trail

---

59   Chesterman et al., 'Changing the Landscape?' See also: Chesterman et al., '"Not Doable Jobs"'; Chesterman et al., 'The Gendered Impact on Organisations of a Critical Mass of Women in Senior Management'.

60   See Joan Eveline, *Ivory Basement Leadership: Power and Invisibility in the Changing University* (Perth: University of Western Australia Press, 2004); Ann Brooks and Alison Mackinnon, eds, *Gender and the Restructured University: Changing Management and Culture in Higher Education* (Buckingham, UK: Society for Research into Higher Education and Open University Press, 2001); A. Toy Caldwell-Colbert and Judith E. N. Albino, 'Women as Academic Leaders: Living the Experience from Two Perspectives', in *Women and Leadership: Transforming Visions and Diverse Voices*, eds Jean Lau Chin, Bernice Lott, Joy K. Rice and Janis Sanchez-Hucles (Maldon, Mass.: Blackwell, 2007).

61   Emmaline Bexley, Richard James and Sophie Arkoudis, *The Australian Academic Profession in Transition: Addressing the Challenge of Reconceptualising Academic Work and Regenerating the Academic Workforce* (Melbourne: Centre for the Study of Higher Education, University of Melbourne, 2011); Simon Marginson and Mark Considine, *The Enterprise University: Power, Governance and Reinvention in Australia* (Melbourne: Cambridge University Press, 2000); Andrew Norton, *Mapping Australian Higher Education* (Melbourne: Grattan Institute, 2012); Tony Coady, ed., *Why Universities Matter: A Conversation about Values, Means and Directions* (Sydney: Allen & Unwin, 2000).

62   Glenda Strachan and Robyn May, 'The Feminisation of the Academy? Statistics, Structures and Stories', Paper presented at the Symposium on Workplace Culture in Higher Education, University of Melbourne, October 2011.

of women in the academic profession in Australia still has a way to go before women attain, if not as the old song ran, the 'land of their dreams', then at least a position of relative equity. In the area of research, we can say numbers of scholars have persisted in cutting-edge research to the point where they have become leaders in their fields and influenced significantly the research endeavours of rising generations in this country and internationally.

References

Academy of Social Sciences in Australia. 'Emeritus Professor Jacqueline Goodnow.' *Academy Fellows.* http://www.assa.edu.au/fellowship/fellow/116.

Allen, Nessy. 'Australian Women in Science: Two Unorthodox Careers.' *Women's Studies InternationalForum* 15(5–6) (1992): 551–62.

Allen, Nessy. 'Helen Newton Turner and the Wool Industry.' *Journal of Australian Studies* 33 (1992): 56–62.

Anderson, Jaynie. 'Ursula Hoff (1909–2005).' http://www.humanities.org.au/Fellowship/Obituaries.aspx.

'ANU Presentation to the Review of the Institute of Advanced Studies 1990.' Typescript.

Australian Academy of Technological Sciences and Engineers (ATSE). Website. www.atse.org.au/.

Australian Academy of Technological Sciences and Engineers (ATSE). 'Women Prominent among New ATSE Fellows.' Media release, 3 November 2011.

Bexley, Emmaline, Richard James and Sophie Arkoudis. *The Australian Academic Profession in Transition: Addressing the Challenge of Reconceptualising Academic Work and Regenerating the Academic Workforce.* Melbourne: Centre for the Study of Higher Education, University of Melbourne, 2011.

Bhathal, Ragbir. 'Mary O'Kane: Computer Engineer.' In *Profiles: Australian Women Scientists*, edited by Ragbir Bhathal, 133–4. Canberra: National Library of Australia, 1999.

Bhathal, Ragbir. 'Mollie Holman: Physiologist.' In *Profiles: Australian Women Scientists*, edited by Ragbir Bhathal, 99–106. Canberra: National Library of Australia, 1999.

Bhathal, Ragbir, ed. *Profiles: Australian Women Scientists.* Canberra: National Library of Australia, 1999.

Bhathal, Ragbir. 'Suzanne Cory: Medical Scientist.' In *Profiles: Australian Women Scientists*, edited by Ragbir Bhathal, 89–98. Canberra: National Library of Australia, 1999.

Blainey, Ann. 'Bassett, Lady Flora Marjorie (Marnie) (1889–1980).' *Australian Dictionary of BiographyOnline*. Canberra: National Centre of Biography, The Australian National University. http://adb.anu.edu.au/biography/bassett-lady-flora-marjorie-marnie-9448/text16613.

Boreham, Paul, Alec Pemberton and Paul Wilson, eds. *The Professions in Australia: A Critical Appraisal*. Brisbane: University of Queensland Press, 1976.

Borrie, Wilfred David. 'Dr Jean Isobel Martin.' In *Annual Report of the ASSA 1978–1979*.

Bourdieu, Pierre. *Homo Academicus*. Paris: Editions de Minuit, 1984.

Brady, Veronica. *South of My Days: A Biography of Judith Wright*. Sydney: Angus & Robertson, 1998.

Brooks, Ann and Alison Mackinnon, eds. *Gender and the Restructured University: Changing Management and Culture in Higher Education*. Buckingham, UK: Society for Research into Higher Education and Open University Press, 2001.

Campbell, K. S. W. and J. S. Jell. 'Dorothy Hill 1907–1997.' *Historical Records of Australian Science* 12(2) (1998): 205–28.

Carey, Jane. 'Departing from their Sphere? Australian Women and Science, 1880–1960.' PhD thesis, University of Melbourne, 2003.

Carey, Jane and Patricia Grimshaw. *Women Historians and Women's History: Kathleen Fitzpatrick (1905–1990), Margaret Kiddle (1914–1958) and the Melbourne History School*. Melbourne: Department of History, University of Melbourne, 2001.

Cass, Bettina. *Why So Few? Women Academics in Australian Universities*. Sydney: University of Sydney Press, 1983.

Chesterman, Colleen, Anne Ross-Smith and Margaret Peters. 'Changing the Landscape? Women in Academic Leadership in Australia.' http://65.54.113.26/Publication/6223987/changing-the-landscape-women-in-academic-leadership-in-australia.

Chesterman, Colleen, Anne Ross-Smith and Margaret Peters. '"Not Doable Jobs": Exploring Women's Attitudes to Academic Leadership Roles.' *Women's Studies International Forum* 28(2) (2005): 163–80.

Chesterman, Colleen, Anne Ross-Smith and Margaret Peters. 'The Gendered Impact on Organisations of a Critical Mass of Women in Senior Management.' *Policy and Society* 24(4) (2005): 69–91.

Coady, Tony, ed. *Why Universities Matter: A Conversation about Values, Means and Directions.* Sydney: Allen & Unwin, 2000.

Coe, Alexis. 'Being Married Helps Professors Get Ahead, but Only if They're Male.' *The Atlantic*, 17 January 2013.

Connell, Raewyn. 'Core Activity: Reflexive Intellectual Workers and Cultural Crisis.' *Journal of Sociology* 42(1) (2006): 5–23.

Connell, Raewyn and June Crawford. 'Mapping the Intellectual Labour Process.' *Journal of Sociology* 43(2) (2007): 187–205.

Crawford, Patricia and Myrna Tonkinson. *The Missing Chapters: Women Staff at the University of Western Australia, 1963–1987.* Perth: Centre for Western Australian History, University of Western Australia, 1988.

Davison, Graeme. 'Phoenix Rising: The Academy and the Humanities in 1969.' *Humanities Australia* 1 (2010): 6–14.

Davison, Graeme and Kate Murphy. *University Unlimited: The Monash Story.* Sydney: Allen & Unwin, 2012.

Dawson, Madge and Heather Radi, eds. *Against the Odds: Fifteen Professional Women Reflect on their Lives and Careers.* Sydney: Hale & Iremonger, 1984.

'Dr John Cole, Interview with Dorothy Hill.' 1981. www.sciencearchive.org.au/fellows/memoirs/hill.html.

Eveline, Joan. *Ivory Basement Leadership: Power and Invisibility in the Changing University.* Perth: University of Western Australia Press, 2004.

Fenner, Frank. *The Australian Academy of Science: The First Twenty-Five Years.* Canberra: Australian Academy of Science, 1980.

Fitzgerald, Tanya, Julie White and Helen M. Gunter, eds. *Hard Labour? Academic Work and the Changing Landscape of Higher Education.* Bingley, UK: Emerald Electronic Resource, 2012.

Fitzpatrick, Kathleen Collection. University of Melbourne Archives, Melbourne.

Fitzpatrick, Kathleen. *Martin Boyd.* Melbourne: Lansdowne Press, 1963.

Fitzpatrick, Kathleen. 'A Cloistered Life.' In *The Half-Open Door: Sixteen Modern Australian Women Look at Professional Life and Achievement*, edited by Patricia Grimshaw and Lynne Strahan, 118–33. Sydney: Hale & Iremonger, 1982.

Fitzpatrick, Kathleen. *Solid Bluestone Foundations and Other Memories of a Melbourne Girlhood 1908–1928*. Melbourne: Macmillan, 1983.

Fowler, Kenneth F. 'Neumann, Hanna (1914–1971).' In *Australian Dictionary of Biography. Volume 15*. Melbourne: Melbourne University Press, 2000.

Gale, Fay. 'Taking on the Academy.' In *Carrying the Banner: Women, Leadership and Activism in Australia*, edited by Joan Eveline and Lorraine Hayden, 136–44. Perth: University of Western Australia Press, 1999.

Goodnow, Jacqueline. Interviewed by Nikki Henningham, 2005, National Library of Australia Oral History and Folklore Collection, ORAL TRC 5547. National Library of Australia, Canberra.

Grimshaw, Patricia and Jane Carey. 'Foremothers VI: Kathleen Fitzpatrick (1905-1990), Margaret Kiddle (1914–1958) and Australian History after the Second World War.' *Gender & History* 13(2) (August 2001): 349–73.

Grimshaw, Patricia and Rosemary Francis. 'Women Research Leaders in the Australian Learned Academies: 1954–1976.' In *Seizing the Initiative: Australian Women Leaders in Politics, Workplaces and Communities*, edited by Rosemary Francis, Patricia Grimshaw and Ann Standish, 223–46. Melbourne: eScholarship Research Centre, University of Melbourne, 2012.

Grimshaw, Patricia and Lynne Strachan, eds. *The Half-Open Door: Sixteen Modern Australian Women Look at Professional Life and Achievement*. Sydney: Hale & Iremonger, 1982.

Grimshaw, Patricia, John Murphy and Belinda Probert, eds. *Double Shift: Working Mothers and Social Change in Australia*. Melbourne: Circa, 2005.

Grimshaw, Patricia, Nell Musgrove and Shurlee Swain. 'The Australian Labour Movement and Working Mothers in the United Nation's Decade for Women, 1975–1985.' In *The Time of their Lives: The Eight Hour Day and Working Life*, edited by J. Kimber and P. Love, 137–52. Melbourne: Australian Society for the Study of Labour History, 2007.

Groves, Matthew, ed. Law and Government in Australia: Essays in Honour of Enid Campbell. Melbourne: Federation Press, 2005.

Groves, Matthew. 'Obituary: Enid Mona Campbell AC, OBE, 1932–2010.' *AIAL Forum* 63 (2009): 1–3.

Harrison, Sharon Maree. 'Clunies Ross, Margaret Beryl.' In *The Encyclopedia of Women's Leadership in Twentieth-Century Australia*, edited by Judith Smart and Shurlee Swain. Australian Women's Archive Project, 2014. http://www.womenaustralia.info/leaders/biogs/WLE0547b.htm.

Harrison, Sharon Maree. 'Cory, Suzanne.' In *The Encyclopedia of Women's Leadership in Twentieth-Century Australia*, edited by Judith Smart and Shurlee Swain. Australian Women's Archive Project, 2014. http://www.womenaustralia.info/leaders/biogs/WLE0541b.htm.

Harrison, Sharon Maree. 'Gale, Gwendoline Fay.' In *The Encyclopedia of Women's Leadership in Twentieth-Century Australia*, edited by Judith Smart and Shurlee Swain. Australian Women's Archive Project, 2014. http://www.womenaustralia.info/leaders/biogs/WLE0574b.htm.

Harrison, Sharon Maree. 'Johnson, Lesley Ruth.' In *The Encyclopedia of Women's Leadership in Twentieth-Century Australia*, edited by Judith Smart and Shurlee Swain. Australian Women's Archive Project, 2014. http://www.womenaustralia.info/leaders/biogs/WLE0552b.htm.

Harrison, Sharon Maree. 'O'Kane, Mary Josephine.' In *The Encyclopedia of Women's Leadership in Twentieth-Century Australia*, edited by Judith Smart and Shurlee Swain. Australian Women's Archive Project, 2014. http://www.womenaustralia.info/leaders/biogs/WLE0666b.htm.

Harrison, Sharon Maree. 'Richardson, Susan (Sue).' In *The Encyclopedia of Women's Leadership in Twentieth-Century Australia*, edited by Judith Smart and Shurlee Swain. Australian Women's Archive Project, 2014. http://www.womenaustralia.info/leaders/biogs/WLE0570b.htm.

Holden, Colin. *The Outsider: A Portrait of Ursula Hoff*. Melbourne: Australian Scholarly Publishing, 2009.

Holman, Mollie. Interviewed by Ragbir Bhathal, 1997, National Library of Australia Oral History and Folklore Collection, ORAL TRC 3600. National Library of Australia, Canberra.

Hooker, Claire. *Irresistible Forces: Australian Women in Science*. Melbourne: Melbourne University Press, 2004.

Horne, Julia and Geoff Sherington. *Sydney: The Making of a Public University*. Melbourne: Melbourne University Publishing, 2012.

'Interview by Professor Bob Crompton with Bernard Neumann.' 1998. www.sciencearchive.org.au/scientists/interviews/n/bn.html.

'Jacqueline Jarrett Goodnow.' In *Women in Psychology: A Biobibliographic Sourcebook*, edited by A. N. O'Connell and M. K. Russo, 134–42. New York: Greenwood Press, 1990.

Kelly, Farley. *Degrees of Liberation: A Short History of Women in the University of Melbourne*. Melbourne: Women Graduates Centenary Committee, University of Melbourne, 1985.

Kelly, Farley. *On the Edge of Discovery: Australian Women in Science*. Melbourne: Text Publishing, 1993.

Kingston, Beverley. *My Wife, My Daughter, and Poor Mary Ann: Women and Work in Australia*. Melbourne: Thomas Nelson, 1975.

'Kramer, Leonie Judith.' In *The Oxford Companion to Australian History*, edited by Graeme Davison, John Hirst and Stuart Macintyre. Melbourne: Oxford University Press, 2000.

'Kramer, Leonie Judith, (1924–).' http://www.womenaustralia.info/biogs/IMP0037b.htm.

Lake, Marilyn. *Getting Equal: The History of Australian Feminism*. Sydney: Allen & Unwin, 1999.

Lamont, Michele. *How Professors Think: Inside the Curious World of Academic Judgment*. Cambridge, Mass.: Harvard University Press, 2009.

Lawler, James. 'Robinson-Valery, Judith Ogilvie (1933–2010).' www.humanities.org.au/Fellowship/Obituaries.aspx.

'McArthur, Norma (1921–1984).' *Obituaries AustraliaOnline*. Canberra: National Centre of Biography, The Australian National University. http://oa.anu.edu.au/obituary/mcarthur-norma-677/text678.

McCalman, Janet. *Journeyings: The Biography of a Middle-Class Generation 1920–1990*. Melbourne: Melbourne University Press, 1995.

McCarthy, Gavan. 'Turner, Helen Alma Newton (1908–1995).' In *Encyclopedia of Australian Science*. www.eoas.info/biogs/P004129b.

Macintyre, Stuart and Richard Selleck. *A Short History of the University of Melbourne*. Melbourne: Melbourne University Press, 2003.

Macintyre, Stuart. *The Poor Relation: A History of the Social Sciences in Australia*. Melbourne: Melbourne University Press, 2010.

Macintyre, Stuart and Peter McPhee, eds. *Max Crawford's School of History*. Melbourne: History Department, University of Melbourne, 2000.

Mackinnon, Alison. *The New Women: Adelaide's Early Women Graduates*. Adelaide: Wakefield Press, 1986.

Mackinnon, Alison. *Love and Freedom: Professional Women and the Reshaping of Personal Life*. Melbourne: Cambridge University Press, 1997.

Mackinnon, Alison. *Women, Love and Learning: The Double Bind*. New York: P. Lang, 2012.

Marginson, Simon and Mark Considine. *The Enterprise University: Power, Governance and Reinvention in Australia*. Melbourne: Cambridge University Press, 2000.

Moyal, Ann, ed. *Portraits in Science*. Canberra: National Library of Australia, 1994.

Newman, Michael and Gordon Wall. 'Hanna Neumann 1914–1971.' *Records of the Australian Academy of Science* 3(2) (1975). http://sciencearchive.org.au/fellows/memoirs/neumann.html.

Norton, Andrew. *Mapping Australian Higher Education*. Melbourne: Grattan Institute, 2012.

Patrick, Alison. 'Fitzpatrick, Kathleen Elizabeth (1905–1990).' *Australian Dictionary of BiographyOnline*. Canberra: National Centre of Biography, The Australian National University. http://adb.anu.edu.au/biography/fitzpatrick/kathleen-elizabeth-12500/text22491.

Pickering, Robert. 'Judith Robinson-Valery, 1933–2012.' *Australian Journal of French Studies* (September 2010).

Poynter, John and Carolyn Rasmussen. *A History of the University of Melbourne, 1935–1975*. Melbourne: J. R. Poynter, 1995.

Richmond, Katy. 'Martin, Jean Isobel (1923–1979).' *Australian Dictionary of Biography. Volume 15*. Melbourne: Melbourne University Press, 2000.

Sherratt, Tim. 'Finding Life in Ancient Corals: Dorothy Hill.' *Australasian Science* (Summer 1995). Australian Science Archives Project. http://www.asap.unimelb.edu.au/bsparcs/exhib/journal/as_hill.htm.

Sinclair, Amanda. *Doing Leadership Differently: Gender, Power, and Sexuality in a Changing Business Culture*. Melbourne: Melbourne University Press, 1998.

Sinclair, Amanda. *Leadership for the Disillusioned: Moving beyond Myths and Heroes to Leading that Liberates*. Sydney: Allen & Unwin, 2007.

Sinclair, Amanda. 'Not Just "Adding Women In": Women Re-Making Leadership.' In *Seizing the Initiative: Australian Women Leaders in Politics, Workplaces and Communities*, edited by Rosemary Francis, Patricia Grimshaw and Ann Standish, 15–36. Melbourne: eScholarship Research Centre, University of Melbourne, 2012.

Strachan, Glenda and Robyn May. 'The Feminisation of the Academy? Statistics, Structures and Stories.' Paper presented at the Symposium on Workplace Culture in Higher Education, University of Melbourne, October 2011.

Thornton, Margaret. 'The Mirage of Merit: Constructing the "Ideal Academic".' Paper presented at the Symposium on Workplace Culture in Higher Education, University of Melbourne, October 2011.

Toy Caldwell-Colbert, A. and Judith E. N. Albino. 'Women as Academic Leaders: Living the Experience from Two Perspectives.' In *Women and Leadership: Transforming Visions and Diverse Voices*, edited by Jean Lau Chin, Bernice Lott, Joy K. Rice and Janis Sanchez-Hucles. Maldon, Mass.: Blackwell, 2007.

Turner, Helen Newton. Interviewed by Ann Moyal, 1993, National Library of Australia Oral History and Folklore Collection, ORAL TRC 2902. National Library of Australia, Canberra.

Walker, Rosanne. 'Hanna Neumann (1914–1971).' *Australasian Science* 22(1) (2001).

Wall, G. E. 'Hanna Neumann.' *Journal of the Australian Mathematical Society* 17(1) (1974): 1–28.

Ward, Beverley. 'The Female Professor: A Rare Australian Species, the Who and How.' PhD thesis, Murdoch University, Perth, 2003.

Webby, Elizabeth. 'Judith Wright McKinney (1915–2000) Obituary.' http://www.humanities.org.au/Fellowship/Obituaries.asp.

Wetherell, David. 'Wedgwood, Camilla Hildegarde (1901–1955).' *Australian Dictionary of Biography Online*. Canberra: National Centre of Biography, The Australian National University. http://adb.anu.edu.au/biography/wedgwood-camilla-hildegarde-11992/text21503.

Witz, Anne. *Professions and Patriarchy*. London and New York: Routledge, 1992.

Wright, Judith. *Half a Lifetime*, edited by Patricia Clarke. Melbourne: Text Publishing, 1999.

Zillman, John W. *ATSE 1975–2005: The First 30 Years—A Short History of the Origins and Development of the Australian Academy of Technological Sciences and Engineering (ATSE)*. Melbourne: ATSE, 2005.

Part V
Women and culture

12. Beyond the glass ceiling: The material culture of women's political leadership

Libby Stewart[1]

In October 1992 a female federal Australian senator made headlines after she displayed a poster that depicted a woman with a smoking gun over the caption 'so many men, so few bullets' in her Parliament House office window. In one newspaper article, titled 'Make My Day', it was reported that Parliament House authorities had received complaints that the poster in question was offensive, and asked for it to be removed.[2] The senator in question, Jocelyn Newman, was a senior parliamentarian from the conservative side of politics who was making a strong statement in favour of women's representation in an overwhelmingly male-dominated parliament, and she refused to take the poster down.

Senator Newman was at one point labelled the most powerful woman in Australian politics and a contender for Australia's first female governor-general. Yet during her period in politics she endured many stereotypical depictions of her gender, including her dress sense and her role as a wife and mother—portrayals that attempted to undermine her authority as a successful female politician. She was not alone in being trivialised in this way; indeed the gendered depictions of Australian women in politics continue to the present. Julia Gillard, Australia's first female prime minister, also endured taunts from her opposition colleagues and the public relating to her status as an unmarried, childless woman in power. An empty fruit bowl in her kitchen that she was photographed in front of in 2005 was singled out as 'evidence' of her lack of authority to hold senior office. To some people the bowl was a symbol of her lack of domestic skills, a sign that she was unqualified for office because she was childless and apparently career-driven, that she lacked empathy, and even that she was 'deliberately barren'.[3]

Objects such as Senator Newman's 'smoking gun' poster and the Gillard fruit bowl can be powerful tools for museums to use in telling the stories of women leaders in politics. This chapter looks at some of the collections of the material culture of women's political leadership that are held by the Museum of Australian Democracy (MoAD) at Old Parliament House in Canberra. Objects

---

1 The Museum of Australian Democracy at Old Parliament House.
2 'Make My Day', *Sun Herald*, 4 October 1992.
3 The 'deliberately barren' statement was made by Queensland Liberal Senator Bill Heffernan in 2007. He was later forced to apologise for the slur.

such as those described above, when displayed in context, showcase the many diverse aspects of women's political activism and political lives. Women who have been successful in achieving political office, as well as women who have been political activists, all have stories that museums can tell through the display of objects like awards, photos, political campaign material, jewellery, clothing, papers and posters. The suffragists of the early twentieth century were some of the first successful users of objects to promote their cause and MoAD has a small collection of these, which it displays as powerful reminders of women's struggle for the vote, both in Australia and in Britain. But the museum also holds collections of more mundane items. Seemingly insignificant, these objects, viewed in context, enable the museum to tell meaningful and important stories of the lives and political actions of Australian women leaders. They also enable the museum to discuss women's different leadership styles—evident in the kinds of objects used to tell each woman's story. Through an examination of a number of the museum's collections it is possible to see how important it is that museum historians and curators search widely and with open minds for collections of objects that tell stories as fascinating as those to be found in collections of documents held in libraries and archives.

The mundane and apparently insignificant nature of some of MoAD's collections that have belonged to Australia's female leaders would appear, at first glance, to reflect some of the ambivalence about the notion of leadership itself. Typical of the mixed feelings about the nature of women's leadership is a comment made several years ago by Pat Giles, the inaugural chair of the Women's Electoral Lobby of Western Australia, and a federal senator for that State for more than 10 years. She said: 'My forte, I think, has been as a facilitator rather than a leader. Leadership has been far from my mind, and even now seems alien, a masculine construct which bears little resemblance to what I have been doing for the last 25 years.'[4]

In her opening chapter of this book, Amanda Sinclair also recognises the feminist ambivalence towards leadership, noting that 'leadership as the lionisation of the achievement of individuals in powerful privileged positions is the antithesis of what many women have fought for'.[5] Women like Giles, who have been politically active and have achieved a great deal as leaders, have often received items such as certificates of appreciation, awards, gifts and plaques in the course of their work. These objects are sometimes dismissed by the recipients as unimportant, perhaps because the women feel ambivalent about the notion of leadership and attribute their success to being part of a wider team or to simply doing their job.

---

4   Quoted in Joan Eveline and Lorraine Hayden, eds, *Carrying the Banner: Women, Leadership and Activism in Australia* (Perth: University of Western Australia Press, 1999), 43.

5   Amanda Sinclair, Chapter 1, in this volume.

There is a strong case, however, for arguing that these objects should be regarded as valuable tools that can enable museums to better tell the stories of these women's leadership journeys. Too many stories of remarkable women in Australia and elsewhere have been lost because papers, photos or objects no longer exist to mark their place in history. An example of this loss lies in the stories of four remarkable Australian women: Vida Goldstein, Nellie Martel, Mary Ann Moore Bentley and Selina Anderson. They were the first women to stand for federal election in 1903—the first occasion at which women were eligible to do so. None was successful, and although the efforts of Vida Goldstein to be elected to Federal Parliament a further four times are well documented in writing, photos and film, the later lives of the other three women, who were without doubt female leaders of their time, are largely unknown to most Australians. This is a great shame because all three were dynamic and courageous: on a platform of equal wages for women and promoting domestic issues, Martel gained a respectable 18,500 votes in 1903, while Moore Bentley was already a writer (having published *A Woman of Mars; or, Australia's Enfranchised Woman* in 1901) and gained nearly 19,000 votes in her bid for the Senate, and Anderson stood for election as an independent protectionist, polling a respectable 18 per cent of the vote. Their stories deserve to be known more widely but any museum would struggle to do so without items of material culture relating to their lives.

Many Australian libraries and museums do hold wonderful collections of material relating to the lives of women, and many also feature regular exhibitions that tell the stories of some of them. It has not been standard practice in Australia, however, to build museums or develop permanent displays devoted to women's lives, as is the practice in many other parts of the world. Only three Australian museums—the Pioneer Women's Hut in Tumbarumba, NSW, the Pioneer Women's Memorial Folk Museum, near Brisbane, and the National Pioneer Women's Hall of Fame in Alice Springs—are wholly devoted to telling the stories of women's personal and professional lives. Of the three, the last has the broadest brief to look at the lives of a wide spectrum of women, as it is 'dedicated to preserving the place of women in history for their special contribution to Australia's heritage'.[6] It also has the closest links to the approximately 40 other women's museums around the world and promotes the importance of women's museums in helping to raise women's status and self-esteem.[7] This small museum in the heart of the country is, however, almost a lone voice amongst larger and better-funded museums that at times marginalise or ignore women's stories.

---

6 National Pioneer Women's Hall of Fame, Alice Springs, NT, website: http://www.pioneerwomen.com.au/index.php.

7 See website (http://www.pioneerwomen.com.au/index.php) for the National Pioneer Women's Hall of Fame's aims and links to international women's museums.

The lack of women's representation in Australian museums has been recognised by industry professionals and in 1993 the National Museum of Australia in Canberra convened a conference on the subject 'Images of Women', to develop recommendations for how the portrayal of women's lives in the public sphere could be improved. In her keynote address at that conference, actor and arts patron Robyn Archer called on Australian museum professionals to try to 'ensure that in the future no less than half of the picture is devoted to what women have done with their time on earth, what they have achieved, what they have endured'. She wanted women's often silent and invisible role in creating the present to be fully acknowledged and respected because, she said, 'due respect for women now ... will only come with the sure recognition that we were always there in all sections of society and that without our extraordinary strength there is no real past, no present and no future'.[8]

One of the conference workshops devoted to looking at women's leadership journeys recommended that museums should enable all women to value their achievements as well as demonstrating the achievements of those who have reached 'the top'. But it also recommended that the definition of 'the top' should include the capacity to contribute to decision-making and effect change. Not only should traditional leadership models be recognised, so too should hidden stories of strength and achievement as they demonstrate a different kind of women's leadership.[9] Nearly 20 years after those recommendations were made, it is, however, apparent that there is still much to be done to improve the representation of women's leadership in Australian museums, libraries, archives and galleries.

What are the kinds of collections that museums can use to tell meaningful stories of women's political lives and leadership? One of the stories of women's political activism already told by MoAD is that of women's suffrage in Australia. The museum discusses the close links between Australian suffragists and their counterparts in countries such as Britain and the United States, where it took much longer for women to achieve the vote. Objects relating to the campaign for women's suffrage in the United Kingdom are visually arresting, and they easily convey the determination and strength of the women who led the campaign through its most militant stages. British suffragists, and in particular the militant suffragettes, became adept at designing and merchandising a wide range of goods to promote their cause and raise funds. MoAD has purchased a number of these objects in order to create a collection that can convey both the British struggle for the female vote and the close connections with Australian suffragists in its exhibitions.

---

8   National Museum of Australia, *Images of Women: Women and Museums in Australia* (Canberra: National Museum of Australia, 1994), 26.
9   Ibid., 90–1.

One such item purchased by the museum is a women's suffrage pendant, which is typical of the type of jewellery worn by many women to indicate their support for the suffrage movement in Britain from the early part of the twentieth century. The inscription on the rear of the pendant, *VFW 1905*, suggests that it was associated with support for the militant British suffragette 'Votes for Women' campaign, which was launched in Manchester in 1905. The colours of the stones in the pendant are those of the constitutional suffragists, adherents of the National Union of Women's Suffrage Societies, who used red and white from as early as 1906 and added green in 1909.

Another women's suffrage group, the militant Women's Social and Political Union (WSPU), also adopted a colour scheme, using purple, white and green in all of its merchandise from 1908 onwards. The formation of the WSPU in 1903 marked a break from the politics of demure persuasion in the earlier period of the suffrage campaign. Frustrated at the lack of progress from years of moderate speeches and promises about women's suffrage from members of parliament, WSPU founder Emmeline Pankhurst and her colleagues decided the only way forward was to abandon these patient tactics in favour of more militant ones. The WSPU opened shops throughout London and in major cities and towns throughout England, selling a wide range of merchandise in their distinctive colours, to raise money and to advertise their cause. One of the most eye-catching, the board game Pank-a-Squith, was sold from 1909 onwards. Named after Emmeline Pankhurst and prime minister Herbert Asquith, an opponent of women's suffrage, the game is a powerful reminder of the hardships endured by many women as they committed acts of violence, were sent to prison and were often force-fed, in their efforts to obtain votes for women.

One British suffragette sent to prison for her part in a window-smashing raid was fifty-six-year-old Charlotte Blacklock. In March 1912, Charlotte turned from passive protest to militancy and was one of dozens of women arrested for using hammers to smash the windows of shops in Piccadilly, Haymarket, Oxford and Bond streets. The incident was widely reported and the damage to property was defended by Emmeline Pankhurst's daughter, Christabel, who said:

> It is a protest against the Government's refusal to legislate in regard to the question of woman suffrage … We are persuaded that the Government will not do anything until they are forced. As they do not yield to the justice of our demand we have been practically forced into adopting these tactics.[10]

Although the event took place in London, so many women were arrested that Charlotte was one of a number of women sent to jail in Birmingham. Like many

---

10 *The Times*, 2 March 1912.

women arrested after a violent demonstration, Charlotte, once sent to prison, went on hunger strike and was force-fed—a brutal and dangerous process that often left women either permanently scarred or fatally injured. Released after her four months' sentence, Charlotte was awarded a hunger strike medal, one of only about 100 produced by the WSPU to recognise the bravery of women who went without food and suffered from being forcibly fed.

The medals were intended to be the suffragists' equivalent of the highest imperial award for bravery under fire, the Victoria Cross (VC). Like the VC, the hunger strike medals featured the words 'For Valour', as well as a metal bar engraved with the dates on which the recipient was arrested. Many of the medals, such as that given to Emmeline Pankhurst, feature a number of bars—a testimony to the women's courage and persistence. Like the others, Charlotte Blacklock's medal features a ribbon in the suffragette colours of purple, white and green, and was purchased by MoAD in 2011; it is one of only three known to be in Australian public collections. A powerful object despite its simplicity, it serves as a graphic reminder of the lengths to which women would go in order to obtain the vote.

Although the museum now has a small but important collection of objects portraying the activism of British suffragists, it has been more difficult to find items that tell the Australian story of women's suffrage. The reasons for this are varied but include the fact that they are fewer in number, many are already held in both private and public collections, and Australian women acquired the vote relatively peacefully. Women in the colony of South Australia became the second in the world (after New Zealand) to be given the vote, and the first to be granted the right to stand for election. Both of these gains took place simultaneously in 1894.

One item the museum has obtained is a rare pamphlet, produced in 1907 by the National Union of Women's Suffrage Societies, which highlights the way in which the early gains by women in New Zealand and Australia were used by British women in support of their claims for suffrage. Keen to reassure men that giving women the vote would not impact negatively on their lives, the Agent-General for South Australia, Sir John Cockburn, is quoted in the pamphlet as saying that 'women sedulously exercise their voting power without neglecting a jot of their domestic duties ... this great reform has been all gain without one single drawback'.[11] The Agent-General for Western Australia, which granted women the vote in 1899, noted the positive effects of the female vote in the 1904 general election: 'The most gratifying features of the whole elections were the close interest exhibited by the women throughout the contest on polling day, and the general recognition by the community that the results justified the change

---

11   National Union of Women's Suffrage Societies, *Women's Suffrage in New Zealand & Australia* (London, 1907), 3.

made.'[12] Another rare item, a suffrage demonstration program from 1910, makes particular mention of the fact that women from around the world, including Australia, were expected to march in the London event, to be held on 23 July. It also contains illustrations of a number of prominent suffragettes, including Adela Pankhurst, who later settled in Australia and became a prominent activist for women's rights.

Although the MoAD places great importance on portraying the history of women's suffrage, its curators and historians are also keen to shed light on the lives of many other women active in the political sphere. In recent years they have collected items from two prominent female Australian politicians: senators Dorothy Tangney and Jocelyn Newman. Both women worked in the building in which the museum is now housed, Old Parliament House. They took leadership roles in their political lives and their collections reflect the complexity and diversity of those roles, as well as the way they were publicly perceived. Dorothy Tangney was a trailblazer, the Australian Labor Party Senator for Western Australia and in 1943 the first woman to be elected to the Senate, some 41 years after women won the right to stand for federal election. Until 1999 she was the longest-serving woman member in an Australian parliament, with a service record of 29 years and nine months. Many of the items in the Tangney collection show a clear leadership path: she received the Secondary School Scholarship Medal in 1919, the Junior University Medal and the Leaving University Medal, in 1920 and 1923 respectively, a Debating Medal in 1933, a Senator's Gold Pass, Jubilee and Coronation medals, a Gold Life Pass (issued to former parliamentarians for rail travel), and finally was made Dame Commander of the Order of the British Empire on her retirement in 1968. These items clearly reflect Dorothy Tangney's abilities, as well as the determination with which she approached her whole career—one she devoted to the causes of health, welfare and women's rights. A woman of both charm and quick wit, she was renowned for stories such as the time she was supposedly accosted by a drunk at a meeting, shouting 'don't you wish you were a man?', and the audience applauding her quick retort: 'No—don't you?'[13]

Although a strong and determined woman, Tangney enjoyed feminine touches in her Parliament House office and always took a tablecloth with her everywhere she went. One of these tablecloths is now held in the museum's collection. But Tangney also had room in her office for something slightly more unorthodox— an object that says much about her position as one of only a handful of women in the Australian Parliament of the 1940s. In December 1944, Tangney officiated at her first boat launching when she travelled to Maryborough, Queensland,

---

12   Ibid.
13   'Dorothy Tangney, Senator 1943–68', *Australian Women's History Forum*, http://www.womenshistory. com.au/image.asp?iID=333.

to launch the navy frigate HMAS *Shoalhaven*. Having smashed the obligatory bottle of champagne against the vessel, she watched as the ship moved slowly down the slipway and into the sea. In line with tradition, Tangney received the remains of the bottle as a souvenir of the day; however, in this case the shipbuilder attached the bottle head to a wooden handle, creating a crude type of axe. Dorothy kept the axe for the rest of her life, displaying it with some pride in her office with the note from the shipbuilders that read: 'To Senator Dorothy Tangney. To be used as and when required.'

Most of the other items in the Tangney collection are not as remarkable or quirky as the champagne bottle axe, however, they convey a sense of the life and personality of the owner equally well. There is a hand-drawn nameplate, a suitcase, a small souvenir purse from Rome, a luggage label from a trip on the *Queen Mary* from New York to London, an election advertising card, and a wishing well given as a gift. With this collection, the museum is able to convey something of the nature of Dorothy Tangney herself, her life as a politician in this house and her life more generally, from her early years to her retirement. Through these objects, the working life of one of the country's trailblazing female politicians will be remembered by many generations of visitors to the museum.

Former senator Jocelyn Newman has donated to the museum a large collection of objects relating to both her own working life and that of her husband, former MP Kevin Newman. Jocelyn Newman began her parliamentary career in 1986 when she was elected a senator for Tasmania. She held the portfolio of defence in opposition, then was appointed Minister for Social Security following the election of the Howard Coalition Government in 1996. In 1998 she was moved to the portfolio of Family and Community Services, and on two occasions held the position of Minister Assisting the Prime Minister for the Status of Women. Described by the Melbourne *Herald* at one stage as both a superwoman and 'the liberated Lib',[14] Newman was, amongst other things, committed to equal education opportunities and equal pay for women.

Unlike Tangney's collection, the objects donated by Jocelyn Newman do not reflect a clear leadership path to the political heights that she eventually reached. Rather, Newman's collection reflects the variety of her life experience, as well as the solid partnership she had with her husband, Kevin. In her early married life with Kevin, who was a career soldier, Jocelyn frequently moved her young family between posts. She also spent a long year without Kevin when he served a tour of duty in Vietnam. As an army wife, she later commented, 'we had to develop the ability to get out and meet people and to make wherever we

---

14 *Herald* [Melbourne], 14 June 1975.

were feel like home'.[15] These were undoubtedly useful qualities for a later life in politics. As well as raising two children, Newman studied law, practising as a barrister and solicitor, and then settled in Launceston when Kevin successfully contested the Bass by-election in June 1975. In Launceston, Jocelyn effectively had a crash course in holding a marginal seat:

> We had a marginal seat so I was just sort of the underling to the local member. I was keeping the family name and the involvement in Bass in front of everybody so that anything that needed to be done or anywhere that needed a speech, I'd go and give it because he would have to be away somewhere.[16]

When a Senate vacancy occurred in 1986, Newman applied for preselection, not really believing she had a chance of winning. This was despite her solid experience: as well as the roles already mentioned, she played a central part in establishing the first women's refuges in Hobart and Launceston, had been prominent in the National Trust and had helped to run a guesthouse. Her credentials must have been regarded as significant because Jocelyn won the seat over a former State president of the Tasmanian Liberal Party, and another man, who had headed the Tasmanian Farmers and Graziers Association.

The items held in the museum's Newman collection, although not remarkable individually, need to be viewed as a whole because together they reflect some of the political achievements Jocelyn Newman was obviously proud of, as well as some of the particular pressures she faced as a woman in federal politics, and the particular leadership style she adopted. A set of her speech notes from 2000 reflects her longstanding interest in women's issues: she covered the topics of women's role in the economy, various aspects of women's paid and unpaid work and women's superannuation, women's health—in particular, breast cancer and the need for access to the most up-to-date contraceptive pills, and the problems associated with domestic violence against women. Another of her items, a framed photo of the women in federal politics in the 1990s, suggests a certain pride in the achievements of Australia's female MPs. Newman mentored younger Liberal women over many years and one of those who benefited, Helen Coonan, said Newman 'was someone who took the role of a friendly face, a kind word and a mentoring approach very seriously. If you don't have any of those it's like you've landed on the moon when you get to Parliament.'[17] Like Tangney, Newman also launched a ship, the Australian Customs Vessel *Storm Bay*, in Hobart in 2000, and she kept a framed memento of that event.

---

15   Ibid.
16   Margaret Fitzherbert, *So Many Firsts: Liberal Women from Enid Lyons to the Turnbull Era* (Sydney: The Federation Press, 2009), 135.
17   Ibid., 164.

From time to time media attention would focus on Newman specifically as a female politician. In a 1996 cartoon, published in the Hobart *Mercury*, she was shown with a rack of aprons behind her, standing in front of a mirror trying another apron for size and thinking, 'Dear oh Dear … (sigh) … A woman's work is never done!' The caption below says, 'Jocelyn ponders what to wear … As another tough day at the office looms.'[18] That she kept a framed copy of the cartoon possibly indicates Senator Newman had a sense of humour about such a portrayal. Perhaps, though, she regarded two newspaper headlines from 1998 and 2000 with more pride. She kept both as framed, full-sized newspaper banners; the first reads 'Our Most Powerful Woman' and the second, 'Newman Tip for Gov-Gen' (governor-general).[19]

Several items in the Newman collection reflect the collaborative nature of Jocelyn and Kevin's marriage. There is a photo album with images showing Kevin at events around the country, often with Jocelyn at his side, as well as one of Jocelyn with young family members in T-shirts that show their support for Kevin at election time. Two portraits of the pair, by artist Audrey Wilson, are significant as a portrayal of one of the very few husband and wife teams in Australian federal politics. Although not of the highest quality as artworks, these paintings convey much of the personality and appearance of two highly successful and influential federal parliamentarians. Jocelyn relied heavily on her husband during two separate battles with cancer in the mid 1990s, and she was bereft when she lost Kevin to illness in 1999. It would be incorrect to depict successful women leaders as if they achieved everything on their own, and with the Newman collection the MoAD is able to tell a subtle but more realistic story of how one woman achieved success in her chosen field.

A few of the museum's smaller collections show how museums can display the diversity of women's leadership experiences through significant objects. In 1975 Parramatta City Council, in Sydney, was awarded an International Women's Year government grant to stage the exhibition 'Fifty Famous Australians'. The one female member of the council, Elizabeth Boesel, organised the exhibition, which consisted of photos and biographies of 50 women, present and past, who were regarded as having been influential in Australian political, social and cultural life. They included Louisa Lawson, Caroline Chisholm, Edith Lyons, Annabelle Rankin and Judith Wright. But the exhibition also had a local touch: two banners were handmade by local Parramatta women and they flew from the front of the Parramatta Post Office building where the exhibition was staged. Local women and girls were also given their voices in exhibition panels, which

---

18   *Mercury* [Hobart], 29 May 1996.
19   *Examiner* [Launceston], 9 November 1998; and *Herald Sun*, 17 October 2000.

capture the spirit of the times during that significant year for women around the world. On one panel, a young local girl, Ceinwen, expressed her hopes for the future:

> I want to be a ballerina; I want to be an architect, or even an engineer. I want to be so many things when I am grown up; I hope I can be the sort of person that I choose to be, because I am learning and doing and being many things. But the thing I like best is being Ceinwen. I am a very special person—a child of golden promise.[20]

Another item that evokes a particular period is a poster by artist Carol Porter, produced for the Victorian Women's Trust after the conservative Howard Government was elected in 1996. It depicts in bright pink words the slogan 'Don't get mad, get elected!' above a giant brunette woman, clad in a tight pink outfit and trainers. She towers over Parliament House in Canberra, while below her tiny suited men run screaming as she clutches one of their colleagues upside down. Porter commented that the poster tapped into a feeling, which was particularly strong at the time, that women should get into power and make a difference,[21] and it followed a move by the Australian Labor Party, which in 1994 had adopted an affirmative action quota in order to get more women into federal politics. The poster was mounted on billboards at prominent intersections around Melbourne, proving to be extremely popular amongst the general community, and generated significant media interest in the issue.[22]

In 2010 the museum received a significant object from the country's first female governor-general, Her Excellency Ms Quentin Bryce AC. Bryce donated a fabric corsage, handed down to her by her mother but originally owned by her grandmother. The corsage is made up of tiny flowers in the suffragette colours of purple, white and green, and was worn by Bryce on significant occasions, such as the swearing in of Julia Gillard as the nation's first female prime minister in 2010. The corsage is highly significant for the museum because it links the views of two generations of feminist women—Bryce and her grandmother—who regarded women's rights and particularly the right of girls to a good education as the foundation stones of democracy. Naturally the corsage highlights the role of Bryce as Australia's first female governor-general, but it also helps the museum to explain the role of the governor-general more broadly—an important exercise because it is a role that is often misunderstood. It is an object that creates a link between the passions and hopes represented by the suffragettes and today's generation of female leaders who also hold high hopes and dreams for Australian women and girls.

---

20 Exhibition panel, Accession Number 2011-1851, Museum of Australian Democracy Collection, Canberra.
21 Tim Richards, 'RedPlanet Revisited', *The Age*, 5 September 2005.
22 Liz McAloon, The Victorian Women's Trust, Email to author, 23 November 2011.

The material culture of women's political activism is varied, multi-layered and fascinating. By taking inanimate objects and incorporating them in displays that are visually exciting, informative and entertaining, much more than we already know about the lives of Australia's leading women and their leadership styles can be revealed. They allow us to think in different ways about what women's leadership looks like; indeed a feminist perspective of these collections reveals, as Amanda Sinclair states, that there is great diversity in how women live their political lives. It allows us to unpeel the layers that sometimes cloak activism in respectability, revealing hidden strengths and collective activism that have allowed these women to achieve much in improving the lives of all women. Although the MoAD will never be devoted entirely to women's stories, a determined effort should be made to ensure that the stories of women's political activism, whether they were played out in the arena of parliament or more informally elsewhere, are woven into the overall story of Australia's democracy. Women's political activism in Australia was alive long before the first female MPs formally entered the front doors of Old Parliament House. Through the collection and display of items such as those discussed here, and much more, this museum can actively respond to Robyn Archer's appeal to ensure that women's efforts and extraordinary strength are recognised and celebrated.

References

'Dorothy Tangney, Senator 1943–68.' *Australian Women's History Forum*. http://www.womenshistory.com.au/image.asp?iID=333.

Eveline, Joan and Lorraine Hayden, eds. *Carrying the Banner: Women, Leadership and Activism in Australia*. Perth: University of Western Australia Press, 1999.

Examiner [Launceston], 9 November 1998.

Fitzherbert, Margaret. *So Many Firsts: Liberal Women from Enid Lyons to the Turnbull Era*. Sydney: The Federation Press, 2009.

Herald [Melbourne], 14 June 1975.

Herald Sun, 17 October 2000.

'Make My Day.' *Sun Herald*, 4 October 1992: 152.

Mercury [Hobart], 29 May 1996.

National Pioneer Women's Hall of Fame, Alice Springs, NT. http://www.pioneerwomen.com.au/index.php.

National Museum of Australia. *Images of Women: Women and Museums in Australia*. Canberra: National Museum of Australia, 1994.

National Union of Women's Suffrage Societies. *Women's Suffrage in New Zealand & Australia*. London, 1907.

Richards, Tim. 'RedPlanet Revisited.' *The Age*, 5 September 2005: 14.

The Times, 2 March 1912.

13. Entertaining children: The 1927 Royal Commission on the Motion Picture Industry as a site of women's leadership

Mary Tomsic[1]

What I object to is the exploitation of our children. I know what the exploitation of natives is, because I have lived among them, and we certainly object to it. I am very sorrowful that we in Australia are willing to exploit our children from a financial aspect or even for our own pleasure.

— Mrs John Jones

Mrs John Jones, president of the Victorian Women's Citizen Movement, presented the above evidence to the Royal Commission on the Moving Picture Industry in Australia in 1927.[2] Jones compared the exploited children with exploited 'natives'—both presumably requiring protection in the form of benevolent control. And it was a particular type and class of woman who could provide such control and guidance. For the women reformers, and also men, who appeared before the commission, the cinema was understood as a public arena in which a novel visual language was spoken. The relative accessibility of the cinema to all classes of people concerned women reformers, and the effects of motion pictures on children were scrutinised in much detail. These women reformers saw a place for themselves in the regulation of film viewing. It was a way in which a 'natural' maternal role, usually private, was made public; they acted as the 'responsible' mothers for the nation's children.

In this collection Amanda Sinclair proposes that we should think about leadership as 'a process of influence', which often aims at 'mobilising people towards change'. Sinclair asks us to consider how women have 'influenced and changed the public agenda and improved the life experience of the people around and following after them'. This definition and question provide a valuable framework to apply to the public activities of women who campaigned

---

1   The University of Melbourne.
2   Mrs John Jones, in Commonwealth of Australia, *Royal Commission on the Moving Picture Industry in Australia*, Minutes of Evidence (Canberra: Commonwealth of Australia, 1927), para. 3328, 107 [hereinafter evidence from this transcript is cited as *RCE*]. This was submitted evidence presented to the Select Committee on 2 May 1927 that was also submitted to the royal commission.

to regulate film viewing for children during the late 1920s in Australia. Women reformers who presented evidence at the royal commission were keen to see changes in the public agenda, specifically in how film-going was regulated for children, how systems of classification could operate and what was suitable screen entertainment for children. From a contemporary perspective, it is easy to question precisely the nature of some of the 'improvements', and it is important that we interrogate the ideologies of social class, gender and race embodied in many of their ideas. But in doing this, there is also value in considering the actions and evidence of these women to more fully interrogate the basis on which they made their claims. I would like to suggest that in considering *how* these women presented their authority of speaking and providing evidence, we can see these women explaining and justifying their gendered form of cultural leadership. Examining these particular women's cultural activism provides evidence of a historical case of women's leadership.

In this chapter I want to examine the evidence of women advocating for children's screen entertainment as examples of leadership, and importantly, consider how this leadership was given currency and authority by invoking the ideology of maternal citizenship. An important element of this is the nature of the way the relationship between women and children is understood and enacted. I will discuss this relationship briefly before looking specifically at the evidence of women reformers. Doing this provides insights into how leadership was enacted by particular women and how they asserted influence in society to mobilise change.

Maternal citizenship

The work of women advocating for children's screen entertainment can be firmly placed in the realm of maternal citizenship. In writing about feminist interpretations of citizenship—in particular, women's relationship with the state—Marilyn Lake suggests that citizens' individual rights were conceptualised in radical ways 'without neglecting citizens' collective responsibilities'.[3] Lake identifies 'the mother' as strategically critical in linking rights with responsibilities in the discourse on maternal citizenship: 'Central … was the insistence on the duty of citizens to protect and care for the more vulnerable, helpless members of the community—hence the campaigns for temperance, censorship of films and books, raising the age of consent, and the state provision of infant and maternal welfare.'[4]

---

3 Marilyn Lake, 'Feminist Creating Citizens', in *Creating Australia: Changing Australian History*, eds Wayne Hudson and Geoffrey Bolton (Sydney: Allen & Unwin, 1997), 104.
4 Ibid.

In addition to this, structurally children in democracies are in an interesting position, as their access to direct political, social and economic citizenship is limited. Theoretically there is considerable difference between guardianship and democracy,[5] but in practice, children require advocates.[6] While both women and men interested in social work and children engaged in public discussions about suitable entertainment for children, often women's presence was linked to the guardianship of children. Either implicitly or explicitly, the category of mother plays a central role in discussions of suitable children's screen entertainment, and has been effectively mobilised by women activists. But as will be shown, this was not necessarily a straightforward invocation of the 'mother'; some detailed attention was paid to the necessary qualifications a woman censor would require. What was not questioned, however, was children's recreation as a civic entitlement. The implied prerogative to leisure and recreation has featured historically in the Australian context. For instance, amusements are included in Justice Higgins' list of items of expenditure he considered suitable for a 'human being living in a civilized community' and in a condition of 'frugal comfort estimated by current human standards' in his Harvester Judgment of 1907.[7] In this way, participating in entertainment is presented as part of being a member of a 'civilised' community. While this right to leisure has been understood in practice as a masculine one,[8] particularly as it played out in discussions about wages and maternal payment allowances, in the context of film-going in the late 1920s, entertainment was taken as granted as appropriate for (female and male) children. While women's advocacy should be understood as part of a project of enacting maternal citizenship and leadership, it could also be understood as contributing to children's social citizenship, albeit with a highly moralistic basis.

Women's role in film censorship

There had been federal film censorship in Australia since 1917, and by 1927 there were (or had been) censorship boards in New South Wales, South Australia and Tasmania. Victoria had made an agreement with the federal authority for

---

5   Francis Schrag, 'Children and Democracy: Theory and Policy', *Politics, Philosophy & Economics* 3(3) (October 2004): 365–6.

6   Schrag discusses ways in which children who are excluded from participation in democracies can be included, with suggestions including a parental vote or appointment of a children's guardian; in ibid.

7   *Harvester Case, Ex parte HV McKay*, 1907, 4 (Canberra: Parliament of Australia, Parliamentary Library), http://www.aph.gov.au/binaries/library/intguide/law/harvester.pdf.

8   Or even as a (male) citizen's duty. See Lake, 'Feminists Creating Citizens', 101; also Marilyn Lake, 'A Revolution in the Family; the Challenge and Contradictions of Maternal Citizenship in Australia', in *Mothers of a New World: Maternalist Politics and the Origins of Welfare States*, eds Seth Koven and Sonya Michel (New York: Routledge, 1993), 391.

it to censor films on Victoria's behalf.[9] All other States maintained the right to independent State censorship. The NSW board was established in the early 1900s and comprised five government officials.[10] South Australia appointed an advisory board of film censors in 1917 to assist the chief secretary in judging films.[11] While there had been pressure to create a State film censorship authority in Tasmania from 1916, it was not until the Federation of Women's Societies for Film Censorship met publicly to lobby for this that regulations were made to appoint local censors.[12] In March 1918 a board of five members, including two women, Edith Waterworth and Mary Taylor, was appointed.[13] Although all the State boards were not in continual operation, they tended to be reactive, responding to current moving pictures being shown or 'offensive' posters displayed. The boards were no longer operating at the beginning of World War II.[14]

Professor Robert Wallace was the chief censor of motion pictures from 1922 to 1927.[15] Wallace, also Professor of English and Literature at the University of Melbourne, was based in Melbourne while the majority of films were imported into Australia in Sydney. So from 1925, Walter Cresswell O'Reilly was appointed the senior Commonwealth film censor in Sydney and was responsible for essentially all of the censoring. Most of the films he examined were from the United States. In 1927, of the 715 feature films imported into Australia, 674 were from the United States and 25 from the United Kingdom. Seven Australian feature films were produced in the same year.[16]

All of the women witnesses who appeared before the royal commission and on behalf of women's organisations supported the presence of women on the proposed censorship boards (somewhere between 20 and 50 per cent).[17] Having formal positions on the boards was understood as particularly important for many of the women's organisations. Mrs Jones stated that her organisation,

9   Diane Collins, *Hollywood Down Under: Australians at the Movies 1896 to the Present Day* (Sydney: Angus & Robertson, 1987), 54; Commonwealth of Australia, 'Report of the Royal Commission on the Moving Picture Industry in Australia', 1, *Commonwealth Parliamentary Papers*, Session 1926–27–28, vol. IV, pt 2, para. 37, 6.
10   Ina Bertrand, *Film Censorship in Australia* (Brisbane: University of Queensland Press, 1978), 41; Commonwealth of Australia, 'Report of the Royal Commission', para. 34, 6.
11   Bertrand, *Film Censorship*, 56.
12   Ibid., 58.
13   Stefan Petrow, 'Leading Ladies: Women and Film Censorship in Early Twentieth Century Tasmania', *Tasmanian Historical Research Association Papers and Proceedings* 41(2) (June 1994): 80.
14   New South Wales ceased in 1923, Tasmania in 1934 and South Australia in 1938. See Bertrand, *Film Censorship*, 59–60.
15   Ursula Bygott, 'Wallace, Sir Robert Strachan (1882–1961)', *Australian Dictionary of BiographyOnline* (Canberra: National Centre of Biography, The Australian National University, 1990), http://adb.anu.edu.au/biography/wallace-sir-robert-strachan-8962/text15767.
16   *Commonwealth Film Censorship Reports, 1925–1939*, in Diane Collins, 'Cinema and Society in Australia 1920–1939' (PhD thesis, Department of History, University of Sydney, 1975), app. A, 461; Andrew Pike and Ross Cooper, *Australian Film* (Melbourne: Oxford University Press, 1981), 178–84.
17   Waterworth (in *RCE*, para. 16923, 590) said on a board of four, two women were needed, and on a board of two, one woman; Muscio (in *RCE*, para. 21730, 804) said at least two women were needed on a board of

the Victorian Women's Citizen Movement, wanted to secure 'representation of women in Parliament and in all boards and commissions' as it is the 'only method of getting a higher moral and spiritual tone in the life of Australia'.[18] This defines women as moral guardians. It explicitly demonstrates the approach taken to carve an area of women's influence in the public arena in maternalistic terms. Representatives of women's organisations believed the impact of these roles to be far reaching. Ruby Rich declared that 'women's organizations throughout the Empire are looking to Australia as the most advanced democracy or the political laboratory of the world, to see what we are doing in that direction'.[19]

The chief censor, Wallace, supported the presence of a woman on a censorship board. He thought a 'woman as a single censor would be undesirable, because the importers would have difficulty in discussing with her matters which they now discuss with us', but as a member of a board 'that difficulty vanishes'.[20] One witness, Elsie Sleeman Reed, secretary of the Young Women's Christian Association (YWCA) in Brisbane, was asked if the presence of a woman on a board would mean that 'it would be difficult to arrive at an agreement'. Unsurprisingly, she disagreed: 'No, she would give them the woman's point of view.'[21] Wallace was asked if a woman's presence on the board would restrict the discussions men could have about a film. Wallace disagreed overall but included specific conditions: 'I have had to discuss these things with women, and the difficulty need not be stressed, provided the woman is of mature experience, and is, preferably, married.'[22]

While women's role in censorship was not focused solely in terms of protecting children, the issue of a woman censor was almost always raised in connection with children. Censorship was widely debated and was a key avenue through which women reformers articulated their desires to influence screen culture and also expressed their beliefs regarding suitable screen material for children.

Ruby Rich was vice-president of the Federated Women's Societies of New South Wales. Organisations included under this umbrella were the Feminist Club of Sydney, the Women's League, the Women's Service League, Women's Christian Temperance Union (WCTU) and the Women's League of Voters.[23] Parts of her evidence were echoed in that of many other witnesses. Rich, speaking in her

---

five and at least one on a board of three; Morris (in *RCE*, paras 16089–91, 560), Rich (in *RCE*, para. 19965, 736) and the Australian Federated Women's Societies of New South Wales proposed that at least one woman should be included on the board.

18   *RCE*, para. 3389, 111.

19   Ibid., paras 19961–4, 736.

20   Ibid., para. 13475, 450.

21   For example, Reed, in ibid., para. 9722, 333.

22   Ibid., para. 13534, 453.

23   Rich reported this organisation was affiliated with the British Commonwealth League and the International Suffrage Alliance. Ibid., para. 19964, 736.

organisational capacity, said that not only is it 'generally conceded that women are the best custodians of the children', but also that '[a] nation is no stronger than the mothers of its people, and we are convinced that with a woman on the censorship board there will be greater protection for the rising generation'.[24] Despite this, she clearly indicated that children were connected not only to women, but also to men. 'Some men', she said, 'appear not to realize that we want a woman to be there to protect *their* children as well as ours'.[25]

Many witnesses at the royal commission were asked about suitable qualifications for a woman censor. Rich, again explicitly on behalf of the organisations she represented, said they did not seek 'the appointment of a "wowser"', but the 'essential qualifications' for both male and female censors were 'a full knowledge of diversified public feeling and a complete understanding of sex psychology'. These would be held by a person with 'a high standard of education, refinement of thought … general understanding of the film industry, a knowledge of the movement of the public pulse, the trend of public outlook, and a comprehensive idea of British ideals'.[26] The commissioners countered this, restating suggestions that appropriate qualifications for a woman should be that she was married, with a family and preferably had travelled 'for the purpose of broadening her mind'. Rich felt these were too restrictive and, should an appointment be made through a women's organisation, an appropriate censor could be found.[27] It was through women's organisations, like the ones Rich represented, that a broad basis of support was publicly presented for women to be formally involved with federal censorship. So while women representing a range of women's groups and organisations were given the opportunity to appear before the royal commission, it seems apparent from the way commissioners asked questions that their focus was more on individual women's specific skills, rather than leaving this to women's groups to put forward suitable female candidates.

The commissioners questioned whether Rich's criteria for a suitable censor would exclude women who had household duties. Rich replied that she doubted 'if a woman who has confined herself to home duties would have the broad view necessary for the duties of a censor of films' for the women of the Empire who attended motion pictures.[28] After being asked again, she said she did not see that marriage and family alone were vital qualifications: 'a thorough knowledge of children' was necessary, but the 'maternal instinct does not arise only from the act of giving birth to a child. It may be highly developed in other women and especially in teachers who have much to do with children.'[29] The issue of

---

24 Ibid., para. 19965, 736.
25 Ibid., emphasis added.
26 Ibid.
27 Ibid., para. 19967, 737.
28 Ibid., para. 19969, 737.
29 Ibid., para. 19970, 737.

travel was also often discussed as a requirement for a woman censor. During this questioning, Rich returned to the domestic sphere. Rich reiterated that domesticity alone did not cultivate the broad range of knowledge she saw as essential for a woman censor's representational requirements: 'The fact that a woman may live a great deal of time in her home does not entitle her to speak on behalf of all the women of Australia.'[30]

Rich presents the case for a woman censor being required as part of claims for equality in citizenship but also because in Australia 'it is estimated that fully one half' of the cinema audience is women and children.[31] In this way, linking the cultural leadership of women to a guardianship function for women and children reveals a practical understanding of women's citizenship; one effectively founded by a cultivation of maternal knowledge. In contrast with this, Edith Alice Waterworth, a welfare worker who was a member of the Picture Censor Board in Hobart, quite explicitly commented on a dual basis for women's public representation in contrast with a singular claim for men: 'Men have their claim as citizens and electors; we have a claim as electors and citizens, and another as mothers.' 'Nature has given us the work of bearing children' and from this women 'necessarily have to give far more careful thought to the rearing of children than is given by a father'.[32] While acknowledging women's individual status as citizens, she nonetheless intimately linked their public representation work to childrearing:

> If the Federal Government considers that we are not capable of judging what is good for our children, it should, to be consistent, take those children from us as soon as they are born and let men rear them. But if we're allowed to bring them up, we should have some say regarding the influences they have to face when they go into the world.[33]

In this statement, motherhood is presented as the key basis for women's civic value—something denied to Indigenous women, with many of their children taken from them in almost precisely the manner Waterworth (improbably) describes.[34]

Mrs John Jones, president of the Victorian Women Citizen Movement, described who she saw as a suitable woman to be on the board of censors. The idea of an advisory board was also discussed (one that would look at production), and the woman representative on that, Jones said, should be

---

30 Ibid., para. 19974, 737.
31 Ibid., para. 19965, 736.
32 Ibid., para. 16905, 588.
33 Ibid., para. 16923, 589–60.
34 Marilyn Lake, 'The Independence of Women and the Brotherhood of Man: Debates in the Labour Movement Over Equal Pay and Motherhood Endowment in the 1920's', *Labour History* 63 (November 1992): 5–6.

an educated and experience[d] woman, preferably a married woman, who understands the child mind, and would be able to lend valuable assistance in consequence of her experience. Such a person ... should have the necessary educational qualifications and should be one which has sufficient leisure to devote time to the uplifting of the people.[35]

Edith Cowan gave evidence in her capacity as a member of the National Council of Women (she was also a member of the Children's Court in Perth at the time). Cowan stated on the inclusion of women on censorship boards that in 'our opinion, the mothers of children have every right to say something in this matter'.[36]

In reading these women reformers' presentations, they are claiming public space for themselves as enfranchised citizens, while simultaneously asserting women's specific skills and expertise as distinct from men, whether they are obtained 'naturally' or professionally. Demanding a place for domestic and maternal knowledge has been aptly described by Ellen Warne as 'civic maternalism'.[37] As explicitly stated by Edith Waterworth, these women's public mothering was for all children including those belonging to 'women who do not care what happens to their children'.[38] So whether censoring films or advising film production, the women giving evidence at the royal commission clearly advocated for their representation on almost all proposed boards. It was acknowledged that this was their right as citizens, but significantly it was primarily as guardians of children that claims were made. If we read the questioning of the commissioners as representing the viewpoint of the state, these women's claims were generally intelligible but were interrogated. The women witnesses were required to staunchly defend their position.

Ultimately, the royal commission recommended that a federal board of film censors and a censorship board of appeal be established with three and five members respectively.[39] Both of these boards were to include one woman. Although the States agreed that uniform legislation was desirable, they were unwilling to surrender their rights for this to be achieved;[40] consequently, when the new legislation took effect in January 1929, all States except Victoria maintained their right to independent State censorship.[41] Many recommendations of the royal commission were not immediately realised after they were handed down

---

35 *RCE*, para. 3428, 114.
36 Ibid., para. 14695, 502.
37 Ellen Warne, 'The Mother's Anxious Future: Australian Churchwomen Meet the Modern World, between the 1890s and the 1930s' (PhD thesis, Department of History, University of Melbourne, 2000), 5.
38 *RCE*, para. 16909, 588.
39 Commonwealth of Australia, 'Report of the Royal Commission', paras. 50 (1) and (7), 8.
40 Bertrand, *Film Censorship*, 79–81.
41 Andrea Allard, 'Grand Gala of Gab (1928–1939)', in *Cinema in Australia: A Documentary History*, ed. Ina Bertrand (Sydney: UNSW Press, 1989), 127.

because the States had not handed powers over to the Commonwealth.[42] In mid 1928, the National Council of Women passed a resolution at their monthly general meeting asking the NSW State Government to hand the appropriate powers to the Federal Government to implement the commission's recommendations.[43] Action on this matter, however, was not swift, which troubled many members of the film industry.[44]

Agreements were finally made and the process of establishing the censorship boards began, with more than 1,000 applications for the positions, and a large number of those came from women.[45] While we can see these formal positions available for at least two women to exert influence in society, this influence, however, was not universally supported. For instance, the motion picture industry paper *Everyones* mocked the credentials listed by female applicants to the censorship board, which they reported 'ranged from domestic duties to a sturdy belief in birth-control'. They despaired: 'God help the two men!'[46] These credentials, and by association the position of women as the prime public guardians of children, were not seen by *Everyones* as a valuable contribution to film culture. The notion of women's 'interference' in the film industry was not limited to the censorship board. For example, a WCTU film investigation in Melbourne was reported with the title 'Well, Ladies Must Talk!' and concluded with 'Doesn't it make you tired?'.[47] *Everyones*, with an air of novelty, did often report favourably on the work of women filmmakers,[48] but they did not see women's explicit political involvement with the regulation of film as anything other than an undeserved and unwanted intrusion. Women's presence, let alone leadership, was not welcomed. In financial terms, women's work on censorship boards was not remunerated equally with that of men. The salary was £3 per day for the male censor and £2 per day for the woman board member.[49] The

---

42   'Control of Films, Conference of States, Wider Powers Sought', *Sydney Morning Herald*, 12 May 1928: 18.

43   'National Council of Women', *Sydney Morning Herald*, 1 June 1928: 5. Although, later in the year at the annual meeting of the federal council of the National Councils of Women, there was much debate as to whether States should retain their powers to censor films locally: 'Federal Conference National Councils of Women', *Sydney Morning Herald*, 19 July 1928: 5; 'Council of Women, Law Anomalies Discussed, Insanity and Divorce', *The Argus* [Melbourne], 19 July 1928: 14.

44   See, for example: 'Editorial', *Everyones*, 24 October 1928: 4.

45   'Film Censorship, Many Women Apply, Powers of Appeal Board', *Sydney Morning Herald*, 31 July 1928: 10; 'Film Censors, 1000 Applications, for Two Positions', *Sydney Morning Herald*, 14 August 1928: 11; 'Censorship of Films. Many Women Applicants', *The Argus* [Melbourne], 31 July 1928: 11; 'Film Censorship, Selection of Board Members', *The Argus* [Melbourne], 5 September 1928: 7.

46   'Women Would A-Censoring Go!', *Everyones*, 1 August 1928: 5; 'Women Rush Censor Job at £2 a Day', *Everyones*, 8 August 1928: 35.

47   Pierce Hodgens, 'Well, Ladies Must Talk!', *Everyones*, 21 November 1928: 40. See also, for example: E. C. Cameron, 'A Woman on the Job', *Everyones*, 20 November 1929: 22.

48   For example: Juliette de la Ruze, 'Along Film Row', *Everyones*, 26 September 1928: 5; McDonaghs, 'Concerning the Future', *Everyones*, 20 June 1928: 5.

49   'Film Censorship, Creating a New Board', *The Argus* [Melbourne], 30 July 1928: 11.

National Council of Women protested against the pay discrepancy,[50] but the acting customs minister justified the inconsistency by stating that the male censor would have more duties to perform than the female censor.[51]

Children's access to entertainment

The other aspect of women's leadership within film culture of the time that I will consider briefly here is the type of entertainment for children that women reformers supported.

The interwar period was a time in which the effects of mass culture on children were fervently debated. The cinema specifically was seen as potentially being able to convince girls to be idle, inebriated and sexual, while boys would desire to be loafers, gamblers and criminals.[52] The report of the royal commission noted that the 'picture theatre seems to have become part of the life of the child, and therefore every possible precaution should be taken to ensure that the child will derive nothing but good entertainment from the picture screen'.[53] Women reformers at the royal commission varied as to how valuable they saw film as a medium for providing entertainment. This was applied specifically to children, but also more broadly. Mrs John Jones said, 'I think it must be admitted that pictures provide the cheapest, most enjoyable, and restful form of amusement available; but it is in the interests of the whole community that they should be of a proper standard'.[54] Mildred Muscio, who was president of the Good Film League, said that films should be used to 'raise the artistic tone of the nation'.[55] Others noted the screen as an important medium of public instruction,[56] the lure of which 'is so great', said Florence Jones, 'that I am wondering what is going to happen'.[57] In placing the importance of film in the national context, and these women actively working towards improving film culture in society at large, they positioned themselves as (indirectly) working for the state.[58] Concern was articulated in terms of the effects of film on audiences, in particular for those who were not 'educated and refined'.[59]

---

50 'Film Censorship Board', *The Argus* [Melbourne], 1 August 1928: 22.
51 'Film Censors, Question of Scale of Fees', *The Argus* [Melbourne], 8 August 1928: 9.
52 Jan Kociumbas, *Australian Childhood: A History* (Sydney: Allen & Unwin, 1997), 191.
53 Commonwealth of Australia, 'Report of the Royal Commission', para. 123, 18.
54 *RCE*, para. 3427, 114.
55 Ibid., para. 21703, 803.
56 Ibid., para. 23999, 919.
57 Ibid., para. 22960, 860.
58 In discussing women's demands for economic independence through a maternal payment, Lake argues that this repositioned women's duty to the state, rather than to an individual master/husband. While different factors are at play in this case, I would suggest these reformers understood their activism as beneficial to individuals but also to the state. See Lake, 'A Revolution in the Family', 388.
59 Waterworth, in *RCE*, para. 16951, 590.

In the case of children specifically, there were concerns (although not always consensus) expressed about the impact of films on crime, copycat behaviour, Americanisation of speech, representations of luxury and stories about sex. But throughout these discussions the understanding was always supported that children should be allowed access to entertainment, even if some women thought outdoor activities would be preferable to the dangers of a darkened picture theatre.

Marriage was an institution that some witnesses felt was under threat from films that mocked and made light of the 'marriage tie'. This was deemed particularly dangerous for children and young adolescents.[60] The fear, as articulated by Edith Waterworth, was that children would believe 'that marriage is not a permanent institution'.[61] Agnes Knight Goode, who was a member of the State Censor Board in South Australia,[62] condemned films more broadly for their insidiousness, which would affect 'the rising generation and our young married women'.[63] Goode described a film she and the other SA female censor wanted to reject because 'childbirth was depicted as a very dangerous thing'.[64] In the unnamed film, a young woman refused to marry a man whom she loved because she had seen two women die in childbirth and 'was terrified that this might happen to her'.[65] While the perspective of these two women censors was not the opinion that was followed, it was an avenue through which they could express what they saw as a fundamentally different outlook to their male counterparts and that they sought to provide entertainment that was aligned to their beliefs to young audience members.

What was shown onscreen was understood as important. Rich explicitly placed her understanding of this in a psychological framework. Films could not be easily forgotten as all 'modern psychologists, including Freud, are unanimous that we are the slaves of our childhood, and that the earlier and plastic years of life are the most important for the development of character'.[66] While most of the women reformers did not use Freudian or psychological language and analysis, they did refer to notions of children as sexual beings requiring sex education, and Rich explicitly postulated on the internal effects of film entertainment on children (and women). In the evidence Jones gave, she described the impact of screen entertainment: 'We are exploiting our children's love of movement

---

60   Waterworth, in ibid., para. 16918, 589; Florence Jones, in *RCE*, para. 22956, 860.
61   Ibid., para. 16918, 589.
62   She was also a justice of the peace and a municipal councillor in Adelaide. *RCE*, 549.
63   Ibid., para. 15845, 549.
64   Ibid., para. 15903, 551.
65   Despite their concerns, the film was passed for exhibition. Ibid., para. 15903, 551–2.
66   Ibid., para. 19986, 737.

and colour and the working of their imagination.'[67] The Saturday matinee was of particular concern to Jones, who was convinced that unsuitable films were shown. She described a picture of

> a divorce scene, with a woman standing behind a screen taking off her garments, including her undergarments one by one, and throwing them over the screen into a part of the room where her husband and another woman were sitting together. We may think that such things are funny, but I do not believe that our children think they are. We are forming their tastes, and when the children see that their parents are amused at such scenes they are amused also.[68]

For Jones, the presence of parents was not always enough to protect children for, as in the example here, they were the ones teaching their children badly. Guardians were required. Jones said: 'If open-air playgrounds have guardians on Saturday afternoons surely the children in picture theatres should be similarly protected.' Women should carry out this work: 'We cannot expect business men to give up their Saturday afternoons to act as guardians of the children in picture theatres, and therefore this work could very well be carried out by women helpers.'[69] In this scenario, men's access to leisure time should not be interfered with, and women's role here is clearly identified as work—work that assisted children in safely participating in leisure activities.

The final report of the royal commission did not engage with the explicitly gendered nature of access to leisure, but noted when commenting on possible age restrictions to cinema attendance that any regulations prohibiting children from cinemas at night would be deemed 'unjust', and if children were required to be accompanied by adults at night screenings this would 'prove a hardship'.[70] It is not clear who, in fact, experiences the hardship—the children or the parents. Most of the women giving evidence acknowledged that completely excluding children from the cinema would be unfair on young parents, as it would mean they would also be unable to attend the theatre if they could not bring their children.[71] But strong statements were made in reference to parents, and specifically mothers, who reportedly prioritised their own leisure before the care of their children. Waterworth believed that a 'worse type of woman is the one who leaves her babies at home whilst she goes to a place of entertainment'.[72] Fanny Cocks, the principal of women police in Adelaide, presented evidence in a report from many people including Miss Lee, a probation officer of the State

---

67 Ibid., para. 3328, 108.
68 Ibid.
69 Ibid.
70 Commonwealth of Australia, 'Report of the Royal Commission', para. 133, 19.
71 *RCE*, para. 21742, 804; also Florence Jones, para. 22970, 860.
72 Ibid., para. 6909, 588.

Children's Department. Lee reported that often children from very poor homes were the ones whose 'drunk parents' gave them money to go to the cinema.[73] Mrs Goode conveyed the story that she had

> heard of little children being sent to the pictures at night by themselves while their mothers have gone to other entertainments. The women police have found little children sitting on the footpath waiting for their mothers to come home from the pictures. I much prefer to see children at pictures than in the congested streets.[74]

These scenarios illustrate the concern that pictures had caused changes in behaviour that resulted in mothers' neglect of their children. In this way mothers' civic right to leisure was in practice understood as of secondary concern to their role in caring for children.

As can be seen in the evidence given by women reformers interested in film culture, they expressed some alarm about this modern medium of entertainment and, in particular, the influence it had on children and adolescents. The reformers constructed a place for themselves within the public debate in maternalistic terms, although how maternal skills were obtained and respected was contested. In examining these reformers' actions we can see how they continually needed to defend their public interventions, to justify their activism. It was through the concept of civic maternalism that they legitimated their interventions as they sought to influence society and mobilise change in the public agenda. Not only in this case study can we see white women's reform work as establishing leadership positions for themselves; in doing this, they were also strongly involved in facilitating children's social citizenship and access to what these women believed would be better entertainment for children.

References

Allard, Andréa. 'Grand Gala of Gab (1928–1939).' In *Cinema in Australia: A Documentary History*, edited by Ina Bertrand, 121–6. Sydney: UNSW Press, 1989.

Bertrand, Ina. *Film Censorship in Australia*. Brisbane: University of Queensland Press, 1978.

---

73 Ibid., para. 16049, 558.
74 Ibid., para. 15889, 551.

Bygott, Ursula. 'Wallace, Sir Robert Strachan (1882–1961).' *Australian Dictionary of Biography Online*. Canberra: National Centre of Biography, The Australian National University, 1990. http://adb.anu.edu.au/biography/wallace-sir-robert-strachan-8962/text15767.

Cameron, E. C. 'A Woman on the Job.' *Everyones*, 20 November 1929: 22.

'Censorship of Films. Many Women Applicants.' *The Argus* [Melbourne], 31 July 1928: 11.

Collins, Diane. 'Cinema and Society in Australia 1920–1939.' PhD thesis, Department of History, University of Sydney, 1975.

Collins, Diane. *Hollywood Down Under: Australians at the Movies 1896 to the Present Day*. Sydney: Angus & Robertson, 1987.

Commonwealth of Australia. *Royal Commission on the Moving Picture Industry in Australia, Minutes of Evidence*. Canberra: Commonwealth of Australia, 1927.

Commonwealth of Australia. 'Report of the Royal Commission on the Moving Picture Industry in Australia.' *Commonwealth Parliamentary Papers*, Session 1926–27–28, vol. IV, pt 2, 1371–1409.

'Concerning the Future.' *Everyones*, 20 June 1928: 5.

'Control of Films, Conference of States, Wider Powers Sought.' *Sydney Morning Herald*, 12 May 1928: 18.

'Council of Women, Law Anomalies Discussed, Insanity and Divorce.' *The Argus* [Melbourne], 19 July 1928: 14.

de la Ruze, Juliette. 'Along Film Row.' *Everyones*, 26 September 1928: 5

'Editorial.' *Everyones*, 24 October 1928: 4.

'Federal Conference National Councils of Women.' *Sydney Morning Herald*, 19 July 1928: 5.

'Film Censors, 1000 Applications, for Two Positions.' *Sydney Morning Herald*, 14 August 1928: 11.

'Film Censors, Question of Scale of Fees.' *The Argus* [Melbourne], 8 August 1928: 9.

'Film Censorship Board.' *The Argus* [Melbourne], 1 August 1928: 22.

'Film Censorship, Creating a New Board.' *The Argus* [Melbourne], 30 July 1928: 11.

'Film Censorship, Many Women Apply, Powers of Appeal Board.' *Sydney Morning Herald*, 31 July 1928: 10.

'Film Censorship, Selection of Board Members.' *The Argus* [Melbourne], 5 September 1928: 7.

Harvester Case, Ex parte HV McKay, 1907, 4. Canberra: Parliament of Australia, Parliamentary Library. http://www.aph.gov.au/binaries/library/intguide/law/harvester.pdf.

Hodgens, Pierce. 'Well, Ladies Must Talk!' *Everyones*, 21 November 1928: 40.

Kociumbas, Jan. *Australian Childhood: A History*. Sydney: Allen & Unwin, 1997.

Lake, Marilyn. 'The Independence of Women and the Brotherhood of Man: Debates in the Labour Movement Over Equal Pay and Motherhood Endowment in the 1920s.' *Labour History* 63 (November 1992): 1–24.

Lake, Marilyn. 'A Revolution in the Family; the Challenge and Contradictions of Maternal Citizenship in Australia.' In *Mothers of a New World: Maternalist Politics and the Origins of Welfare States*, edited by Seth Koven and Sonya Michel, 378–95. New York: Routledge, 1993.

Lake, Marilyn. 'Feminist Creating Citizens.' In *Creating Australia: Changing Australian History*, edited by Wayne Hudson and Geoffrey Bolton, 96–105. Sydney: Allen & Unwin, 1997.

'National Council of Women.' *Sydney Morning Herald*, 1 June 1928: 5.

Petrow, Stefan. 'Leading Ladies: Women and Film Censorship in Early Twentieth Century Tasmania.' *Tasmanian Historical Research Association Papers and Proceedings* 41(2) (June 1994): 74–83.

Pike, Andrew and Ross Cooper. *Australian Film*. Melbourne: Oxford University Press, 1981.

Schrag, Francis. 'Children and Democracy: Theory and Policy.' *Politics, Philosophy & Economics* 3(3) (October 2004): 365–6.

Warne, Ellen. 'The Mother's Anxious Future: Australian Churchwomen Meet the Modern World, between the 1890s and the 1930s.' PhD thesis, Department of History, University of Melbourne, 2000.

'Women Rush Censor Job at £2 a Day.' *Everyones*, 8 August 1928: 35.

'Women Would A-Censoring Go!' *Everyones*, 1 August 1928: 5.

14. Women's leadership in writers' associations

Susan Sheridan[1]

In thinking about women, leadership and literature, I have passed up the opportunity to celebrate writers like Henry Handel Richardson, Christina Stead and Judith Wright, whose creative achievements call for the discourse of heroic individualism. Rather, in accord with the feminist challenges to conventional concepts of leadership outlined by Amanda Sinclair's leading chapter in this book, I looked for women who have sought to influence public opinion about literary matters and advocate in various ways for writers. In Australia women's literary activism of this kind includes furthering the cause of Australian literature, as Miles Franklin did throughout her life, or forming writers' associations which work to ensure the political, literary and economic independence of writers. Specifically feminist literary activism involves drawing attention to the previously neglected traditions of women's writing and nurturing contemporary female writers, as feminist publishers, booksellers and academics have done since the 1970s.

In this chapter I want to draw attention to some of the women who have been active in writers' associations—the Fellowship of Australian Writers (formed in 1928), PEN Australia (formed in 1931) and the Australian Society of Authors (formed in 1963). All three organisations continue to exist today. They have both social and practical purposes: while an important result of their formation was to bring writers out of their individual isolation and into contact with one another, the major work they have undertaken to date has involved lobbying government and other bodies to further their aims of protecting the rights and enhancing the opportunities and income of writers.

Women were prominent in the formation and running of all three groups, and in some cases achieved positions of formal leadership. What was new about women's leadership in these three organisations was that they were not organising on their own behalf as women, but as writers, for writers of both sexes. In many ways the women activists in writers' organisations could be said to be working to achieve for all writers what Virginia Woolf had deemed the basic necessities for women writers to ensure their intellectual and material independence: 'a room of their own' and an adequate income (in her day, £500

---

1   Flinders University.

a year).[2] In Australia, with its relatively small population and a publishing industry dominated by the major Anglophone economies of Britain and the United States, it has always been difficult if not impossible for writers of most kinds of literature to earn a living wage.

Nineteenth and early twentieth-century literary societies had been informal by comparison with these later organisations, and did not have any of their 'craft union' features. They had held discussion meetings and social events, and had been, by and large, gender segregated. The notorious 'Bohemians of the Bulletin', for example, met at smoking rooms and pubs, or else gentlemen's clubs. Ladies had their own literary and debating societies, and a few clubs, such as the Lyceum Club and the Feminist Club (Sydney, 1914). The 1920s saw the formation of two women's organisations with a feminist slant: the Zonta Club and the Society of Women Writers, both of which still exist today.[3] Mixed literary salons, like those Rose Scott held in Sydney, increased during the interwar years, and as the twentieth century went on and there was a marked increase in the social mingling of the sexes,[4] this was reflected in writers' organisations.

The Fellowship of Australian Writers (FAW) was established in 1928. Mary Gilmore—already the grande dame of Australian literature, though she would live for another 30 years—was one of its two founding patrons, along with Roderick Quinn. It aimed to promote the *development* of literature and theatre, and the *study* of Australian literature, and to 'render aid and assistance to Australian authors, artists and dramatists'.[5] Prominent members included women as different from one another as bohemian Dulcie Deamer and feminist Miles Franklin. During the 1930s, when many members saw its role as defending democracy against encroaching fascism, the FAW was dominated by Flora Eldershaw, Marjorie Barnard and Frank Dalby Davidson. Eldershaw was president of the FAW in 1935 and again in 1943. The FAW had some success in lobbying for government support for literature through the Commonwealth Literature Fund (CLF), and in the postwar years its central strategy was to seek market protection for writers.[6]

PEN (originally standing for 'poets, essayists, novelists') was founded in 1921 in London by English novelist Amy Dawson Scott, to encourage intellectual

---

2   Virginia Woolf, *A Room of One's Own* (London: Hogarth Press, 1928).

3   Jane Hunt, 'Fellowing Women: Sydney Women Writers and the Organisational Impulse', *Australian Cultural History* 23 (2004): 175–99.

4   Jill Julius Matthews, *Dance Hall and Picture Palace: Sydney's Romance with Modernity* (Sydney: Currency Press, 2005), 88–90.

5   Len Fox, *Dream at a Graveside; History of the Fellowship of Australian Writers, 1928–1988* (Sydney: FAW, 1989), 18.

6   Pat Buckridge, 'Clearing a Space for Australian Literature', in *The Oxford Literary History of Australia*, eds Bruce Bennett and Jennifer Strauss (Melbourne: Oxford University Press, 1998), 180.

cooperation among writers and with a particular brief to defend freedom of expression internationally. Ten years later, PEN Australia was established, the work of a triumvirate of women writers: Mary Gilmore (again), Ethel Turner and Dorothea Mackellar. The Melbourne PEN Club was also established, to which Vance and Nettie Palmer belonged. Its formation in 1931 suggests it was also a response to the rising tides of political censorship of the period, but there is as yet no history of this organisation in Australia.

The writers' organisations of the 1930s were formed during a time when there was a growing conviction in Australia that government should assist the evolution of a national literature, and so the FAW's central strategy was lobbying for government patronage for writers. The Commonwealth Literary Fund, formed in 1908 as a modest pension scheme for writers, was expanded in 1939, largely due to agitation by the FAW. It took on a range of activities promoting and assisting the production of Australian literature. The CLF was replaced in 1973 with the Literature Board of the Australia Council, with a budget four times larger than the old CLF, and incorporated literature into a national program of support for the arts. This came about in part as the result of pressure from the Australian Society of Authors (ASA), founded in 1963. As literary historian David Carter concludes from his account of the burgeoning of Australian writing in the 1960s and 1970s:

> It is impossible to untangle the influence of the Literature Board from other developments [that made a difference to Australian literature]— the growth of new publishers, the formation of the Australian Society of Authors, the expansion of university teaching, the generational shift in terms of higher levels of education, or the arrival of cheaper offset printing which allowed new entrants into the publishing game.[7]

In this period of growth and change, the need for the ASA's work to protect and extend authors' rights was all the greater.

Major changes in the postwar publishing industry required a greater professionalisation of literary production in Australia, and this was reflected in the ASA's focus on contracts and copyright. Its concern was with writing of all kinds, not just 'literature': 'writers on astrology or astronomy, or on Baudelaire or Badminton, are equally eligible' for membership, as their early publicity flyer put it. Its principal business was with publication, payment and distribution. It offered legal and business advice to writers, and acted on behalf of the profession 'by negotiating for fair minimum terms and conditions with those who buy the

---

7   David Carter, 'Publishing Patronage and Cultural Politics', in *The Cambridge History of Australian Literature*, ed. Peter Pierce (Melbourne: Cambridge University Press, 2010), 377.

author's work'.[8] It met regularly with the Australian Publishers Association on such matters. It was also concerned with law reform, especially in relation to copyright law and liberalising the law in relation to obscenity, defamation and libel. More generally, it was concerned with raising the status of the writer in society, and had contacts with equivalent associations, the Authors League of America Incorporated and the Society of Authors (London).[9]

The ASA's first campaign was to abolish the 'colonial royalty' by which British publishers paid Australian authors the full 10 per cent royalty on copies of their books sold in the United Kingdom but only half that rate for sales in Australia, which were considered 'export sales'. Some of its other early successes included negotiating with the Australian Broadcasting Commission (ABC) for better rates of pay for scripts, with newspapers and periodicals for payment on acceptance, and with publishers for repeat fees for anthologies. It published a newsletter (which became the journal *Australian Author*) and a guide to book contracts, as well as *The Australian and New Zealand Writer's Handbook* (1975). It was involved in setting up the National Book Council, making a foundation grant for that purpose. It also made a foundation grant to finance the McNair Survey into writers' incomes in 1969, with additional support from Ampol, the Bank of New South Wales and the CLF—evidence that its fundraising activities extended into the commercial world.[10] The results of this survey included five recommendations for action, beginning with a call for a public lending right— something the British Society of Authors was also seeking.[11]

In tandem with the Publishers Association, the ASA waged a long and ultimately successful campaign for the Public Lending Right (PLR), which was agreed to in 1975 (although it was not actually established in legislation until 1985).[12] This is the government-funded scheme to compensate writers for royalty income they lose through the availability of their books in public libraries. It, and the Educational Lending Right set up in 2000, is an innovation from which writers and illustrators of all descriptions benefit. The ASA worked towards the Copyright Amendment Bill (1980), which granted authors a page-by-page fee for photocopying in educational institutions—a world first. It was also instrumental in setting up the Copyright Agency Limited (CAL) and the Australian Copyright Council. In 1989 CAL made its first distribution payments to authors of $1 million—a sum that tripled by the next year's distribution.

---

8   Jill Hellyer, 'Publicity flyer', n.d., Australian Society of Authors (ASA) Papers, Barr Smith Library Special Collections, Adelaide University [hereinafter ASA Papers], folder 1.

9   'President's letter 1963 to Fellow Members', Jill Hellyer Papers, NLA MS 6814, National Library of Australia, Canberra [hereinafter Hellyer Papers], Folder 1.

10   'Chairman's letter 10 April 1969', in ibid., folder 3.

11   'Survey of Earnings May–August 1969', Press release, September 1969, in ibid., folder 3.

12   Barbara Jefferis, 'Public Lending Right: "Our precious child is legitimate"', *Australian Author* (July 1988): 11–12.

Such achievements as these involved the ASA taking on an educative role. As Dale Spender put it on the occasion of its thirtieth anniversary, it has led the way in teaching the community, as well as authors, about 'new ways of seeing the relationship between money, books and authors': not just politicians but also librarians and writers themselves were the ones who needed to be convinced that these new arrangements would 'extend the possibilities (and payments!) for writers, rather than reduce them'.[13]

The Australian Society of Authors, as the first real business organisation of writers, set out to establish a national structure. The FAW, on the contrary, was a decentralised series of State-based associations. This difference was an important one, and the founders of ASA were anxious to convince the older members of the FAW that it was a parallel organisation, not intended to supersede the fellowship. The FAW had, during the Cold War period, experienced major disagreements about whether it should take a political stand, and if so, how far to the left that should be. These political issues lie behind the following account of the society's formation:

> It all started with the then President of the NSW Federation of Australian Writers, Walter Stone, inviting delegates from all other writers' societies to a meeting in Sydney in October 1962 to discuss the formation of a national organisation to represent professional authors. A series of meetings followed culminating in the formation of the ASA on 15 May 1963, and the acceptance of a provisional constitution on 26 June 1963.
>
> Much of the work in those early years was done by a largely unsung group of visionaries. Chief among them was the indefatigable, Miles Franklin Award-winning author the late Dal Stivens, who became the founding President of the ASA in 1963 and who invested many hours of his productive life to making sure the organisation survived those early years.
>
> Another of the founders, Jill Hellyer, the ASA's first Secretary, tells the story of how Frank Hardy was dispatched by a Melbourne push (headed by Judah Waten) to torpedo the first ASA meeting, and how he almost succeeded until Dymphna Cusack saved the day with the speech of her life and the passing round of somebody else's hat for donations. Frank Hardy later became an office-holder of the society.[14]

Women were well represented in the early years of the ASA. Among the list of new members to be approved for admission at the first AGM in July 1964 were Henrietta Drake-Brockman, Ernestine Hill, Mavis Thorpe Clark, Hesba

---

13   Dale Spender, 'Passionate Gratitude', *Australian Author Thirty Years* (Spring 1993): 36–8 at 38.
14   ASA website: www.asauthors.org.

Brinsmead, Thelma Forshaw, K. S. Prichard, Kath Walker and Dorothy Hewett.[15] This is indicative of the spread of writers, both popular and more literary—and the inclusion of Prichard and Hewett indicates that the ASA was supported by members of the Communist Party of Australia, no longer suspicious, as Hardy and Waten had been, that it was out to supplant the FAW. Other women who joined in 1964 included writers Jessica Anderson, Dorothy Auchterlonie (Green), Rosemary Dobson, Elsa Chauvel, Joyce Nicholson, Aileen and Nettie Palmer, and academics Leonie Kramer and Kathleen Fitzpatrick.

The organisational structure, as well as its membership, involved many women as activists. Its first secretary, Jill Hellyer, had spent the whole year before the society's foundation, in her role as secretary of the FAW, in delicate negotiations with interstate groups and individuals. This 'resulted in my first ulcer', she later wrote. Many people anticipated endless wrangling, and she wrote to reassure them that this would not happen. She also had to hose down notorious troublemakers like Xavier Herbert. She was secretary of the ASA for its first seven years for £10 a week, operating out of her own home at Mount Colah north of Sydney: 'I worked from home, sitting on a fruit box, and my children spent their weekends folding circulars. The phone rang seven days a week.' She added: 'The ASA gave me a job when I needed one, and several of the many writers I was to meet became my friends.'[16]

The ASA Council (which attempted to represent all the States) included from the outset Judith Wright (Queensland) and Nancy Cato (South Australia), later joined by Katharine Susannah Prichard (Western Australia). The Management Committee—which did most of the legwork, its members taking on particular portfolios, such as copyright or contracts—included more women. Betty Roland, Joan Clarke and Grace Perry were members of the first committee, soon joined by Barbara Jefferis. Quarterly general meetings were at first held in the Feminist Club, 77 King Street, Sydney;[17] perhaps this constituted a link with the earlier all-women literary societies. The Committee of Management, however, met in members' homes—Betty Roland's flat, for instance, or in Beatrice Davis's office at Angus & Robertson.

Australian Author, the society's magazine, which started up in 1968, was first edited by a woman, Barrie Ovenden. She, like Hellyer, worked from home. Later, Nancy Keesing edited it for several years. She also assembled *Transition* (1970), an anthology of literary work donated by members, which the society published and sold to raise funds, as well as to raise its public profile. Keesing left the ASA editorship in 1974 when she was appointed to the Literature Board

---

15   *1964 Annual Report*, in ASA Papers.
16   Jill Hellyer, 'My First Ulcer', *Australian Author Thirty Years* (Spring 1993): 22.
17   Deidre Hill, *A Writer's Rights: The Story of the Australian Society of Authors 1963–1983* (Sydney: Australia and New Zealand Book Company, 1983), 86.

of the Australia Council, which she chaired for five years, the first woman to do so. In 1971 she and Barbara Jefferis had appeared as 'star defence witnesses' in the test case obscenity trial of *Portnoy's Complaint*. 'I sometimes wonder if one reason for our selection was that we are respectable, sensible housewives', she wrote later in her memoir.[18]

Housewife or not, Barbara Jefferis in 1973 became the ASA's first woman president, and her leadership in the society deserves attention. In this period of growth in Australian literature, with proliferating literary magazines and publishing enterprises, increased state support for the arts and the spread of Australian literature as a subject of study in schools and universities, the leaders in these enterprises were predominantly male.[19] Keesing and Jefferis were among the first women to join the ranks of the major protagonists.

Barbara Jefferis was a Sydney writer, who, by the early 1960s when she helped form the ASA, had published several well-reviewed novels. She contributed a regular column to the *Australian Women's Weekly* called 'At Home with Margaret Sydney', as well as writing reviews for the newspapers and radio plays and dramatised documentaries for the ABC. Married to the film critic John Hinde, she was very familiar with the conditions for writers in the media industries. She had started out as a journalist at the Sydney *Daily News*, having left her native Adelaide in 1939, at the age of twenty-two, for the city.[20] After working on various papers and magazines, she decided when her only child was born in 1944 that she could 'make writing a full-time job, one that would not interfere with bringing up her child and looking after her husband'—as the *Weekly* put it in a 1959 feature about her.[21]

This situation—having no journalist or academic salary to fall back on—was no doubt a strong motivation for her to pursue rights for writers. She and Hinde were friends and colleagues with the talented group of people who wrote for the ABC, including Ruth Park and D'Arcy Niland, Diana and Mungo MacCallum, Charmian Clift, George Johnston and Colin Simpson—although only Simpson seems to have been active in the ASA, along with Barbara. As a member of the Committee of Management, she took on the portfolio for contracts and wrote the book about them, with founding president, Dal Stivens: *Guide to Book Contracts* (1967).

During her time as ASA president (1973–76), she was able not only to welcome the establishment of the PLR but also to preside over not one but two 'victory

---

18   Nancy Keesing, *Riding the Elephant* (Sydney: Allen & Unwin, 1988), 207.

19   Susan Sheridan, *Nine Lives: Postwar Women Writers Making their Mark* (Brisbane: UQP, 2011), 11–12.

20   Nadia Wheatley, 'The Long Haul of Devotion to Writers and their Rights', Obituary, *Sydney Morning Herald*, 23 January 2004, http://www.smh.com.au/articles/2004/01/23/1074732602894.html.

21   A Best-Seller', *Australian Women's Weekly*, 25 November 1959: 29, http://trove.nla.gov.au.

dinners' to celebrate, with Prime Minister Gough Whitlam as guest of honour—one held at the Sydney Opera House, the other at the Windsor Hotel in Melbourne. Here is what she wrote to ASA members on learning that Whitlam's Government intended to accept the Literature Board's advice and set up the Public Lending Right:

> This is a triumph for the Australian Society of Authors. It is a government decision of a different quality from the decision to make generous grants available to writers. Grants are, in the best sense of the word, an act of patronage. The PLR decision is a recognition of the author's absolute right to some recompense for the public's use of his work.[22]

She was an eloquent advocate. She was also good at straight talking: her 1989 survey of ASA members' experiences with Australian publishers is called The Good, the Bad and the Greedy. In terms of naming and shaming, publishers were not going to like being named, she wrote, 'any more, perhaps, than writers like being framed'.[23] She recalled that

> Australian contracts were appalling when the ASA began … Not many books were being published and it was hard for writers to be anything but passionately grateful to publishers who wanted to publish their work. Naturally that made it hard for them to niggle over terms and that's why the ASA was needed.[24]

There are, of course, still writers who resist such union-style activities. Dal Stivens recalled his 'membership drives', writing to anyone who had a book published. Some refused to join: 'I suspect some were literary snobs or free-loaders', he wrote.[25] A pamphlet issued during Jefferis's presidency, 'How the ASA Helps Writers', ends on a rousing note: 'We need more members to provide the sinews of war.'[26] I like to think this was her answer to the snobs and freeloaders. 'I'm in it for the long haul', she told a younger colleague, Nadia Wheatley, when they first met at the ASA, and indeed she was. She remained an active member of the ASA Management Committee for almost 40 years, until she suffered a stroke in 2001, at which time she was rewriting the guide to book contracts. She had held the Contract Advisory Service portfolio since its inception, and the PLR portfolio from 1981 to 1989, during part of which time she represented writers' interests on the Government's PLR Committee.

Jefferis, like many professional women of her generation, did not identify as a feminist in her youth, when the term was out of fashion. But by the 1980s she

---

22 Hill, *A Writer's Rights*, 69.
23 Barbara Jefferis, 'Publishers Who Break their Code of Practice', *Australian Author* (July 1987).
24 Spender, 'Passionate Gratitude', 36.
25 Dal Stivens, 'The Work of the ASA', *Australian Author* 1(3) (1969): 45–6.
26 'How the Australian Society of Authors Helps Writers', April 1973, in ASA Papers, folder 3.

certainly did. She wrote a biography of three generations of talented women, *Three of a Kind* (1982), and published it with the feminist publisher McPhee Gribble. It is fitting that she should be remembered by an award named after her, drawn from a bequest by her husband, John Hinde, and administered by the ASA. The Barbara Jefferis Award is made each year for the best novel written by an Australian author that depicts women and girls in a positive way or otherwise empowers the status of women and girls in society.

Her ASA colleagues Jill Hellyer and Nancy Keesing did not go on record as regarding women as particularly disadvantaged in society. Nancy Keesing's International Women's Year speech denied that women writers were disadvantaged, though she conceded that women academics and publishers were. Using evidence from Johnston's *Annals of Australian Literature*, she argued that good and persistent writers do get published 'sooner or later'.[27] But when she later published a book on the slang used by Australian women and their families, she speculated about the reasons for women's slang being so poorly represented in collections of Australian idiom.[28] While Keesing was a prominent public figure in the literary world, Hellyer was less well known; in fact, as becomes clear from articles she wrote later about her family, she was sole supporting parent of three children, two of whom were disabled.[29] After a succession of publishing disappointments during the 1970s, at the suggestion of her mentor, A. D. Hope, she contacted the feminist publishing house Sisters.[30] In 1981, they published her *Song of the Humpbacked Whales*, one of their first single-author volumes of poetry.

In these ways the heroines of the Australian Society of Authors all participated to some extent in the assertion of women's literary presence in the early 1980s. Yet their contributions to the ASA were made on behalf of all writers, not just women. Were they, in fact, playing a traditional female role and doing the profession's housework, as well as the wifely work of organising its social life? Jane Hunt frames the activities of most Australian women's organisations in the early twentieth century as forms of 'maternal citizenship'—that is, taking on a specialised and inevitably secondary role in public life, akin to their traditional maternal role.[31] Was the ASA yet another case of women serving as the handmaidens of literature? A woman writer friend to whom I spoke about the idea for this chapter said: 'Well of course those women never get the rewards, they just do the legwork—so surely they're an example of failed leadership?' In the course of researching their activities, I became convinced that, on the

---

27 Keesing, *Riding the Elephant*, 209.
28 Nancy Keesing, *Lily on the Dustbin: Slang of Australian Women and their Families* (Melbourne: Penguin, 1982).
29 Copy of article from *Contact* magazine (15 April 1980), in Hellyer Papers, folder 13.
30 'Letter ADH to JH 7 February 1980', in ibid., folder 39.
31 Hunt, 'Fellowing Women', 194.

contrary, the women leaders of the ASA were outstandingly successful in enabling worthwhile things to happen. The power they wielded was not that of a large institution with major economic interests, and they could scarcely be said to have become household names for their efforts. But they applied what pressure they could, where they could, and by persistence achieved policy changes that made a significant difference to the political, literary and economic independence of their fellow writers. In doing so, they exercised leadership in the best sense, which supports and expands human possibility.[32]

These writers' organisations, especially the ASA, have achieved immense and lasting gains. Their relatively democratic structures ensured that women could and did occupy those seats of power and were recognised for their work (Jill Hellyer, Nancy Keesing and Barbara Jefferis were all made honorary life members of the ASA, for instance). The ASA was different from its predecessors to the extent that it was a professional organisation, a 'craft union' (its preferred designation). Yet it represents an unstructured and immensely varied profession, one that exercises a degree of cultural clout but has no major investment in social or economic power. Unlike more prestigious professions such as law and medicine, literature has not been for centuries an exclusively male arena. In some respects the writers' associations have more in common with community organisations than with professional bodies. This may explain why women became prominent in them many years before they began to make headway in leadership of the other professions.

At the 'Women, Leadership and Democracy' conference held in Canberra in December 2011, then Governor-General, Quentin Bryce, described in her opening speech the situation of women of her generation who were young wives and mothers in the 1960s, typically fighting off maternal guilt as they took on roles outside the family as part-time workers and community leaders. This captures very well the situation of the women who played major roles in the ASA. They were modern women of the postwar era, wives and mothers as well as professional writers. Their attitudes and values, too, bore the stamp of postwar culture: they did not identify as feminists, and their attitudes to censorship bore no traces of maternal feminism; they advocated solidarity in pursuing the Society's aims but beyond that they did not identify politically as socialists. Pragmatic, stoical, hardworking, altruistic and modest they were— but very clear about their values and the value they set upon their work.

The value of that work, and the kind of leadership it required, is well captured in Nadia Wheatley's obituary for Barbara Jefferis:

---

32 Sinclair, Chapter 1, in this volume.

Her work for authors has been extremely important, not just to her colleagues, but to our whole society. Copyright … public lending right … educational lending right … somehow the words tend to sound worthy but dull. They do not have the emotional ring of, for example, human rights or civil rights or women's rights. Yet if a society is to have those more universal rights, a precondition is the right of authors, not just to write and publish their opinions freely, but to gain a decent living from their writing.

References

'A Best-Seller.' *Australian Women's Weekly*, 25 November 1959: 29. http://trove. nla.gov.au/ndp/del/page/4830410.

Australian Society of Authors (ASA). Papers. Barr Smith Library Special Collections, Adelaide University, Adelaide.

Buckridge, Pat. 'Clearing a Space for Australian Literature.' In *The Oxford Literary History of Australia*, edited by Bruce Bennett and Jennifer Strauss, 169–92. Melbourne: Oxford University Press, 1998.

Carter, David. 'Publishing Patronage and Cultural Politics.' In *The Cambridge History of Australian Literature*, edited by Peter Pierce, 360–90. Melbourne: Cambridge University Press, 2010.

Fox, Len. *Dream at a Graveside: History of the Fellowship of Australian Writers, 1928–1988*. Sydney: FAW, 1989.

Hellyer, Jill. Papers. NLA MS 6814. National Library of Australia, Canberra.

Hellyer, Jill. 'My First Ulcer.' *Australian Author Thirty Years* (Spring 1993): 22.

Hill, Deidre. *A Writer's Rights: The Story of the Australian Society of Authors 1963–1983*. Sydney: Australia and New Zealand Book Company, 1983.

Hunt, Jane. 'Fellowing Women: Sydney Women Writers and the Organisational Impulse.' *Australian Cultural History* 23 (2004): 175–99.

Jefferis, Barbara. 'Publishers Who Breach their Code of Practice.' *Australian Author* (July 1987): 7–8.

Jefferis, Barbara. 'Public Lending Right: "Our precious child is legitimate".' Australian Author (July 1988): 11–12.

Keesing, Nancy. *Lily on the Dustbin: Slang of Australian Women and their Families*. Melbourne: Penguin, 1982.

Keesing, Nancy. *Riding the Elephant*. Sydney: Allen & Unwin, 1988.

Matthews, Jill Julius. *Dance Hall and Picture Palace: Sydney's Romance with Modernity*. Sydney: Currency Press, 2005.

Sheridan, Susan. *Nine Lives: Postwar Women Writers Making their Mark*. Brisbane: UQP, 2011.

Spender, Dale. 'Passionate Gratitude.' *Australian Author Thirty Years* (Spring 1993): 36–8.

Stivens, Dal. 'The Work of the ASA.' *Australian Author* 1(3) (1969): 45–6.

Wheatley, Nadia. 'The Long Haul of Devotion to Writers and their Rights.' Obituary. *Sydney Morning Herald*, 23 January 2004. http://www.smh.com.au/articles/2004/01/23/1074732602894.html.

Woolf, Virginia. *A Room of One's Own*. London: Hogarth Press, 1928.

Part VI
Movements for social change

15. Collectivism, consensus and concepts of shared leadership in movements for social change

Marian Sawer[1] and Merrindahl Andrew[2]

In the 1970s, 'leadership' was a dirty word for many in the women's movement. Journalists trying to find a 'spokesman' complained of how upset women became if they were labelled as leaders. Leadership was associated with hierarchy and hierarchy was seen as inextricably linked with the patriarchal domination of women. To liberate themselves from patriarchy, women were trying to organise without hierarchy, through collectives and networks. Instead of there being leaders and followers, women would empower themselves through taking responsibility for decisions, which would be reached by consensus.

At first there were attempts not only to resist the idea of leaders but also to do without structure at all. It was soon realised, however, that this could lead to unacknowledged and unaccountable leadership as informal power relations emerged. In an influential essay, American feminist Jo Freeman called this the 'tyranny of structurelessness'. Freeman's essay was roneoed and distributed widely within the women's movement, both in the United States and in Australia. It proved an important influence in the development of feminist organisational philosophy: it was better to have democratic structures than none at all. Freeman's democratic principles included delegating authority for specific tasks, requiring accountability to the group, distributing authority as widely as possible, rotating tasks and ensuring access by all members to information and other resources.[3]

The new feminist experiments with organisational structures were seen as a model by those like Bruce Kokopeli and George Lakey who were seeking alternative structures to fulfil the functions of leadership in movements for social change. They described the feminist approach as one of 'shared leadership' and as demonstrating that while leadership was needed, leaders were not.[4] Leadership was seen not as an attribute of individuals but rather as a number of functions that could be shared flexibly among members. Functions could be

---

1   The Australian National University.
2   The Australian National University.
3   Joreen Freeman, 'The Tyranny of Structurelessness', Reprinted from *The Second Wave* 2(1) (Sydney: Words for Women, 1972).
4   Bruce Kokopeli and George Lakey, *Leadership for Change: Towards a Feminist Model* (Philadephia: New Society Publishers, 1978), 7.

divided between the task functions of goal-setting and goal accomplishment and the morale functions of nurturing the group through attention to process and emotional climate. A valuable aspect of the feminist model was to make morale functions a central part of leadership. Too often this function had been invisible in the older models of leadership, leaving it to women to do the emotion work without any corresponding leadership status.[5]

In this chapter we explore the initial rejection by second-wave feminists of the concept of leadership, the development of the concept of shared leadership, and later compromises that built on both feminist organisational philosophy and the expectation that women would do leadership differently because of their socialisation and family roles. We look at how these philosophies and expectations were also carried into other movements for social change and to what extent more collaborative ideas of leadership with emphasis on empowering others are being carried forward in these movements.

Rejecting masculine models of leadership

Because of the extent of the discursive shift that has taken place in Western democracies and the current pre-eminence of individualistic norms, it can be a shock to rediscover the collectivist frames that were so common in the 1970s. A good example can be found in a Penguin book published in Melbourne in 1975, a collection called *The Other Half: Women in Australian Society*, edited by Jan Mercer. The contributors included a number of future university professors and one future vice-chancellor. But far from presenting themselves as academic leaders, these outstandingly talented women did not even attach their names to their contributions. The book explained:

> The names of contributors are not listed on the contents page or linked with the contributions in the body of the book, as it is the ideas themselves rather than who presented them that is crucial. Nor is it relevant to indicate the academic status of individual writers because these have been allocated in terms of a male dominated and defined system of rewards.[6]

The second wave of the women's movement was in part reacting to the way in which gender hierarchy had reasserted itself in the radical movements of the 1960s. Men had taken the microphone and expected women to type the minutes. In the new women's services that were springing up from 1974, women sought to replace individual leaders by democratically sharing the functions of

---

5   Ibid., 16–20.
6   Jan Mercer, ed., *The Other Half: Women in Australian Society* (Melbourne: Penguin, 1975), 5.

leadership within the group. Functions included not only setting and achieving goals but also maintaining group morale and nurturing members. The concept of shared leadership was embodied in the flatter structures adopted by women's movement organisations (matrices rather than hierarchies) and the emphasis on democratic process and consensus decision-making. This philosophy was seen as reflecting preferred female ways of organising and as supporting the empowerment of women. Even when the consensus model was modified, it was through the horizontal delegation of routine decision-making, with major decisions continuing to be decided by consensus—the preferred route to empowerment through everybody 'winning'.[7]

The emphasis on consensus was part of what the late activist and academic Wendy Weeks describes as a distinctive form of organising, characterised by the 'pursuit of collectivity'.[8] This pursuit, Weeks argues, is rooted in the long histories of women's involvement in family, neighbourhood and community, but became politicised in the 1970s in Western countries including Australia. Feminists developed a form of organising that emphasised leadership acts, which could be shared by a number of people, rather than viewing leadership as synonymous with charismatic individuals.[9] Accordingly, 'negotiations of the social order' needed to be ongoing and invite questioning, rather than closing off debate in order to achieve a goal.

The refusal to separate means and ends and an ethic of continual feminist analysis involve 'locating theory and practice within the tension between the diverse individual women's experiences … and an analysis of the economic, political and social arrangements, processes and related ideas and beliefs'.[10] As Brown observes in relation to the UK Women's Centres, '[o]rganising activity … makes reference to the values of the autonomous women's movement, but … the relationship between values and action is one which is continually negotiated by participants'.[11] This means that no one leader can be taken to embody the values of the movement, and attempts at such representation have often been vigorously contested.

Such demanding principles certainly make it difficult for women's movements to operate in a broader social order that values individual success and goal attainment over all. Yet this very difficulty has been part of the reasoning behind feminist organising: the challenges faced by women in creating alternative models

7   Kathleen P. Iannello, *Decisions without Hierarchy: Feminist Interventions in Organization Theory and Practice* (New York: Routledge, 1992), 120–1.

8   Wendy Weeks, 'Democratic Leadership Practices in Australian Feminist Women's Services: The Pursuit of Collectivity and Social Citizenship?', *International Review of Women and Leadership* 2 (1996): 19–33.

9   Helen Brown, *Women Organising* (London: Taylor & Francis, 2002 [first published 1992]).

10   Wendy Weeks, 'Feminist Principles for Community Work', *Women in Welfare Education*, 7 (October 2004): 1–16 [reprinted from *Women in Welfare Education* 1 (1994)].

11   Brown, *Women Organising*, 53.

of collective action are seen to prefigure the struggle to bring about broader changes in society as a whole. This conflict is acute in relation to principles of leadership. The conventional vision of leadership maintains that, as well as embodying the vision and goals of the movement, leaders provide 'someone who can speak with authority on behalf of the movement' to governments and the public.[12] This expectation has been a challenge for women's movements, emerging as conflict over 'media stars' and questions of who can legitimately speak for whom.

Operationalising ideas of shared leadership

Ideas of shared leadership had a very broad influence in the women's movement in the 1970s as activists called on women to 'stop mirroring men's institutions and behaviours'.[13] The determination to avoid hierarchy was true even of the second-wave organisations most dedicated to 'reformist' goals of influencing government. This was in contradiction to received wisdom on effective lobbying, which suggested that organisations should mirror the agencies of government they were trying to influence. For example, when the Women's Electoral Lobby (WEL) held its first national conference immediately after the 1972 federal election, the NSW paper on how WEL should be organised reported: 'We are determined to avoid having leaders—either convenors or permanent spokeswomen or any form of power hierarchy.'[14]

These ideas were not only being put into practice in advocacy organisations and women's services; there were also attempts to carry them into government. Sara Dowse, the first head of the Women's Affairs Branch in the Australian Department of Prime Minister and Cabinet, told of the discomfort of the new feminist bureaucrats (femocrats) with the hierarchical ladder they were given. In protest, when the next woman on the ladder was promoted she said she would not accept the promotion unless the woman below her was promoted as well, which also led to promotions for others.[15] Another early femocrat spoke of the unresolved issue of how to 'get from the values we hold dear—of collective,

---

12   Karen O'Connor and Alixandra B. Yanus, 'Overview: History of Women Leaders in Social Movements', in *Gender and Women's Leadership: A Reference Handbook. Volume 1*, ed. Karen O'Connor (New York: Sage, 2010), 182.

13   Weeks, 'Feminist Principles for Community Work', 10; Marian Sawer and Abigail Groves, '"The Women's Lobby": Networks, Coalition Building and the Women of Middle Australia', *Australian Journal of Political Science* 29 (1994): 441.

14   Marian Sawer, *Making Women Count. A History of the Women's Electoral Lobby in Australia* (Sydney: UNSW Press, 2008), 94.

15   Sara Dowse, 'Address to WEL–ACT Dinner', Canberra, 5 June 1989.

non-hierarchical democratic behaviour—to the outcome we seek, of a peaceful world safe for women … without sacrificing these values in the rush to seize and use power on behalf of feminist ends'.[16]

In New Zealand the first head of the Ministry of Women's Affairs tried to minimise hierarchy. She practised collectivism and decisions were talked through until consensus was reached. At the weekly staff meeting time was allocated for staff to mention issues that were impinging on their public role, such as children who were teething.[17] As we have seen, the emphasis on emotion work as part of leadership was intrinsic to feminist organisational philosophy; this meant relating to the whole person and particularly to the roles fulfilled by women outside the organisation. Setting aside time to ensure that personal concerns could be shared was one aspect of this.

Attempts to import feminist values into a somewhat unreceptive bureaucracy led to numerous cultural clashes. For example, a WA premier tried to find who was 'in charge' of his Women's Information and Referral Exchange (WIRE) and hence who could be held responsible for sending out letters about a women's peace camp through the premier's department. Being frustrated by WIRE's flat structure and not being able to find anyone in charge, he shouted 'you're all fired'.[18]

In Victoria as well, the Women's Information and Referral Exchange was established under the premier's department in 1983–84. The original proposal was put forward by WEL and the Young Women's Christian Association (YWCA). After the Office of Women's Affairs in the premier's department conducted consultations with some 200 women's organisations, a constitution was adopted that included the purposes of upholding the principles of feminism and functioning 'within a democratic non-hierarchical organisational structure which includes flexibility and collective decision-making'. It did not have a coordinator, instead having a series of collectives to perform coordination and other functions. Tasks involved in collective meetings were all rotated and until 1988 WIRE annual reports did not reveal who belonged to any of the collectives, in accordance with a policy of attributing all work to the collective rather than naming individual members.[19] No wonder it was described as 'a libertarian classroom in an authoritarian school', given the very different organisational values of the government departments which funded it.[20]

---

16   Hester Eisenstein, *Gender Shock* (Boston: Beacon, 1992), 3.
17   Marian Sawer, 'Femocrats and Ecorats: Women's Policy Machinery in Australia, Canada and New Zealand', in *Missionaries and Mandarins: Feminist Engagement with Development Institutions*, eds Carol Miller and Shahra Razavi (London: Intermediate Technology Publications, 1998), 130.
18   Marian Sawer, *Sisters in Suits: Women and Public Policy in Australia* (Sydney: Allen & Unwin, 1990), 203.
19   Ibid., 197.
20   Sara Dowse, 'The Bureaucrat as Usurer', in *Unfinished Business: Social Justice for Women in Australia*, ed. Dorothy Broom (Sydney: Allen & Unwin, 1984), 154.

As noted, at the height of women's movement mobilisation there were attempts to import the anti-hierarchical spirit of the women's movement even into the heart of government. Sara Dowse claimed at an International Women's Year conference in 1975 that the wheel model of women's affairs, with its hub in a central coordinating department and spokes in functional departments, was in harmony with feminist organisational philosophy.[21] She thought that in society at large one could generalise that there was a central autonomous women's movement and then feminist caucuses in places such as the media, the public service and the unions, which related back to the central autonomous movement. The same model could apply within the public service, with a central core linked to caucuses in every other area of the public service. This wheel of women's affairs, which was about to come into existence at the federal level, became the Australian model for women's policy machinery: it was a centre–periphery model, rather than one characterised by vertical integration. Of course the term 'feminist caucuses' would not be used in organisational charts, but rather 'women's desks', 'women's units' or, later, 'gender focal points'. Nonetheless, in the late 1980s senior federal bureaucrats were still referring to the oldest of the women's units, the Women's Bureau, as 'the feminist collective'.

Women in management: Making a difference?

Meanwhile, during the 1980s a literature emerged on women in management, much of it inspired by Rosabeth Moss Kanter's *Men and Women of the Corporation*.[22] Kanter made the case for the importance of relative proportions. While there were still only token numbers of women in an organisation they experienced dynamics such as boundary heightening, reminders of difference and loyalty tests, and there were enormous pressures to conform to the culture of the dominant group. Kanter argued that a shift in relative proportions and the achievement of 'critical mass' could mean that minorities were able to initiate serious change in the culture of the organisation. Kanter's work inspired Danish political scientist Drude Dahlerup to investigate whether the concept of critical mass could be useful in analysing under what circumstances women politicians were able to make a difference. She found that the concept was not really transferable to parliament, where critical actors were more important in achieving change than numbers alone.[23]

---

21   Sara Dowse, 'Power in Institutions—The Public Service', Transcript of discussion at the Women and Politics Conference 1975, National Library of Australia, Canberra, 1975, 12.

22   Rosabeth Moss Kanter, *Men and Women of the Corporation* (New York: Basic Books, 1977).

23   Drude Dahlerup, 'From a Small to a Large Minority: Women in Scandinavian Politics', *Scandinavian Politics Studies* 11 (1988): 275–97.

Nonetheless the concept of critical mass lived on to inspire a worldwide movement for electoral quotas to ensure there were enough women elected to parliaments to bring about change. It was widely believed that because of the roles women played in the family they would bring a more consensus-seeking approach to politics and that, once there were enough of them, political culture would shift away from more confrontational styles. This gendered expectation of what might be possible when women became 'a large minority' in organisations was also reflected in the new literature on women in management.

For example, in 1990 Judy Rosener published a famous article in the *Harvard Business Review* arguing that women managers were now feeling freer to depart from the masculine styles that had been the norm of successful management and which the first women executives had felt obliged to follow. The masculine leadership style had been one of command and control, using organisational status and manipulation of rewards (something labelled in the 1970s as a 'transactional' form of leadership).[24]

Rosener found that women were now relying more on their interpersonal skills and using them to motivate others through sharing power and information, encouraging participation and affirming others' contributions. Her interviewees made constant reference to creating mechanisms to make people feel part of the organisation—something Rosener described as an interactive and inclusive style of leadership. She argued that women were succeeding, particularly in fast-changing and growing organisations, because of, rather than despite, characteristics generally regarded as 'feminine' and hitherto as inappropriate in a leader.[25]

Rosener's article stimulated a range of reactions. Cynthia Fuchs Epstein suggested it reflected bias in the self-reporting of management styles: both male and female managers were reporting what they saw to be a gender-appropriate management style.[26] The confirmation that shared leadership was seen as a 'feminine' management style and transactional leadership as a 'masculine' style was itself interesting, highlighting the pressures on women and men to define themselves in relation to these stereotypes.[27] Rosener's article had many resonances for those who wished to demonstrate that there was a feminist way of doing leadership, that women should not shrink from exercising power and

24 James McGregor Burns, *Leadership* (New York: Free Press, 1978).
25 Judy Rosener, 'Ways Women Lead', *Harvard Business Review* (November–December 1990): 120.
26 Cythia Fuchs Epstein, 'Ways Men and Women Lead: Debate', *Harvard Business Review* (January–February 1991): 150–1.
27 Joyce K. Fletcher, 'The Paradox of Postheroic Leadership: An Essay on Gender, Power, and Transformational Change', *Leadership Quarterly* 15(5) (2004): 650.

that women could make a difference. Naomi Wolf later wrote a bestseller setting out a case for 'power feminism' called *Fire with Fire: The New Female Power and How to Use It*.[28]

In Australia, Amanda Sinclair, soon to become foundation professor of management (diversity and change) at the University of Melbourne, was arguing that organisations needed to build in more diversity in order to facilitate flexibility and adaptability. As women moved up the organisational hierarchy, they tended to reject their own distinctive managerial traits in order to better fit into male models of leadership and managerial success. This discouragement of diversity meant a loss of organisational effectiveness, particularly in terms of capacity to respond and adapt to rapidly changing circumstances.[29] Another sign of the times was the establishment in 1995 of the journal *International Review of Women and Leadership* by feminist management expert Leonie Still.

WEL advocate and public intellectual Eva Cox joined in with the book *Leading Women: Tactics for Making a Difference*. She began by discussing the discomfort many women felt with the concepts of power and leadership, even women being groomed for senior levels in the public service. She found that for many women the concepts of power and leadership were 'so identified with certain masculine values that they found it difficult even to discuss them'.[30] She went on to urge feminists to become more comfortable with power. As part of her argument, she referred to how the models of shared leadership associated with the women's movement were now being taken up by management manuals that advocated flatter structures and having time for family and community.[31]

Judy Wajcman presented a less sanguine view in the same year (1996). Reporting on a survey she had conducted of male and female managers in five multinational companies, she found that in an economic climate of downsizing and a context of strong organisational imperatives, women were conforming to older male norms of management. While both male and female managers used the rhetoric of consultative and people-oriented management, in fact there had been a return to macho management styles.[32]

But feminists continued to hope that an alternative form of leadership was possible. Joan Kirner, the first woman Premier of Victoria, published a book together with human rights advocate Moira Rayner that drew on many of her experiences in government. It was called *The Women's Power Handbook* and

28   Naomi Wolf, *Fire with Fire: The New Female Power and How to Use It* (London: Chatto & Windus, 1993).
29   Amanda Sinclair and Fern Marriott, 'Women in Management—Advantage through Adversity', *Asia Pacific Human Resource Management* 28 (1990): 14–25.
30   Eva Cox, *Leading Women: Tactics for Making the Difference* (Sydney: Random House, 1996), 24.
31   Ibid., 256.
32   Judy Wajcman, 'Desperately Seeking Differences. Is Management Style Gendered?', *British Journal of Industrial Relations* 34 (1996): 333–49.

sought to establish that women were more likely to use power in a democratic way, to empower others. The authors suggested women were most likely to be seen exercising power 'through networking: acting collectively, persuading, consulting and influencing'.[33] Kirner drew on EMILY's List research to argue that it was not just a matter of different leadership preferences but also of voter expectations: women voters expected that women in parliament would ensure decision-making processes were more democratic and inclusive of women.[34]

Hybrid organisations

In women's services, the pressures of neoliberal reform and generational change led to the development of an innovative 'hybrid' form of organisation. This can be seen through the case of WIRE in Victoria, discussed earlier as an example of feminist organisational philosophy and collectivist practice. Like other women's services, WIRE eventually moved to a more traditional governance structure, with a chief executive officer from 2002, but retained strong elements of feminist organisational philosophy. There was a 'conscious effort to maintain the collaborative and participatory elements that were an integral part of the WIRE culture'.[35] These included the time set aside at the beginning of board meetings for the discussion of personal issues, reflecting the feminist emphasis on holistic rather than purely role-based relationships within organisations.

Like WIRE, the Canberra Rape Crisis Centre (CRCC) has gone through extensive changes since its establishment as a collective in 1976. Having debated the risks of government funding, in the early 1980s CRCC eventually accepted funds sufficient for one and a half workers—but then decided to share the funds equally between several workers, giving them an exceptionally low wage for full-day shifts that often extended to 8 pm.[36] More insidious from a feminist point of view was the way that State agencies promoted individualised responses to rape (the 'treatment model') at the expense of the 'political analysis, activism and work to change social relations' for which rape crisis centres were founded.[37] Despite this change, however, and the shift from a collective to a governance model in 2005, CRCC, like rape crisis centres generally, has maintained aspects of participatory decision-making and has continued to pursue a social change agenda.

---

33 Joan Kirner and Moira Rayner, *The Women's Power Handbook* (Melbourne: Penguin, 1999), 4.
34 Ibid., 236.
35 Kerry Jeanne Tanner, 'Emotion, Gender and the Sustainability of Communities', *Community Informatics: A Global E-Journal* 1 (2005), http://ci-journal.net/index.php/ciej/article/view/208/165.
36 Veronica Wensing, 'What's Behind a Name? The Organisational Identity of Rape Crisis Centres: Positioning the Canberra Rape Crisis Centre as a Feminist Organisation in the 21st Century', Unpublished paper, 2009, 8.
37 Ibid., 12.

The development of a 'hybrid' form of management is part of a broader pattern among women's services facing pressures from outside and within to adopt more formal structures of governance. Organisational scholar Karen Lee Ashcraft argues that feminist organisations have had to forge a compromise between a feminist commitment to collectivism and the need to keep organisations viable and effective over the long term, leading to 'organized dissonance', blending 'hierarchical and egalitarian models of power'.[38] In this form of organisation, the need to respond to conflicting imperatives creates a series of 'strategic tensions—pushes and pulls that become a check-and-balance system'.[39] In some ways, this embracing of tension carries forward the early women's liberation philosophy of continual questioning and ongoing feminist analysis (described above); however, this attempt to merge bureaucratic form and egalitarian practice faces some deep problems, including the tendency for bureaucracy to take over when 'relations of dominance/submission carry more cultural weight' in the broader society 'than those of equality'.[40]

Feminist organisations also highlight the importance of emotion in feminist concepts of leadership, in contrast with the rationality-centric approaches to management that have dominated Western countries in the twentieth century. While organisational theorists and sociologists have long challenged the overemphasis on rational decision-making,[41] feminist services exemplify a fully developed practice of embracing emotion. These services confront the potential conflict between organisational imperatives and personal experience. One case study of WIRE, for example, contrasted 'the barren emotional landscape of many organisations with the vibrancy and warmth of a feminist community organisation [WIRE]', which 'manifests a skilful blending of rational and emotional elements'.[42]

In the new discursive environment of neoliberalism, where collectivist ideas were rarely heard anymore, leadership emerged as something the women's movement could embrace, even while promoting ideas that women's leadership could be different from the old masculine models. In 2010 the Australian Sex Discrimination Commissioner identified women and leadership as one of the five priority areas for achieving gender equality. There was also a proliferation of initiatives with titles such as Women and Leadership Australia, Centre for

---

38   Karen Lee Ashcraft, 'Organized Dissonance: Feminist Bureaucracy as Hybrid Form', *Academy of Management Journal* 44 (2001): 1301.

39   Ibid., 1304.

40   Ibid., 1304.

41   See, for example, Herbert Simon's concept of 'bounded rationality'. Herbert A. Simon, 'A Behavioral Model of Rational Choice', *Quarterly Journal of Economics* 69 (1955): 99–118. On rationality and emotion in social movement organisations, see also Merrindahl Andrew, 'Social Movements and the Limits of Strategy: How Australian Feminists Formed Positions on Work and Care' (PhD dissertation, The Australian National University, Canberra, 2008), https://digitalcollections.anu.edu.au/handle/1885/49281, 189–207.

42   Tanner, 'Emotion, Gender and the Sustainability of Communities'.

Leadership for Women and the Women's Leadership Institute Australia. It was not just a matter of having women at the top; it was also thought that women's leadership could be more democratic and information-sharing or transformational rather than transactional.

Movements for social change

Compared with research on women's leadership in corporate and political life, there has until now been only limited analysis of women's leadership in social movements. Internationally, research in this area has explored four main themes. First, there have been studies of the leadership roles played by individual women. Second, research has documented the way gendered expectations continue to constrain women's leadership, even in supposedly 'progressive' movements for social change. Third, scholars have considered the often invisible emotional and relational work of women in social movements, thereby expanding our understandings of what leadership is. Finally, some researchers have considered how feminist organisational philosophy may have affected leadership practices in social movements.

The leadership roles played by individual women in social movements have attracted some attention and this is perhaps the most thoroughly researched aspect of the field. In Australia, for example, *Local Heroes* tells the stories of various people, most of them women, who have led local environmental campaigns such as those against pollution and industrial contamination.[43] Editor Kathleen McPhillips notes that gender may be a significant factor, because of women's fears for their children's health.[44] Jane Elix and Judy Lambert (this volume) confirm the significant role of maternal identity in motivating Australian women's environmental activism, while international evidence also suggests that collective identity as mothers can easily be mobilised in support of activism around issues such as industrial or nuclear contamination.[45]

The second theme explored by the literature is that of the constraints imposed on women's leadership roles by gendered expectations, even in movements for social change. Social movement scholars Aldon D. Morris and Suzanne Staggenborg argue that focusing too much on individual leaders risks overlooking 'the structural opportunities and obstacles to collective action'. The focus on leaders not only distracts attention from what enables collective action but also unfairly

---

43   Kathleen McPhillips, ed., *Local Heroes: Australian Crusades from the Environmental Frontline* (Sydney: Pluto Press, 2002).
44   Kathleen McPhillips, 'Introduction', in ibid., xi–xxiv, xix–xxii.
45   Alison E. Adams and Thomas E. Shriver, 'Collective Identity and Gendered Activism in the Czech Environmental Movement: The South Bohemian Mothers' Struggle against Nuclear Power', *Research in Social Movements, Conflicts and Change* 32 (2011): 163–89.

relegates the actual membership of movements to the category of 'followers'.[46] Accordingly, they argue that we should look at social movement leadership within its structural contexts and acknowledge the different levels of leadership and roles of participants.

Gender is central to this critique. The North American authors observe that the 'degree of gender inequality in the community of a challenging group is one of the main determinants of gender inequality in top levels of leadership in social movements'.[47] They observe that women's lower status has typically been reproduced in movements' leadership profiles, with men taking on roles as public spokespeople (viewed as a leadership equivalent in social movements, where decentralisation may make it less clear who is actually 'in charge'). As prominent women's movement scholar Verta Taylor argues, '[e]mpirical research by feminist social scientists suggests that gender hierarchy is so persistent that, even in movements that purport to be gender-inclusive, the mobilisation, leadership patterns, strategies, ideologies and even the outcomes of social movements are gendered'.[48]

In line with leadership research generally, discussions about women leading movements for social change have often focused on the question of whether women have a distinctively feminine 'leadership style'. As Amanda Sinclair has argued, however, to focus on this question has inherent limits and can perpetuate oppressive gendered stereotypes, especially concerning caring and family responsibilities.[49] Instead, we might ask what social pressure (for example, family responsibilities) and resources (such as friendships and networks) must be considered when analysing the role of women in movements. How have women leaders themselves conceptualised their roles, particularly in those cases where they have been engaged in the double struggle of trying to make their movements more gender-sensitive and women-friendly, while working towards the other goals of the movement?

The third type of literature on women leading social movements focuses on the relatively invisible emotional and relational work performed by women in these movements, which has not been part of more traditional concepts of leadership. In many cases the different roles taken in social movement activities are what mark out the different status of participants. In her study of African-American

46   Aldon D. Morris and Suzanne Staggenborg, 'Leadership in Social Movements', in *The Blackwell Companion to Social Movements*, eds David A. Snow, Sarah A. Soule and Hanspeter Kriesi (Malden, Mass.: Blackwell, 2004), 171.

47   Ibid., 176.

48   Verta Taylor, 'Gender and Social Movements: Gender Processes in Women's Self-Help Movements', *Gender and Society* 13 (1999): 8–9.

49   Amanda Sinclair, 'Not Just "Adding Women In": Women Re-Making Leadership', Paper delivered at Women, Leadership and Democracy in Australia Conference, Museum of Australian Democracy, Canberra, 1–2 December 2011.

women in the civil rights movement, Belinda Robnett notes that while men tended to occupy formal roles as spokespeople/leaders, women often acted as 'bridge leaders', forming an 'intermediate layer of leadership, whose task includes bridging potential constituents and adherents, as well as potential formal leaders to the movement'.[50] She also argues that, in this bridging role, women have done much of the 'emotion work' of movements. As we noted earlier, part of the feminist critique of traditional concepts of leadership was the way in which such emotion work, essential to nurturing any organisation, was rendered invisible.

The way in which 'emotional gender rules' affect the distribution of leadership roles may be made explicit within social movements rather than simply remaining at the unconscious level. For example, the animal rights movement deliberately chose men to make its arguments in public, believing the movement's credibility would be undermined by women's 'emotional' claims.[51] But it is not only the distribution of leadership roles but also the repertoires of social movements that are affected by emotional gender rules. This effect is illustrated by women's self-help practices in women's health movements as contrasted with the use of violent tactics in male-dominated nationalist, left-wing and right-wing movements.[52]

Finally, research has begun to analyse the influence of feminist organisational philosophy on the way leadership is practised in social movements. In doing so, such research steps back from the focus on individual leaders to consider the models of collective action in social movements. It looks not only at the organisational practices of the women's movement but also at the extent to which such practices have been carried into other movements for social change. For example, Suzanne Staggenborg argues that 'feminist organizations have been the main carriers of the "participatory democratic" mode of social movement organization since the 1960s and feminists have been influential in spreading this form of organization to other movements with similar concerns such as the antinuclear power movement'.[53]

---

50   Belinda Robnett, *How Long? How Long? African American Women in the Struggle for Civil Rights* (New York: Oxford University Press, 1997), 191.

51   Jeff Goodwin, James M. Jasper and Francesca Polletta, 'Emotional Dimensions of Social Movements', in *The Blackwell Companion to Social Movements*, eds David A. Snow, Sarah A. Soule and Hanspeter Kriesi (Malden, Mass.: Blackwell, 2004), 424.

52   Verta Taylor and Nella van Dyke, '"Get Up, Stand Up": Tactical Repertoires of Social Movements', in *The Blackwell Companion to Social Movements*, eds David A. Snow, Sarah A. Soule and Hanspeter Kriesi (Malden, Mass.: Blackwell, 2004), 276.

53   Suzanne Staggenborg, 'Can Feminist Organizations be Effective?', in *Feminist Organizations: Harvest of the New Women's Movement*, eds Myra Marx Ferree and Patricia Yancey Martin (Philadelphia: Temple University Press, 1995), 339.

A study of the 1980s peace movement, for example, found that the ways in which the women's movement had influenced the peace movement included the adoption of organisational structures designed to avoid hierarchy.[54]

To what extent has the entry of feminists resulted in similar influences in other social movements? As the late Jane Elix points out, feminist organisational philosophy may make leadership a very complex issue. In the environment movement, as in other movements with limited material resources, charismatic leadership is highly valued but at the same time leaders are often expected to 'recognise and work within low hierarchy structures, favouring extensive internal consultation and inclusive decision-making'.[55] To the extent that distinctively feminist models of organising have influenced these movements, can such influences be sustained as social movement organisations become professionalised? These questions remain largely un-researched in the area of Australian social movements but certainly in the environment movement there is a perceived departure by peak bodies from the collaborative organisational models found in grassroots campaigns.

Finally, we should consider how feminist organisational philosophies interact with the mainstream shift to 'post-heroic' ideas about leadership in corporate life. On the face of it, post-heroic leadership has much in common with feminist practices of organisation, envisioning as it does a shift 'from individual to collective, from control to learning, from "self" to "self-in-relation", and from power over to power with'.[56] In practice, however, heroic models of leadership are proving to be very resilient in corporate and political life, with rewards and promotions continuing to flow to those demonstrating traditionally 'masculine' leadership traits.

For decades now, non-profit and social movement organisations have been urged to adopt best practice from the corporate world, while government and corporate bodies have to some extent moved towards the more decentralised networks characteristic of social movements. Given that at least some social movement organisations have been influenced by feminist critiques of hierarchy and domination, have these organisations been able to transform leadership beyond the impasse of continued masculine privilege, and what factors have enabled or impeded this process? The inherently critical and questioning nature of social movements might predict a capacity to identify and change the gendered dynamics of leadership, but as we have seen, there are crosscutting

---

54 David S. Meyer and Nancy Whittier, 'Social Movement Spillover', *Social Problems* 41 (1994): 277–98.

55 Jane Elix, 'Leadership by Another Name: Women Coordinating, Influencing and Enabling within the Australian Environment Movement', Paper presented to the Women, Leadership and Democracy in Australia Conference, Museum of Australian Democracy, Canberra, 1–2 December 2011.

56 Fletcher, 'The Paradox of Postheroic Leadership', 650.

pressures from professionalisation. Forty years on from the arrival of second-wave feminism's ideas of shared leadership, it is still too early to tell whether these can be sustained within and beyond the women's movement.

References

Adams, Alison E. and Thomas E. Shriver. 'Collective Identity and Gendered Activism in the Czech Environmental Movement: The South Bohemian Mothers' Struggle against Nuclear Power.' *Research in Social Movements, Conflicts and Change* 32 (2011): 163–89.

Andrew, Merrindahl. 'Social Movements and the Limits of Strategy: How Australian Feminists Formed Positions on Work and Care.' PhD dissertation, The Australian National University, Canberra, 2008. https://digitalcollections.anu.edu.au/handle/1885/49281.

Ashcraft, Karen Lee. 'Organized Dissonance: Feminist Bureaucracy as Hybrid Form.' *Academy of Management Journal* 44 (2001): 1301–22.

Brown, Helen. *Women Organising*. London: Taylor & Francis, 2002 [first published 1992].

Cox, Eva. *Leading Women: Tactics for Making the Difference*. Sydney: Random House, 1996.

Dahlerup, Drude. 'From a Small to a Large Minority: Women in Scandinavian Politics.' *Scandinavian Politics Studies* 11 (1988): 275–97.

Dowse, Sara. 'Power in Institutions—The Public Service.' Transcript of discussion at the Women and Politics Conference 1975, National Library of Australia, Canberra, 1975.

Dowse, Sara. 'The Bureaucrat as Usurer.' In *Unfinished Business: Social Justice for Women in Australia*, edited by Dorothy Broom, 139–160. Sydney: Allen & Unwin, 1984.

Dowse, Sara. 'Address to WEL–ACT Dinner.' Canberra, 5 June 1989.

Eisenstein, Hester. *Gender Shock*. Boston, Mass.: Beacon, 1992.

Elix, Jane. 'Leadership by Another Name: Women Coordinating, Influencing and Enabling within the Australian Environment Movement.' Paper presented at the Women, Leadership and Democracy in Australia Conference, Museum of Australian Democracy, Canberra, 1–2 December 2011.

Fletcher, Joyce K. 'The Paradox of Postheroic Leadership: An Essay on Gender, Power, and Transformational Change.' *Leadership Quarterly* 15(5) (2004): 647–61.

Freeman, Joreen. 'The Tyranny of Structurelessness.' Reprinted from *The Second Wave* 2(1), Sydney: Words for Women, 1972.

Fuchs Epstein, Cynthia. 'Ways Men and Women Lead: Debate.' *Harvard Business Review* (January–February 1991): 150–1.

Goodwin, Jeff, James M. Jasper and Francesca Polletta. 'Emotional Dimensions of Social Movements.' In *The Blackwell Companion to Social Movements*, edited by David A. Snow, Sarah A. Soule and Hanspeter Kriesi, 413–32. Malden, Mass.: Blackwell, 2004.

Iannello, Kathleen P. *Decisions without Hierarchy: Feminist Interventions in Organization Theory and Practice*. New York: Routledge, 1992.

Kirner, Joan and Moira Rayner. *The Women's Power Handbook*. Melbourne: Penguin, 1999.

Kokopeli, Bruce and George Lakey. *Leadership for Change: Towards a Feminist Model*. Philadephia: New Society Publishers, 1978.

McGregor Burns, James. *Leadership*. New York: Free Press, 1978.

McPhillips, Kathleen. 'Introduction.' In *Local Heroes: Australian Crusades from the Environmental Frontline*, edited by Kathleen McPhillips, xi–xxiv. Sydney: Pluto Press, 2002.

McPhillips, Kathleen, ed. *Local Heroes: Australian Crusades from the Environmental Frontline*. Sydney: Pluto Press, 2002.

Mercer, Jan, ed. *The Other Half: Women in Australian Society*. Melbourne: Penguin, 1975.

Meyer, David S. and Nancy Whittier. 'Social Movement Spillover.' *Social Problems* 41 (1994): 277–98.

Morris, Aldon D. and Suzanne Staggenborg. 'Leadership in Social Movements.' In *The Blackwell Companion to Social Movements*, edited by David A. Snow, Sarah A. Soule and Hanspeter Kriesi, 171–96. Malden, Mass.: Blackwell, 2004.

Moss Kanter, Rosabeth. *Men and Women of the Corporation*. New York: Basic Books, 1977.

O'Connor, Karen and Alixandra B. Yanus. 'Overview: History of Women Leaders in Social Movements.' In *Gender and Women's Leadership: A Reference Handbook. Volume 1*, edited by Karen O'Connor, 181–7. New York: Sage, 2010.

Robnett, Belinda. *How Long? How Long? African American Women in the Struggle for Civil Rights*. New York: Oxford University Press, 1997.

Rosener, Judy. 'Ways Women Lead.' *Harvard Business Review* (November–December 1990): 119–25.

Sawer, Marian. *Sisters in Suits: Women and Public Policy in Australia*. Sydney: Allen & Unwin, 1990.

Sawer, Marian. 'Femocrats and Ecorats: Women's Policy Machinery in Australia, Canada and New Zealand.' In *Missionaries and Mandarins: Feminist Engagement with Development Institutions*, edited by Carol Miller and Shahra Razavi, 112–37. London: Intermediate Technology Publications, 1998.

Sawer, Marian. *Making Women Count. A History of the Women's Electoral Lobby in Australia*. Sydney: UNSW Press, 2008.

Sawer, Marian and Abigail Groves. '"The Women's Lobby": Networks, Coalition Building and the Women of Middle Australia.' *Australian Journal of Political Science* 29 (1994): 435–59.

Simon, Herbert A. 'A Behavioral Model of Rational Choice.' *Quarterly Journal of Economics* 69 (1955): 99–118.

Sinclair, Amanda. 'Not Just "Adding Women In": Women Re-Making Leadership.' Paper presented at the Women, Leadership and Democracy in Australia Conference, Museum of Australian Democracy, Canberra, 1–2 December 2011.

Sinclair, Amanda and Fern Marriott. 'Women in Management—Advantage through Adversity.' *Asia Pacific Human Resource Management* 28 (1990): 14–25.

Staggenborg, Suzanne. 'Can Feminist Organizations be Effective?' In *Feminist Organizations: Harvest of the New Women's Movement*, edited by Myra Marx Ferree and Patricia Yancey Martin, 339–55. Philadelphia: Temple University Press, 1995.

Stivers, Camilla. 'Women as Leaders in the Progressive Movement.' In *Gender and Women's Leadership: A Reference Handbook. Volume 1*, edited by Karen O'Connor, 188–95. New York: Sage, 2010.

Tanner, Kerry Jeanne. 'Emotion, Gender and the Sustainability of Communities.' *Community Informatics: A Global E-Journal* 1 (2005). http://ci-journal.net/index.php/ciej/article/view/208/165.

Taylor, Verta. 'Gender and Social Movements: Gender Processes in Women's Self-Help Movements.' *Gender and Society* 13 (1999): 8–33.

Taylor, Verta and Nella van Dyke. '"Get Up, Stand Up": Tactical Repertoires of Social Movements.' In *The Blackwell Companion to Social Movements*, edited by David A. Snow, Sarah A. Soule and Hanspeter Kriesi, 262–93. Malden, Mass.: Blackwell, 2004.

Wajcman, Judy. 'Desperately Seeking Differences. Is Management Style Gendered?' *British Journal of IndustrialRelations* 34 (1996): 333–49.

Weeks, Wendy. 'Feminist Principles for Community Work.' *Women in Welfare Education*, 7 October 2004: 1–16 [reprinted from *Women in Welfare Education* 1 (1994)].

Weeks, Wendy. 'Democratic Leadership Practices in Australian Feminist Women's Services: The Pursuit of Collectivity and Social Citizenship?' *International Review of Women and Leadership* 2 (1996): 19–33.

Wensing, Veronica. 'What's Behind a Name? The Organisational Identity of Rape Crisis Centres: Positioning the Canberra Rape Crisis Centre as a Feminist Organisation in the 21st Century.' Unpublished paper, 2009.

Wolf, Naomi. *Fire with Fire: The New Female Power and How to Use It*. London: Chatto & Windus, 1993.

16. Passionate defenders, accidental leaders: Women in the Australian environment movement

Jane Elix[1] and Judy Lambert[2]

The environment movement, like many other social change movements, is not easy to define or delineate. Individuals within a movement may hold extremely diverse views on goals, strategies and even philosophies, but 'a shared sense of moral outrage'[3] builds alliances within and between the different organisations that form part of the environment movement.

Women have been active in seeking protection of the environment since Federation and even before 1900. Those in the historical record include Georgiana Molloy (1805–43) and Elizabeth Gould (1804–41), both of whom played a significant role in supporting the scientific endeavours of their male colleagues, while Jane Franklin (1791–1875), Ellis Rowan (1847–1922) and Amalie Dietrich (1821–91) were explorers and scientific adventurers in their own right. We might fairly assume that other endeavours went quietly unrecorded. After them came a string of women who were enthusiastic bushwalkers, either with other women (Ethel Lun and her two friends) or in mixed company (Marie Byles, Dorothy Butler, Jessie Luckman and Hattie Clark).

This particular research on female environment movement leaders is built around interviews with 34 women who have filled leadership roles in the movement since its emergence in the 1970s as a force for social change. The interviewees, subject to their availability, were selected to provide a representative sample from across the spectrum of organisations and their locations that together make up the Australian environment movement. The sample captures the views of women of different ages, backgrounds and interests who have filled a diversity of roles within the movement. The interviews were conducted throughout 2011, each completed using a semi-structured set of questions as a starting point for a broader-ranging discussion. Wherever possible, the interviews were held in

---

1   Formerly Jane Elix Consulting and The Australian National University. Jane Elix conducted the research and prepared an initial overview of this chapter in 2011. In December 2011 Jane became seriously ill and was unable to complete the project. She briefed her friend and former business partner Judy Lambert, who took up the challenge of completing Jane's commitment to the project. The work is a tribute to Jane, who passed away in July 2012, and whose own contribution to leadership by and mentoring of women in the environment movement is worthy of powerful recognition.

2   Community Solutions.

3   Drew Hutton and Libby Connors, *A History of the Australian Environment Movement* (Melbourne: Cambridge University Press, 1999), 5.

the home of the interviewee, or within the region that was the focus of their involvement in the environment movement. The personal stories of these women and their relationships to wider perspectives on leadership guide this chapter.

Consistent with the findings of Drew Hutton and Libby Connors, the environment movement has a different meaning for almost every person interviewed.[4] So, in using the term 'Australian environment movement', this research focused on the work of leaders in organisations that

- have originated in Australia; or
- have been embedded in Australia for a long time and have a specific Australian identity
- have a clearly stated objective of changing political and industry policies and practices on environmental protection and management
- have a membership base of either individuals or organisations (the latter being peak bodies).

Generally not included are women in

- organisations whose principal activities are education, scientific investigation, recreation, networking and information exchange or planning
- organisations which have a very recent presence in Australia, but whose bases lie overseas.

Many of the women leaders who have been part of this project have moved between organisations that fit the four criteria above and those that do not. While there are many other women who meet these criteria for leadership, the intention of this research was to gather a representative sample of environmental leadership across the decades since Federation.

Defining leadership

Definitions of leadership vary widely over time and context. Amanda Sinclair, in her rethinking of leadership, describes it as 'a relationship, in which leaders inspire and mobilise others to extend their capacity to imagine, think and act in positive new ways'.[5] She goes on to stress that leadership is not a weighty responsibility usually borne by men and played out through the individual performances of interlocking elites. 'Leadership is not a job or a position, but a way of influencing others towards ends recognised as valuable and fulfilling.'[6]

---

4 Ibid., 4.
5 Amanda Sinclair, *Leadership for the Disillusioned* (Sydney: Allen & Unwin, 2007), xvi.
6 Ibid., xvii.

While many women in the environment movement have sought an inclusive, collaborative approach to leadership, ample evidence exists suggesting that many remain bound by societal expectations aligned with a more directive leadership style usually associated with men.

Leadership styles

Participatory democracy was a catchcry of social change in the 1960s. Carol Mueller identifies three key elements of this early push for 'participatory democracy': 1) grassroots involvement in decision-making; 2) minimisation of hierarchy 'with expertise and professionalism as a basis for leadership'; and 3) a call for direct action.[7] In the preceding chapter, Marian Sawer and Merrindahl Andrew identify the hopes and expectations of feminism of the 1970s that hierarchical male-dominated leadership styles would be replaced with a new collective-based approach in which functions were shared democratically within the organisation or group. This change in leadership was expected to replace male management or leadership styles in business, in government, in politics and in the non-governmental (third) sector. Areas of social change that held similar or complementary values, including in the environment movement, were expected to become part of this change.

Male styles were described as 'command and control, using organisational status and manipulation of rewards' and called *transactional*. In contrast, Judy Rosener and others describe the female collaborative approach as *transformational*, 'enhancing other people's sense of self-worth and energizing followers'.[8]

Sinclair describes, however, how over recent decades 'transformational leadership' has been adopted by mainstream leadership trainers and gurus. 'A sizable genre of leadership writing, from the 1980s through to the present, pines after leadership that is fused with goodness, caring and a "servant" mentality.'[9] In this literature, the 'transformational' leadership model has been linked not to the outcomes that are envisaged by feminists, but rather to the capitalist values of large material achievement, competition and conquest. The transformational model of leadership has been coopted and corrupted by what Sinclair refers to as 'McDonaldized leadership'.

Sinclair identifies an important place for charisma in leadership in recent times. Like leadership, charisma may derive from a diversity of qualities that inspire

---

7   Carol Mueller, 'Ella Baker and the Origins of "Participatory Democracy"', in *The Black Studies Reader*, eds Jaqueline Bobo, Cynthia Hudley and Claudine Michel (New York: Routledge, 2004), 79.
8   Judy R. Rosener, 'Ways Women Lead', *Harvard Business Review* (November–December 1990): 122, Reprint No. 90608, 4.
9   Sinclair, *Leadership for the Disillusioned*, 24.

others. Dennis Perkins and his colleagues in their examination of leadership based on Antarctic explorer Ernest Shackleton emphasise the importance of optimism in the charismatic leader.[10] In the environment movement, high value is placed on charismatic leadership—for men at least—and allowances are made for charismatic leaders who can inspire optimism even when they are not good managers. It is not unusual for a male leader to surround himself with women with high interpersonal skills to buttress his organisational roles.

'Male' leadership in the environment movement

The language attached to male-dominated 'command and control' transactional leadership and its contrast with the more collaborative transformational leadership style posed as an alternative may seem simplistic and bound to stereotypes that feminism was seeking to overcome; however, when asked about differences between men's and women's leadership in the environment movement, the language used by many of those interviewed reflects these characteristics of female and male leadership.

Margaret Blakers commented that '[m]en are more prepared to put themselves in the front row of representing the group or being recognised. And that's society's expectation too, I think it's very deeply embedded—still.'

This is a view reinforced by comments from Brigid Dowsett: 'Women come in hoping and believing that the environment movement is going to be different— less hierarchical—but in the end it's really no different from the way the rest of society functions.'

Hannah Aulby, a much younger environmental leader, says: 'Women push their agenda along a bit more quietly and carefully … It's hard to generalise, but men are maybe a bit less conscious of the consequences of their decisions, more single focused, more focused on the few things that they've decided to pursue.'

This male model may be changing, according to Louise Crossley:

> Increasingly the concept of leadership of being out front and having everyone else follow is not the way it works. Usually two or three brains are better than one, and it's that kind of collaborative leadership that works best, and the sum becomes greater than the parts, and that's the excitement of it.

---

10 Dennis Perkins, Margaret Holtman, Paul R. Kessler and Catherine McCarthy, *Leadership at the Edge: Leadership Lessons from the Extraordinary Saga of Shackleton's Antarctic Expedition* (New York: AMACOM, 2000).

The leadership that women are quite good at is cooperative, collegial and it's not leadership by command.

Barriers to women's leadership

That the concept of 'leadership' is problematic for many women from the environment movement is perhaps one of the barriers to their greater uptake of traditional leadership roles. When interviewed, many expressed views such as 'I never thought of myself as a leader'. Few stepped forward to claim identified leadership roles. Most who took on such roles did so only after being persuaded by others.

Typifying this pathway is Beth Schultz (b. 1936), who for the past 36 years has worked in a voluntary leadership capacity for the WA environment movement, many of those years as chair of the WA Conservation Council. Beth is now an icon for younger women environmentalists, but her comments still reflect a discomfort with the label of leadership. 'I've never thought of myself as a leader—you don't put yourself out there—it just happens. You wait to be invited or there's nobody else doing it.' To this reluctance can be added the influence of family circumstances. Among the almost three-quarters of interviewees currently in a long-term relationship, support from partners varied across the spectrum from working together in an organisation and extensive support and encouragement to partner perceptions of commitment to environmental campaign jobs as being 'selfish', with little support being provided in household activities and caring for children.

The challenges of juggling environmental leadership roles and caring for children were a significant factor for many interviewees. Some chose to take up more local roles so they could spend time with children and for others this challenge was identified as a factor contributing to the breakdown of marriage or long-term relationships.

Of the women interviewed, 14 (41 per cent) were childless by choice or circumstance, and none had four or more children. Each of these is a significantly higher proportion than in the general population.[11] For some, this was a deliberate choice made for environmental reasons. For others, it was a response to a perceived need 'to make a choice in life'. One interviewee captured the sentiment of others in her comment that '[t]he challenge is trying to incorporate the nurturing, family-oriented role that most women aspire to with the focus that you've got to have if you're really trying to make a difference'.

---

11   Australian Bureau of Statistics (ABS), *Australian Social Trends*, ABS Publication 4102.0 (Canberra: Australian Bureau of Statistics, 2008).

Conditions under which women have assumed leadership

Since the nineteenth century, when an interest in the natural sciences was the preserve of 'gentlemen'—pastoralists, merchants and professionals such as clergymen, lawyers and doctors—there have always been some women who exerted their influence in their own ways.

From the early 1900s, people began to seek escape from the industrialisation of towns and cities through bushwalking in more remote areas. While the early bushwalking clubs admitted only male members, women were soon knocking on their doors and by the 1920s women were joining these activities and campaigning for the protection of their favoured natural areas.

As these clubs were joined, in the 1950s and 1960s, by national parks associations, National Trust groups and others combining outdoor recreation with campaigns for areas under threat, women continued to play an active role.

By the early 1970s, an unsuccessful campaign to protect Lake Pedder in Tasmania's south-west wilderness and the highly successful Kelly's Bush campaign against inappropriate development in a Sydney harbourside suburb were setting new agendas for environmental protection, with women filling some leadership roles.

The 1980s saw the national campaign against damming of the Franklin River in Tasmania become a touchstone for a whole generation of people who cared about the natural environment. The environment movement gained a strong political voice, in which women took some key roles—initially as volunteers and only later in paid positions.

Since the 1990s, the Federal Government's Ecologically Sustainable Development process, the Decade of Landcare and subsequent developments have seen much more emphasis on partnerships, networks and international environmental initiatives.

The contributions of key women in the evolving environment movement are captured in summary in Table 16.1.

Table 16.1 The Environment Movement: An evolving force for social change in Australia

Prior to Federation	Early 1900s	1950s & 1960s	1970s	1980s	1990 & beyond
Gentleman 'naturalists'	Bushwalking: respite from suburbia	Rise of the 'intellectuals'	Saving special places	A strong voice; a political player	Networks; international environmentalism; more forests

Women leaders: there from the start					
Supporting male colleagues: Georgiana Molloy (1805–43) Elizabeth Gould (1804–41) Scientific exploration: Jane Franklin (1791–1875) Ellis Rowan (1847–1922) Amalie Dietrich (1821–91) Writing & advocating for the environment: Louisa Anne Meredith (1812–95) Louisa Atkinson (1834–72)	Doing their own walks: Ethel Lun & two colleagues (1909) Joining male groups: Marie Byles Dorothy Butler (1930s onward) Jessie Luckman (1930s onward) Hattie Clark Advocating for the environment: Irene Longman (1877–1974)	Wildlife Preservation Society Qld (1962–): Judith Wright, Kathleen McArthur & David Fleay Australian Conservation Foundation (1965–): Penny Figgis (1970s–) Tricia Caswell (1990s) Little Desert (1968): Valerie Honey & Gwynnyth Taylor	Lake Pedder (1971–72): Brenda Hean & others Kelly's Bush Battlers (1971): Kath Lehaney & other middle-class urban residents Millers Point/ The Rocks (1970s–): Nita McCrae, Shirley Ball & Millicent Chalmers (from 1990s) SW Forests Defence WA (1975–): Beth Schultz Animal Liberation (1976–): Christine Townend	Franklin River (1970s–1982): Karen Alexander, Margaret Robertson, Judy Lambert, Janet Rice, Linda Parlane, Christine Milne Antinuclear campaigns: Jo Vallentine Land Release Study Group (WA): Rosemary Jasper, Brenda Newbey & Heather Pearce Australian Rainforest Conservation Society (1982–): Aila Keto NSW Wilderness Act (1987): Margaret Robertson Wesley Vale pulp mill (1988): Christine Milne	Federal Ecologically Sustainable Development process (early 1990s): Jane Elix, Imogen Zethoven, Lyn Goldsworthy Decade of Landcare (1990–2000): Jane Elix, Colma Keating National Threatened Species Network: Di Tarte (National Coord.), Vicki-Jo Russell (SA Coord.), Peg Putt (Tas Coord.), Giz Watson (WA Coord.) State & regional environment groups: Rachel Siewert (WA Conservation Council, 16 years) Judy Messer (NSW Conservation Council Chair, 16 years) Michelle Grady (Conservation Council of SA, 12 years) Liz Bourne, Rosie Crisp, Imogen Zethoven, Felicity Wishart (Queensland Conservation Council Coordinators, 1980s & 1990s), Kelly O'Shannassy (Victoria, 2011–present) Maria Mann (Environs Kimberley, 12 years) Jill Redwood (East Gippsland forests, 1980s–present) Private land acquisition & conservation management (2000s): Judy Henderson (Bush Heritage Australia, co-founder) Philippa Walsh International science-based environmental NGOs (2000s): Imogen Zethoven, Michelle Grady (Pew Trusts)

Source: Authors' compilation.

Many of these women did not see themselves as 'leaders' but all were part of an evolving force for social change in Australia.

The women interviewed as part of the Australian Women and Leadership project often said they fell into leadership roles in the environment movement either by filling a gap or by working harder than others. In other words, they saw themselves as 'accidental leaders'.

For example, Margaret Blakers described the way she operates as: 'I see a gap— something that needs to be done—and then, if I can, I work out how to make it happen.' Brigid Dowsett explains: 'For me, it was never assuming a leadership mantle. It was more being ready and willing to take on responsibility at a certain level and make some decisions about the way I felt things should be managed, or volunteer to do something that no one else was available to do.'

Millicent Chalmers (b. 1934), who has been included on Australia's honours list for her service to the community, is very reluctant to identify herself as a leader. 'I'm really a nursemaid. People say—Millicent will fix it. Millicent will do something.'

Hard work comes through clearly as a strong personal value for many of the women leaders interviewed, and it is to hard work that much of their success as leaders is attributed. Several long-term and well-respected leaders said they work up to 18-hour days almost every day of the week. In some cases, this relates to paid work, in others as a volunteer, and for many it is a mix of both.

Another more emotive driver for these women who are leaders in the environment movement was a sense of outrage at the loss of special places (the 'shared sense of moral outrage' identified by Hutton and Connors).[12] This sense of outrage turned them into passionate defenders. Long-time Environs Kimberley coordinator Maria Mann was moved to action for the environment because she 'felt a sense of outrage … at the proposal to dam the Fitzroy River'. Co-founder of The Wilderness Society's Victorian branch Karen Alexander says her involvement was 'built on the anger of the loss of Lake Pedder'. Peace activist and former senator Jo Vallentine described being mobilised by her anger at WA Premier Charles Court's announcement that Western Australia would be the first State in Australia to have a nuclear power plant.

At a deeper level, and consistent with Amanda Sinclair's[13] observations about the influences of early childhood on our leadership styles and aspirations,

---

12   Hutton and Connors, *A History of the Australian Environment Movement*, 5.
13   Sinclair, *Leadership for the Disillusioned*.

an early appreciation of the natural environment resulting from bushland experiences or a rural upbringing played an important role for one-third of the women interviewed.

Role models and mentors

Few of the women interviewed as leaders in the environment movement identified formal mentors, but those who did so felt they had gained significant benefit from the relationships. Several of the interviewees mentioned individuals (both male and female) as role models.

Of the 34 women interviewed, 27 identified one or more aspects of their early life as having influenced their involvement in the environment movement. These factors varied widely, with mothers, fathers and grandmothers identified as important in shaping this aspect of their lives. School and/or teachers were also influential for almost half of the interviewees; for a majority of these women this came from Catholic schools or nuns and the values they imbued in their young charges. Although many of these women later moved away from their Catholic upbringing, the values persisted.

For instance, Colma Keating sees her time at a Catholic school as 'giving her the impetus to think of others, but also understanding that women are not second-rate citizens'. She says the nuns instilled in her 'a sense of being capable of doing things in the world'. Christine Milne reinforces this perception, indicating that her time under the guidance of the nuns imbued her with 'a strong work ethic, a belief that one should have the courage of one's own convictions and a very strong sense of social justice', but also 'a stoic capacity for incredible self-contained resilience'. Jo Vallentine sees her education in Catholic boarding school as 'one contributing factor in my sense of self-identity'. Although from a younger generation, Gemma Tillack also sees her current values as still influenced by the values of community and giving that come from her time growing up in a strong Irish Catholic family.

Female or feminist support groups

Informal networks such as ad-hoc Green Girls Drinks groups that met informally for breakfast in Canberra or after work in Sydney played an important role for some in demanding positions in the environment movement; however, women in the environment movement have tended not to explicitly emphasise either female or feminist support when they reflect on their experiences. Nor is there evidence of women acting for women as they campaigned for the conservation of special places in Australia's environment. In the interviews conducted for the

Australian Women and Leadership in a Century of Australian Democracy project, women in the environment movement more frequently focused on conserving the environment for present and future generations—for their children rather than for other women. This is a driver of environmental activism also reported by Yulia Maleta in her study of grassroots activist women in the environment movement.[14]

Critical moments and changes

The decade from 1983 was a period of substantial gains for the environment movement. This period began with the High Court decision to stop a proposed hydroelectric power supply dam on Tasmania's Franklin River. It included the early 1990s, when the Australian Government showed leadership at the United Nation's Rio Earth Summit, signing on to Agenda 21 and also the Conventions on Biological Diversity and Climate Change. At that time and well into the 1990s, there was a significant, perhaps close to equal, involvement of women in designated leadership positions both at the national level and in State-based peak bodies. The previous gender imbalance in recognised leadership of the movement has, however, returned.

Despite the significant contribution the environment movement has made to social change in Australia, it is today just as male dominated in its recognised leadership as it was in the late 1980s. In 2011, men outnumbered women 7:1 in the (executive) director positions of the conservation councils—the peak bodies for environment groups in each State and Territory. At the same time in 2011, there was only one female CEO among the four major national environment groups: the Australian Conservation Foundation, The Wilderness Society, Greenpeace and the Worldwide Fund for Nature (WWF). The environment movement is more inclusive of women in its board positions, the major national organisations variously having between 18 per cent and 36 per cent women compared with 8.4 per cent in industry and 34 per cent on government-controlled boards.[15] It is, however, important to recognise that while industry pays its board members and governments generally provide some financial recompense for their work, those on the boards of environment organisations fill voluntary positions. As in government and industry, the environment movement's involvement of women in identified leadership positions has a long way to go before equality is achieved.

---

14 Yulia Maleta, 'Activism as a Barrier and Gender Dynamics within Australian Third-Sector Environmentalism', *Third Sector Review* 13(1) (2012): 77–98.

15 Government of Australia, *Women Towards Equality* (Canberra: Department of Foreign Affairs and Trade, 2011).

Nevertheless, many women in the environment movement—including many younger women—provide significant leadership outside the mainstream perspectives embodied in the concept of 'transactional' leadership. For these women, social influence directed to accomplishing a common task is achieved through the collaborative approaches characteristic of 'transformational' leadership.

Some have moved into Greens politics (Christine Milne, Rachel Siewert, Giz Watson, Janet Rice, Margaret Blakers), others into international and national philanthropic organisations operating in Australia but not generally seen as part of Australia's environment movement (for example, Imogen Zethoven and Philippa Walsh) and some (Karen Alexander, Judy Lambert, Judy Henderson) into more collaborative local and regional environmental initiatives, frequently working closely with local government and younger women in local communities.

It is in these other areas, rather than in the mainstream environment movement, that these women see leverage for the greatest level of change for their efforts; however, at a time when the environment movement faces increased pressure from the resources and other sectors and from government agendas, it is important that the contribution of women to the movement's leadership is also strengthened.

As Sinclair identifies: 'Only by challenging the assumptions on which leadership is based will we be equipped to seriously anticipate the "transformation" so often promised by leadership.'[16]

Acknowledgments

Jane would not have allowed this chapter to go to publication without an expression of appreciation to the wonderful women who made this project possible by giving generously of their time and experiences. Logistical support from Heather Pearce throughout the project is also greatly appreciated.

References

Australian Bureau of Statistics (ABS). *Australian Social Trends*. ABS Publication 4102.0. Canberra: Australian Bureau of Statistics, 2008.

Government of Australia. *Women Towards Equality*. Canberra: Department of Foreign Affairs and Trade, 2011.

---

16 Sinclair, *Leadership for the Disillusioned*, 33.

Hutton, Drew and Libby Connors. *A History of the Australian Environment Movement*. Melbourne: Cambridge University Press, 1999.

Maleta, Yulia. 'Activism as a Barrier and Gender Dynamics within Australian Third-Sector Environmentalism.' *Third Sector Review* 13(1) (2012): 77–98.

Mueller, Carol. 'Ella Baker and the Origins of "Participatory Democracy".' In *The Black Studies Reader*, edited by Jaqueline Bobo, Cynthia Hudley and Claudine Michel. New York: Routledge, 2004.

Perkins, Dennis, Margaret Holtman, Paul R. Kessler and Catherine McCarthy. *Leadership at the Edge: Leadership Lessons from the Extraordinary Saga of Shackleton's Antarctic Expedition*. New York: AMACOM, 2000.

Rosener, Judy R. 'Ways Women Lead.' *Harvard Business Review* (November– December 1990): 119-125, Reprint No. 90608.

Sinclair, Amanda. *Leadership for the Disillusioned*. Sydney: Allen & Unwin, 2007.

17. Consuming interests: Women's leadership in Australia's consumer movement

Jane Elix[1] and Kate Moore[2]

Political consumerism is on the rise. It is a form of activism in which women have played significant roles at least since the eighteenth century. They continue to do so today.

This chapter describes female leadership in the emergence and growth of the modern consumer movement, and in particular the health consumer movement. It is a sector in which women play many leading roles in different ways, according to their own preferences and values and to the circumstances in which leadership is needed. It is a sector that amply demonstrates the need for a broader understanding and reconceptualisation of leadership, as identified by Amanda Sinclair in this volume.

The consumer movement has been largely neglected in the social movement and public policy literature, but in writing this chapter we have drawn on the small amount of literature available, interviews we conducted with 15 women leaders and our own experiences of working in and with consumer organisations.[3]

The consumer movement emerged from the failure of markets. Traditional economic theories assume that consumers are sovereign in the marketplace, that they will make rational choices based on full information and that perfect competition will prevail. In practice, producers (often large corporations) and providers of services have much greater political influence, economic resources and access to information. Some have abused this power through exploitative employment practices, unethical marketing or production of shoddy goods and services.

Citizens have responded through individual and collective actions targeting a range of consumer products and services. The twentieth century saw the

---

1 Formerly Jane Elix Consulting and The Australian National University. Jane Elix conducted much of the research on the broad consumer movement. She and Kate Moore presented the original findings in a paper at the Women, Leadership and Democracy Conference in Canberra in December 2011. Later that month, Jane became seriously ill and was unable to complete the project.

2 The Australian National University.

3 Jane Elix was director of the Australian Federation of Consumer Organisations from 1991 to 1993. Kate Moore was the executive director of the Consumers' Health Forum of Australia from 1991 to 1999. She now represents the organisation on several committees.

formation of an organised consumer movement that 'seeks to identify, expose and remedy incidences where manufacturers, retailers or service providers mislead, deceive or place consumers at risk of disadvantage'. It also lobbies governments to legislate for consumer protection and adequate regulatory standards for business and industry.[4]

Political consumerism

Formally defined, political consumerism is the choice of producers and products with the aim of changing ethically or politically objectionable institutional or market practices.[5] It is a form of activism that appears to be increasing. It also appears from the limited research in this area that women have a stronger preference for this form of participation than men.[6]

Even before women had the vote and significant access to independent financial means, boycotts mobilised the power and leadership of women. For example, in the late eighteenth century abolitionists in the United Kingdom organised a boycott of sugar produced using slave labour. They were primarily supported by female anti-slavery associations, which provided an early form of feisty female leadership.[7] Notably, in 1824, Elizabeth Heyrick wrote a pamphlet entitled 'Immediate, Not Gradual Abolition'. In it, she had the temerity to criticise the principal (male) anti-slavery campaigners, including William Wilberforce, as being overly cautious and slow in their dealings with the West Indian planters, saying they 'have shown a great deal too much politeness and accommodation towards these gentlemen'. Her pamphlet sold thousands of copies and caused much discussion in various parts of England.[8]

In the early 1900s, Florence Kelly, leading the National Consumers League (NCL) in the United States, campaigned to use women's purchasing power to improve conditions for working-class women, by granting its White Label to stores that met the NCL's standards for minimum wages, maximum working hours and decent working conditions.[9]

4   Jane Brown, *A History of the Australian Consumer Movement*, ed. Fiona Marsden (Melbourne: Consumers' Federation f Australia, 1996), 8.

5   Michele Micheletti and Dietlind Stolle, 'Concept of Political Consumerism', in *Youth Activism—An International Encyclopaedia*, ed. Lonnie R. Sherrod (Westport, Conn.: Greenwood Publishing, in press).

6   Dietlind Stolle, Marc Hooghe and Michele Micheletti, 'Politics in the Supermarket: Political Consumerism as a Form of Political Participation', *International Political Science Review* 26(3) (2005): 245–69.

7   The Abolition Project, http://abolition.e2bn.org/campaign_17html.

8   'Elizabeth Heyrick', Wikipedia, http://en.wikipedia.org/wiki/Elizabeth_Heyrick#Early_life.

9   National Women's History Museum, 'The National Consumers League', http://www.nwhm.org/online-exhibits/progressiveera/consumerleague.html.

Many early forms of political consumerism were directed at producers who used exploitative employment practices; later the role of protecting workers was increasingly assumed by trade unions, at least in developed countries. In the meantime, there were close links between political consumerists and unions. For example, in the 1930s Esther Petersen, a union organiser for textile sweatshop workers in the United States, developed close alliances with the women's movement and the emerging consumer groups in order to gain better conditions for the women workers she represented.[10]

Political consumerism was a common form of political action throughout the twentieth century. Some campaigns targeted businesses in order to criticise governments—for example, boycotts by American business of French products, as a means of protesting about the French Government's opposition to the US-led war in Iraq.[11] In the 1970s and 1980s, boycotts of South African products and sporting events were successful in pressuring governments to stop support for the apartheid regime in that country. Other campaigns have been used directly to target the products of big companies including oil companies, and footwear and clothing manufacturers.[12] The international boycott against the marketing by Nestlé of its baby-milk products in developing countries involved a number of women's groups which had not previously been involved in political consumerism. Australian groups which participated included the Nursing Mothers Association, Parents' Centres Australia and the Childbirth Education Association.[13]

Survey data published in 2005 show that political consumerism is on the rise and that a growing number of citizens are turning to the market to express their political and moral concerns.[14] Recent advances in communications technologies such as email, Facebook and Twitter are enhancing the abilities of consumer activists to gain support for actions against producers who are seen to behave unethically. In Australia, the successful online campaign in 2012 to persuade companies to stop advertising on the Alan Jones 2UE radio program is but one recent example. Women were in the forefront of this campaign, which focused attention, in part, on misogynist behaviour.[15]

---

10 Eileen Baldry, 'The Development of the Health Consumer Movement and its Effect on Value Changes and Health Policy in Australia' (PhD thesis, University of New South Wales, Sydney, 1992), 62.

11 Remi Barroux, 'Le Medef s'inquiete des consequences pour les entreprises des tensions franco-americaines', *Le Monde*, 17 April 2003, quoted in Stolle et al., 'Politics in the Supermarket', 246.

12 Stolle et al., 'Politics in the Supermarket', 245–69.

13 Baldry, 'The Development of the Health Consumer Movement', 111.

14 Stolle et al., 'Politics in the Supermarket'.

15 Larissa Nicholson, 'Online and Outraged: The People Begin to Talk Back', *Sydney Morning Herald*, 9 October 2012, http://www.smh.com.au/national/online-and-outraged-the-people-begin-to-talk-back-20121008-279q8.html.

The modern consumer movement

The modern consumer movement—described by Brown as 'the intensification of organised consumer activity throughout Western developed nations from around 1960'[16]—developed alongside other movements that used political consumerism as part of their repertoire. These included anti-racist, feminist and environment movements in addition to self-help and support group movements.

The earliest organised groups dealing specifically with consumer issues were formed in the first half of the twentieth century in the United States.[17] As unions came to recognise themselves as representing consumers as well as workers, they joined forces with organisations of housewives during the Depression to challenge exorbitant prices for essential items and poor-quality products.

With the growth of affluence in the mid 1930s, middle-class women and professional men demanded better quality control and some form of redress over badly made goods and dangerous products.[18] This led to the formation of the modern consumer movement, characterised by a range of small and large groups campaigning for better products and services.

The focus was initially on product testing and production of information for consumers. In the United States, the Consumers Union was formed in 1936, relying solely on membership subscriptions. It began testing products and publishing the reports of those tests, a model followed in 1957 by the Consumers Association in the United Kingdom and in 1959 by the Australian Consumers' Association (ACA). In 1960 ACA began publication of Choice, disseminating the results of product testing in the same way as its UK and US counterparts.[19] Shortly afterwards, the International Organisation of Consumer Unions (IOCU) was formed at a meeting in Holland, with the organisations from Australia, the United States, the United Kingdom, the Netherlands and Belgium as founding members.

Women were active within both the national organisations and the IOCU. They led the way in broadening the focus of the organisations to encompass concerns of people in developing countries. For example, US consumer activist Florence Mason was at the forefront of efforts to involve developing countries in the international movement and to 'shift the consumer movement internationally away from a consumption oriented "western" attitude—and to focus on basic human needs such as clean water and housing'.[20] After 22 years on the staff of the Consumers Union of the USA, at the age of sixty-five, she became an education

---

16   Brown, *A History of the Australian Consumer Movement*, 7.
17   Baldry, 'The Development of the Health Consumer Movement', 61.
18   Ibid.
19   Ibid., 62.
20   Ibid., 68.

officer with the IOCU. This role broadened and led to the IOCU presence at the United Nations, and a vital link between the many struggling consumer groups in developing countries. She was succeeded as the IOCU representative to the United Nations by Esther Petersen, 'exemplifying the connections and interdependence between the union, women's and consumer movements'.[21]

Women's leadership in the growth of the Australian consumer movement

In Australia, in the late nineteenth and early twentieth centuries, women's organisations were a driving force behind the fledgling consumer movement that emerged within the broader social reform and women's movements.[22] Although the modern movement developed in the 1960s, these early links remain important through both connections with women's organisations and the movement's interests in welfare and social justice issues.[23]

The Housewives Cooperative Association was formed in 1915, in response to spiralling prices, and aimed to bring the consumer and producer into direct contact. In 1931, the Federated Association of Australian Housewives was formed and was, at its peak, the largest women's organisation in Australia,[24] with a membership of 115,000 in a population of only seven million. It appealed both to female economic interests and to altruism. For the leaders, altruism in the form of a secularised Christian charity and moral duty was the dominant imperative, although ambition and the desire for political influence also played a part.[25] Although the Housewives Association's primary function was to reduce the cost of living and control 'profiteering', they did identify themselves as 'political', although always non-party.[26]

The National Council of Women also established itself at the national level in 1931 and its agenda included a range of what are now regarded as consumer issues: health, nutrition, food safety, pricing, shopping hours and inflation.[27] The Country Women's Association also has taken on many consumer campaigns in its advocacy for services for rural families.

Australia's consumer movement is now part of an international web of organisations that gather under the umbrella of Consumers International. In

21   Ibid., 61.
22   Brown, *A History of the Australian Consumer Movement*, 18.
23   Ibid.
24   Ibid., 3.
25   Judith Smart, 'The Politics of Consumption: The Housewives Associations in Southeastern Australia before 1950', *Journal of Women's History* 18(4) (2006): 13–39.
26   Ibid., 16.
27   Brown, *A History of the Australian Consumer Movement*, 18.

Australia the largest individual consumer organisation is Choice (formerly the Australian Consumers' Association), whose flagship magazine receives extensive media coverage. The foundation members of Choice included many women's organisations. Ruby Hutchison was the first woman member of the WA Legislative Council and was very active in the early stages of the ACA in 1959–60. Although the ACA pursued the narrow course of product testing and submissions to government inquiries on products for many years, Hutchison also fought for the more basic consumer rights to protection, information and participation in decision-making in Australian society.[28] She was active in early health consumer forums as founder (in 1962) and president of the WA Epilepsy Association. She is described as 'a fiery speaker and a tenacious crusader for democratic reform, women's rights and social justice'.[29]

Women were not only involved in founding Choice, but also have played important and high-profile roles in its senior executive and board positions ever since. The organisation has seen a number of significant women take on the CEO role—particularly Philippa Smith and Louise Sylvan—and in 2012 the board was chaired by Jenni Mack.

By the end of the 1970s most States had consumer bodies—with Canberra Consumers the first established (by three men). The Australian Federation of Consumer Organisations (AFCO) was founded in 1974 as a peak body for these State groups, as well as for the more specialised consumer advocacy organisations. Its establishment meant the consumer movement had a national profile and voice, which, in its early days was predominantly male, but since the early 1990s has tended to be female.

Between 1974 and 1996, AFCO grew in strength and influence, its policy priorities changing with the political and social issues of the day. In the 1970s the focus was on establishing product standards and trade practices law, and social justice and the effects of inflation on consumers. In the 1980s attention turned to product labelling, competition, media ownership and health, and during the 1990s the focus was on National Competition Policy, media ownership, environmental issues, product safety, tobacco control, financial services and banking and deregulation.[30] By 1994, when AFCO was renamed the Consumers' Federation of Australia (CFA), it had nine paid staff. It coordinated consumer representation on dozens of industry and government committees, and had a significant profile in the media.

---

28   Baldry, 'The Development of the Health Consumer Movement, 93.
29   *Australian Dictionary of Biography Online* (Canberra: National Centre of Biography, The Australian National University, 2006), http://adbonline.anu.edu.au/.
30   'Consumers' Federation of Australia', Wikipedia, http://en.wikipedia.org/wiki/Consumers%27_Federation_of_Australia.

One of the first actions of the incoming Coalition government under John Howard in 1996, however, was to defund the CFA. In 2012 the CFA was a shadow of the earlier organisation, with no paid staff and a volunteer board of 10, of whom seven are women. It had representatives on eight major government or industry bodies (of whom eight are women and seven are men) as well as volunteer representatives on Standards Australia technical committees.

One of the key functions AFCO performed in the 1980s was to encourage the development of specialist consumer groups, which have now grown to take on advocacy in a range of specialised consumer policy areas. Women played a key leadership role in the early days of these emerging organisations, including Philippa Smith and Louise Sylvan in the Consumers' Health Forum (see below), Elizabeth Morley and Edwina Deakin in the Consumers' Telecommunications Network, Carolyn Bond in the consumer credit legal services, and Kate Harrison and Anne Davies in the Communications Law Centre.

Governments responded to the growing influence of the consumer movement by establishing consumer protection measures including the Federal Bureau of Consumer Affairs and the consumer component of the Australian Competition and Consumer Commission (ACCC). At the federal level, ministerial responsibility for consumer affairs, which might be seen as a 'nurturing' portfolio, is often linked with an economic 'competition' portfolio and tends to be held by a man. Jeannette McHugh was a notable exception in 1992–96. As at July 2012, all eight State and federal consumer affairs ministers were male.

Defining the 'the consumer movement' today

The contemporary consumer movement retains a focus on equity and social justice, and targets a range of products and services including food, product safety, financial services, insurance and legal and health services.

With the exception of the health consumer movement, however, very little has been written about the consumer movement in Australia. There is also no real agreement on the limits or extent of what might be defined as 'the consumer movement'.

Since the establishment of the Australian Consumers' Association, the relationships between the different parts of the movement have changed considerably. For example, legal and financial services advocacy organisations have grown and become less reliant on volunteers in representing consumer interests as they receive funding from a variety of sources, particularly a range of government agencies. These organisations now provide women with employment as lawyers, financial counsellors, advocates and managers, and many of these organisations have predominantly female staff. They invariably grew out of 'the consumer movement' as an initiative of individuals and small groups with a concern about a consumer injustice but now form part of a network of professional service providers and advocacy organisations. It would be fair to say, therefore, that the broad consumer movement has become professionalised to the extent that it is now a totally different entity from what it was in the 1960s and 1970s.

The one consumer area where women's participation has increased and strengthened, as paid professional leaders but more significantly as volunteer activist leaders, is in the health consumer area. The 1970s, 1980s and 1990s support group and self-help movements at the core of the strong health consumer movement that we see today grew and proliferated. They have been predominantly led by, and comprise, women.

The health consumer movement

In the late eighteenth and nineteenth centuries, the growth of a number of social movements, including the labour movement and movements for the emancipation of women, led to increased activism by women around the health care they were subjected to.[31]

In the 1960 and 1970s, women's health groups such as the Nursing Mothers Association, Parent Centres Australia and the Childbirth Education Association advocated for women's right to have control over the way they gave birth and nurtured their children.[32]

The emergence of feminism in the 1960s and 1970s gave rise to a substantial women's health movement. Some women's health groups specifically rejected the medical model of illness care and embraced the World Health Organisation (WHO) view of health as involving physical, mental and social wellbeing. The Whitlam Government's National Women's Health Conference in 1975 was seen as a landmark because of the breadth of issues discussed, encompassing many aspects of health and resulting in dozens of recommendations that indicated a consumer orientation.[33]

Indeed, women's activism has been one of the foundations of today's health consumer movement—and has been well documented by Eileen Baldry[34]

---

31 Hilda Bastian, 'Speaking Up for Ourselves: The Evolution of Consumer Advocacy in Health Care', *International Journal of Technology Assessment in Health Care* 14(1) (1998): 10.
32 Baldry, 'The Development of the Health Consumer Movement', 110.
33 Ibid., 127.
34 Ibid.

and Gwen Gray.[35] The movement was part of a much broader and relatively conventional international health reform push, which included the 'new' public health movement, the community health centre movement and, in Australia, the Aboriginal health movement, all of which were critical of the way medical systems had been organised during the twentieth century.

By the early 1980s, as the Coalition Government led by Malcolm Fraser reduced healthcare spending, a range of groups were actively challenging established models of care and mobilising to redress inequities of access to care and inequalities of power between the medical profession and the lay population;[36] however, there was little national coordination.

The major consumer organisations, Choice and the Consumers Federation, service organisations such as the Australian Council of Social Service, as well as some State-based consumer and community health organisations, were raising health issues. The scope of the issues and the division of responsibilities between federal and State governments meant they could only tackle issues in a somewhat piecemeal way.[37] They initiated a process, led by Philippa Smith of Choice, which resulted in moves to create a formal mechanism to represent health consumers.[38]

The federal health minister in the Hawke Labor Government, Neal Blewett, supported these moves and provided funding for what became the Consumers' Health Forum (CHF). It was led by a general committee, chaired by Philippa Smith, and was broadly representative of the women's, service provider, environmental, consumers' and health movements. It elected, from among its members, a smaller executive committee, with six of the seven members being women.

The creation of the CHF was a pivotal point in the development of the health consumer movement. The new national organisation provided a focal point for federal activism, and enabled a range of organisations to come together with a common interest. While many of the groups which instigated the establishment of the CHF had a focus on broad public health issues such as tobacco marketing and use, environmental health, equity, and social services, others were concerned with specific issues such as the medicalisation and disempowerment of women in childbirth and other aspects of reproductive health. After much discussion and debate, there was broad agreement that the forum should initially focus on the health issues that were the responsibility of the Federal Government:

35　See Gwendolyn Gray Jamieson, *Reaching for Health: The Australian Women's Health Movement and Public Policy* (Canberra: ANU E Press, 2012), http://epress.anu.edu.au/?p=165181, 8–98.
36　Stephanie Short, interview, quoted in Hans Löfgren, Michael Leahy and Evelyne de Leeuw, eds, *Democratizing Health: Consumer Groups in the Policy Process* (Cheltenham, UK: Edward Elgar, 2011), 177.
37　Baldry, 'The Development of the Health Consumer Movement', 144.
38　Louise Sylvan, 1989 interview, quoted in ibid., 146.

financing of health care, medicines policy, consumer rights and mental health.[39] Underpinning all their work was a strong commitment to ensuring that consumers, whether as citizens or as individual recipients of healthcare services, should play a major role in determining how health services should be delivered.

While the emergence of the forum was met by considerable hostility from the medical profession, it is now largely (if grudgingly in some circles) accepted as part of the health policy landscape. Its work is resulting in significant changes to the way health care is provided and consumed. The health consumer sector continues to grqw so that as well as having a national voice, there are now peak health consumer groups in Western Australia, South Australia, Queensland, New South Wales and the Australian Capital Territory, all of which receive support from State or Territory governments. In Victoria, the Health Issues Centre has provided a voice for consumers since 1985.

The sector's leadership was, and continues to be, predominantly female; however, men are starting to play a more significant role, which is perhaps attributable to a number of factors, such as the rise of the men's health movement, the activism by gay men around HIV/AIDS during the 1980s and 1990s expanding to an interest in the broader health system, and a greater awareness of men's health issues such as prostate cancer.

Women have largely led the CHF. They held the role of CEO for all but four years of its existence, and women held the position of chair until 2000, when men stepped into the chairing role. In 2012 Karen Carey was elected as chair of the governing board, which had equal numbers of men and women, and Carol Bennett was CEO. A large majority of the staff have always been female.

One of the sector's most significant activities, and one in which leadership of the sector is nurtured and drawn, are the consumer representatives programs. These operate at both national and State/Territory levels and represent a large, voluntary workforce—predominantly female. Some of the positions are paid a sitting fee, although this is more common at the national than the local level. The CHF's latest annual report, for 2011–12, shows that the majority of consumer representatives sitting on more than 100 national government, professional and industry bodies are women.[40]

---

39   Baldry, 'The Development of the Health Consumer Movement', 173.
40   Consumers' Health Forum of Australia, *Annual Report 2011–2012* (Canberra: Consumers' Health Forum of Australia, 2012), 38.

From representation to leadership

Leadership within the health consumer movement is of two kinds. It can be seen in the few structured leadership positions available in the sector, such as CEO or chair of a board. More importantly, however, much of the leadership tends to be organic, emerging 'from within a community of interest to represent the views and concerns of that community'.[41]

Sinclair's emphasis on reconceptualising leadership is important in understanding and identifying consumer leadership in health. She points out that '[m]ost theorists recognise leadership is not a position or a person but a process of influence'.[42] Leadership is demonstrated in the process of influence whereby new values, ideas and behaviours are adopted. This is how leadership emerges from the health consumer movement. It is the 'process of influence' that leads health services to change and improve the quality of the service, so they are focused on the needs of consumers rather than providers.

Over the years, many women who represent consumers on government and professional bodies have engaged in the 'process of influence'. Their leadership extends beyond their work within consumer organisations, leading health systems and services to adopt more consumer-focused policies and practices. Examples of the leading roles played by women are highlighted in Box 17.1.

Unfortunately, this leadership is largely unrecognised either within the health consumer sector or within professional and government bodies. Within the consumer sector, there is unease about the notion of leadership, possibly because of the 'consumer ethic of an inclusive and supportive group of equals'[43] and the traditional concepts of leadership as 'the out-front, tough and stoic male hero'.[44] In spite of this, some individual health consumer advocates have been nominated from within the health sector for awards that recognise the leading roles they have played. Also, publications from within the sector sometimes contain articles about individuals that implicitly recognise their leadership roles.[45]

---

41 Victorian Quality Council, *Consumer Leadership: Report of the Findings of a Literature Review and Consultation Process into Consumer Leadership* (Melbourne: Victorian Quality Council, 2007), 14.
42 Amanda Sinclair, 'Not Just "Adding Women In": Women Re-Making Leadership', in *Seizing the Initiative: Australian Women Leaders in Politics, Workplaces and Communities*, eds Rosemary Francis, Patricia Grimshaw and Ann Standish (Melbourne: eScholarship Research Centre, University of Melbourne, 2012).
43 Victorian Quality Council, *Consumer Leadership*, 16.
44 Sinclair, 'Not Just "Adding Women In"'.
45 Victorian Quality Council, *Consumer Leadership*, 16.

Box 17.1 Insights from interviews with female leaders

Leadership as a process of influence

- Janne Graham, Jan Donovan, Linda Adamson and Yong Sook Kwok successfully advocated for the National Medicines Policy that now guides Australia's approach to the regulation and financing of medicines—and in turn our access to medicines and the information and education about their use. Graham later became deputy chair of the Australian Pharmaceutical Advisory Council—an appointment that recognised the leadership she was providing beyond the consumer movement to the health sector. Donovan went on to become one of the founding board members of the National Prescribing Service, and led that organisation to focus its work on consumers as well as prescribers.
- Hilda Bastian campaigned tirelessly on a range of issues including a better, more rigorous research base to underpin health care. Both in her drive for better birthing statistics and in her involvement in the international Cochrane Collaboration, she has contributed significantly to the consumer focus of significant research organisations in Germany and the United States.
- In the mid 1990s, Lyn Swinburn and Sue Lockwood campaigned about the poor quality of treatment received by women with breast cancer. They established the National Breast Cancer Network (BCNA), which has bought about a significant increase in public awareness of, and attitudes to, breast cancer as well as much needed improvements in treatments. The BCNA is now an established organisation. It advocates for good, evidence-based treatments and trains women to act as consumer representatives on a range of decision-making committees—including scientific research committees. Importantly, that organisation provides a model for other cancer consumer groups to emulate.
- Anne McKenzie is a consumer advocate on a range of committees. Her advocacy started as a result of her experience as a mother of a child with disabilities. She now chairs the Health Consumers Council of Western Australia. She also plays a leading role with the University of Western Australia's School of Population Health and the Telethon Institute for Child Health Research, where she is employed as the consumer advocate. Her role is to increase consumer and community participation in health and medical research within those institutions.

Source: Authors' compilation.

As part of the Women, Leadership and Democracy in Australia project, we conducted interviews with 14 women leaders from the consumer movement. Those interviews provide some important insights into aspects of women's leadership.[46] Most of the women we interviewed did not set out to be leaders or even now see themselves as being leaders. Responses to the requests for interviews were often met with a sense of discomfort at being identified as a leader. Most were modest, seeing themselves as a part of a movement and acknowledging the hard work put in by many in the sector. Most of the women we interviewed could be described as transformational leaders (facilitative and collaborative). They all enjoyed working with other people, working through

---

46 A list of the women who were interviewed is included in the Acknowledgements. Profiles of these women can be seen on Jane Elix's blog: http://janeelix.wordpress.com. Short profiles of the women can also be seen in Judith Smart and Shurlee Swain, eds, *The Encyclopedia of Women and Leadership in Twentieth-Century Australia* (Australian Women's Archive Project, 2014) http://www.womenaustralia.info/leaders/index.html.

ideas and learning from others; as Sally Crossing puts it, 'the way we work is to spark off and learn from each other. It's very rewarding and exciting to do it that way, and you can have confidence that you are doing the right thing.'

The women we interviewed were all motivated by a passionate commitment to social justice and to good policy. For some, motivation comes from their own lived experience of poor products and services and their desire to ensure that other people do not have similar experiences. Jenni Mack was charged exorbitant fees by a financial adviser.[47] After experiencing breast cancer, Sally Crossing gave up her career to start off in a new direction of 'giving back and creating something that needed to be created'. Anne McKenzie's and Marg Brown's experiences of raising children with disabilities led them into the health consumer sector. Janne Graham was driven by anger at her own (and her husband's) experience of illness and health care, but channelled this into a constructive energy that enabled her to become an important and effective leader.

Courage is a quality that all the interviewees displayed in different ways. Leaders in the consumer movement are constantly challenging powerful, entrenched and vested interests and at times find themselves facing strong resistance, hostility and personal attacks. Louise Sylvan emphasises that she has 'never seen the task as being liked'. She stresses that she never attacks the person who is attacking her because, she says, 'people who do that have already lost the argument— they are scared at that point … they are out of things to do. So I take that as quite a positive thing.' Carol Bennett stresses that challenging the practices of health professionals and industry is not easy: 'You are putting yourself on the line, and it does make yourself vulnerable to retaliation.' Her advice is to 'hold the line, hold your nerve and believing in what you are doing and why'.

The interviewees who were employed in paid positions within consumer organisations had thought carefully about how they could be in meaningful paid employment in ways that suited them. For Teresa Corbin, working in the community sector gave her flexibility and family-friendly environments. Jenni Mack left a traditional career path and took up a range of board appointments, which enabled her to do interesting work, engage her mind, make a difference and still have time for her children.

Most interviewees agreed there is a difference between male and female leaders. Comments were that 'women are probably better facilitators and men are better dictators' (Susan Nulsen); 'Men tend to have a lot more ego on the table. That's the nature of our society' (Louise Sylvan); 'Men see work as a role and are more matter-of-fact about it. For women, it's more about doing their job as the person they are' (Carol Bennett).

---

47 'Profile: Jenni Mack', *Sydney Morning Herald*, 2 March 2011, http://www.smh.com.au/money/planning/profile-jenni-mack-20110301-1bcba.html.

Conclusion

Much of the leadership literature relating to formal organisational hierarchies in commerce, industry and the services sector does not adequately describe the richness or complexity of women's leadership in the consumer sector. In the community and consumer sectors, leadership is seen as a more inclusive concept and operating in different ways and at different levels.[48] As Amanda Sinclair has elucidated,[49] this means that leadership can be exercised by people without formal authority, as much as by CEOS or prime ministers. In contrast with understandings of leadership that focus on the ongoing control of resources and tasks, leadership within movements like the consumer movement involves challenging the status quo and bringing about changes in attitude and behaviour.

This reconceptualisation is helpful in understanding leadership in the consumer sector, where leadership is not dependent on hierarchical structures. Rather, it emerges from within a community of interest and is not reliant on formal leadership positions, although a limited number are available. As well, consumer leadership focuses on challenging and changing established practices and processes within the sector targeted by consumer advocacy and not just within the organisation from which the leadership has emerged.[50] This can, in turn, mean that women lead change within the sector targeted by consumer advocacy. It is a function that is not recognised in the formal literature and yet is an important factor in social and economic changes that affect all our lives.

In any analysis, women's leadership in the establishment and growth of the various elements of the consumer movement has been crucial. That leadership has been exercised both within consumer organisations and within the wider world of the production of goods and services. Women have fought for, and succeeded in improving, many of the products and services on which we depend. Yet that leadership goes largely unrecognised.

It will only be by reconceptualising leadership, and by understanding that leadership takes different forms and is exercised in many different ways, that the work of the many women in this sector will be recognised.

Acknowledgments

Many thanks go to the following wonderful women who gave so generously of their time to be interviewed for this project.

---

48   Victorian Quality Council, *Consumer Leadership*, 15.
49   Sinclair, 'Not Just "Adding Women In"'.
50   Victorian Quality Council, *Consumer Leadership*, 17.

Carol Bennett: CEO of the Consumers' Health Forum of Australia.

Margaret Brown: Campaigner for the rights of health consumers in rural and remote Australia.

Carolyn Bond: Campaigner for consumer rights in banking, financial and legal services.

Anne Cahill Lambert: High-profile campaigner on oxygen supplies and organ donation issues.

Teresa Corbin: Campaigner for consumer rights in telecommunications technologies.

Sally Crossing: Relinquished her career to become an advocate for better-quality cancer treatments and services.

Mary Draper: Feminist, writer, thinker and advocate for quality health care.

Janne Graham: Former chair of the CHF and leading advocate for health consumer rights.

Jenni Mack: Chair of Choice and former CEO of Consumers' Federation of Australia.

Anne McKenzie: Consumer research advocate at the University of Western Australia and Telethon Institute of Child Health Research.

Susan Nulsen: Former chair of Consumers' Federation of Australia, who now works in the consumer protection area of the WA Department of Commerce.

Louise Sylvan: Long-term campaigner for consumer-centred policy and practice through CHF and Choice.

References

Australian Dictionary of Biography Online. Canberra: National Centre of Biography, The Australian National University, 2006. http://adbonline.anu.edu.au/.

Baldry, Eileen. 'The Development of the Health Consumer Movement and its Effect on Value Changes and Health Policy in Australia.' PhD thesis, University of New South Wales, Sydney, 1992.

Bastian, Hilda. 'Speaking Up for Ourselves: The Evolution of Consumer Advocacy in Health Care.' *International Journal of Technology Assessment in Health Care* 14(1) (1998): 3–23.

Brown, Jane. A History of the Australian Consumer Movement. Edited by Fiona Marsden. Melbourne: Consumers' Federation of Australia, 1996.

'Consumers' Federation of Australia.' Wikipedia. http://en.wikipedia.org/wiki/Consumers%27_Federation_of_Australia.

Consumers' Health Forum of Australia. Annual Report 2011–2012. Canberra: Consumers' Health Forum of Australia, 2012.

'Elizabeth Heyrick.' Wikipedia. http://en.wikipedia.org/wiki/Elizabeth_Heyrick#Early_life.

Gray Jamieson, Gwendolyn. Reaching for Health: The Australian Women's Health Movement and Public Policy. Canberra: ANU E Press, 2012. http://epress.anu.edu.au/?p=165181.

Löfgren, Hans, Michael Leahy and Evelyne de Leeuw, eds. Democratizing Health: Consumer Groups in the Policy Process. Cheltenham, UK: Edward Elgar, 2011.

Micheletti, Michelle and Dietlind Stolle. 'Concept of Political Consumerism.' In Youth Activism—An International Encyclopaedia, edited by Lonnie R. Sherrod. Westport, Conn.: Greenwood Publishing, in press.

National Women's History Museum. 'The National Consumers League.' http://www.nwhm.org/online-exhibits/progressiveera/consumerleague.html.

Nicholson, Larissa. 'Online and Outraged: The People Begin to Talk Back.' Sydney Morning Herald, 9 October 2012. http://www.smh.com.au/national/online-and-outraged-the-people-begin-to-talk-back-20121008-279q8.html.

'Profile: Jenni Mack.' Sydney Morning Herald, 2 March 2011. http://www.smh.com.au/money/planning/profile-jenni-mack-20110301-bcba.html.

Sinclair, Amanda. 'Not Just "Adding Women In": Women Re-Making Leadership.' In Seizing the Initiative: Australian Women Leaders in Politics, Workplaces and Communities, edited by Rosemary Francis, Patricia Grimshaw and Ann Standish. Melbourne: eScholarship Research Centre, University of Melbourne, 2012.

Smart, Judith. 'The Politics of Consumption: The Housewives Associations in Southeastern Australia before 1950.' Journal of Women's History 18(4) (2006): 13–39.

Smart, Judith and Shurlee Swain, eds. The Encyclopedia of Women and Leadership in Twentieth-Century Australia. Australian Women's Archives Project (2014). http://www.womenaustralia.info/leaders/index.html.

Stolle, Dietlind, Marc Hooghe and Michele Micheletti. 'Politics in the Supermarket: Political Consumerism as a Form of Political Participation.' *International Political Science* 26(3) (2005): 245–69.

The Abolition Project. http://abolition.e2bn.org/campaign_17html.

Victorian Quality Council. *Consumer Leadership: Report of the Findings of a Literature Review and Consultation Process into Consumer Leadership.* Melbourne: Victorian Quality Council, 2007.

Conclusion: Gender and leadership

Joy Damousi[1] and Mary Tomsic[2]

We began this volume with quotations from Julia Gillard, Australia's first female prime minister (2010–13), and Australia's first female governor-general, Quentin Bryce (2010–14). During the course of preparing this volume of essays, both positions have now been occupied by men—respectively, Tony Abbott and Peter Cosgrove. Time will tell whether the fact that women occupied the most powerful positions in the country in the early twenty-first century was an aberration in relation to what went before or whether we will see this elevation of women to the seat of power once again. This is a vital question and one that has provided the contemporary framework for the questions that have been pursued in this volume.

The significance of the sex of the people who hold these two positions of leadership must also be considered in relation to the style of leadership they enact and the ways in which they are presented and understood as leaders. The valorisation of a masculine heroic mode of leadership is clearly seen in Greg Craven's recent praise of Peter Cosgrove's appointment as governor-general. Craven said: 'Cosgrove is less qualified for the job than *designed for it*. He is a general; a war hero (he won the Military Cross in Vietnam); a civic hero (he oversaw the reconstruction of North Queensland after Cyclone Larry); and an international figure (for leading the peacekeeping force in East Timor).'[3] While the suggestion here is not that such a career and experience preclude Cosgrove from being a good governor-general, what is noteworthy is the statement that Cosgrove is 'designed for' the job; this reflects the type of leadership Craven envisages as desirable. Additionally, whether intentional or not, it is difficult not to read such a statement in contrast with the experiences and qualifications of the outgoing governor-general. Most of the roles Cosgrove has held were not and, in practice, will probably not be open to women. What Craven's discussion reveals is a particularly narrow conception of leadership. This example brings into focus the esteem in which masculine heroic leadership continues to be held,[4] with the effect of silencing or devaluing other modes of leadership, which are often enacted by women.

---

1   The University of Melbourne.
2   The University of Melbourne.
3   Emphasis added. Greg Craven, 'Peter Cosgrove, Groomed by a Life of Service to be Our GG', *The Conversation*, 29 January 2014, http://theconversation.com/peter-cosgrove-groomed-by-a-life-of-service-to-be-our-gg-22499.
4   See also Amanda Sinclair's chapter in this volume.

Craven's article concludes by saying:

> Cosgrove also brings with him a rare bonus in his wife, Lynne. As clever and as funny as her husband, she is the veteran of innumerable parades, fund-raisers and graduations. With three children of her own and a newly minted grandson, she is another people-lover who will make the Cosgroves a very Australian gubernatorial combination. All in all, Australia has the very model of a modern governor-general.

The position Craven affords Lynne Cosgrove is defined in supporting and maternal roles. While this is not necessarily of any particular importance, in light of Craven declaring Peter Cosgrove being 'designed' to be governor-general, the place for a woman within such a conception is limited to a support role only.

The question of women and leadership continues to be vital in our times.

Beyond the state of play of women's role in positions of high public office, but informed by it, in this volume we have attempted to show the range and variety of women's social and political leadership across a variety of enterprises and activities within democratic political structures. We want to unsettle common conceptions of leadership and challenge readers to think broadly about what leadership can and does look like; to see the range of ways women have sought to influence others, to work towards social change.

Through an examination of a diversity of women's experiences in a number of historical and contemporary settings, this volume of essays has examined the complexity, fluidity and varied nature of women's leadership through the twentieth century. But this volume has sought not only to document women's achievements but also to highlight several distinctive aspects of women's leadership. The first is the remarkable diversity of women's leadership across time and place. By adopting a range of themes—feminist perspectives and leadership; Indigenous women's leadership; local and global politics; leadership and the professions; women and culture and movements for social change—this volume has demonstrated the significant activities women have engaged in to bring about change. Second, while women themselves have often eschewed the term 'leadership', the ways in which women have undertaken roles and activities that required leadership—however loosely defined—invite an analysis of the term that goes beyond the traditional and conventional masculine understandings of leadership. Finally, this is a timely publication, which highlights the factors that have enhanced and limited women's opportunities to exercise leadership in a range of political, cultural and social fields, both in the past and for the future.

Women's leadership in everyday life and on issues of immediate concern is also scrutinised in this volume. It is valuable to conclude with commentary on a contemporary event that highlights the gendered aspect of leadership at an everyday level. Recent research has revealed that some people experienced significant conflict as to how they should respond to the dangerous conditions of the 2009 Black Saturday bushfires in Victoria. The conflict revolved around gender, with some men wanting to stay to defend their homes and women wanting to leave. There was a masculine heroism attached to staying and defending property despite the heightened risk of death. In stark contrast with this, the women involved in the study in all cases preferred to pack the car and leave. Meagan Tyler, who conducted this research, observed 'society should not make heroes of the blokes who stay on with a garden hose to defend the pub in shorts and thongs, but instead celebrate the man who listens to his wife and helps pack up the car well before the fire arrives'. 'Men are significantly more likely to die during bushfire in Australia, because of their propensity to stay in the thick of the action.' In fact, the '2009 Victorian Bushfires Royal Commission revealed text messages and phone conversations where entire families had died after spouses disagreed over whether to defend the home or leave'.[5]

In this context, staying and defending property are valorised as heroic and often interpreted as acts of leadership. Conversely, the actions of women in evacuating (or wanting to leave) are interpreted as passive and weak, rather than as exercising leadership. The gendered dynamics and meanings associated with these actions are 'quite literally, a life or death issue'.[6] In the case of bushfire survival in Australia, 'history has conclusively shown the woman to be right'.[7] We would contend that precisely these types of research and analysis where models of leadership are challenged along gender lines are what will shed light on the diversity of leadership: the limits of elevating a masculine model and spotlighting how women often exercise leadership in ways that are very different to men and not labelled as such.

The stories and analysis presented here are part of an important conversation that interrogates ideas about leadership. We wish to encourage a critical use of the term—for us to think about when the term leadership is applied to someone and/or their actions: what are the tacit assumptions behind this? In contrast, what acts of leadership do we see, which go publicly unidentified as leadership? Any why? In bringing a critical eye to the category of leadership, we hope this volume provided an opportunity to reflect on the diverse ways leadership has been enacted by women in the past and present, and the range of ways women have publicly and privately worked to influence others and for social change.

---

5 Aisha Dow, 'Firefighting Macho Men are Sometimes, Well, Stupid', *The Age*, 11 February 2014, http://www.theage.com.au/victoria/firefighting-macho-men-are-sometimes-well-stupid-20140211-32f2e. html#ixzz2t8xkau4B. Also Megan Tyler and Peter Fairbrother, 'Gender, Masculinity and Bushfire: Australia in an International Context', Australian Journal of Emergency Management 28(2) (April 2013): 23.

6 Tyler and Fairbrother, 'Gender, Masculinity and Bushfire', 24.

7 Dow, 'Firefighting Macho Men are Sometimes, Well, Stupid'.

References

Craven, Greg. 'Peter Cosgrove, Groomed by a Life of Service to be Our GG.' *The Conversation*, 29 January 2014. http://theconversation.com/peter-cosgrove-groomed-by-a-life-of-service-to-be-our-gg-22499.

Dow, Aisha. 'Firefighting Macho Men are Sometimes, Well, Stupid.' *The Age*, 11 February 2014. http://www.theage.com.au/victoria/firefighting-macho-men-are-sometimes-well-stupid-20140211-32f2e.html#ixzz2t8xkau4B.

Marshall, T. H. *Citizenship and Social Class: And Other Essays*. Cambridge: Cambridge University Press, 1950.

Tyler, Megan and Peter Fairbrother. 'Gender, Masculinity and Bushfire: Australia in an International Context.' *Australian Journal of Emergency Management* 28(2) (April 2013): 20–5.

Epilogue: Reflections on women and leadership through the prism of citizenship

Kim Rubenstein[1]

Looking at questions about women and leadership also provides an excellent frame through which to reflect upon the way women leaders have expressed their citizenship. The word 'citizenship' is an important term to think about from the experience of women, and I begin these concluding comments by explaining what I mean when using the term. I am also interested to conclude this collection by asking: what does this tell us about women leaders as citizens?

The term citizenship is used in a range of interdisciplinary contexts. Different discussions occur when thinking of citizenship as a legal formal notion, compared with citizenship as a normative concept. The legal formal notion is primarily concerned with the legal status of individuals within a nation-state. So, for instance in Australia, citizens are contrasted with permanent residents, temporary residents and unlawful non-citizens. Legal issues associated with the formal status include the acquisition and loss of citizenship, the criteria for citizenship by application, dual or multiple citizenship and discrimination based upon citizenship status. All of these legal issues have had an impact, historically, and to a certain extent currently, in various countries around the world, in discriminatory ways upon women. For instance, there was a period in Australia's citizenship law history when a woman's formal legal status was entirely dependent upon her husband's.[2]

The normative notion of citizenship, in contrast, is not solely concerned with these legal questions, but rather it sees membership as something more comprehensive and less formally constrained. For instance, citizenship is discussed in the non-legal, normative frameworks in a variety of ways— primarily in terms that look to the material circumstances of life within the polity, notably to questions of social membership and substantive equality.[3]

---

1 The Australian National University.
2 Kim Rubenstein, *Australian Citizenship Law in Context* (Sydney: Lawbook Company, 2000). See also Helen Irving, *When Women Were Aliens: The Neglected History of Derivative Marital Citizenship*, Research Paper No. 12/47, 2012, Sydney Law School, http://ssrn.com/abstract=2110546.
3 Kim Rubenstein and Daniel Adler, 'International Citizenship: The Future of Nationality in a Globalised World', *Indiana Journal of Global Legal Studies* 7(2) (2000): 519.

Indeed, Linda Bosniak has identified three other ways that the scholarship conceives of citizenship beyond legal status: citizenship as rights, citizenship as political activity and citizenship as identity.[4]

The concept of citizenship as identity relates more to how an individual thinks of herself as part of a community. To some extent one's formal legal status can reflect one's own sense of identity, but there were many women historically who were deprived of their formal citizenship status, but that had no real impact on their own identification with their home. And as this collection highlights, many women's identity was affirmed through a transnational, international environment, taking their self-identity well beyond the domestic concerns of a single nation-state.

In thinking about citizenship as rights and political activity and identity, we can see the normative notion is often much broader than the legal notion in that it looks to membership in ways that are not necessarily dependent upon legal status. In fact, there is often a disjuncture between the legal notion—which is an exclusive one—and the normative notion that in certain contexts seeks to be inclusive and universal.

But what is common to them all is the sense that citizenship represents a form of membership—and it is women's membership in society broadly and in the public and private spheres that feminist work on citizenship has been directed to for some time and that this volume adds rich material to by considering women's leadership.

What does this tell us about women leaders as citizens?

This volume informs our understanding about women's participation in society through the leadership experiences of women and it also illustrates how women have expressed their citizenship. It helps us conceive of women's citizenship in terms of their own life experiences—in both legal and normative terms. Indeed, the six-part structure has captured the complexity and nuance of women's expressions of citizenship in a mix of historical and contemporary contexts.

Amanda Sinclair's chapter and the first part on feminist approaches to leadership remind us why women have a strong interest in the broader phenomena of leadership. She affirms the value of this collection in its contribution to making us think about how women have influenced and changed the public agenda and improved the life experiences of the people around and following after them. In the same way that Bosniak discusses how citizenship is a powerful discourse, Sinclair argues that precisely because leadership has become such a powerful

---

4   Linda Bosniak, 'Citizenship Denationalised', *Indiana Journal of Global Legal Studies* (2000): 447.

discourse, with people at all levels of society being urged to do more leadership, it is vital to deconstruct, interrogate and reapproach leadership from a feminist point of view.[5]

This feminist approach also reminds us that feminists have long challenged the universal nature of citizenship often promoted. Margaret Thornton has illustrated that feminists must also think of citizenship beyond the formal legal context because:

> Liberal legalism is strewn with universalised concepts that deny the particularity of difference. Citizenship is a paradigmatic example of such a universal, for it requires the citizen to erase all facets of his or her identity. Within legal discourse, 'the citizen' is not only an individual who is de-sexed, de-raced and de-classed, but he or she is also dehistoricised. The one characteristic of identity that the juridical concept of citizenship purports not to suppress is that of nationality. Citizenship is therefore grounded in a very distinctive way. It signals homogeneity and a sense of belonging, but the community to which the citizen belongs is exclusively determined in relation to the nation state. The familiar communities of everyday life, such as those congregated around the workplace, club, school and suburb, are invisible to the juridical gaze. Indeed, this gaze is pathologically incapable of seeing multiplicitous and heterogeneous interests at all.[6]

This collection forces us to think of women's leadership—women's expressions of their citizenship—in these multiple and broader ways. In the second part, the focus on Indigenous women's leadership also resonates with a citizenship story. Not only does it inform us of the important leadership contributions and active citizenship and participation of the Indigenous women whose lives we read about, citizenship as rights and political participation, but it also intersects with the citizenship struggles in Australia that Indigenous women and men have been engaged with. In Australia, Indigenous Australians have formally been full legal members of the community—first as British subjects and then, when the *Australian Citizenship Act* (1948) came into force, as Australian citizens.[7] But their life experiences have highlighted the disjuncture between citizenship as a formal status and citizenship as rights, participation and identity.[8]

In the third part, on local and global politics, we are reminded of how citizenship has always, in practice, been discussed and engaged with as both a national

---

5   Ibid.

6   Margaret Thornton, 'Historicising Citizenship: Remembering Broken Promises', *Melbourne University Law Review* 20 (1996): 1072.

7   Rubenstein, *Australian Citizenship Law in Context*.

8   John Chesterman and Brian Galligan, *Citizens without Rights: Aborigines and Australian Citizenship* (Cambridge and Melbourne: Cambridge University Press, 1997).

and a transnational activity. While the formal concept is linked to the singular nation-state (although people can hold more than one formal citizenship), the normative concept has discussed rights, participation and identity as something more open and fluid. Citizenship issues arise throughout this part through women's activism on legislative reform issues and rights struggles, and in the language of political participation as in those lives we read about of women with disability. And the gaze also heads beyond the national borders as we hear more about those women who have participated in the international sphere through their leadership on both the national and the international stages.

We are reminded with the final three parts of the collection of how important it is to look at leadership beyond the formal political governance structures and sites of civic citizenship, to the other sites of influence and power in society to highlight participation in its myriad ways. The fourth section on leadership and the professions enlarges our thinking beyond women's experiences in the professional public world to activity and leadership in the factory houses, in the philanthropic and social worlds and in academia. Once again, we see the multiple ways in which citizenship as membership through different associations and professional communities plays out through the experiences of those women. When we move in the fifth part to leadership and women and culture, we are encouraged to think about women's voices and influence in those other powerful aspects of society—through representations of leadership for those women who did hold formal leadership roles to those women who have led the way in fighting about entertainment policy and issues, and also into the literary world, which is often a world that represents our lives back to ourselves. These all play into citizenship as identity—for our identities as women are informed both by the issues covered in this section and by the way in which women have engaged with them. And finally, when reading about movements for social change, we are reminded of the different styles and ways in which participation and leadership can be expressed. The women's movement, the environment movement and the consumer movement are all illustrative of how different associations have seen different women's citizenship experiences play out. They resonate with the view that citizenship activity occurs as much in civil society and in broader social issues and is not reliant on the formal expressions of citizenship through voting and political office.

In conclusion, I am reminded that the purpose of the book included identifying outstanding women leaders to demonstrate their significance in inspiring the actions of others within a range of activities, and also to consider the fragility of women's capacity to take up leadership roles after they gained formal expressions of citizenship. By doing so, this book has contributed to understanding a different kind of leadership culture, challenging the masculine model on which leadership is conventionally based. In this epilogue, I have argued that we have also seen that in fulfilling their purpose those women's voices and experiences have expanded and added to both formal and normative understandings of citizenship. This can be seen by the stories showing how women's participation and influence have often directly influenced the formal national governance sphere in ways that have broadened who is included in its citizenry, but also in our thinking about leadership as political activity. It has also shown us that citizenship as rights activity and rights protection has been subject to significant women's influence. Finally, all of this material enlarges our collective national and international identity and understanding as human beings, as fellow citizens of the world, connected to one another.

References

Bosniak, Linda. 'Citizenship Denationalised.' *Indiana Journal of Global Legal Studies* 7 (2000): 447-509.

Chesterman, John and Brian Galligan. *Citizens without Rights: Aborigines and Australian Citizenship*. Cambridge and Melbourne: Cambridge University Press, 1997.

Irving, Helen. *When Women Were Aliens: The Neglected History of Derivative Marital Citizenship*. Research Paper No. 12/47, Sydney Law School, 2012.

Rubenstein, Kim. *Australian Citizenship Law in Context*. Sydney: Lawbook Company, 2002.

Rubenstein, Kim and Daniel Adler. 'International Citizenship: The Future of Nationality in a Globalised World.' *Indiana Journal of Global Legal Studies* 7(2) (2000): 519–48.

Thornton, Margaret. 'Historicising Citizenship: Remembering Broken Promises.' *Melbourne University Law Review* 20 (1996): 1072–86.

www.ingramcontent.com/pod-product-compliance
Lightning Source LLC
Chambersburg PA
CBHW061242270326

41928CB00041B/3365